Contents

Data Section

A Race for Pokémon Knowledge

Pokémon are a major part of life in the land of Sinnoh, but little real research has been done on the area's native species. Prof. Rowan is out to change this, and he's asking brave and talented Pokémon Trainers to help him track down all of Sinnoh's native Pokémon. Unfortunately, the professor is already a step behind—a mysterious organization known as Team Galactic (also researching Pokémon) seems to have learned something that will allow them to reshape Sinnoh forever. . . .

A Companion Pokédex

This book will guide you through your quest to defeat Team Galactic and find each of the 150 Pokémon needed to complete the Sinnoh Pokédex. After you accomplish these goals, you'll earn the National Pokédex, several new areas will become accessible, and new Pokémon will begin to appear in previously visited areas. For coverage of these areas, updated information on areas you've already visited, and complete Pokédex details for all 490 Pokémon, consult the Ultimate National Pokédex published by Nintendo Power.

Controls

Pokémon Diamond and Pokémon Pearl make full use of the touch screen, so even Pokémon veterans should familiarize themselves with the new controls.

L Button

In the default control scheme, the L Button has no function. But the Button Mode menu in the Option screen allows you to make it a copy of the A Button—a useful option when holding the Nintendo DS with your left hand and using the stylus with your right.

Touch Screen

In many menu screens you can save time by simply tapping your selection on the touch screen. Menus that involve long lists of options (such as item pouches and the Pokédex) often feature a large Poké Ball-shaped wheel on the touch screen. Spinning the wheel with your finger or the stylus lets you scroll through the list quickly.

On the field, the touch screen has no function until you earn the Pokétch. Then you can use it to control and switch between a variety of simple programs known as Pokétch apps.

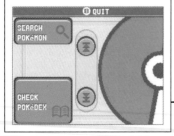

Control Pad

Use the Control Pad to move your character on the field and to navigate menu screens.

Y Button

The Y Button can be used as a shortcut to instantly use any item from your Bag's Key Item pouch. To do so, highlight an item, press the A Button, and select "Register." The words "Y Set" should appear by the item's name. Now you can tap the Y Button to hop on your Bicycle, cast a fishing rod, or look at your Town Map without navigating any menus.

X Button

The X Button opens and closes the main menu.

A Button

The A Button confirms menu selections. On the field you can use it to speak to other characters, examine objects, or search for hidden items.

B Button

The B Button cancels a menu selection, returning you to the previous menu. After you obtain the Running Shoes, you can run on the field by holding down the B Button as you move your character. When riding a Bicycle, press the B Button to change gears.

Select Button

The Select Button allows you to reorder items in certain lists. For example, to put a favorite item at the top of an item list, highlight it and press Select. Then scroll to the top of the list and press Select or the A Button to place it in position. You can also use the Select Button to switch the order of a Pokémon's four moves, but only when the Moves menu appears during combat.

Start Button

In the default control scheme, the Start Button has no function. But the Button Mode menu in the Option screen allows you to make it a copy of the X Button.

The Cast of Characters

You can't save Sinnoh by yourself! Team up with a wide variety of Trainers and mentors—and even your rival—to foil Team Galactic's nefarious plans.

Your Character

You are the hero, and you have the freedom to choose both a gender and a name for your character. The two character models do not differ in Trainer ability, but they do have minor aesthetic differences. (Each has a different Bag design, for example.) The name you choose will be used by all game characters and will be the name by which other players will come to know you. It will also be added to the OT (Original Trainer) field of any Pokémon you catch.

Boy Character

Girl Character

Professor Rowan's Assistant

The character of the gender you do not choose will appear in the game as Prof. Rowan's assistant. So if you select the boy hero, the girl hero will appear as a Trainer working for Prof. Rowan.

Your Online Persona

It would be confusing if everyone looked the same when communicating with other players through local wireless and Nintendo Wi-Fi Connection. So in Oreburgh City you'll have the opportunity to choose a Trainer style for your character. That will determine how you appear to others online. See page 38 for details.

Your Rival

Your rival is your childhood best friend, a neighbor from your home town of Twinleaf. Your friendship is strong, but your rival has a competitive nature and will strive to reach Gyms before you do and to raise a stronger Pokémon team than yours. To test your strength, your rival will abruptly challenge you to Pokémon battles when your paths cross. You may choose any name you like for this character.

A True Competitor

Your rival is always looking to one-up you, and early in the game he will choose whichever Pokémon starter has a type advantage against the starter you chose. That will make a big difference early on, when your roster is small, so strive to catch a Pokémon that trumps his starter as soon as possible!

Friends and Allies

Sinnoh is full of friendly people that will help you on your quest. Most remain in their homes, offering assistance to respectful travelers, but some are traveling Trainers on quests of their own. You may run into them at unexpected times and in unexpected places!

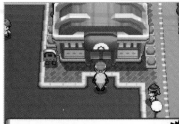

> They have some ancient books that you might find interesting.

Cynthia is a Trainer with her own agenda. She will offer you helpful items and advice, but may ask for favors in return.

Professor Rowan

Prof. Rowan is a leading Pokémon expert. He has spent many years studying the Pokémon in other lands, and has recently returned to his Sinnoh laboratory in Sandgem Town to study the Pokémon of his native land. His first priority is field research, so he's looking for ambitious and talented Trainers to gather data on local Pokémon with his specially developed Pokédex.

> I heard from Dawn that you used our Pokémon?

Prof. Rowan's lab employs many gifted scientists. At times, he'll send them out to find you and give you valuable items and Pokédex upgrades that will aid in your research.

Trainer Camaraderie

In particularly difficult areas Trainers may put aside their desire to challenge you, and instead team up with you for a series of Double Battles against common foes and wild Pokémon.

Team Galactic

Team Galactic is a mysterious group of Trainers with a military-style power structure. They are rumored to be involved in criminal enterprises ranging from Pokémon kidnapping to energy theft. Their heavily guarded compounds are popping up all over Sinnoh. What could they possibly be up to?

Team Galactic Grunts

Team Galactic has hired a small army of ne'er-do-wells to do its bidding. The ones that prove themselves are given Pokémon so they can challenge meddling Trainers like you. Whenever you see a Galactic Grunt, something dirty is afoot.

The Trainer's Path

True Pokémon Trainers don't just accumulate Pokémon; they use them as tools to fight evil and protect the helpless—human and Pokémon alike.

The First Step on the Path

Your career as a Pokémon Trainer begins when you choose your very first Pokémon from Prof. Rowan's briefcase (see page 48). The Pokémon you select will be the foundation of a team that will constantly grow and change as you collect more Pokémon. The starter is the only Pokémon you will ever be given—you must earn all other Pokémon by capturing them in the wild, trading for them with friends, evolving them from other Pokémon, or hatching them from carefully bred Pokémon Eggs. The more Pokémon you can gather, the more options you'll have when assembling a team of six strong fighters to protect Sinnoh or challenge the Pokémon League.

Complete the Pokédex

Every time you encounter a new Pokémon, its information will be saved in a digital catalog known as a Pokédex. Prof. Rowan wants you to see every one of Sinnoh's 150 native Pokémon, and you won't be able to complete the game until you do.

Protect Sinnoh

As a skilled Trainer with a roster of powerful Pokémon, you have a duty to use your strength to protect your homeland. Most of the Trainers you meet are good people who simply want to practice their skills, but a few are using their Pokémon for evil. Uncover their villainous plan and put a stop to their crimes!

Become the Champion

The ultimate goal for a Trainer is to become the Pokémon League Champion. To do so, you'll need to prove your skills by earning a badge from each of Sinnoh's eight Gyms. Only then will you have earned the right to challenge Sinnoh's top Trainers: the Elite Four and the current Pokémon League Champion.

The Choice Is Yours

Your quest begins when you run into Prof. Rowan at the shore of Lake Verity. There you'll be given the choice of three powerful Pokémon with which to start your team (these are commonly referred to as the "starters"). Each can evolve twice, and will ultimately become one of the game's strongest Pokémon. Additionally, your starter Pokémon will likely be your companion for the entire game, so consider your choice carefully.

Eh...? Which one do you want, then?

Getting the Other Two Starters

The three starters do not appear in the wild, but by breeding and trading you can acquire the two you did not choose. Breeding a starter Pokémon with a Ditto will create an Egg that will hatch into the starter's first Evolutionary form. Canny traders should breed their own starter so they can trade their starter's offspring for the offspring of other players' starters. See the breeding section on page 32 for more detail.

Which Starter Is Right for You?

You can read all about the three starters on the pages that follow. Before making your choice, carefully consider each starter's type, stats, moves, and abilities. Or skip all that and just choose the one that's most adorable! You can't go wrong with any of them.

① Pokémon Name and Type

Here you'll find the Pokémon's name and type. See page 13 for more information about Pokémon types.

② Strategy Notes

This section provides a bit of insider information that will help you understand each starter's strengths and weaknesses.

③ Ability, Egg Group, and Stats

Each Pokémon has an inherent ability that influences its encounters with other Pokémon. Each Pokémon also has stats in six categories that influence the damage it can deal, receive, and endure. Every Pokémon belongs to an Egg Group (shown as "Egg" in the charts) and can breed with any Pokémon of an opposite gender that is within the same Egg Group (see page 32 for details). Finally, this section lists the implications of your choice: Which Pokémon types your starter will have advantages and disadvantages against, and which starter you'll cause your rival to choose.

④ Level-Up and Egg Moves

Each Evolutionary form has its own move chart that shows which moves it learns at which levels. You'll also see each move's type, category, (Physical, Special, or Other—see page 15 for details), contest type, and Appeal Points (AP), the latter two of which are relevant only in Pokémon Super Contests (see page 34). Egg Moves are moves of Egg-hatched Pokémon that are inherited from their parents. See page 33 to learn how Pokémon inherit Egg Moves.

⑤ Evolved Forms

Each starter Pokémon can evolve into two other forms by leveling up, and may gain a new type and access to new moves when it does. See page 22 to learn more about Evolution.

Turtwig Type: Grass

If You Choose Turtwig

Turtwig specializes in HP-draining Grass-type attacks, but will also learn Ground- and Dark-type attacks that increase the number of types it can trump. Turtwig is somewhat lacking in attack power early on, so focus on leveling it up quickly so it will learn some good Grass-type moves by the time you face the first Gym.

Ability: Overgrow
Egg: Monster / Grass
Size: 1'04" Weight: 22.5lbs

HP	
Attack	
Defense	
Speed	
Special Attack	
Special Defense	

Strong against: Water, Ground, Rock
Weak against: Fire, Ice, Poison, Flying, Bug
Rival's Pokémon: Chimchar

Level-up, Egg Moves

Turtwig

#	ATTACK	CAT	TYPE	CONTEST	AP
01	TACKLE	P	NRM	TOUGH	+3
05	WITHDRAW	O	WTR	CUTE	+2
09	ABSORB	S	GRS	SMART	+1
13	RAZOR LEAF	P	GRS	COOL	+3
17	CURSE	O	???	TOUGH	–
21	BITE	P	DRK	TOUGH	+2
25	MEGA DRAIN	S	GRS	SMART	+1
29	LEECH SEED	O	GRS	SMART	–
33	SYNTHESIS	O	GRS	SMART	–
37	CRUNCH	P	DRK	TOUGH	+2
41	GIGA DRAIN	S	GRS	SMART	+1
45	LEAF STORM	S	GRS	CUTE	+2
EGG	WORRY SEED	O	GRS	BEAUTY	+2
EGG	GROWTH	O	NRM	BEAUTY	–
EGG	TICKLE	O	NRM	CUTE	+2
EGG	BODY SLAM	P	NRM	TOUGH	+3
EGG	DOUBLE-EDGE	P	NRM	TOUGH	–
EGG	SAND TOMB	P	GRD	SMART	–
EGG	SEED BOMB	P	GRS	SMART	+3
EGG	THRASH	P	NRM	TOUGH	+2
EGG	AMNESIA	O	PSY	CUTE	–
EGG	SUPERPOWER	P	FTG	TOUGH	+2

Grotle

#	ATTACK	CAT	TYPE	CONTEST	AP
01	TACKLE	P	NRM	TOUGH	+3
01	WITHDRAW	O	WTR	CUTE	+2
05	WITHDRAW	O	WTR	CUTE	+2
09	ABSORB	S	GRS	SMART	+1
13	RAZOR LEAF	P	GRS	COOL	+3
17	CURSE	O	???	TOUGH	–
22	BITE	P	DRK	TOUGH	+3
27	MEGA DRAIN	S	GRS	SMART	+1
32	LEECH SEED	O	GRS	SMART	–
37	SYNTHESIS	O	GRS	SMART	–
42	CRUNCH	P	DRK	TOUGH	+2
47	GIGA DRAIN	S	GRS	SMART	+1
52	LEAF STORM	S	GRS	CUTE	+2

Torterra

#	ATTACK	CAT	TYPE	CONTEST	AP
01	WOOD HAMMER	P	GRS	TOUGH	+2
01	TACKLE	P	NRM	TOUGH	+2
01	WITHDRAW	O	WTR	CUTE	+2
01	ABSORB	S	GRS	SMART	+1
01	RAZOR LEAF	P	GRS	COOL	+3
05	WITHDRAW	O	WTR	CUTE	+2
09	ABSORB	S	GRS	SMART	+1
13	RAZOR LEAF	P	GRS	COOL	+3
17	CURSE	O	???	TOUGH	–
22	BITE	P	DRK	TOUGH	+3
27	MEGA DRAIN	S	GRS	SMART	+1
32	EARTHQUAKE	P	GRD	TOUGH	+2
33	LEECH SEED	O	GRS	SMART	–
39	SYNTHESIS	O	GRS	SMART	–
45	CRUNCH	P	DRK	TOUGH	+2
51	GIGA DRAIN	S	GRS	SMART	+1
57	LEAF STORM	S	GRS	CUTE	+2

Evolution family

Evolves at Level 18 — Grotle Grass

Evolves at Level 32 — Torterra Grass Ground

Chimchar Type: Fire

If You Choose Chimchar

Chimchar gains its second type as soon as it evolves into Monferno at Level 14. The combination of Fire- and Fighting-types isn't worth much on defense, but offers many powerful attacks. Unless you can evolve it quickly, Chimchar will struggle with the very first Gym, but it should be smooth sailing after that.

Ability: Blaze
Egg: Field / Human-Like
Size: 1'08" Weight: 13.7lbs

HP
Attack
Defense
Speed
Special Attack
Special Defense

Strong against: Grass, Ice, Bug, Steel
Weak against: Water, Ground, Rock
Rival's Pokémon: Piplup

Level-up, Egg Moves

Chimchar

#	ATTACK	CAT	TYPE	CONTEST	AP
01	SCRATCH	P	NRM	TOUGH	+3
01	LEER	O	NRM	COOL	+2
07	EMBER	S	FIRE	BEAUTY	+3
09	TAUNT	O	DRK	SMART	–
15	FURY SWIPES	P	NRM	TOUGH	+2
17	FLAME WHEEL	P	FIRE	BEAUTY	+2
23	NASTY PLOT	O	DRK	CUTE	–
25	TORMENT	O	DRK	TOUGH	–
31	FACADE	P	NRM	CUTE	+2
33	FIRE SPIN	S	FIRE	BEAUTY	–
39	SLACK OFF	O	NRM	CUTE	–
41	FLAMETHROWER	S	FIRE	BEAUTY	+2
EGG	FIRE PUNCH	P	FIRE	BEAUTY	+2
EGG	THUNDERPUNCH	P	ELC	COOL	+2
EGG	DOUBLE KICK	P	FTG	COOL	+2
EGG	ENCORE	O	NRM	CUTE	+1
EGG	HEAT WAVE	S	FIRE	BEAUTY	+2
EGG	FOCUS ENERGY	O	NRM	COOL	–
EGG	HELPING HAND	O	NRM	SMART	+1
EGG	FAKE OUT	P	NRM	CUTE	+2
EGG	BLAZE KICK	P	FIRE	BEAUTY	+2
EGG	COUNTER	P	FTG	TOUGH	+2

Monferno

#	ATTACK	CAT	TYPE	CONTEST	AP
01	SCRATCH	P	NRM	TOUGH	+3
01	LEER	O	NRM	COOL	+2
01	EMBER	S	FIRE	BEAUTY	+3
07	EMBER	S	FIRE	BEAUTY	+3
09	TAUNT	O	DRK	SMART	–
14	MACH PUNCH	P	FTG	COOL	+2
16	FURY SWIPES	P	NRM	TOUGH	+2
19	FLAME WHEEL	P	FIRE	BEAUTY	+2
26	FEINT	P	NRM	BEAUTY	–
29	TORMENT	O	DRK	TOUGH	–
36	CLOSE COMBAT	P	FTG	SMART	+2
39	FIRE SPIN	S	FIRE	BEAUTY	–
46	SLACK OFF	O	NRM	CUTE	–
49	FLARE BLITZ	P	FIRE	SMART	+2

Infernape

#	ATTACK	CAT	TYPE	CONTEST	AP
01	SCRATCH	P	NRM	TOUGH	+3
01	LEER	O	NRM	COOL	+2
01	EMBER	S	FIRE	BEAUTY	+3
01	TAUNT	O	DRK	SMART	–
07	EMBER	S	FIRE	BEAUTY	+3
09	TAUNT	O	DRK	SMART	–
14	MACH PUNCH	P	FTG	COOL	+2
17	FURY SWIPES	P	NRM	TOUGH	+2
21	FLAME WHEEL	P	FIRE	BEAUTY	+2
29	FEINT	P	NRM	BEAUTY	–
33	PUNISHMENT	P	DRK	SMART	+1
41	CLOSE COMBAT	P	FTG	SMART	+2
45	FIRE SPIN	S	FIRE	BEAUTY	–
53	CALM MIND	O	PSY	SMART	–
57	FLARE BLITZ	P	FIRE	SMART	+2

Evolution family

Evolves at Level 14

Monferno Fire Fighting

Evolves at Level 36

Infernape Fire Fighting

Piplup Type: Water

If You Choose Piplup

Piplup is the most defense-oriented starter. It doesn't learn many strong attacks, but it will ultimately evolve into a Water-and-Steel-type Pokémon with resistance to 12 different types. Its Water-type moves will give you an edge in the first Gym, but will be a liability in the second Gym.

Ability: Torrent
Egg: Water 1 / Field
Size: 1'04" Weight: 11.5lbs

HP	▓▓░░░░
Attack	▓▓░░░░
Defense	▓▓▓░░░
Speed	▓▓░░░░
Special Attack	▓▓▓░░░
Special Defense	▓▓░░░░

Strong against: Fire, Ground, Rock
Weak against: Electric, Grass
Rival's Pokémon: Turtwig

Level-up, Egg Moves

Pilup

#	ATTACK	CAT	TYPE	CONTEST	AP
01	POUND	P	NRM	TOUGH	+3
04	GROWL	O	NRM	CUTE	+2
08	BUBBLE	S	WTR	CUTE	+2
11	WATER SPORT	O	WTR	CUTE	+2
15	PECK	P	FLY	COOL	+3
18	BIDE	P	NRM	TOUGH	+2
22	BUBBLEBEAM	S	WTR	BEAUTY	+2
25	FURY ATTACK	P	NRM	COOL	+2
29	BRINE	S	WTR	SMART	+2
32	WHIRLPOOL	S	WTR	BEAUTY	−
36	MIST	O	ICE	BEAUTY	+2
39	DRILL PECK	P	FLY	COOL	+3
43	HYDRO PUMP	S	WTR	BEAUTY	+2
EGG	DOUBLE HIT	P	NRM	SMART	+2
EGG	SUPERSONIC	O	NRM	SMART	+2
EGG	YAWN	O	NRM	CUTE	+2
EGG	MUD SPORT	O	GRD	CUTE	+2
EGG	MUD-SLAP	S	GRD	CUTE	+3
EGG	SNORE	S	NRM	CUTE	+3
EGG	FLAIL	P	NRM	CUTE	+2
EGG	AGILITY	O	PSY	COOL	+2
EGG	AQUA RING	O	WTR	BEAUTY	−
EGG	HYDRO PUMP	S	WTR	BEAUTY	+2

Prinplup

#	ATTACK	CAT	TYPE	CONTEST	AP
01	TACKLE	P	NRM	TOUGH	+3
01	GROWL	O	NRM	CUTE	+2
04	GROWL	O	NRM	CUTE	+2
08	BUBBLE	S	WTR	CUTE	+2
11	WATER SPORT	O	WTR	CUTE	+2
15	PECK	P	FLY	COOL	+3
16	METAL CLAW	P	STL	COOL	+2
19	BIDE	P	NRM	TOUGH	+2
24	BUBBLEBEAM	S	WTR	BEAUTY	+2
28	FURY ATTACK	P	NRM	COOL	+2
33	BRINE	S	WTR	SMART	+2
37	WHIRLPOOL	S	WTR	BEAUTY	−
42	MIST	O	ICE	BEAUTY	+2
46	DRILL PECK	P	FLY	COOL	+3
51	HYDRO PUMP	S	WTR	BEAUTY	+2

Empoleon

#	ATTACK	CAT	TYPE	CONTEST	AP
01	TACKLE	P	NRM	TOUGH	+3
01	GROWL	O	NRM	CUTE	+2
01	BUBBLE	S	WTR	CUTE	+2
04	GROWL	O	NRM	CUTE	+2
08	BUBBLE	S	WTR	CUTE	+2
11	SWORDS DANCE	O	NRM	BEAUTY	−
15	PECK	P	FLY	COOL	+3
16	METAL CLAW	P	STL	COOL	+2
19	SWAGGER	O	NRM	CUTE	+2
24	BUBBLEBEAM	S	WTR	BEAUTY	+2
28	FURY ATTACK	P	NRM	COOL	+2
33	BRINE	S	WTR	SMART	+2
36	AQUA JET	P	WTR	BEAUTY	+2
39	WHIRLPOOL	S	WTR	BEAUTY	−
46	MIST	O	ICE	BEAUTY	+2
52	DRILL PECK	P	FLY	COOL	+3
59	HYDRO PUMP	S	WTR	BEAUTY	+2

Evolution family

Evolves at Level 16 → **Prinplup** Water

Evolves at Level 36 → **Empoleon** Water Steel

Pokémon Battles

Surviving the wilds of Sinnoh will require not just strength and courage, but also a keen wit and a proper grasp of combat mechanics.

Master the Combat Basics

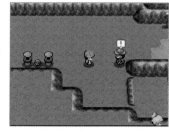

Whether it's wild Pokémon fighting to protect their territory or rival Trainers fighting to prove a point, you'll face Pokémon battles at every stage of your journey. The only way to triumph is to capture a wide assortment of wild Pokémon, hone them into champion fighters, and learn how to use their diverse abilities to overcome any challenge on the battlefield.

Wild Pokémon Encounters

When walking on certain types of terrain, wild Pokémon will attack you at random intervals. You can defeat these Pokémon to gain Exp. Points, or capture them with a Poké Ball to add them to your own team. Wild Pokémon tend to be lower-level, weaker, and less evolved than trained Pokémon.

Tall Grass

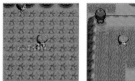

Early in your quest you can fill out your roster by tramping through tall grass in search of wild Pokémon. If you prefer to avoid combat, stay in the short grass!

Caves and Building Interiors

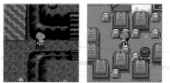

Some types of wild Pokémon make their homes in caves or certain buildings. There's no way to avoid combat in such locations, so be ever ready for a fight.

Water

You'll encounter wild aquatic Pokémon while using the Surf move to cross lakes, rivers, and seas.

Marsh

You'll find a patch of wet marshland on Route 212. Wild Pokémon live in this gunk as well as in the tall grass.

Seeking Wild Pokémon

Although you'll encounter most wild Pokémon by walking through their native habitats, there are a few other ways to provoke a Pokémon encounter. You'll never fill out your Pokédex if you don't master these methods!

Fishing

You can dip a fishing pole into any body of water, and if you're lucky, you just might get a nibble—press the A Button when the "!" appears to reel it in!

Honey Trees

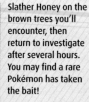

Slather Honey on the brown trees you'll encounter, then return to investigate after several hours. You may find a rare Pokémon has taken the bait!

The Safari Game

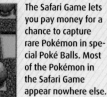

The Safari Game lets you pay money for a chance to capture rare Pokémon in special Poké Balls. Most of the Pokémon in the Safari Game appear nowhere else.

Trainers and Gym Leaders

Wild Pokémon battles present an opportunity to expand your roster, but they don't pose much of a challenge. For that, you'll have to battle other Trainers who have their own teams of well-trained Pokémon. Amateur Trainers tend to hang out in routes and caves, while groups of professionals populate Pokémon Gyms.

Trainers

Trainers will challenge you throughout your quest, and most of these battles are unavoidable. Win them all to progress through the area and earn money and Exp. Points.

Pokémon Gyms

Many towns have a Pokémon Gym where the area's best and brightest Trainers fight. Defeat Gym Leaders to earn badges that allow you to use new HMs and manage higher-level Pokémon.

Rival Battles

Your best friend shares your interest in Pokémon training, and will soon grow into one of your most skilled rivals. While you can challenge other Trainers at your own convenience, your rival will appear to challenge you without warning. Keep your team in fighting shape at all times!

The Fundamentals of Pokémon Combat

Past Pokémon games have relied on a series of pop-up menus, but Diamond and Pearl keep the action on the upper screen and the commands on the lower screen. Highlight commands with the Control Pad and press the A Button to confirm, or simply tap commands with the stylus.

The Battle Begins

Battles begin with the top Pokémon in each Trainer's roster being summoned to the battlefield. You can then choose your move, swap Pokémon, use an item, or flee the battle.

Fight

When you choose the Fight command, the lower screen will display a list of your active Pokémon's moves. Select the one to use or choose Cancel to return to the previous screen. See page 15 to learn more about moves.

Bag

Choose the Bag command to access the HP/PP Restore, Poké Balls, Status Healers, and Battle Items sections of your backpack. Using a single item will take up your whole turn, but the item will take effect immediately, before your foe has a chance to take action. See page 28 to learn more about items.

Run

Choose Run to attempt to flee from a battle against wild Pokémon. Running away doesn't always work, and if you fail it will cost you your turn.

You Can't Run from Trainer Battles

You can run only from wild Pokémon. Any attempt to flee from a Trainer (including via special moves) will always fail.

Pokémon

Switching Pokémon allows you to choose the best teammate for the situation, and rotating your Pokémon allows each to gain a share of the Exp. Points. Switching Pokémon with the Pokémon command will cost you your turn, but you can do it for free when your active Pokémon is KO'd.

The Turn-Based Battle

The battles in Pokémon Diamond and Pearl are turn-based, so you can take all the time you need to select your command. When both Trainers select a move, the order in which the moves occur will be decided by the Speed scores of the active Pokémon (moves and Abilities may also affect who gets to go first).

The Spoils of Combat

When an enemy Pokémon is KO'd, every conscious Pokémon who participated in the battle will receive an equal share of Exp. Points (even if it was switched out before it used any moves), as will any non-participating Pokémon with the Exp. Share item. If you defeat all of a Trainer's Pokémon, that Trainer will reward you with a prize purse of Poké Dollars. When all of a player's Pokémon are knocked out, the player will lose some money and be sent back to the last visited Pokémon Center. There you can heal all your wounded Pokémon and shake up your party to ensure that you don't lose a second time!

Type-Trumping Basics

The most important strategy in Pokémon battles is to pick the right type of Pokémon to defeat each opponent. Every Pokémon has a type (or two) that makes it vulnerable to foes of certain types, but that gives it an edge when battling against foes of other types. Learn this system well!

Moves Have Types Too

Each Pokémon move also has a type. Moves of a certain type will deal additional damage to foes that are weak to that type, but will do reduced damage to foes that are resistant to that type, and no damage to foes that are immune to that type!

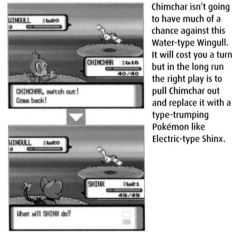

Chimchar isn't going to have much of a chance against this Water-type Wingull. It will cost you a turn, but in the long run the right play is to pull Chimchar out and replace it with a type-trumping Pokémon like Electric-type Shinx.

Type-Trumping Example

When a Pokémon uses a move that is especially effective against its target's type, we call it "type-trumping." Here are a few examples.

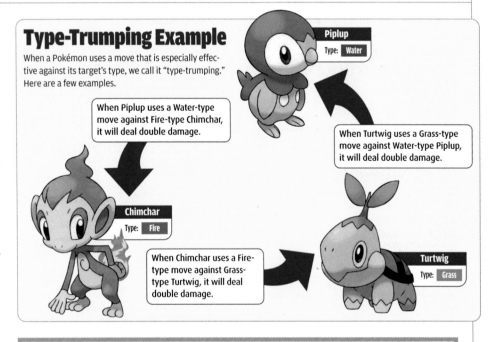

When Piplup uses a Water-type move against Fire-type Chimchar, it will deal double damage.

When Turtwig uses a Grass-type move against Water-type Piplup, it will deal double damage.

When Chimchar uses a Fire-type move against Grass-type Turtwig, it will deal double damage.

Piplup — Type: Water

Chimchar — Type: Fire

Turtwig — Type: Grass

A Second Type Can Help . . . and Hurt

Having dual types mitigates some vulnerabilities, but increases others. For example, Water-type Pokémon are weak to Grass-type moves, while Flying-type Pokémon are resistant to them, so a Grass-type attack will deal normal damage to a Water-and-Flying-type Pokémon like Wingull. But both Water- and Flying-type Pokémon are vulnerable to Electric-type moves, so an Electric-type move would hit Wingull for *quadruple* damage. Ouch!

Same-Type Bonuses

Damage bonuses consider not just the move's type and the target's type, but the user's type as well. A Pokémon gets a 50% damage bonus when using a move whose type matches the type of the Pokémon using it. This bonus is in addition to all of the other bonuses!

How Base Damage Is Calculated

The way type bonuses work hasn't change, but Diamond and Pearl have introduced a radical change in how base damage is calculated. In past games, types like Normal and Fighting were considered "physical," which meant they did damage based on the user's Attack score and the target's Defense score; types like Water and Fire were considered "special" and used the Special Attack and Special Defense stats instead. Now it's *moves* that are considered to be either physical or special, not types.

Moves that involve striking a foe now tend to be physical, while ranged attacks are usually special, unless they involve throwing a physical object. For example, the move Fire Punch is now a physical attack, but Fire Blast remains a special attack. You can tell whether an attack is physical or special based on its category icon on the Battle Moves description screen (see the next page for details). Longtime Pokémon players will have to reevaluate old Pokémon based on this new rule. For example, Hitmonchan is a lot stronger now that it can power its Fire Punch, Ice Punch, and Thunderpunch attacks with its high Attack stat instead of its mediocre Special Attack stat.

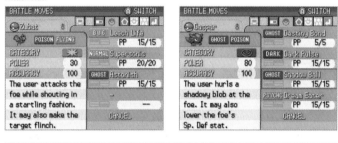

Other Factors that Affect Combat Damage

While move types and stats are important factors in combat, other factors may influence combat damage. Held items, Abilities, other moves, and even weather can influence the effectiveness of your attacks.

Understanding Pokémon Stats

Six simple stats determine how much damage your Pokémon can deal and how much it can endure. Although stats may not be as memorable as flashy moves or Abilities, they can mean the difference between success and failure. View the summaries of a Pokémon's stats before determining if the ally is worth using, and permanently boost the stats of favored Pokémon with items like Calcium and Zinc.

HP	When a Pokémon is damaged, it loses HP. When its HP runs out, it faints and can no longer fight.
Attack	The higher a Pokémon's Attack stat, the more damage it inflicts with physical attacks.
Defense	The higher a Pokémon's Defense stat, the less damage it suffers from physical attacks.
Special Attack	The higher a Pokémon's Special Attack stat, the more damage it inflicts with special attacks.
Special Defense	The higher a Pokémon's Special Defense stat, the less damage it suffers from special attacks.
Speed	The higher a Pokémon's Speed, the more likely the Pokémon will get to act before its opponent in battle.

Damage Multipliers in Action

The bonuses of type-trumping can be huge, allowing even the weaker, lower-level Pokémon to easily dispatch tougher opponents. Here's an example of how the multipliers can add up.

Example:
Pachirisu uses the Spark move

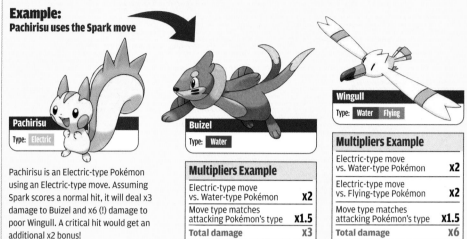

Pachirisu
Type: Electric

Pachirisu is an Electric-type Pokémon using an Electric-type move. Assuming Spark scores a normal hit, it will deal x3 damage to Buizel and x6 (!) damage to poor Wingull. A critical hit would get an additional x2 bonus!

Buizel
Type: Water

Multipliers Example

Electric-type move vs. Water-type Pokémon	**x2**
Move type matches attacking Pokémon's type	**x1.5**
Total damage	**x3**

Wingull
Type: Water Flying

Multipliers Example

Electric-type move vs. Water-type Pokémon	**x2**
Electric-type move vs. Flying-type Pokémon	**x2**
Move type matches attacking Pokémon's type	**x1.5**
Total damage	**x6**

The Combat Chart

This chart is the greatest weapon in a Pokémon Trainer's arsenal. If you use the right attacks to exploit a Pokémon's weaknesses, even your opponent's highest-level Pokémon won't last more than a few turns. Much of it is common sense; Fire melts Ice, for example, while Water douses Fire. Other type relations are more complicated, so refer to this chart often. You can also use the new Pokétch Move Tester app to see what attack types will be useful against a certain Pokémon type that is giving you trouble.

Your attack type \ Opponent's Pokémon type	NORMAL	FIRE	WATER	ELECTRIC	GRASS	ICE	FIGHTING	POISON	GROUND	FLYING	PSYCHIC	BUG	ROCK	GHOST	DRAGON	DARK	STEEL
NORMAL													-	=			-
FIRE		-	-		+	+						+	-		-		+
WATER		+	-		-				+				+		-		
ELECTRIC			+	-	-				=	+					-		
GRASS		-	+		-			-	+	-		-	+		-		-
ICE		-	-		+	-			+	+					+		-
FIGHTING	+					+		-		-	-	-	+	=		+	+
POISON					+			-	-				-	-			=
GROUND		+		+	-			+		=		-	+				+
FLYING				-	+		+					+	-				-
PSYCHIC							+	+			-					=	-
BUG		-			+		-	-		-	+			-		+	-
ROCK		+				+	-		-	+		+					-
GHOST	=										+			+		-	-
DRAGON															+		-
DARK							-				+			+		-	-
STEEL		-	-	-		+							+				-

Damage Multipliers

x2	Damage for **+** attacks
x2	Extra damage from randomly occurring critical hits
x1.5	Damage when the attack type matches the attacking Pokémon's type
x0.5	Damage for **−** attacks
x0	Damage for **=** attacks

Managing a Pokémon's Moves

A Pokémon can possess only four battle moves. If it knows four moves and is about to learn a new one, you'll have to choose whether to have it forget an existing move or pass up the new one. Base your decision on the new move's stats, its category, and the level of versatility it will add to your Pokémon. Moves acquired at higher levels aren't necessarily better than low-level moves, so don't blindly replace old moves with new ones!

Move Stats

When viewing moves in a Pokémon's Battle Moves summary screen, highlight each move to see its Category and its Power, Accuracy, and PP stats. These stats combine with the Pokémon's base stats to determine the move's damage and odds of connecting with its target.

Power	Power determines the base amount of damage an attack will inflict. This number is then modified by the Pokémon's Attack or Special Attack (depending on the move's category) and damage modifiers to determine how effective the move will be. Generally, you should replace low-power moves with high-power moves whenever you have the opportunity.
Accuracy	It doesn't matter how powerful a move is if it doesn't hit its target! Each Pokémon should know at least one high-Accuracy move (the max Accuracy is 100) to ensure a hit against Pokémon that are near fainting, or to give you a fighting chance at hitting Pokémon who have used a move to increase their Evasiveness (a hidden combat stat that lowers attacker's Accuracy).
PP (Power Points)	Power Points (PP) show how many times a Pokémon can use a move before the move is tapped out. When a Pokémon refreshes at a Pokémon Center, all PP are replenished. Many of the game's best moves have only 5 or 10 PP, so make sure each Pokémon has a few reliable high-PP moves to use against lesser foes.

Three Move Categories

The Battle Moves summary screen now has a Category field in which you'll see one of the three icons shown below. This is a new feature designed to make it easy to tell physical attacks from special attacks.

 Physical moves derive their power from the user's Attack stat and the target's Defense stat. These are typically close-range fighting moves in which the attacker physically strikes the defender.

 Special moves derive their power from the user's Special Attack stat and the target's Special Defense stat. These are typically long-range moves in which the attacker unleashes some sort of damaging energy.

 The third category includes moves that heal wounded Pokémon, alter stats, inflict conditions, and cause other effects. This category also includes unconventional moves that deal damage based on stats other than Attack, Defense, Special Attack, and Special Defense.

Learning New Moves

Most Pokémon will know at least two moves when you catch them in the wild, hatch them from an Egg, or receive them in trades. There are three main ways in which they can then learn new moves:

By Leveling Up

Most Pokémon can learn new moves when they reach certain levels. Unevolved Pokémon typically learn new moves at lower levels than their evolved versions, and some moves can be learned only by evolved or unevolved forms.

From a TM or HM

You can use items known as TMs or HMs to teach specific moves to certain Pokémon. A TM can be used only once before it is destroyed, but an HM can be used to teach the same move to any number of Pokémon. Pokémon Diamond and Pearl feature 92 TMs and 8 HMs in all.

From Move Tutors

A few people in the Sinnoh region will offer to teach moves to your Pokémon. Some will do it out of the kindness of their heart, and others require compensation. Take advantage of their services whenever you have the opportunity.

Using Unusual Moves Effectively

While its possible to play through the game using nothing but simple attack moves and stat boosters, many Pokémon learn moves that are a little less straightforward. Every move has a purpose, and strange effects that initially seem like drawbacks can work to your advantage in the right situation or in combination with other moves. Expert Trainers should experiment with these moves to discover their true strengths and weaknesses.

Recurring Attacks

Some moves, like Ice Ball or Rollout, do damage over a few turns while keeping a foe trapped or building up power. The catch is that you can't change the attacking Pokémon's move until the effect is over.

Health-Stealing Moves

Moves like Leech Seed or Giga Drain draw health from your opponent and add it to your Pokémon's HP. These moves are among the Grass-type's greatest strengths.

Fly, Dig, and Dive

Moves like Fly, Dig, and Dive will cause the attacker to leave the field for one turn and strike on the next. If you time the move correctly, factoring in your opponent's Speed, you can use it to avoid an attack on the first turn.

Multiple-Hit Attacks

Attack with a move like Fury Swipes to hit an enemy two to five times in one turn. These moves usually do less damage per hit, but five hits in a row can devastate your foes!

Confusion and Trickery

Swagger and Flatter confuse an opponent while boosting its attack stats. It can backfire, but if the target turns its attacks on itself, it's in for a world of self-hurt.

Weather Moves

Many Pokémon types have a weather move that boosts the power of same-type attacks. Rain Dance boosts Water-type moves, for example. In combination with specific moves, these may have other positive effects!

Trap an Opponent

Moves like Fire Spin, Wrap, or Constrict deal continuous damage to a target and prevent it from escaping. The damage may be small, but you can compound it with other status conditions, such as Poison.

Level-Based Moves

Night Shade and Seismic Toss are great for high-level Pokémon. They do damage equal to the user's level, regardless of type-based weaknesses and resistances!

Helping Moves

In Double Battles, you can have one Pokémon use Helping Hand or Follow Me to boost its partner's strength or protect it for the duration of the turn.

Mess with Your Opponent's Moves

Encore forces an opposing Pokémon to repeat its last move for a few turns. Conversely, Disable prevents the last move from being used again for a few turns.

Keep a Diverse Move List

There are 17 types of Pokémon you can face, but you have room for only six Pokémon on your team. That means each Pokémon should be prepared to deal with an array of enemy types. Choose moves that have a variety of types and effects, but pick only attacks that play to the Pokémon's strengths—a Pokémon with a high Attack score should learn physical moves, not special ones.

Use Your TMs and HMs Wisely

TMs can be rare, so you don't want to waste them on Pokémon you may not use in the future. HMs have useful effects on the field, so teach them to Pokémon you plan on traveling with.

Put Dual-Types to Good Use

The best aspect of dual-type Pokémon is their ability to effectively use attacks of two different types. Make sure your dual-types know at least one good attack for each of their types.

Choose Moves that Work Well Together

Some moves make sense only when combined with other moves or abilities. For example, Dream Eater is nearly useless if you don't also have a way of putting your foes to sleep.

Status Conditions

Damage isn't the only peril that a Pokémon may face in combat—many moves inflict status conditions that can sap a Pokémon's health or impair its ability to fight. Of course, your Pokémon can use these moves as well, and a clever strategist can use them to cripple difficult bosses and to improve the odds of catching wild Pokémon.

Condition	Effect on Afflicted Pokémon
Burn	Lowers Attack strength and loses HP each turn
Confuse	Sometimes attacks itself instead of the target
Flinch	Can't use a move on the turn
Freeze	Can't use moves until the condition is cleared
Infatuate	If opposite gender of attacker, moves will fail 50% of the time
Paralyze	Can't use moves 25% of the time, and Speed stat is lowered
Poison	Loses HP each turn
Sleep	Can't use most moves until the condition is cleared

Curing Status Conditions

Sometimes you'll want to tough out a battle with sickened Pokémon, but some conditions are too serious or too long-lasting to ignore. There are remedies for every condition in the game, but they won't always be cheap or easy to find.

Condition	Item-Related Cures	Other Cures
Burn	Burn Heal, Full Heal, Full Restore, Heal Powder, Lava Cookie, Lum Berry, Old Gateau, Rawst Berry	Aromatherapy, Heal Bell, Refresh, Rest
Confuse	Full Heal, Full Restore, Heal Powder, Old Gateau, Persim Berry, Yellow Flute	Remove Pokémon from battle or wait a few turns for the condition to fade
Faint	Max Revive, Old Gateau, Revival Herb, Revive, Sacred Ash	No move-related cure—restore Pokémon at Pokémon Center
Flinch	None	No cure—wait for next move
Freeze	Aspear Berry, Full Restore, Full Heal, Heal Powder, Ice Heal, Lava Cookie, Lum Berry, Old Gateau	Aromatherapy, Heal Bell move, any Fire-type attack except Will-o-Wisp and Sunny Day, or wait a few turns for the condition to fade
Infatuate	Mental Herb, Old Gateau, Red Flute	Remove Pokémon from battle
Paralyze	Cheri Berry, Full Heal, Full Restore, Heal Powder, Lava Cookie, Lum Berry, Old Gateau, Paralyze Heal	Aromatherapy, Heal Bell, Refresh, Rest, Smellingsalt
Poison	Antidote, Full Heal, Full Restore, Heal Powder, Lava Cookie, Lum Berry, Old Gateau, Pecha Berry	Aromatherapy, Heal Bell, Refresh, Rest
Sleep	Awakening, Blue Flute, Chesto Berry, Full Heal, Full Restore, Heal Powder, Lava Cookie, Lum Berry, Old Gateau	Aromatherapy, Heal Bell, Wake-Up Slap, or wait a few turns for the condition to fade

Using Status Conditions to Catch Wild Pokémon

Use status conditions to make catching wild Pokémon a lot easier. Virtually any status condition will increase your odds of success when using a Poké Ball, but Poison, Burn, and Confuse might backfire by KO'ing your target. Paralyze is a better choice, and Sleep and Freeze conditions are the best of all.

Condition-Inflicting Moves

Condition	Move	Effect AC*
Burn	Will-o-Wisp	75
Confuse	Confuse Ray	100
	Supersonic	55
	Sweet Kiss	75
	Teeter Dance •	100
Infatuate	Attract	100
Paralyze	Glare	75
	Stun Spore	75
	Thunder Wave	100
Poison	Poison Gas	55
	Poisonpowder	75
	Toxic ••	85
	Toxic Spikes •	100
Sleep	Dark Void	80
	Grass Whistle	55
	Hypnosis	70
	Sing	55
	Sleep Powder	75
	Spore	100
	Yawn •	100
Special	Psycho Shift	90

Damage- and Condition-Inflicting Moves

Effect	Move	Effect AC*
Burn	Blaze Kick	10
	Ember	10
	Fire Blast	10
	Fire Punch	10
	Flame Wheel	10
	Flamethrower	10
	Heat Wave	10
	Lava Plume	30
	Sacred Fire	50
Confuse	Chatter •	varies
	Confusion	10
	Dizzy Punch	20
	Dynamicpunch	100
	Psybeam	10
	Signal Beam	10
	Rock Climb	20
	Water Pulse	20
Flinch	Air Slash	30
	Astonish	30
	Bite	30
	Dragon Rush	20
	Dark Pulse	20
	Extrasensory	10
	Fake Out •	100
	Fire Fang	10
	Headbutt	30
	Ice Fang	10
	Iron Head	30
	Needle Arm	30
	Rock Slide	30
	Rolling Kick	30
	Sky Attack	30
	Snore •	30
	Stomp	30
	Thunder Fang	10
	Twister	20
	Zen Headbutt	20

Effect	Move	Effect AC*
Freeze	Blizzard	10
	Ice Beam	10
	Ice Fang	10
	Ice Punch	10
	Powder Snow	10
Paralyze	Body Slam	30
	Bounce	30
	Discharge	30
	Dragonbreath	30
	Force Palm	30
	Lick	30
	Spark	30
	Thunder	30
	Thunderbolt	10
	Thunderpunch	10
	Thundershock	10
	Thunder Fang	10
	Zap Cannon	100
Poison	Cross Poison	10
	Gunk Shot	30
	Poison Fang •	30
	Poison Jab	30
	Poison Sting	30
	Poison Tail	10
	Sludge	30
	Sludge Bomb	30
	Smog	40
Special	Tri Attack •••	20
	Secret Power ••••	30

• Move has an additional effect or special usage condition. See the Battle Moves list on pages 158-173.

•• Move afflicts target with more-serious damage each turn.

••• Move can cause a Paralyze, Freeze, or Burn condition randomly.

•••• Move effect changes by location.

* Effect AC (Accuracy) is the percent chance that the move will cause a status condition.

Caring for Afflicted Pokémon

If you cannot immediately heal an afflicted Pokémon during a fight, the next best strategy is to switch it out of battle. This will cure some status conditions like Infatuate and Confuse, and status conditions such as Poison and Burn will not continue to harm the switched-out Pokémon. However, once the battle is finished, Poison will resume causing damage as the player walks around.

Stat-Altering Moves

Some moves can temporarily affect a Pokémon's stats. While these moves are of little use in short fights, they can be part of a powerful strategy in longer, more difficult battles. For example, by lowering an opponent's Defense, you effectively increase the power of all the physical attacks your team will use throughout the fight. Use stat-altering moves as early as possible for best results.

Moves that Raise the Attacker's Stats

Effect	Move
Attack +	Belly Drum •
	Howl
	Meditate
	Swords Dance
Defense +	Acid Armor
	Barrier
	Defend Order
	Defense Curl
	Harden
	Iron Defense
	Withdraw
Special Attack +	Growth
	Nasty Plot
	Tail Glow
Special Defense +	Amnesia
Speed +	Agility
	Rock Polish
	Tailwind
Attack + / Defense +	Bulk Up
	Curse •
Attack + / Speed +	Dragon Dance
Defense + / Special Defense +	Cosmic Power
Special Attack + / Special Defense +	Calm Mind
Evasion +	Double Team
	Minimize
Special	Acupressure
	Heart Swap
	Guard Swap
	Power Swap
	Power Trick
	Psych Up ••

Moves that Inflict Damage and Raise the Attacker's Stats

Effect	Move	Stat AC*
Attack +	Metal Claw	10
	Meteor Mash	20
Defense +	Skull Bash	100
	Steel Wing	10
Special Defense +	Charge Beam	70
All +	Ancientpower	10
	Ominous Wind	10
	Silver Wind	10

Moves that Inflict Damage and Reduce the Attacker's Stats

Effect	Move	Stat AC*
Attack - / Defense -	Superpower	100
Special Attack -	Draco Meteor	100
	Leaf Storm	100
	Overheat	100
	Psycho Boost	100
Defense - / Special Defense -	Close Combat	100
Speed -	Hammer Arm	100

• Move has an additional effect or special usage condition. See the Battle Moves list on pages 158-173.

•• Duplicates the target's stat modifications.

Moves that Reduce the Defender's Stats

Effect	Move	Stat AC*
Attack -	Charm	100
	Featherdance	100
	Growl	100
Defense -	Leer	100
	Screech	85
	Tail Whip	100
Special Attack -	Captivate •	100
Special Defense -	Fake Tears	100
	Metal Sound	85
Speed -	Cotton Spore	85
	Scary Face	90
	String Shot	95
Attack - / Defense -	Tickle	100
Attack - / Special Attack -	Memento •	100
Accuracy -	Flash	70
	Kinesis	80
	Sand-Attack	100
	Smokescreen	100
Evasion -	Sweet Scent	100

Moves that Inflict Damage and Reduce the Defender's Stats

Effect	Move	Stat AC*
Attack -	Aurora Beam	10
Defense -	Acid	10
	Crush Claw	50
	Iron Tail	30
	Rock Smash	50
Speed -	Bubble	10
	Bubblebeam	10
	Constrict	10
	Icy Wind	100
	Mud Shot	100
	Rock Tomb	100
Special Attack -	Mist Ball	50
Special Defense -	Bug Buzz	10
	Crunch	20
	Earth Power	10
	Energy Ball	10
Accuracy -	Flash Cannon	10
	Focus Blast	10
	Luster Purge	50
	Psychic	10
	Shadow Ball	20
	Mirror Shot	30
	Mud Bomb	30
	Muddy Water	30
	Mud-Slap	100
	Octazooka	50

* Stat AC (Accuracy) is the percent chance that the move will affect a Pokémon's stats.

Holding Berries and Items

Every Pokémon can hold a single item, and you'll be wasting an opportunity if you leave them empty-handed. Using held items never requires a turn, or even a command—your Pokémon will automatically use them when necessary.

Berries cure status conditions or recover lost HP, but can be used only once. They'll trigger as soon as your Pokémon becomes afflicted or seriously wounded.

Certain held items provide benefits constantly without being consumed. Held items like Leftovers, which restores HP every turn, are highly prized by Trainers.

Lead Pokémon

You'll begin every fight by sending your lead Pokémon into battle. This guarantees it a share of the Exp. Points in every fight, but you'll have to waste a lot of turns switching it out if it isn't a good match for the Pokémon in the area.

The Pokémon on the upper-left corner of your roster is your lead Pokémon. If it has fainted, the Pokémon to its right will become the lead Pokémon, and so on. Select a Pokémon and choose Switch to change its place in your roster.

Switching Pokémon in Battle

Switching out your active Pokémon wastes a turn, but there are many situations in which the sacrifice is worth it. A well-timed switch can save a wounded Pokémon, hasten an opponent's defeat, or simply provide an experience boost to a low-level team member.

Offensive Switching

A well-made team should include at least one Pokémon with an advantage against any given type. When battling difficult foes, it's worth wasting a turn to replace a vulnerable Pokémon with one that has a type advantage. But if the situation is truly dire, you may wish to let your active Pokémon get KO'd so your opponent doesn't get a free hit against your MVP.

Defensive Switching

When a crucial Pokémon is badly wounded, pulling it off the front lines is the best way to guarantee it doesn't get KO'd. Switching Pokémon is also a good way to shake temporary conditions like Confuse and Infatuate.

Countering Stat-Altering Moves

The effects of stat-altering moves are temporary, so affected Pokémon will regain their normal stats at the end of the battle. If one of your Pokémon is severely weakened, swapping it out is usually the best solution, but there are a few moves that can restore reduced stats (such as Golbat's Haze). You can prevent status reductions entirely by using a Guard Spec at the beginning of the battle.

Double Battles

Some Trainers battle in teams, deploying two Pokémon on the field at once. You'll respond by sending out your top two to create a 2-on-2 battle. Many moves and abilities affect multiple Pokémon, so having your Pokémon work together opens up new areas of strategy.

Choose Your Leads Carefully

The first two Pokémon in your roster (the ones on the top row) will be your lead Pokémon in a Double Battle. Consider this when choosing your roster—you don't want your top two Pokémon to share a weakness, and a diverse selection of move types is a definite plus.

Some Attacks Affect Multiple Pokémon

Many moves affect both of your opponents' Pokémon, but a few—Earthquake, Eruption, Magnitude, Selfdestruct, and Teeter Dance—hit everyone except the user, including the user's teammate! If you intend to use these moves, pair the user with a Pokémon that is expendable, type-resistant, or can save itself with a move like Protect.

GRAVELER used Selfdestruct!

Some Abilities Benefit Multiple Pokémon

In addition to its moves, every Pokémon has an innate Ability that may be able to affect multiple Pokémon. For example, Intimidate will reduce the Attack of all opponents, and Cloud Nine will protect both of your Pokémon from weather effects. Lightningrod and Storm Drain will draw Electric-type and Water-type attacks, respectively, away from your more vulnerable teammates. And you can mix Abilities that cause weather (for instance, Snow Warning, which causes hail) with Abilities that benefit from weather (like Ice Body, which restores HP during hail) for easy team combos.

Wide-Area Attacks With Status Effects

Status conditions are especially powerful in Double Battles, because they diminish the power of one opponent and allow you to concentrate on the other. The moves on the chart to the right damage both foes and have a chance of inflicting a status condition as well. (The Accuracy is checked individually against each foe, so a condition may affect one, both, or neither of the targets.)

Effect	Move	Effect AC
Burn	Heat Wave	10
	Lava Plume	30
Flinch	Rock Slide	30
	Twister	20
Freeze	Powder Snow	10
	Blizzard	10
Paralyze	Discharge	30
Accuracy	Muddy Water	30
Defense	Acid	10
Speed	Bubble	10
	Icy Wind	100

Wide-Area Support Moves

Several of the stat-boosting, stat-lowering, and recovery moves can affect both Pokémon on a team. The moves shown here improve dramatically in Double Battles.

Move	Effect
Aromatherapy •	Heals all conditions of all Pokémon in your party
Gravity	Makes moves involving flying unusable and negates Levitate
Growl	Reduces the Attack stat of foes by one level
Haze •	Returns stats of all active Pokémon to normal
Heal Bell •	Heals all conditions of all your active Pokémon
Imprison	Prevents foes from using moves the user knows
Leer	Reduces foes' Defense stat by one level
Light Screen •	Halves damage from foes' special attacks for five turns
Mist •	Prevents all stat reduction
Reflect •	Halves damage from foes' physical attacks for five turns
String Shot	Reduces foe's Speed stat by one level
Sweet Scent	Reduces foe's Evasiveness stat by one level
Tail Whip	Reduces foe's Defense stat by one level
Tailwind	Boosts the Speed of all Pokémon in the user's party for three turns

• These moves will always succeed.

Move Combos

When selecting moves, consider how they'll interact with the Pokémon's Ability, held item, and other moves. Some moves can have their powers boosted dramatically when used in clever combinations, and Double Battles increase the combo potential even further.

Single-Battle Combos

You can set up battle combos by combining a move with an Ability, a held item, or a follow-up move you'll use on a subsequent turn. Here are a few examples.

Toxic Spikes and Roar

The Toxic Spikes move scatters poisonous spikes, damaging any foe who enters the battlefield. Follow it up with repeated uses of Roar or Whirlwind to cycle through your foe's roster until everyone on the opposing team is poisoned!

Hypnosis and Dream Eater

Use Hypnosis (or any other Sleep-inflicting move, like Dark Void), then follow it up with Dream Eater to inflict heavy damage and restore the user's HP. If your Pokémon has the Bad Dreams ability, you'll deal even more damage to your slumbering foe.

Belly Drum, Rest, and Chesto Berry

This one is a Snorlax classic. Start with Belly Drum to max out your Attack stat at the cost of half your HP. Restore the lost HP by using Rest, which will heal the user but put it to sleep. If it is holding a Chesto Berry, it will immediately wake up to dish out the hurt.

Rain Dance and Thunder

Summon a storm with Rain Dance to raise the damage of all Water-type attacks. The rain will also boost the Accuracy of the powerful but notoriously inaccurate Thunder move—when you use Thunder on a rainy day, it will always hit! Since the rain sticks around for several turns, you'll have plenty of time to bring in an Electric-type.

Double-Battle Combos

The combination of two Abilities and two move lists enable countless Double Battle combos. For example, you can have a Pokémon use a move that hits everyone, like Confuse-causing Teeter Dance, while its teammate uses a move, held item, or Ability (such as Own Tempo) to protect itself.

Sunny Day and Solarbeam

A solo Pokémon can use this combo if it has both moves, but it will take two turns to get the combo started. In a Double Battle, a fast teammate can use Sunny Day while a slower Pokémon casts Solarbeam with no lag. It's even better if one (or both) Pokémon uses Fire-type attacks (which will be powered up) or has Abilities that are sunlight-triggered.

Follow Me and Focus Punch

Focus Punch can do serious damage if it connects. However, it forces the attacker to move last in the turn, and if the Focus-Punching Pokémon is hit before using the move, it will flinch and lose its attack. Have another Pokémon use Follow Me to draw the attacks away while its teammate gathers its focus.

Guts, Status Conditions, and Facade

If a teammate has the Guts ability, you can power it up by having your other Pokémon hit the gutsy Pokémon with a status condition. Even better, you could then have the afflicted Pokémon use the Facade move to double the damage.

Belly Drum and Psych Up

The Belly Drum move maxes out the user's Attack score at the expense of half its HP. The Psych Up move allows a second Pokémon to gain the benefit without the drawback!

Switcheroo and Pluck

Switcheroo allows a Pokémon to switch held items with a foe. If the Switcheroo user trades off a berry, it can still eat it before its foe by attacking with the Pluck move.

Assurance and Quick Attack

Assurance deals double damage to a foe that has already been damaged during the turn. It's easy to exploit in Double Battles, in which you can have your other Pokémon use Quick Attack or any other "strike first" move to guarantee the extra damage.

Catching and Raising

Your Sinnoh Pokédex has room for 151 Pokémon, and who knows how many exist beyond that? It's time to start catching!

Using Poké Balls to Catch Pokémon

The basic method of catching a wild Pokémon hasn't changed. Reduce its health as much as you can without KO'ing it, then throw a Poké Ball from your bag. If you succeed, the Pokémon will join your party. (If your party is full, it will be sent to computer storage.)

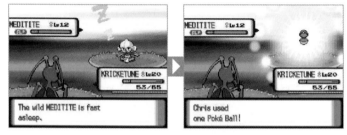

Even if you do everything right, catching high-level Pokémon is rarely easy. You can improve your odds of success by using better Poké Balls (see the chart below), knocking your target down to 1 HP with the False Swipe attack, and afflicting it with a status condition like Sleep or Paralyze.

A Poké Ball for Every Occasion

Strong Pokémon are easier to catch if you use the right Poké Balls. With 16 diferent kinds of Poké Balls, one is sure to be ideal for whatever Pokémon you've set your sights on.

	Ball Type	Description	Availability
	PokéBall	The basic ball to catch Pokémon	Can be puchased at any Pokémart
	Great Ball	Provides a higher Pokémon catch rate than a standard Poké Ball	Can be purchased at any Pokémart
	Ultra Ball	Provides a higher Pokémon catch rate than a Great Ball	Can be purchased at any Pokémart
	Master Ball	Catch any wild Pokémon without fail	Given to you by Cyrus in Veilstone City
	Dive Ball	Works especially well on Pokémon that live in the sea	Can be purchased at certain Pokémarts
	Dusk Ball	Makes it easier to catch wild Pokémon at night or in dark places, such as caves	Can be purchased at certain Pokémarts
	Heal Ball	Restores the captured Pokémon's HP and eliminates any status problem	Can be purchased at certain Pokémarts
	Luxury Ball	Makes a captured wild Pokémon grow friendly quickly	Can be purchased at certain Pokémarts
	Nest Ball	Works especially well on weaker Pokémon in the wild	Can be purchased at certain Pokémarts
	Net Ball	Works especially well on Water- and Bug-type Pokémon	Can be purchased at certain Pokémarts
	Premier Ball	A Poké Ball specially made to commemorate an event of some sort	Received after buying 10 Poké Balls
	Quick Ball	Provides a better capture rate if it is used at the start of a wild encounter	Can be purchased at certain Pokémarts
	Repeat Ball	Works especially well on Pokémon that were previously caught	Can be purchased at certain Pokémarts
	Safari Ball	A special Poké Ball used only in the Great Marsh	Available only in the Great Marsh Safari Game
	Timer Ball	Becomes progressively better the more turns there are in a battle	Can be purchased at certain Pokémarts

Finding Pokémon on Your Journey

You'll encounter most wild Pokémon in random battles on certain types of terrain, but you can also fish for them in lakes and streams, lure them to trees with Honey, hatch them from Eggs, and receive them in trades from friends and certain game characters.

Where the Wild Pokémon Roam

You'll encounter wild Pokémon simply by walking in their natural habitats. In the outdoors, most Pokémon live in tall grass. Others live in caves or certain buildings. When you gain the ability to use HM03 (Surf), you'll encounter aquatic Pokémon as you ride the waves.

In Tall Grass, Caves, and Water

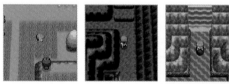

See page 12 for more details on wild-Pokémon encounters in various kinds of terrain.

Using a Fishing Rod

You can use a fishing rod to catch Pokémon in almost any body of water. Stand at the water's edge and select your fishing rod from your Bag to cast a line. When the exclamation point appears over your character's head, reel in the Pokémon by quickly tapping the A Button.

Slather Honey Trees

You can purchase Honey from the groundskeeper at Floaroma Meadow. Use the Honey to slather the bark of brown trees, and you may lure over a reclusive Pokémon. It will take roughly 12 hours before a Pokémon appears, and sometimes one won't take the bait at all, so this tactic requires a fair amount of patience. However, if you wait *too* long, the Pokémon will leave the tree.

Different trees may summon different Pokémon, so set your Honey traps in a wide variety of locations. There are several Pokémon that can be caught only this way, including one that is exclusive to each version of the game.

Other Ways to Acquire Pokémon

You can't be expected to find all of Sinnoh's Pokémon by yourself, especially since several are exclusive to either the Diamond or Pearl version of the game. Cooperate with friends to find and catch them all.

Trade with Other Trainers

Once the Pokémon Center is up and running, you'll be able to trade Pokémon with friends locally via the DS wireless connection or around the world with Nintendo Wi-Fi Connection (see page 38 for details). You'll also meet NPCs (non-playable characters) in some towns who are looking to trade for certain Pokémon.

Hatch a Pokémon Egg

Some NPCs will give you Pokémon Eggs that you can hatch by keeping them in your roster and walking a certain number of steps. You can also produce your own Eggs at the Pokémon Day Care. (See page 32 for details.)

> #### Importing from Other Pokémon Versions
> To import Pokémon from Game Boy Advance Pokémon games, you'll need to first complete the Pokémon Diamond or Pearl story by defeating the Elite Four. You'll then gain access to Pal Park, where you can import up to six Pokémon a day from Pokémon Ruby, Sapphire, Emerald, FireRed and LeafGreen games.

Traded Pokémon Will Grow Faster

The Pokémon that you receive in trades gain a significant boost from the trade—they'll gain 50% more Exp. Points in battle than Pokémon you capture yourself! Trading is also the only way to evolve certain Pokémon.

Version-Exclusive Pokémon

The Diamond and Pearl versions of the game each have 20 exclusive Pokémon that cannot be captured in the other version. To acquire these Pokémon you'll have to rely on friends who own the other version. Study the list of Pokémon that are exclusive to your game—they'll be the ones that your friends want in trade!

Version	Exclusive Pokémon
Diamond	Seel, Dewgong, Scyther, Murkrow, Scizor, Larvitar, Pupitar, Tyranitar, Poochyena, Mightyena, Aron, Lairon, Aggron, Kecleon, Cranidos, Rampardos, Honchkrow, Stunky, Skuntank, Dialga
Pearl	Slowpoke, Slowbro, Pinsir, Slowking, Misdreavus, Houndour, Stantler, Spheal, Sealeo, Walrein, Bagon, Shelgon, Salamence, Shieldon, Bastiodon, Mismagius, Glameow, Purugly, Palkia

Passage of Time

Pokémon Diamond and Pearl have a full 24-hour day-and-night cycle based on the internal clock in your Nintendo DS. So when it's morning in the real world, it should be morning in Sinnoh, and so on (if it's not, you may want to check the clock settings on your DS).

The game divides each 24-hour cycle into three time periods: morning, day, and night. Many wild Pokémon can be found only during certain periods, and some can evolve only during a specific period. There is even a special Dusk Ball that has a better chance of catching Pokémon after the sun has set.

Several events occur based on the passage of time. Honey takes around 12 hours to attract a Pokémon when slathered on a tree, berry trees take set amounts of time to grow, and areas like the Great Marsh Safari Game cycle their Pokémon anew every day.

When you use the Area feature of your Pokédex to see where a certain Pokémon can be found, you'll notice a sun at the bottom of the screen. Move it across the screen with the stylus; the map will change along with the time, revealing where the Pokémon can be found at each phase of the day.

Times of Day

The lighting changes to reflect the time of day. The screenshots below depict morning, day, afternoon (which counts as day), evening (which counts as night), and night.

Abilities Can Affect Encounters and Growth

As introduced in Pokémon Emerald, in Pokémon Diamond and Pokémon Pearl some Pokémon Abilities have an affect on the field. This is vital information for those hunting wild Pokémon—the Abilities listed to the right may affect what kind of Pokémon you encounter and how often you meet them! However, only the Ability of your lead Pokémon will be active, with a few exceptions—Sand Veil, Snow Cloak, Flame Body, and Magma Armor work from any position in your roster.

Ability	Effect in the field
Arena Trap / Illuminate	Increases the chance of meeting wild Pokémon
Suction Cups / Sticky Hold	Increases the chance of meeting Pokémon while fishing
Magnet Pull	Increases the chance of meeting Steel-type Pokémon
Synchronize	Increases the chance of meeting Pokémon with the same Nature as yours
Static	Increases the chance of meeting Electric-type Pokémon
Hustle / Pressure / Vital Spirit	Increases the chance of meeting higher-level Pokémon
Compoundeyes	Increases the chance of meeting Pokémon with held items
Cute Charm	Increases the chance of meeting Pokémon of opposite gender from yours
Quick Feet / No Guard / White Smoke	Decreases the chance of meeting wild Pokémon
Flame Body / Magma Armor	Hatches Eggs in half the time
Intimidate / Keen Eye	Decreases the chance of meeting low-level Pokémon
Sand Veil	Decreases the chance of meeting wild Pokémon when in a sandstorm
Snow Cloak	Decreases the chance of meeting wild Pokémon when in snow, blizzard, or fog

Filling Out the National Pokédex

The Sinnoh Pokédex has room for the 150 Pokémon you'll encounter on your mission from Prof. Rowan, but what about the other 300+ Pokémon (plus the hidden character, Manaphy)? They each have a place in a special National Pokédex that you'll receive after you defeat the Elite Four. When you receive the National Pokédex, hundreds of previously unavailable Pokémon will begin to appear throughout Sinnoh. Finding all the new arrivals won't be easy—you'll have to use several new tactics to seek them out. When you have the National Pokédex you will also be able to import Pokémon from your Game Boy Advance cartridges at the Pal Park.

Dual-Slot Pokémon

If you continue to play the game with a copy of Pokémon Ruby, Sapphire, Emerald, FireRed, or LeafGreen in the GBA cartridge slot of your Nintendo DS, you may encounter exclusive Pokémon from that game on your travels. Each of the five cartridges adds five or six different Pokémon to certain regions of Sinnoh.

Pokémon Swarms

As in past games, Pokémon will begin to swarm after you beat the game. Talk to your rival's sister every day; she'll tell you where a large quantity of rare Pokémon has begun to appear. Catch them while you can—a different variety will be swarming the next day.

Route 216! They said there's a whole bunch of DELIBIRD there!

Poké Radar Exclusives

Along with the National Pokédex, you'll receive an item known as a Poké Radar. Use this item in any field of tall grass to make a small patch begin to rustle. Step into the rustling patch to provoke a Pokémon battle—it may be against a normally occuring Pokémon, or it may be an exclusive Pokémon that can be found only with the Poké Radar! The more the grass rustles, the rarer the Pokémon will be.

New Stuff Everywhere!

Once you have the National Pokédex, you'll also find new Pokémon in the Safari Game and the Pokémon Mansion yard, and new Pokémon Fossils in The Underground!

Control Limitations

Although you can acquire high-level Pokémon by trading with your friends, you can't simply cheat through the game with a friend's Level-90 Infernape. A Pokémon won't obey you unless you can impress it with a prestigious Gym Badge. You'll need the badges shown below to control high-level Pokémon you receive in trades.

Badge	Effect
Forest Badge	Pokémon at or below Level 30 will obey you
Fen Badge	Pokémon at or below Level 50 will obey you
Mine Badge	Pokémon at or below Level 70 will obey you
Beacon Badge	Pokémon at or below Level 100 will obey you

Boosting Stats with Items

Gaining levels isn't the only way to improve your Pokémon's basic stats. Items like Calcium and Zinc can permanently boost a particular stat. But such items are extremely pricey, so give them only to Pokémon you plan on using throughout the game.

Item	Permanent Effect
Calcium	Raises Special Attack stat
Carbos	Raises Speed stat
HP Up	Raises HP
Iron	Raises Defense stat
Protein	Raises Attack stat
Rare Candy	Raises Pokémon's level by one
Zinc	Raises Special Defense stat

Exp. Points

Whenever you defeat an opponent's Pokémon, your Pokémon will earn Exp. Points. When they accumulate enough, they'll level up and gain a bonus to many of their stats. They may also learn a new move or even evolve into a new form! To check on your Pokémon's progress, view its stats on its Summary screen.

Distributing Experience

Pokémon will gain Exp. Points only if they participate in a winning battle without getting KO'd. That works out great for strong Pokémon, but not so well for weak ones. Use the strategies below to gain experience for low-level Pokémon that are unlikely to survive serious combat.

Quick Switches

To get a share of the Exp. Points, a Pokémon need only appear in battle. That means that if you put your weakest Pokémon in the lead slot and switch it out immediately at the beginning of every battle, it will gain a share of Exp. Points in every fight.

Using Exp. Share

You'll find the invaluable Exp. Share item early in your journey. A Pokémon that's in your roster and holds the Exp. Share will get a full half of the Exp. Points earned in battle. If it actually participates in the fight, it will receive a standard share on top of that! See the chart below for examples.

Standard Experience Division

After your team defeats a Pokémon, all battle participants will get an equal share of the Exp. Points. Pokémon that did not enter the battlefield will get nothing.

60 Experience Points	60		Pokémon 1 20 fought	Pokémon 2 20 fought	Pokémon 3 20 fought
			Pokémon 4 00 not used	Pokémon 5 00 not used	Pokémon 6 00 not used

Division If the Pokémon with Exp. Share Doesn't Fight

When a Pokémon holds Exp. Share but doesn't enter the battle, it will still receive half of the total Exp. Points. The remainder will be divided up among battle participants.

60 Experience Points	30 / 30		Pokémon 1 10 fought	Pokémon 2 10 fought	Pokémon 3 10 fought
			Pokémon 4 30 Exp. Share / not used	Pokémon 5 00 not used	Pokémon 6 00 not used

Division If the Pokémon with Exp. Share Does Fight

When a Pokémon holds Exp. Share and enters the battle for any length of time, it will receive half of the Exp. Points, plus an equal share of the remaining Exp. Points divided among all the participants.

60 Experience Points	60		Pokémon 1 40 Exp. Share / fought	Pokémon 2 10 fought	Pokémon 3 10 fought
			Pokémon 4 00 not used	Pokémon 5 00 not used	Pokémon 6 00 not used

Pokémon Day Care

If you want to level up a Pokémon but can't make room for it in your roster, take it to Pokémon Day Care in Solaceon Town. There it will steadily gain Exp. Points based on the number of steps you take until you return to pick it up. And if you leave it with a Pokémon of the opposite gender, you might return to find that an Egg has appeared!

Which Pokémon should we raise for you?

Evolution

Pokémon usually gain strength steadily by leveling up, but sometimes they take a drastic leap forward and transform into an entirely new Pokémon in the blink of an eye! Evolving your Pokémon fills two purposes: strengthening your Pokémon and filling out your Pokédex.

What?
LUXIO is evolving!

Pros and Cons of Evolution

Evolution is usually welcome, but it has disadvantages as well. Evolved Pokémon like Staravia typically learn new moves more slowly than their unevolved counterparts (see the table to the right), so if you're waiting to learn a particular move, you may want to delay their Evolution. Other Pokémon, like Chimchar, learn entirely different moves in their Evolved forms—sometimes for the better, and sometimes for the worse. However, all Pokémon will enjoy a substantial boost to their stats when they evolve.

Starly
Type: Normal Flying

Evolves at Level 14 ▸ **Staravia**
Type: Normal Flying

Moves	Starly	Staravia
Endeavor	Level 17	Level 18
Whirlwind	Level 21	Level 23
Aerial Ace	Level 25	Level 28
Take Down	Level 29	Level 33
Agility	Level 33	Level 38
Brave Bird	Level 37	Level 43

Evolving a Second Type

Several single-type Pokémon will gain a second type when they evolve. (This is true of all three of the Diamond and Pearl starters.) This adds another wrinkle to consider; while evolving a new type may increase your ability to type-trump your foes, it will also give your Pokémon new vulnerabilities. There may be situations in which such vulnerabilities outweigh the benefits of Evolution.

Chimchar
Type: Fire

Evolves at Level 14 ▸ **Monferno**
Type: Fire Fighting

Moves	Chimchar	Monferno
Mach Punch	–	Level 14
Nasty Plot	Level 23	–
Feint	–	Level 29
Facade	Level 31	–
Close Combat	–	Level 36
Flamethrower	Level 41	–
Flare Blitz	–	Level 49

Stopping Evolution

If you want to prevent your Pokémon from evolving, press and hold the B Button during the Evolution animation that plays when they reach the necessary level. That will halt the Evolution for the moment, but the Pokémon will attempt to evolve again the next time it levels up.

Evolve to Complete the Pokédex

Outside of trading, Evolution is the only way to acquire certain Pokémon. If you're serious about completing the Sinnoh Pokédex, you'll want to encourage Evolution whenever possible.

Other Methods of Evolution

While many Pokémon evolve by level alone, others won't evolve unless certain conditions are met. The most common methods of Evolution are listed below.

Trade Evolution

Some Pokémon evolve immediately after they are traded to another player, regardless of their level. These Pokémon often learn moves at the same rate as their unevolved forms, so arrange a trade with a friend as soon as possible.

What?
GRAVELER is evolving!

Stone Evolution

Some Pokémon will evolve when you use a certain Evolution Stone that you've collected on your journey (they're easiest to find in The Underground). However, some of these Pokémon won't be able to learn new moves after they evolve, so hold off for as long as you can!

Evolution Stones
Dawn Stone
Dusk Stone
Fire Stone
Leaf Stone
Moon Stone
Shiny Stone
Sun Stone
Thunderstone
Water Stone

Held-Item Evolution

If certain Pokémon (such as Gligar, Sneasel, and Happiny) are holding a specific item when they gain a level, they may evolve into a new form. But as an added twist, these held-item Evolutions can happen only at certain times of day.

Held Items That Help Evolution
Oval Stone
Razor Claw
Razor Fang

Friendship Evolution

Pokémon will like you more if you keep them in your roster, give them items to hold, feed them Poffins, and don't let them faint in battle. When this hidden friendship level is at its peak, certain Pokémon will evolve when they level up!

Item + Trade Evolution

Trading isn't always enough. Several Pokémon must be holding a specific item when traded in order to evolve.

Trade-Evolution Items
Deepseascale
Deepseatooth
Dragon Scale
Dubious Disc
Electrizer
King's Rock
Magmarizer
Metal Coat
Protector
Reaper Cloth

Gender Evolution

Some of the new Sinnoh Pokémon evolve differently based on their gender. For example, male Burmy evolve into Mothim, while female Burmy evolve into Wormadam. And only female Combee can evolve at all, making the rarer female Combee an especially desirable catch.

Move-Based Evolution

Several new Pokémon can evolve only when they learn a certain move. They'll learn the moves by leveling up, but if you choose not to learn their trademark move, the Evolution won't happen at all!

Area-Based Evolution

Particularly finicky Pokémon can evolve only in a certain area of Sinnoh. If such a Pokémon levels up after a battle anywhere within that area, it will evolve into a new form.

Abilities

In addition to its moves and stats, each Pokémon has a single ability that may give it a significant advantage in combat.

What Are Abilities?

Each individual Pokémon has a single Ability that gives it an advantage in a particular situation. Some of these Abilities provide a minor boost that rarely matters, whereas others may be a Pokémon's defining trait. You can see the name and description of each Pokémon's ability on the Pokémon Skills page of its Summary screen.

Many Kinds of Abilites

There are 123 different Abilities in the world of Pokémon. Although there are several unique Abilities in that number, most Abilities fall within one of the following categories.

Type-Negating Abilities

Some Abilities can change the rules of how types interact with each other. For example, the Levitate Ability negates all Ground-type attacks. Even better are absorbtion Abilities like Volt Absorb and Water Absorb—they don't just negate the damage of certain attack types; they convert it into HP recovery instead. The Scrappy Ability can even allow a Pokémon to hit a Ghost-type with Normal- or Fighting-type moves.

Contact Abilities

Some Abilities discourage foes from making physical contact in battle. For example, Pichu's Static Ability may automatically paralyze any foe that touches it by using certain physical attacks. Another example is Budew's Poison Point, which has a chance of inflication the Poison condition on any foe who makes physical contact.

Stat-Altering Abilities

Many Abilities will alter the stats of Pokémon on the field. The Attack-boosting Huge Power is a simple example, but Abilities like Hustle are a mixed blessing, boosting one stat while lowering another. Other Abilities provide larger boosts, but only under certain circumstances, like when an opponent is of the same gender (Rivalry) or under certain weather conditions (Chlorophyll).

Reactive Abilities

Some Abilities provide a bonus when a Pokémon is in a "pinch," which occurs when it's down to 1/3 of its max HP. Other Abilities trigger in response to enemy actions; Steadfast boosts Speed after a Pokémon is caused to Flinch, and Anger Point boosts Attack to max after a Pokémon is damaged by a critical hit.

Status-Condition Protection

Many Pokémon have Abilities that protect them from specific status conditions. For example, Thick Fat will prevent a Pokémon from being burned or frozen, and Vital Spirit provides immunity to the Sleep condition. Other Abilities provide general protections; for instance, Shield Dust protects from status conditions inflicted by damage-dealing moves.

Field Abilities

Many Abilities now work outside of battle, affecting the quantity and types of Pokémon you encounter on the field (see page 20 for the complete list). These Abilities usually have a different (but often related) effect in battle. For example, Magnet Pull increases the odds of meeting Steel-type Pokémon in the wild and prevents those Pokémon from escaping in combat. Most in-game Ability descriptions list the combat effect only.

Unique Abilities

There are several Abilities that cannot be easily categorized—they provide significant and complicated effects that are unique to a very small group of Pokémon. Some examples are listed below.

Mold Breaker

Mold Breaker allows a Pokémon to attack without being affected by a foe's special properties, effectively negating the following Abilities: Battle Armor, Clear Body, Damp, Dry Skin, Filter, Flash Fire, Flower Gift, Heat Proof, Hyper Cutter, Immunity, Inner Focus, Insomnia, Keen Eye, Leaf Guard, Lightningrod, Limber, Magma Armor, Marvel Scale, Motor Drive, Oblivious, Own Tempo, Sand Veil, Shell Armor, Shield Dust, Simple, Snow Cloak, Solid Rock, Soundproof, Sticky Hold, Storm Drain, Sturdy, Suction Cups, Tangled Feet, Thick Fat, Unaware, Vital Spirit, Volt Absorb, Water Absorb, Water Veil, White Smoke, and Wonder Guard.

Pickup

A Pokémon with the Pickup Ability has a 10% chance of finding an item after defeating a foe. The item is determined at random—it is not based on the kind of Pokémon you defeat, but the opponent's level does affect its quality. The items you can obtain with Pickup include Dawn Stone, Dusk Stone, Elixir, Escape Rope, Ether, Full Heal, Full Restore, Great Ball, Hyper Potion, King's Rock, Leftovers, Max Elixir, Max Revive, Nugget, Potion, PP UP, Rare Candy, Repel, Revive, Shiny Stone, Super Potion, TM01, TM26, TM44, Ultra Ball, and White Herb.

Soundproof

Soundproof makes a Pokémon immune to moves that have a sonic component, negating the effects of Bug Buzz, Chatter, Grasswhistle, Growl, Heal Bell, Hyper Voice, Metal Sound, Perish Song, Roar, Screech, Sing, Snore, Supersonic, and Uproar.

Wonder Guard

This makes Shedinja immune to all damage except from attacks that trump its own type.

Different Abilities in the Same Pokémon

Some Pokémon species can only ever know a single Ability (for example, all Ninetales have Flash Fire), but most species can have one of two different Abilities. You may need to catch several wild Pokémon of the same species before you find one with the Ability you want.

Breeding Abilities

When breeding Pokémon, Abilities are inherited from the mother. So if you want your hatchling to have a particular Ability, choose its mom carefully! See page 32 for more information on breeding Pokémon.

Pokémon Nature

A Pokémon can have one of 25 different Natures that define its individual personality and its strengths in combat.

Natures

Each individual Pokémon has one of 25 Natures, chosen at random regardless of species. Its Nature defines which stats gain the most improvement each time it levels up, and can have a significant effect throughout the Pokémon's life. A Pokémon's Nature also determines what Poffin flavors it prefers—see page 29 for more information on that topic.

The Trainer Memo Summary screen is full of useful information for serious Pokémon Trainers. In addition to a Pokémon's Nature, you'll see a personality trait such as "Likes to run," "Thoroughly cunning," or "Proud of its power." These descriptions provide a hint about that Pokémon's fastest-growing stat, which may not be the one suggested by its Nature. (See page 156 for the complete list of character traits.)

Benefits and Drawbacks of Natures

Nature	Effect	Nature	Effect
Adamant	Attack + / Special Attack -	Lonely	Attack + / Defense -
Bashful	—	Mild	Special Attack + / Defense -
Bold	Defense + / Attack -	Modest	Special Attack + / Attack -
Brave	Attack + / Speed -	Naive	Speed + / Special Defense -
Calm	Special Defense + / Attack -	Naughty	Attack + / Special Defense -
Careful	Special Defense + / Special Attack -	Quiet	Special Attack + / Speed -
Docile	—	Quirky	—
Gentle	Special Defense + / Defense -	Rash	Special Attack + / Special Defense -
Hardy	—	Relaxed	Defense + / Speed -
Hasty	Speed + / Defense -	Sassy	Special Defense + / Speed -
Impish	Defense + / Special Attack -	Serious	—
Jolly	Speed + / Special Attack -	Timid	Speed + / Attack -
Lax	Defense + / Special Defense -		

Managing Your Pokémon

You'll gather information on hundreds of different Pokémon during your journey. Count on your trusty Pokédex to keep all this data organized.

The Sinnoh Pokédex

Early in your quest, Prof. Rowan will give you the Sinnoh Pokédex, an advanced dual-screen computer that collects data on every Pokémon you meet. By using the stylus and the lower screen of your DS, you can easily access information on any Pokémon you've encountered.

Filling the Pokédex

As you encounter Pokémon in the wild and in Trainer battles, your Pokédex will fill with information about them that you can access at any time after the fight. The Pokémon that you've caught, evolved, or received in trades will appear with a Poké Ball symbol next to their name (even if they're no longer in your possession). Pokémon that you've faced in combat but haven't yet captured will also appear, but crucial data will be missing from their entries. The Pokémon that you have yet to meet will be respresented by "-----." But this lack of information can be useful in itself. Pokémon typically appear in Evolution order, so a perpetually blank entry suggests that there may be a way to evolve the Pokémon that comes before it.

Rapidly scroll through your Pokédex entries by spinning the Poké Ball-esque wheel on the right side of the lower screen.

The National Pokédex

After you defeat the Elite Four and rise to Pokémon Champion status, you'll be given an expanded Pokédex known as the National Pokédex. This will reorder the Pokémon in your Sinnoh Pokédex to make room for the several hundred Pokémon from previous games in the series. At the same time, most of those Pokémon will begin appearing in the land of Sinnoh. Your work has only just begun!

Searching for Information in the Pokédex

The Info screen of each Pokémon entry offers a description of the Pokémon as well as information about its type, height, and weight. Press the Area button to find out where the Pokémon can be found in the wild. Drag the sun across the screen to see at what times of day you can find it.

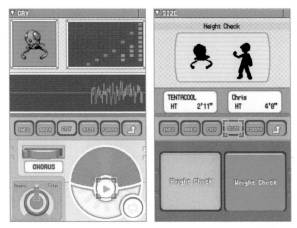

The Cry button allows you to listen to each Pokémon's cry, and even adjust various sound-output settings. Press Size to see how that Pokémon's height and weight compare to your hero's.

By using the Pokédex's Search Pokémon function, you can reorder the Pokémon alphabetically or by size. You can also search for Pokémon that have a particular name, type, or body style.

Use the Pokédex to Locate Elusive Pokémon

The area locator is one of the Pokédex's most useful features. Even if you've seen a Pokémon only in the roster of some other Trainer, your Pokédex will be able to tell where the Pokémon's natural habitat is and what times of day it can be found there. However, not all Pokémon can be caught—if "Area Unknown" pops up, that Pokémon may not exist in the wild. (At least not in your version of the game.)

Use the Pokédex to Find a Specific Type

When you get stuck at a difficult Gym, you may realize that your roster is in desperate need of a certain Pokémon type. Instead of wandering aimlessly, select Search Pokémon on your Pokédex and then hit the Type button. Choose a type to see entries on all the Pokémon of that type that you've encountered, then use the area function to find the ones you desire most.

Forming a Team of Six

You can store over 500 Pokémon on the Pokémon Center PC, but you can bring only six with you at any one time, forcing Trainers to make hard strategic decisions. Pick a team that gives you an edge against as many Pokémon types as possible, and has few vulnerabilities in common. Bring several strong Pokémon you can rely on, but don't forget to save a slot or two for new recruits or unhatched Eggs—raising new talent is important too.

To arrange your team, access Bebe's PC (aka "Someone's PC") at a Pokémon Center, and use the Withdraw Pokémon and Deposit Pokémon commands to move Pokémon between their boxes and your roster.

Maintain a Bench of Usable Pokémon

Use a diverse team when exploring unfamiliar areas, but when challenging Gyms and type-themed areas, you may want to build a more narrowly focused team with several Pokémon of the same type. This will require a varied bench with several usable Pokémon, so don't limit yourself by raising only a handful of favored Pokémon. It pays to have a few high-level Pokémon of every common type.

A Well-Balanced Pokémon Team

When exploring new areas and battling unfamiliar Trainers, it pays to have a diverse assortment of Pokémon with a wide variety of attack types and—more importantly—no shared vulnerabilities.

An Effective Team

The Prinplup-led team to the right can effectively use attacks of 10 different types, providing a solution to almost every challenge. It also has a wide variance in stats; quick, heavy hitters like Roserade and Heracross can take out foes quickly, and strong defenders like Graveler can stall foes while the Trainer tends to the wounded.

An Ineffective Team

The Psyduck-led team shown here can exploit only four types of attacks, leaving it unable to type-trump several popular types. Worse yet, every single member of the team shares a weakness to Electric-type attacks. A single strong Electric-type Pokémon could knock out all six team members without breaking a sweat.

Traveling in Sinnoh

Sinnoh is a vast and wild land, known for steep mountains, thick forests, and harsh weather. Getting around won't be easy.

Navigating the Wilds

You'll need a two-speed bike, a few ferry tickets, and several talented Pokémon to overcome the rocky terrain and harsh weather of the Sinnoh region.

Traveling on Foot

You'll begin your journey on nothing but your own two feet. Luckily you'll soon receive a pair of Running Shoes that will allow you to move much faster by holding the B Button. The Running Shoes are always on your feet and don't need to be used or registered as other items do.

The New Two-Speed Bike

Every Pokémon adventure involves acquiring a Bicycle, but the one in Diamond and Pearl is a lot fancier than the ones that came before. Hop on by selecting it from the Key Items pouch of your bag, then switch between third and fourth gear (there's no first and second) by tapping the B Button. Third gear offers good maneuverability, and fourth gear has poor maneuverability but allows you to build up the speed necessary to ascend steep ramps.

Leaping off Ledges

You'll find short ledges, like the ones shown to the right, throughout Sinnoh. You can jump off a ledge safely, but there is no way to climb back up. These one-way routes can save time, but you may need to take a long trip around them on the way back.

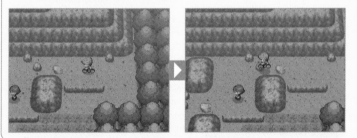

Bike Jumps and Ramps

The fourth gear of your Bicycle is used for more than just ascending steep ramps. You'll also encounter jumps that can send you flying over obstacles, but you'll need to hit the jumps with speeds that can be reached only in fourth gear.

Travel by Sea

You can use HM03 (Surf) to cross shallow water, but at some points in your journey a passenger ship will be the only way to cross deep water.

The Town Map

Select the Town Map to see how Sinnoh's many towns and cities are connected. Highlight any area and press the magnifying glass on the lower screen to bring up a Guide Map with a full description of the area. This is a great feature when you can't remember what town the Day Care is in, or where the Berry Master lives.

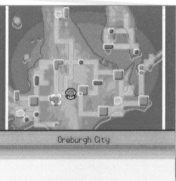

Oreburgh City

Player Location

Your current location is displayed as a small icon of your character's head.

Direction of Travel

The orange-and-white circles show what direction you're coming from, a great feature for when you've lost your bearings.

Towns and Cities

Towns are displayed in blue, and cities in red. Towns and cities that you haven't yet visited are grey.

Pokétch Map Apps

The Town Map provides the best general overview of Sinnoh, but a few Pokétch apps display maps that offer additional information. See page 30 for details.

Guide Map Locations

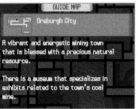

When you view the Guide Map of a city, you'll see a small diagram of its roads with the Pokémart shown as a blue dot and the Pokémon Center shown as a red dot.

Some Moves Are Useful for Travel

Though all Pokémon moves can be used in combat, a few can be used on the field to clear obstacles, allow you to travel on new types of terrain, or transport you around the world.

HM Travel Moves

HM items can be used to teach important moves to your Pokémon, but you won't be able to use them outside of combat until you've earned a particular Gym Badge. Once you have, you can use the move by pressing the A Button near a target object or by selecting the Pokémon who knows it from your Pokémon menu.

Badge	HM Unlocked
Coal Badge	HM06 Rock Smash
Forest Badge	HM01 Cut
Cobble Badge	HM02 Fly
Fen Badge	HM05 Defog
Relic Badge	HM03 Surf
Mine Badge	HM04 Strength
Icicle Badge	HM08 Rock Climb
Beacon Badge	HM07 Waterfall

HM01 Cut

The Cut move can take down the two-limbed trees that often block your path in wilderness areas.

HM02 Fly

In the blink of an eye, the Fly move can take you to any town you've already visited.

HM03 Surf

The Surf move will allow you to ride your Pokémon over lakes and rivers, allowing you to reach otherwise-inaccessible areas.

HM04 Strength

Use the Strength move to push aside the heavy grey rocks that often block paths in caves.

HM05 Defog

When thick fog leaves you unable to see where you're going, use Defog to clear the mists and restore normal visibility.

HM06 Rock Smash

The cracked brown rocks can't be pushed aside with Strength, but they can be smashed apart with Rock Smash.

HM07 Waterfall

The Surf move allows you to swim, but you'll need the Waterfall move to climb up waterfalls that may impede your progress.

HM08 Rock Climb

Use the Rock Climb move to climb up or down the footholds that have been carved in certain mountain walls.

Other Helpful Travel Moves

The following moves can be learned from TMs or by leveling up certain Pokémon. They aren't required to complete the game, but they will come in handy at times.

Teleport

The Teleport move can return you directly to the last Pokémon Center you've visited, but it won't work in caves or buildings.

Dig

When exploring a cave, use the Dig command to return to whatever entrance you entered from.

Sweet Scent

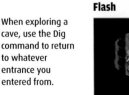

If you're tired of tramping through tall grass, you can initiate a wild-Pokémon fight by using the Sweet Scent move.

Flash

Some caves are so dark that you can't see more than a few feet ahead of you. Use Flash to light up the area.

Weather and Weather Effects

You'll encounter a wide variety of weather on your journey. Some Pokémon enjoy harsh conditions, but it will dampen the spirits—and Abilities—of others. As in real life, it pays to be prepared.

Rain

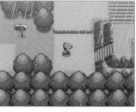

Rain falls often in Sinnoh, which makes life easy for Water-types by providing a 50% power boost to Water-type moves. But Fire-types prefer to stay dry, and will suffer a 50% cut in the power of Fire-type moves. Rain also boosts the accuracy of the Thunder move and heals Pokémon that have the Dry Skin ability.

Snow

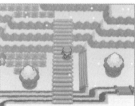

Snow doesn't affect any moves directly, but most Ice-type Pokémon seem to enjoy it. Where you encounter snow, you're likely to encounter wild Pokémon that use moves to create hail effects and to increase the efficiency of Ice-type moves like Blizzard.

Thick Fog

Thick fog is an annoyance that will sharply reduce your visibility until you use a Pokémon that has learned HM05 (Defog) to clear it. In combat, thick fog cuts the accuracy of all moves to 60% of their normal values.

Weather that Damages Pokémon

Hail continues to fall.

Some moves and Abilities can summon damaging weather effects like hail and sandstorms. Sandstorms damage all but Rock-, Steel-, and Ground-type combatants every turn. Hail hurts just as much, but spares only Ice-types. If you can't change to a Pokémon that's immune to certain weather, try switching the weather to something more agreeable.

Travel Items

There are several items that will prove useful on your journey. You may not need them to complete the game, but using them will make things a whole lot easier.

Vs. Seeker

The Vs. Seeker will point you to defeated Trainers who are ready for a rematch.

Repels, Super Repels, and Max Repels

Repel items prevent wild Pokémon from attacking you for a set number of steps. Super Repels last longer than normal ones, and Max Repels last the longest of all.

Pokétch

The Pokétch has at least 19 separate functions that are accessible on the DS's lower screen. See page 30 for full details.

Explorer Kit

The Explorer Kit is a key item that allows you to enter a secret area of Sinnoh known as The Underground. Read more about it on page 38.

Item Use and Held Items

Expert Trainers keep an assortment of useful gear in their Bags, and one quality item in each Pokémon's hot little hands.

A Bag Worthy of a Hero

Every item you find will automatically be sent into one of your Bag's eight compartments. With the Bag's impressive capacity and the touch-screen ball providing an easy way to scroll through your inventory, there is no longer any need to store excess items in PCs.

Badges and Item Availability

Some items (marked with a red dot in the Pokémart tables in the walkthrough) are available only after you've earned a certain number of badges.

Badges	Items that Become Available
0 Badges	Antidote, Paralyze Heal, Poké Ball, Potion
1 or 2 Badges	Awakening, Burn Heal, Escape Rope, Ice Heal, Repel, Super Potion
3 or 4 Badges	Great Ball, Revive, Super Repel
5 or 6 Badges	Full Heal, Hyper Potion, Max Repel, Ultra Ball
7 Badges	Max Potion
8 Badges	Full Restore

The Veilstone Department Store

You can purchase basic supplies at the Pokémart located in every town, but for selection it's hard to beat the Veilstone Department Store. In addition to a wide selection of recovery items, the store sells TMs, combat items, stat-boosting nutrients, stationery, Seals, and even furniture for your Secret Base.

Finding Treasures

Many items have been scattered throughout the routes and caves of Sinnoh. Most are in Poké Balls that are clearly visible, but are invisible to the naked eye. Ferret out these hidden treasures with the Dowsing Machine Pokétch app or just press the A Button to search suspicious spots.

Item Use in the Field

You'll use items mostly when in the field and in town areas between battles. To reach into your backpack, select Bag from the main menu and then cycle through the pockets by pressing left or right or tapping their icons on the touch screen.

Key Items

Your most important items go into the Key Items pouch, including such commonly used items as the Town Map, Bicycle, and Good Rod. You can register a single commonly used item by selecting it from the Key Items menu and choosing Register. You will then be able to use that item at any time by simply pressing the Y Button.

Care for Your Pokémon

You can use recovery items like Potions in combat, but it will cost you a turn that you may not be able to afford to lose. It's best to save your healing until the battle is over, and then tend to your wounded Pokémon before you end up in another fight. But don't waste healing items if you're near a Pokémon Center, where healing is free.

TMs and HMs

You can use HMs and TMs any time outside of battle. Once you fire one up, you'll see a list of all the Pokémon in your roster and an Able or Unable tag by each one. If you can't teach the move to the Pokémon you wanted to, press the B Button to back out without wasting the item. Note that while you can teach HM moves at any time, you won't be able to use the moves outside of combat until you earn a particular Gym Badge.

Item Use in Battle

Of the eight compartments in your Bag, only items in the Medicine, Poké Balls, and Battle Items compartments can be used in combat. Use them only when necessary—employing any item in combat will consume your entire turn.

Potions

There isn't much point healing a Pokémon that is taking heavy damage, so swap it out for a hearty defender before you break out the Potions.

Status Healers

Incapacitating conditions like Sleep must be dealt with quickly in tough fights. Less-serious conditions like Paralyze can usually wait until after the battle.

Poké Balls

You never know when you'll run into a rare wild Pokémon, so keep a wide variety of Poké Balls on hand, and always buy the most powerful Poké Balls you can afford.

Battle Items

Special battle items like X Defend, Dire Hit and Guard Spec. should be used only in major battles, and only on Pokémon that you expect to use for several turns in a row.

Held Items

The items in your Berry pouch and most of the items in your Item pouch aren't for your human character—they can be used only by a Pokémon. Each Pokémon can be given a single item while on the field, and the Pokémon will use the item automatically without any further orders from its Trainer.

Enhancement Items

Most of the items in your Item pouch are non-consumable held items that boost a Pokémon's stats, increase the power of a certain move type, enable a new form of Evolution, or impart any one of a number of strange and (usually) useful abilities to its holder. These items are most often found in Poké Balls or given as prizes.

Berries

Berries are much easier to find, and can be picked right off of trees in most of the game's connecting routes. A Pokémon that holds a restorative berry will consume it to recover HP or heal a status condition when necessary—and it won't waste its turn to do so.

Berries that Cure Status Conditions

When battling foes who inflict a specific status condition frequently, it may help to give all of your Pokémon berries that cure that condition. Here's a full list of what cures what.

Condition	Berry
Burn	Lum Berry, Rawst Berry
Confuse	Persim Berry
Freeze	Aspear Berry, Lum Berry
Paralyze	Cheri Berry, Lum Berry
Poison	Lum Berry, Pecha Berry
Sleep	Chesto Berry, Lum Berry

Berries and Poffins

Wild berries allow traveling Trainers to live off the land. Replant the ones you pick—the berries will multiply and prosper.

Collecting Berries

There are 52 berry varieties that grow wild in the soft soil of Sinnoh. Some can be held by Pokémon for useful one-shot effects in combat, whereas others can be used only as ingredients in Poffins.

Berry Plants and Soft Soil

You'll find most berries by simply picking them off of plants. Berries grow in soft soil, and when you first encounter a berry plant it will typically have only one berry on its branches. But if you replant that berry and check on it in a few days, you'll find two (or more) berries instead. Take one, replant the other, and the cycle will continue forever.

It's soft, earthy soil.

Growing and Caring for Berry Plants

If you pluck every berry you see without replacing it, Sinnoh will soon run out of berries. To ensure a long-term supply, replant the ones you pick, and care for them throughout your quest. The maximum yield and growth rates of berry plants varies by variety—some take only eight hours to produce fruit, but others take as long as 72 hours. All 52 varieties enjoy watering and a bit of mulch.

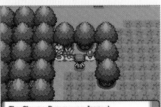

The Chesto Berry was planted in the soft, earthy soil.

Use the Sprayduck to Water Plants

You'll receive the Sprayduck watering can early on your adventure. Use it to water the soft soil after you plant a berry, or to water a flowering berry plant. This will keep the soil healthy and reduce the amount of time it takes for the berry plant to produce fruit.

Use the Pokétch to Find Berries

With soil patches scattered all over Sinnoh, it can be hard to keep track of where you've planted your berries. Fortunately, there's a Berry Searcher Pokétch application that can display a map of Sinnoh with all of the planted berries that are ready to harvest.

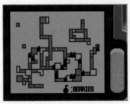

Use Mulch to Fertilize the Soil

On your quest you'll find gardeners who will offer to sell you mulch. Apply mulch to the soft soil where you plant your berries to increase the yield and keep the soil healthy. Mulch is particularly important for players who can't check in on their berries often.

Mulch Type	Effect
Damp Mulch	Slows the growth of berries and causes the soil to dry more slowly
Gooey Mulch	Ups the number of times new plants grow where mature plants withered
Growth Mulch	Speeds up the growth of berries and causes the soil to dry faster
Stable Mulch	Extends the time ripened berries remain on plants before falling

The Berry Master

The Berry Master lives in Route 208, just west of Hearthome City. Visit him every day to receive a free berry, which you can then plant outside of his home. You can also buy mulch from one of his family members.

Everyone seems to call me the Berry Master.

Poffins and Pokémon Conditions

In addition to their other effects, all berries can be used to make Poffins. When fed to Pokémon, Poffins will boost the stats that are used in Pokémon Super Contests—Cool, Tough, Beauty, Smart, and Cute. Each Pokémon has its own flavor preferences, and you can make Poffins in a wide variety of flavors.

Baking Poffins at the Poffin House

The Poffin House in Hearthome City has a mixing pot where Trainers who have been given a Poffin Case can cook their berries. Speak to the woman by the pot, choose your berry, and select Check Tag to see what kind of flavors the berry can produce. If you're trying to boost the stats of a specific Pokémon, make sure the flavors match the preferences listed on its Summary screen!

To cook the berry, use your stylus to stir the pot in the direction indicated on the screen. Early on stir slowly, but quicken your pace as the batter begins to darken. Make sure it doesn't burn (if you stir it too slowly) or overflow (if you stir it too quickly), and you'll create a tasty Poffin.

More Cooks in the Kitchen

If you choose to cook "in a group" up to four players can team up over the DS wireless connection. More cooks means tastier Poffins!

Put Your Berries to Good Use

Early in the game, focus on planting held-item berries that restore HP or remove status conditions. When berries become less important in combat, focus on varieties that make for tasty Poffins or can be exchanged for accessories.

Using Berries as Held Items

Each Pokémon can hold one item. Give Pokémon berries to hold, and they'll eat them when necessary to restore HP, remove status conditions, or reduce the damage from certain types of attacks.

Exchanging Berries for Accessories

At the Floaroma Flower Shop you can trade accumulated berries for accessories that can be used to dress up your Pokémon in Super Contests. Some accessories require hundreds of berries, so start planting early!

The Pokétch

The Pokétch can put dozens of simple apps at a Trainer's fingertips. No wonder it's all the rage in Sinnoh!

Finding Pokétch Apps

You'll receive a Pokétch in Jubilife City, and will find new "apps" (applications) throughout your quest. The Pokétch will fill the lower screen of your Nintendo DS throughout your quest, and you can toggle between its apps by pressing the red touch-screen button at any time on the field. The Pokétch comes with only a few apps—to earn new ones you'll have to talk to everyone you meet and return to Jubilife frequently to speak with the staff of the Pokétch Company.

I'm the president of the Pokétch Company!

The Pokétch uses the DS touch screen exclusively. Press the red button at the right side of the touch screen to toggle between apps, and use the stylus to press the touch-screen buttons within each app.

Analog Watch

If digital watches leave you cold, you can use this app to track time analog-style. As with the Digital Watch, you can tap the screen to light it up.

Berry Searcher

The Berry Searcher displays a map of Sinnoh with berry icons wherever a berry plant is ready for harvest. Tap the screen to refresh it.

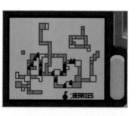

Calendar

This app displays the days of the current month. To mark a day, tap it with your stylus.

Calculator

One of the first Pokétch apps is a touch-screen calculator that can add, multiply, subtract and divide.

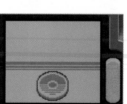

Coin Toss

Trying to resolve a disagreement with a friend? Tap the coin to flip it and have your friend call "Poké Ball" or "Magikarp."

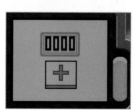

Counter

Tap the plus key to raise the counter by one. Note that the counter will be zeroed out if you switch to any other app.

Day Care Checker

Use this handy app to keep tabs on the current levels of the Pokémon you've sent to Day Care.

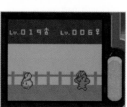

Digital Watch

The Digital Watch displays the current time, based on the time settings of your Nintendo DS. Tap the screen to make the panel light up!

Dot Artist

Tap each pixel of the screen to toggle it between one of four colors. Create your own original Game Boy-style artwork!

Dowsing Machine

To search for hidden items, tap the Dowsing Machine screen to send out a radar wave. If an item is nearby, you'll get a blip that will point you to it.

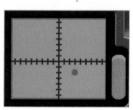

Friendship Checker

To check on the frienship status of a Pokémon in your roster, tap its icon with the stylus. The more hearts that appear, the happier the Pokémon.

Link Searcher

Touch the DS icon to search for any players within wireless range that are currently in a Union Room, the Colosseum, or The Underground.

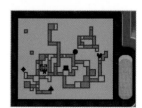

Marking Map

This handy app displays a Sinnoh map and a bunch of icons. Drag an icon to the map to remind yourself of places you intend to return to.

Memo Pad

To write a note, tap the pencil icon and scribble on the touch screen. To write something new, tap on the eraser icon and rub out the old note.

Pedometer

This app records the number of steps you've walked—useful information for when you're trying to hatch an Egg. Tap the C Button to reset it to zero.

Pokémon List

This handy app lets you view your roster and see the current HP of all the Pokémon on your team. Tap a Pokémon to hear its cry.

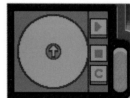

Move Tester

Can't remember what trumps what? Input the type of the move and the type of the defender to see how effective an attack will be.

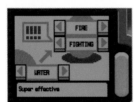

Pokémon History

This app displays the icons of the last 12 Pokémon you've captured.

Roulette

This strange mini-game allows you to sketch out your own roulette wheel. Press the triangle to start it spinning, and the square to make it stop.

Visiting Pokémon Centers

Whether you're connecting with friends or just healing weary Pokémon, Pokémon Centers are an invaluable resource for traveling Trainers.

Pokémon Centers Aren't Hard to Find

You'll find a Pokémon Center in every town in Sinnoh (except Twinleaf Town), so you'll never be far from the resources you need. Each center has different customers to talk to, but they all have the same resources and layout.

The Ground Floor

The ground floor is where you'll find the reception desk. Hand your Poké Balls to the staff behind the counter to restore all of your Pokémon to full health—for free!

OK, I'll take your Pokémon for a few seconds.

Downstairs

The Pokémon Wi-Fi Club is in the basement of every Pokémon Center. Speak to the staff to register Friend Codes, learn your own Friend Code, and to sign on to Nintendo Wi-Fi Connection to trade Pokémon or battle with friends around the world. Wi-Fi Internet access and a properly configured Nintendo DS are required to use the Pokémon Wi-Fi Club.

Upstairs

If you want to battle or trade with nearby friends, head upstairs to the Pokémon Wireless Club. Speak to the clerk at the center counter to enter the Union Room, where you can interact with other players over a local wireless connection. To arrange a Pokémon battle over a local wireless connection, speak to the clerk at the counter on the right.

The Pokémon Center PC

You'll find a public PC terminal on every floor of the Pokémon Center. You can use the PC to connect to three different computer networks, where you can arrange your Pokémon roster, decorate your Poké Balls, and check in with Prof. Rowan. Note that there is no longer any need to use your PC for item storage—everything is now capable of fitting in your Bag.

Bebe's PC

Bebe's PC (which is known as "Someone's PC" until you meet Bebe) is where all of your extra Pokémon are stored. It contains 18 Pokémon boxes with a capacity of 30 Pokémon each, which you may use to organize your Pokémon in any way you please. New features include the ability to mark Pokémon for organizational purposes and switch a Pokémon's held items without adding the Pokémon to your roster. A Compare Pokémon option allows you to view the stats of two Pokémon side-by-side.

Your PC

Your can store up to 20 pieces of personal mail on your own PC. You can also use the Ball Capsules function to decorate your Poké Balls with Seals that you've found or purchased during your quest.

Rowan's PC

Access Prof. Rowan's PC to upload your Sinnoh Pokédex and receive words of encouragement from the good professor.

Hall of Fame

When you defeat the Elite Four, your winning team will be recorded forever in the Hall of Fame.

Breeding Pokémon

Some rare Pokémon can never be caught—they must be bred from their Evolved forms and hatched from an Egg. Can you master the art of Pokémon breeding?

Where Do Eggs Come From?

When two Pokémen of opposite genders are left at the Pokémon Day Care in Solaceon Town, they may produce an Egg. Figuring out which Pokémon you'll produce and what traits it will inherit from its parents is tricky, but worth it; Pokémon raised from Level 1 have the potential to be the strongest possible Pokémon of their species. Breeding is also the only way to earn certain rare Pokémon.

Pokémon Day Care
Let Us Raise Your Pokémon

Leave the Parents at Day Care

Bring a male Pokémon and a female Pokémon from the same Egg Group to the Day Care Center. Leave them with the Day Care Lady, then speak to her husband outside to see if the two are compatible. If his prediction sounds promising, return later to see if an Egg has appeared (the waiting period is based on steps walked, not time passed).

Money
₱154838

Fine, we'll raise your MEDICHAM for a while.

Collect and Hatch the Egg

If the two Pokémon have hit it off and produced an Egg, you'll see it on your Pokétch Day Care Checker. Collect the Egg from the Day Care Lady's husband (you'll need an extra slot in your roster) and walk several thousand steps with the Egg in your party to hatch it.

Your Pokémon was holding an Egg!

TRAINER MEMO

⊙ Egg

Mar. 8, 2007
A mysterious Pokémon Egg received from Day-Care Couple.

"The Egg Hatch"
What will hatch from this? It doesn't seem close to hatching.

Item
None

The Day Care Man will tell you if an Egg has been found. If no Egg has been produced, he'll merely comment on the compatibility of the Pokémon in Day Care.

Once an Egg has been found, you can add it to your roster and read its status on its Summary screen. The more the Egg is moving, the sooner it will hatch.

Not All Pokémon Can Breed

Not all Pokémon can breed—especially Legendary Pokémon (which may be the only member of their species) and "baby" Pokémon like Pichu and Azurill.

Pokémon Egg Groups

There are 12 Pokémon Egg Groups, and a Pokémon can breed only with a member of its same group (or with Ditto). To see a Pokémon's Egg Group, check the Sinnoh Pokédex on pages 126-143 or the Egg Group charts on pages 174 and 175. Note that some Pokémon may be members of multiple Egg Groups.

Egg Groups	
Amorphous	Human-like
Bug	Mineral
Ditto	Monster
Dragon	None
Fairy	Water 1
Field	Water 2
Flying	Water 3
Gender Unknown	

Day Care Man's Predictions

Just because two Pokémon *can* breed doesn't mean they will. When you drop off a pair of Pokémon, talk to the Day Care Lady's husband; he'll tell you how well they're getting along. His comment will reveal the odds of the pair producing an Egg (see the table below). If he doesn't seem optimistic, there's no point wasting time—pull out one of the Pokémon and try a new combination.

The two prefer to play with other Pokémon more than with each other.

Egg Probability	Day Care Man's Message
Not a chance	"The two prefer to play with other Pokémon more than with each other."
Not very likely	"The two don't seem to like each other much."
Somewhat likely	"The two seem to get along."
Extremely likely	"They're very friendly."

Breeding Pre-Evolution Pokémon

Some Pokémon have pre-Evolution or "baby" forms that can be acquired only through breeding. However, producing a pre-Evolution Pokémon isn't as simple as pairing up two of its Evolved forms. To ensure a pre-Evolution form, give one parent a certain held item (see the table to the right). For example, breeding two Marill will usually produce another Marill. But if one Marill is holding Sea Incense, you'll end up with a rare, pre-Evolution Azurill instead.

Baby Pokémon	Item Needed
Azurill	Sea Incense
Bonsly	Rock Incense
Budew	Rose Incense
Chingling	Pure Incense
Happiny	Luck Incense
Mantyke	Sea Incense
Mime Jr.	Odd Incense
Munchlax	Full Incense
Wynaut	Lax Incense

Gender Issues

Ditto has no gender and can breed with any Pokémon (except for those in the "none" group). This makes it an essential breeding partner for Pokémon in the Gender Unknown group (like Bronzor) and Pokémon like Mothim or Vespiquen, which come in only a single gender. Aspiring breeders should get ahold of a Ditto as early as possible.

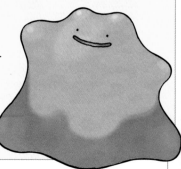

The Products of Successful Breeding

You're certainly free to throw two compatible Pokémon into a room together and hope for the best, but if you're looking to create a Pokémon of a specific species, with a specific Ability, or with specific starting moves, it pays to understand how breeding works. Breeding is full of surprises, but the way traits are passed from parent to child is well-understood.

A Basic Pairing

Breeding Pokémon of the same species keeps things simple, but isn't strictly necessary—A Pokémon gets it species from its mother (unless its mother is a Ditto)—so, for instance, a Bidoof can be bred by pairing a female Bibarel with a Ditto or with any male Pokémon in the Water 1 or Ground group.

Bibarel ♂
Type: Normal Water
Ability: **Simple**
Egg Group: **Water 1 / Field**

Bibarel ♀
Type: Normal Water
Ability: **Unaware**
Egg Group: **Water 1 / Field**

Father

Bidoof ♂ or ♀
Type: Normal Water
Ability: **Unaware**
Egg Group: **Water 1 / Field**

Mother

Pokémon typically produce offspring of their earliest Evolutionary form, so these two Bibarel will produced a Bidoof, not another Bibarel.

Passing Abilities to Offspring

When breeding two of the same Pokémon, the offspring will always receive its Ability from its mother, so it's important to choose a mother with the most desirable Ability possible. In the example above, Unaware is generally more desireable than Simple, so the breeder has done right by its newborn Bidoof.

Passing Moves to Offspring

While the mother contributes her ability and Evolutionary line, the father is the primary contributor to the Pokémon's starting move list. It will pass on any move it has learned from a TM (assuming the offspring is capable of learning that move) and any move it knows that is on the offspring's Egg Move list (a special category of moves that each species can learn only from breeding). However, a father cannot pass down a move that it has learned by leveling up unless the mother also knows that move and it is a move that the offspring could learn naturally through leveling up. A detailed example of how moves are passed down is shown below.

◎ Floatzel's Ice Fang move happens to be on Shinx's Egg Move list, so the Shinx will already know it when it hatches. The Shinx cannot learn moves from its mother in this manner.

◎ Floatzel has learned Toxic from TM06. Since Toxic is on Shinx's TM list, Shinx will inherit the ability to use Toxic from its father.

◎ Shinx can naturally learn the move Crunch when it hits Level 29. But since both parents already know Crunch, it will be born with the ability to use that move.

◎ Having inherited three moves from its parents, Shinx has only one slot left for its traditional starting moves. But Shinx has only one starting move anyway: Tackle.

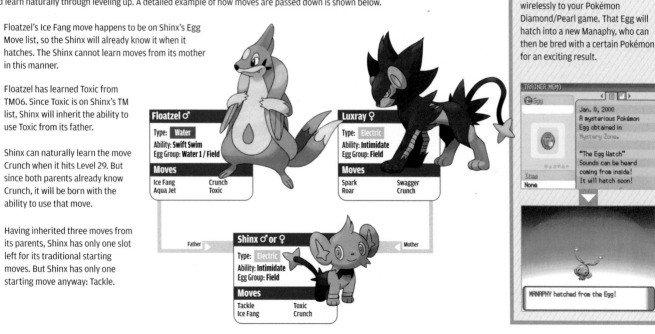

Floatzel ♂
Type: Water
Ability: **Swift Swim**
Egg Group: **Water 1 / Field**
Moves
Ice Fang   Crunch
Aqua Jet   Toxic

Luxray ♀
Type: Electric
Ability: **Intimidate**
Egg Group: **Field**
Moves
Spark   Swagger
Roar   Crunch

Father

Shinx ♂ or ♀
Type: Electric
Ability: **Intimidate**
Egg Group: **Field**
Moves
Tackle   Toxic
Ice Fang   Crunch

Mother

Hatching Pokémon Eggs

To hatch an Egg, you'll have to walk several thousand steps with the Egg in your possession—riding your Bicycle up and down a long route is the fastest way to pass the time if you simply can't wait for nature to takes its course. You can also speed up the process by keeping a Pokémon with the Flame Body or Magma Armor ability in your roster—either move will cut the number of required steps in half. When your Egg does hatch, you'll be prompted to watch the momentous occasion and choose a name for your new recruit.

Producing More Eggs

If you're trying to create multiple copies of a specific Pokémon, why break up a winning team? If you pick up an Egg and leave the parents in Day Care, the parents will once again begin the process of courtship that may—or may not—produce another Egg. But they can't get started until you pick up the first Egg.

Manaphy

If you earned a special Egg in Pokémon Ranger, you can transfer it wirelessly to your Pokémon Diamond/Pearl game. That Egg will hatch into a new Manaphy, who can then be bred with a certain Pokémon for an exciting result.

Super Contests

In addition to combat, Pokémon are skilled at acting, dancing, and being just plain adorable. Enter the Super Contests to watch yours shine!

Hearthome's Pokémon Contest Hall

The Pokémon Contest Hall in Hearthome City hosts Pokémon talent competitions all day, every day. Here you can practice in the Visual, Dance, and Acting categories individually, or test your skills in a full-blown Pokémon Super Contest. Use Poffins and accessories to boost your chances of victory, and climb through the Super Contest ranks to earn ribbons and rare accessories.

The Three Challenges of a Super Contest

There are three competition phases in a Super Contest, and your scores in all three will be tabulated to determine the winner. If you want to practice a particular phase without the pressure of real competition, speak to the clerk at the counter on the right.

Visual

This competition is based on the Pokémon's visual appeal, and scoring is based on audience response. Pokémon are scored in two categories; Condition Points and Dress-Up Points. Condition scoring is based on the Pokémon's condition stats—Cool, Beauty, Cute, Smart, and Tough—which can be boosted by feeding a Pokémon Poffins. Dress-Up Points are awarded based on how skillfully you can arrange accessories to match the contest's theme.

Dance

In the Dance competition, the four entrants take turns being the main dancer, with the other three acting as backup dancers. The main dancer chooses the dance steps, and the backup dancers must match those steps as you press buttons along with the rhythm. Match the main dancer as closely as possible to earn the best score.

Acting

In an Acting competition, each contestant takes turns performing moves in front of the judges. Instead of dealing damage, each of a Pokémon's combat moves has properties that can impress the judges in a variety of different categories. Matching your moves to the theme of the contest (using Cool moves in Cool competitions, for example) will give you a boost in some situations.

Winning a Super Contest

At the end of a Super Contest, the points are tallied in all three competitions and a winner is declared. Only the first-place winner will get the prize of an exclusive accessory and a ribbon that allows the winning Pokémon to compete in the next-highest rank of Super Contests. There are four ranks in all: Normal, Great, Ultra, and Master.

Linked Super Contests

You can replace any number of computer-controlled Super Contest participants with real-life friends playing over the DS wireless link. See page 38 for more details on how to set up a multiplayer Super Contest.

Pokémon Condition

When you enter a Super Contest, you can choose in which field you wish to compete: Cool, Tough, Beauty, Smart, or Cute. Most Pokémon start with low stats in all five categories, so you should pick a condition for the Pokémon you hope to enter, work hard to boost that condition, and enter that Pokémon only in contests associated with that type. As a rule, you should pick the condition that best matches a Pokémon's taste preferences.

Feed Your Pokémon Poffins

To boost a Pokémon's condition stats you'll need to feed it Poffins of a particular flavor. Use the Check Tag option when deciding which berry you'll cook to see what its final flavor will be. For more information on making Poffins, see page 29.

Taste	Condition Raised
Bitter	Smart
Dry	Beauty
Sour	Tough
Spicy	Cool
Sweet	Cute

Each Pokémon has a taste preference that can be viewed on the Trainer Memo page of its Summary screen. Any Pokémon can benefit from eating any Poffin, but feeding it Poffins that match its preference will result in faster growth of a condition.

Stat-Boosting Scarves

After boosting a particular condition stat in your Pokémon, put it in your lead roster slot and bring it to Pastoria City. If its best stat is high enough, a man there will offer you a scarf that will further boost that stat when held by a Pokémon. Boost different stats in different Pokémon to collect all five scarves.

Consider Move Types

Ideally, a Pokémon who excels at Beauty should have at least two Beauty Contest Moves. (You can view moves' contest types in a Pokémon's Contest Moves Summary screen.) Having two moves that match the contest type allows you to exploit the voltage mechanic in Acting competitions (see the next page), but it is not necessary to do so to win.

Round One: Visual Competition

In the Visual competition you'll be given a theme and 60 seconds in which to decorate your Pokémon with accessories to match that theme. Use your stylus to drag accessories from the panels on the left to your Pokémon. The winners are judged by the crowd reaction, which is measured by the hearts that float up from the audience on the lower screen.

Use the arrows below the accessory panels to scroll through your collection in search of items that fit the theme.

You aren't judged on placement, so concentrate instead on attaching as many appropriate accessories as you can.

Collecting Accessories

Accessories can be won through Super Contest victories (one prize per rank in each condition category), found at random by walking your Pokémon in Amity Square, discovered when you give a Pokémon a massage in Veilstone City (maximum of once per day), or earned by trading berries at the Floaroma Flower Shop. A few others can be received in special in-game events.

Round Two: Dance Competition

Watch carefully as the main dancer sets a pattern of dance moves, visible as colored dots on the bottom-left corner of the top screen. Then comes the backup dancers' time to shine—match the set pattern by hitting the buttons of the same colors at the right times.

Hit the colored buttons slightly in advance of the cue to ensure proper timing.

When you're the main dancer, set your moves at the first and last beats of the song for maximum challenge.

Round Three: Acting Competition

In the Acting competition your goal is to impress the judges with your Contest Moves. You get additional points by selecting a judge that no one else chooses to appeal to, and you can score a huge number of points by maxing out a judge's "voltage."

In each of the four turns you will choose a move and a particular judge as a target. Your moves will earn you as many hearts as you see in the move description, and may have other effects as well. At the end of the round, judges will award additional hearts to the Pokémon who targeted them—if you were the only contestant to choose a given judge, you'll earn all of that judge's bonus points, but when multiple Pokémon choose the same judge, each Pokémon will receive smaller bonuses. After the points are tallied everyone moves on to the next turn, in which the Pokémon act in order of lowest-scoring to highest-scoring. Note that you can't use the same move twice in a row, so make sure your contestant has at least two high-appeal Contest Moves.

When a Pokémon uses a move that matches the contest type (a Beauty move in a Beauty contest, for example) it raises the target judge's "voltage." The first four voltage points are meaningless, but whoever scores the fifth voltage point with a single judge will get a huge heart bonus that could turn the entire contest around. Aiming for voltage is risky—since there are only four turns, multiple contestants will need to compete for the same judge to raise its voltage to five, and only the Pokémon who scores the fifth voltage point will earn the bonus. Try to anticipate when the judge will give its fourth bonus point, and intentionally do poorly that turn. That way you'll get to go first and score the fifth voltage point on the next turn!

Moves with High Appeal

It's hard to win in the Acting competition without two moves that have high appeal. However, some moves have other properties that may indirectly aid you by harming opponents or affecting the turn order. Here are some of the best moves in each category:

Category	High-Appeal Moves
Beauty	Ember, Fire Fang, Night Slash, Powder Snow, Power Gem, Power Whip, Tri Attack
Cute	Aqua Tail, Mud Slap, Sleep Talk, Snore, Water Gun
Cool	Air Cutter, Brick Break, Cut, Cross Poison, Crush Claw, Dragon Rage, Drill Peck, Gunk Shot, High Jump Kick, Horn Attack, Hyper Voice, Ice Fang, Jump Kick, Magnet Bomb, Peck, Razor Leaf, Rolling Kick, Slash, Sonic Boom, Spark, Steel Wing, Submission, Thundershock, Twister, Vine Whip, Wing Attack
Smart	Acid, Astonish, Confusion, Gust, Knock Off, Needle Arm, Night Shade, Poison Gas, Psywave, Seed Bomb, Thunder Fang
Tough	Bite, Body Slam, Bone Club, Clamp, Egg Bomb, Headbutt, Karate Chop, Low Kick, Pound, Rock Slide, Rock Throw, Scratch, Seismic Toss, Slam, Smog, Stomp, Strength, Super Fang, Tackle, Take Down, Vicegrip, Waterfall

The Underground

You never know what—or who—you might come across in the subterranean network of tunnels that spans the entirety of Sinnoh.

What Is the Underground?

You'll meet a famous spelunker named the Underground Man in Eterna City. He'll give you the Explorer Kit, which you can use at any time to tunnel down to The Underground. Whenever you enter The Underground, DS wireless communications will be launched so you can explore The Underground with friends, and possibly even run into nearby strangers who are down there too!

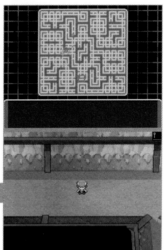

Going underground is quite easy. Simply use your Explorer Kit.

Reading the Underground Map

All of the action in The Underground takes place on the lower screen of your Nintendo DS. The upper screen shows a map of the labyrinthine tunnel network, with your position marked by a red circle. Other players are marked by orange crosses, while walls concealing hidden items are marked by bursts of orange light. If you've established a Secret Base, it will be marked by a red square.

The Underground Menu

Instead of launching the usual menu, the X Button will open a special menu with Underground-exclusive options. The menu divides your Underground inventory into Traps, Spheres, Goods, and Treasures. You can also select your name to see a list of your Underground accomplishments, and choose Go Up to return to the surface world.

Unique Items

The Underground is full of items that are rare or impossible to find in the suface world. Treasure hunters can discover Evolution stones, rare held items such as Plates, Shards that can be traded for TMs (see page 85), and even Pokémon Fossils!

Things to Do in the Underground

There are plenty of things to do in The Underground, but they're all optional—you can spend hundreds of hours down here, or skip this part of the game entirely.

Complete the Training Missions

After giving you the Explorer Kit, the Underground Man will ask you to accomplish a series of short missions (see the list on page 65). Not only are these a great way to learn how The Underground works, but the Underground Man will reward you with valuable items.

Go Treasure Hunting

The walls of The Underground are studded with treasure, and if you're willing to put some time and energy into it, you can excavate all sorts of great loot. The rare finds include Evolution stones, held items, and Fossils, but you'll mostly find colored spheres of various sizes. You can redeem these spheres for various items from vendors in The Underground, or bury them in the ground, where they'll slowly grow into larger and more-valuable spheres.

Underground Vendors

You'll find three kinds of vendors in The Underground. Goods Vendors and Trap Vendors offer items in exchange for your excavated spheres ("goods" are furniture and decorative objects you can set in your Secret Base). On the other hand, Treasure Traders want your excavated Treasures and will give *you* spheres in return. Each vendor has different stock, so find them all!

The Many Regions of the Underground

When you first use your Explorer Kit in Eterna City, you'll end up in The Underground's central area. This is a vast maze that comprises most of The Underground, but it doesn't connect to the isolated regions at each corner of the map. To reach those, you'll have to use your Explorer Kit from the corresponding regions at the four corners of Sinnoh. The four corners of The Underground are the only places you'll find Treasure Traders.

Make Your Own Secret Base

One of the rewards from the Underground Man is the Digger Drill, a one-shot item that allows you to bore a room-sized cave into any section of the tunnel. You can use the resulting cave as a Secret Base, and decorate it any way you like.

The Hood Dresser was placed.

Decorating Your Base

You can decorate your Secret Base with items received in trade from Goods Vendors, purchased at the Department Store, or won as prizes. But you'll need to upgrade your flag to remove the large boulders that litter your Secret Base.

Using the Underground PC

Once you earn decorations, you'll need to store them in your Secret Base's PC, and then use the PC's Decorate options to place, move, or store your items.

DECORATE
STORE GOODS
RECEIVE GOODS
CHECK FLAGS
EXIT

Check your collection of Flags.

Stealing Flags from Other Bases

Every Secret Base comes with a PC and a flag beside it. If you find a friend's base in The Underground, sneak in and steal the flag—the more flags you steal, the more you level up your own flag. At higher levels you can remove more boulders from your base, display more decorations, and even earn special item-finding radar programs for your PC!

Flag	Rewards
Bronze (1 flag)	Remove 1 boulder and display 12 decorations
Silver (3 flags)	Remove up to 5 boulders and display 15 decorations
Gold (10 flags)	Remove up to 10 boulders and receive radar functions for your PC
Platinum (50 flags)	Remove all boulders

Digging Treasures out of the Walls

The walls of The Underground are studded with gemlike spheres, rare items, and even Pokémon Fossils! These treasure veins are indicated on your map by glowing orange bursts. Approach them, then tap on the lower screen to send out a radar signal that will reveal their exact positions as glittering sparkles. Approach the sparkles and press the A Button to bring up your excavation tools. Work together with friends to make excavation even easier.

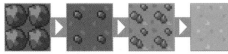

You can hit a wall only so many times before it cracks and collapses. So choose your actions carefully; use the hammer to reveal the treasures' locations, then carefully free them by removing the remaining rock with the pick.

Rock-Wall Density

All treasure is at the lowest levels, buried under as many as four layers of rock. Aim for shallow treasures—the wall won't last long if you're pounding through multiple layers of rock.

Spheres and Other Treasures

While you can dig up all sorts of great stuff, spheres are the most common find. Their value is based on their size, but even small ones can gain value if you then bury them in the floor of The Underground and give them time to grow. The best treasures are, of course, Pokémon Fossils—at first you can find only one in each version of the game, but after you earn the National Pokédex several new Fossils and items will become available.

Traps

Tired of friends sneaking into your base and stealing your flag? You can protect it by leaving traps outside of your base! Traps have all sorts of nasty effects, such as filling an infiltrator's screen with smoke that they must wipe away, or creating a storm of leaves that can be cleared only by blowing into the DS microphone. No one gets hurt—it's all in good fun!

Blow the Trap away!

You can discover and disarm enemy traps the same way you discover treasure: by tapping on the touch screen.

Extras and Fun Stuff

In addition to Super Contests and The Underground, Sinnoh offers a wide variety of diversions for Trainers who want a break from their quest.

TV Interviews

Jubilife TV is at the forefront of the Sinnoh Trainer scene, and there's nothing they'd love more than to interview a rising star like you. If you're willing, give brief interviews—they'll be broadcast on TV later in the game. If you're in a group, your friends will see your TV interviews, and you can see theirs as well.

May I hit you up for a quick interview?

Poké Ball Seals

If you like, you can decorate a favorite Pokémon's Poké Ball with Seals that can make letters, symbols, and even special effects appear on the screen when it is deployed in combat. You can earn letter Seals in Solaceon Town and purchase other kinds in Sunyshore City.

You may set or edit capsules for decorating Poké Balls.

After you earn the Seal Case, you can visit a Pokémon Center and use the Ball Capsules function of your PC. To apply Seals, drag them from the case onto the Poké Ball.

Game Corner

If you want to kill some time and make some money (maybe), play the slot machines at Veilstone City's Game Corner. Once the rollers start spinning, you can stop them individually with the Y, B, and A Buttons, and if you have the right timing, you can earn plenty of coins. If you can score a big jackpot when Clefairy is on the lower screen, you can begin a bonus game in which you can win repeatedly by stopping the rollers in the order Clefairy points to. Your coins can be redeemed for prizes next door—see page 83 for full details on the Clefairy bonus game and the list of prizes.

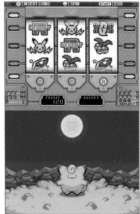

The Daily Loto

Jubilife City hosts a free daily "Loto" in which a five-digit number is drawn and compared to the ID numbers of the Pokémon in your possession. You can win prizes if even a single digit matches, but to earn the big prize—a Master Ball—they need to match exactly. Visit Jubilife City and try your luck every day!

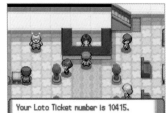

Your Loto Ticket number is 10415.

Connectivity

Pokémon is all about connectivity. Trade, battle, and chat with friends and friends-to-be worldwide.

Local Connections and Wi-Fi Networking

The Pokémon Centers of Sinnoh each host a Union Club on the top floor and a Wi-Fi Club in the basement. The Union Club allows you to connect with friends over a local wireless connection, while the Wi-Fi Club offers a Pokémon first—the ability to trade and battle with Pokémon Diamond and Pearl players around the world!

The Pokémon Center Wi-Fi Club

You'll find the Wi-Fi Club at the basement level of any Pokémon Center. To participate, you'll need a properly configured Nintendo DS and access to a wireless network (see your Nintendo DS manual for more details), as well as a Pal Pad and at least one registered friend. When you're ready to connect, talk to the center clerk in the Wi-Fi Club.

Welcome to the Pokémon Wi-Fi Club!

Once You Are Connected

Once you have connected to the Wi-Fi network, you'll see a list of available friends. You may now use voice chat, share group records, or invite a friend for a battle or a trade.

Single Battle or Double Battle

You may challenge your online friends to either a Single or Double Battle with the Pokémon in your roster. If you invite someone to a Level-50 or Level-100 battle, all participating Pokémon will have their stats scaled up or down to the designated level, ensuring a fair fight. (Their levels will return to normal afterward.) If you want to battle with your teams as is, choose the Free battle option.

Trading in the Wi-Fi Club

The Wi-Fi Club allows you to trade with friends around the world as easily as if they were right by your side—you can even use voice chat as you do it!

Connected-Friend Icons

You'll see icons by the names of each of your connected friends, indicating their status and proclivities. You can't interrupt while they're trading or battling, so wait until they return to idle status before you issue an invitation.

- Friend is idle
- Friend is looking for a battle
- Friend is in a battle
- Friend is looking to trade Pokémon
- Friend is in the process of trading
- Voice chat is disabled

The Pal Pad

In the basement of the Pokémon Center in Oreburgh City, a clerk named Teala will give you a Pal Pad. This device lets you keep track of your online friends so you can connect with them online at the Wi-Fi Club. When online, you can communicate with only the friends that have been registered with your Pal Pad.

Obtain Your Friend Code

Visit the desk in the basement of any Pokémon Center and talk to the center clerk to sign on to the Wi-Fi Club for the first time. After you successfully connect, your Pal Pad will be updated with a Friend Code that will allow others to register you as a friend.

Register Your Friends

Once you have obtained a Friend Code, you can share it with other players who can then input it in their Pal Pads manually. However, if a friend is local, it's much easier to exchange Friend Codes—simply meet in the Union Room and use the Register function. That will update both players' Pal Pads with the appropriate codes.

Choose an Avatar

Players may select an online avatar instead of their normal hero appearance. A customer on the ground floor of the Oreburgh City Pokémon Center will ask you how you perceive yourself, and provide a choice of Trainer types. The one you select will appear by your name in friends' Pal Pads, and it's how you will appear to others in Union Rooms.

Voice Chat

Once you connect with friends over Wi-Fi, you'll be able to use the Nintendo DS microphone to speak to them directly! Voice chat is active by default; use the X Button to toggle it on and off. You may also use voice chat during trades and battles if the host of the session enables that option.

Making New Friends

Whenever you trade with a friend in the Union Room or compete in a Colosseum battle, you'll be prompted to register that friend. If you both agree, Friend Codes will be exchanged and you can communicate further at the Wi-Fi Club. It's good to make friends, but be forewarned: Your Pal Pad has room for only 32 people.

The Battle Tower Wi-Fi Room

Those who attain the rank of League Champion will gain access to the Battle Tower. The Battle Tower has a Wi-Fi Room where you can go online and battle against the teams that other users have registered in their Halls of Fame (but which are now controlled by the computer). If you participate, people around the world will be given the chance to battle your team of Champions!

The Pokémon Center Union Room

When you want to connect with other players that are within wireless range, have all your friends visit the upper floor of any Pokémon Center and enter the Union Room. There you can trade Pokémon, swap Friend Codes, and engage in simple battles. Visiting the Union Room does not require Wi-Fi service or any setup.

Chatting with Other Players

When you use the X Button to open the main menu in the Union Room, you'll find a new Chat option at the top of the menu. Using the game's vocabulary system, you can select a word and broadcast it to all players in the room, who will see it as a line in the chat log on the lower screen. To locate a player who has spoken recently, tap that person's dialogue; a red circle will appear around the person's character. You can scroll through the chat log by using the bar and movement arrows on the right side of the touch screen.

Sign Your Trainer Card

Speak to the clerk at the left desk in the Union Room to use the stylus to sign your digital Trainer Card or change your card's existing signature. Other players will be able to see your signature when they use the Greet command in the Union Room.

Interacting with Other Players

Once you've located a friend with whom you'd like to battle or trade, approach the friend and press the A Button. A menu that'll open contains the following communication options.

Greet

Trainers greet each other by exchanging Trainer Cards. If your friend agrees, both players will get to see a card on the upper screen showing the character's avatar, name, play time, and other information. On the lower screen, tap the button below the Gym Leaders' faces to reveal which Gym Badges that player has won. For more information, press the A Button to see the back of a Trainer Card, with a signature and the person's link-trade and link-battle data.

Battle

Battles in the Union Room have very strict conditions. Each player can use only two Pokémon at Level 30 or under. If that isn't what you had in mind, arrange a fight at the battle counter instead.

Trade

Trading Pokémon with a friend in the Union Room is a simple process. Each player is allowed to see the other player's roster before choosing a single Pokémon to offer in trade, which will be shown on the DS's lower screen. If both players confirm the offer, the Pokémon and their held items will be exchanged.

Share Records

Group members can use this option to sync their records. Up to five group members in the Union Room may join in. See "Groups and Records" on page 40 for more information.

Drawing

The Draw option allows up to five players to draw pictures that will appear on the touch screen simultaneously. Each player's pen will have a number above it to show who's doing what. Change colors by tapping the color palette on the bottom of the screen and change the line width of your pen by tapping the dots along the top.

Pokémon Communication Club Colosseum

To arrange a full-fledged wireless battle, visit the upper floor of a Pokémon Center and speak to the clerk on the right. She'll allow you to arrange a free battle with up to three friends, or test your team-building mettle by competing with a single friend in one of five cup categories. To begin, have everyone approach the counter, then have the host choose Become Leader and the other participants choose Join Group.

BATTLES FOR TWO
▶ SINGLE BATTLE
  DOUBLE BATTLE
  MIX BATTLE
BATTLES FOR FOUR
  MULTI BATTLE
  INFO
  EXIT

Which Battle Mode would you like to play?

Battles for Four

All four-player battles are free battles with no restrictions. Each player selects a teammate and a battle roster of three Pokémon. You'll fight with your teammate in a Double Battle in which each player has one Pokémon deployed on the field at a time.

Garmy sent out SHINX!
Capey sent out LUXRAY!

Battles for Two

If you select a Single Battle or Double Battle, you'll be allowed to choose a set of rules from the chart below. Once both players agree to the terms, they'll be allowed onto the combat field. Take a position at either side to begin the fight.

Single Battle

Single Battles allow Trainers to engage in standard one-on-one competition in which each Trainer places one Pokémon on the field at a time.

Double Battle

Double Battles require each player to have at least two Pokémon in his roster. Double Battles allow each Trainer to deploy two Pokémon at once, enabling all sorts of clever team combos.

Mix Battle

In a Mix Battle, each Trainer makes a battle roster of three Pokémon. Then each player chooses one Pokémon from the opponent's roster to fight on his side instead! Players then battle with the swapped Pokémon and the remaining two in their rosters.

Competing for the Cups

The various battle modes allow players to compete on an even playing field, but require a bit of preparation. Make a separate box on your PC for your cup fighters so you can quickly swap out your team for a specialty team of low-level or lightweight Pokémon. Note that all special battle modes ban the use of multiple Pokémon of the same species and duplicate held items.

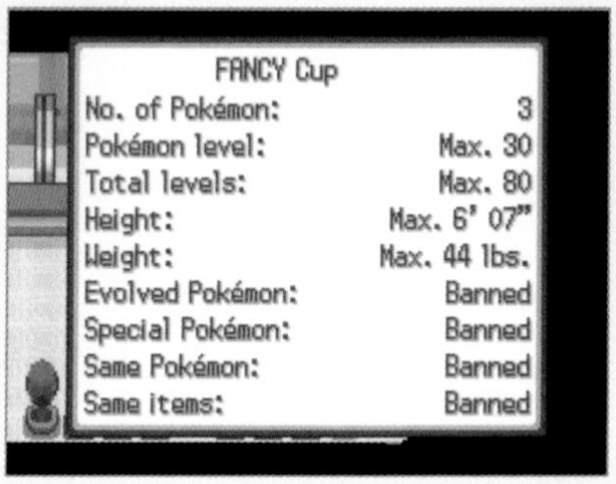

FANCY Cup
No. of Pokémon: 3
Pokémon level: Max. 30
Total levels: Max. 80
Height: Max. 6' 07"
Weight: Max. 44 lbs.
Evolved Pokémon: Banned
Special Pokémon: Banned
Same Pokémon: Banned
Same items: Banned

Rules for Various Battle Modes

Rules	No Restrictions	Standard Cup	Fancy Cup	Little Cup	Light Cup	Double Cup
Number of Pokémon	6	3	3	3	3	4
Pokémon Level	No restrictions	Level 50	Level 30	Level 5	Level 50	Level 50
Max. Total of Pokémon Levels	No restrictions	No restrictions	80	No restrictions	No restrictions	No restrictions
Max. Height Total	No restrictions	No restrictions	6' 07"	No restrictions	No restrictions	No restrictions
Max. Weight total	No restrictions	No restrcitions	44 lbs.	No restrictions	218 lbs.	No restrictions
Evolved Pokémon	No restrictions	Permitted	Banned	Banned	Banned	Permitted
Special Pokémon *	No restrictions	Banned	Banned	Banned	Banned	Banned
Same Pokémon	No restrictions	Banned	Banned	Banned	Banned	Banned
Same Items	No restrictions	Banned	Banned	Banned	Banned	Banned

* Restricted special Pokémon include Celebi, Deoxys (all formes), Dialga, Groudon, Jirachi, Kyogre, Ho-Oh, Lugia, Manaphy, Mewtwo, Mew, Palkia, and Rayquaza.

Groups and Records

You can form a group in Jubilife City (see page 50), or join a friend's group when you meet in the Union Room. When you mix records, certain random game elements will become fixed throughout the group so that its members can share information about where to catch a Feebas or which slot machine pays off best. You'll also see your group members on TV interviews and see pictures of their Pokémon at the Jubilife City TV station.

Oh, you want to make a new group? Sure thing!

Sending Mail

To send a message to another Trainer, start by buying a piece of Stationery, which is usually sold by the left clerk at Pokémarts. Give that to any Pokémon, which will allow you to begin writing. Compose a message by selecting words from the game's vocabulary system, then "send" the mail by trading that Pokémon to your friend.

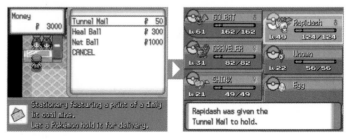

Money
₽ 3000

Tunnel Mail   ₽ 50
Heal Ball   ₽ 300
Net Ball   ₽1000
CANCEL

Stationery featuring a print of a dimly lit coal mine.
Let a Pokémon hold it for delivery.

GOLBAT   ♂
Lv61 162/162
Rapidash   ♂
Lv49 124/124
GRAVELER
Lv31 82/82
Unown
Lv22 56/56
SHINX
Lv21 49/49
Egg

Rapidash was given the Tunnel Mail to hold.

Linked Super Contests

At the Pokémon Contest Hall in Hearthome City, you can compete with up to three friends. To arrange a contest, have everyone visit the Contest Hall and speak to the clerk at the left counter. Pick a contest type (everyone must choose the same one) and then tell the clerk you're ready to begin. Any missing players will be replaced by NPC entrants.

Making Poffins Together

You can meet up to three friends in the Poffin House in Hearthome City and work together to cook Poffins. Each player chooses a different berry, then they all stir the batter at the same time. The mixture of berries will create higher-level Poffins than a single player could make, and the more players that participate, the more Poffins each player will earn!

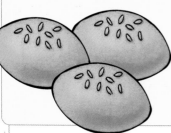

Underground Multiplayer

When you meet other players in The Underground, you can invade each other's Secret Bases to steal flags. By stealing flags you can improve your own base–don't pass up an opportunity to do so! However, it won't be any fun if you make it easy for friends to infiltrate your base, so set traps to slow them down and allow you to reach their base first. You can trade spheres for traps with the Trap Vendors in The Underground.

Trap	Effect
Alert Trap 1	Stepping on this trap sends greetings to everyone near you.
Alert Trap 2	Stepping on this trap sends farewells to everyone near you.
Alert Trap 3	Stepping on this trap tells all nearby that you are going to the Union Room.
Alert Trap 4	Stepping on this trap alerts everyone to gather around you.
Big Smoke Trap	This trap releases billowing smoke. The smoke can be rubbed away.
Bubble Trap	This trap releases a mass of bubbles. Pop them to get free.
Confuse Trap	Stepping on this trap scrambles the victim's movements.
Ember Trap	This trap releases immobilizing embers. Blow the embers away to get free.
Fire Trap	This trap releases billowing flames. Blow the flames away to get free.
Flower Trap	This trap releases immobilizing fireworks. Blow the fireworks away to get free.
Foam Trap	This trap releases bubbles. Pop the bubbles to get free.
Hole Trap	A pit opens up underneath the trap to immobilize the victim.
Hurl Trap (down)	Stepping on this trap sends the victim flying downward.
Hurl Trap (left)	Stepping on this trap sends the victim flying to the left.
Hurl Trap (right)	Stepping on this trap sends the victim flying to the right.
Hurl Trap (up)	Stepping on this trap sends the victim flying upward.
Leaf Trap	This trap releases immobilizing leaves. Blow the leaves away to get free.
Move Trap (down)	Stepping on this trap sends the victim flying downward.
Move Trap (left)	Stepping on this trap sends the victim flying to the left.
Move Trap (right)	Stepping on this trap sends the victim flying to the right.
Move Trap (up)	Stepping on this trap sends the victim flying upward.
Pit Trap	A huge pit opens up underneath the trap to immobilize the victim.
Reverse Trap	Stepping on this trap reverses the victim's movements.
Rock Trap	This trap makes blocking boulders. Break the boulders to get free.
Rockfall Trap	This trap makes big boulders. Break the boulders to get free.
Smoke Trap	This trap releases obscuring smoke. The smoke can be rubbed away.

GTS Wi-Fi: Global Trade Station

The Global Trade Station is in the southwest corner of Jubilife City. There players can trade Pokémon over the Wi-Fi network with people from all over the world. Post a Pokémon that you're willing to trade or search through the list of Pokémon offered by other Trainers. You may end up with a Pokémon from another country!

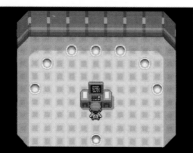

Register on the Geonet Globe

The lobby of the Global Trade Station is dominated by the massive Geonet Globe. Input your location by selecting it from a series of menus, and it will be marked on the map. Now whenever you communicate or trade with anyone in the world, your location will be marked on their globe and vice versa.

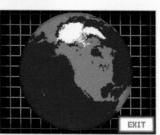

Offer Pokémon

When you offer a Pokémon for trade, you'll be asked which Pokémon you want in return, and if you have any gender or minimum-level requirements. If someone else has already offered that Pokémon for the one you're offering now, the trade will go through immediately! If not, you can leave your Pokémon at the Global Trade Station until the right deal comes along.

Seek Pokémon

If you just want to browse through the Pokémon offered by other players, select Seek Pokémon. You can search for any Pokémon and specify a gender or minimum level. All the matching Pokémon will appear, along with what Pokémon the offering player seeks in return. If you have what they want and are willing to make the trade, you can grab that Pokémon from the nearby PC.

Using the Walkthrough

The walkthrough that follows will take you from your first Pokémon through your final battle to become League Champion. Here's how to make sense of it all.

Checklist

Each section has a checklist of the special things you can do in that area, numbered to correspond to that section's tips. When you can't do everything on your first visit, the list will be divided into First Visit and Return Visit.

Maps

Each section features a full map of the area, with numbered labels that correspond to the tips for that section. You'll also find labels for Gyms, Pokémon Centers, and Pokémarts, as well as labels that reveal the contents of the Poké Balls in the area. Some maps also have letter labels that show how multiple map sections connect to each other.

Tips

Each checklist item and numbered map label corresponds to a tip that provides detailed information on unusual shops, interesting characters, and special events. Any items you can gain during the course of the tip are indicated in orange tags. If a tip refers to an event that occurs later in the game or an area that you can't yet reach, it will be in a darker-tinted Return Visit section.

Event Battles

Boxes like this highlight special Event Battles in which you'll face off against your rival or a commander from Team Galactic. These boxes provide special strategies as well as lists of your opponent's Pokémon and suggestions for which types of Pokémon you should use when you face them.

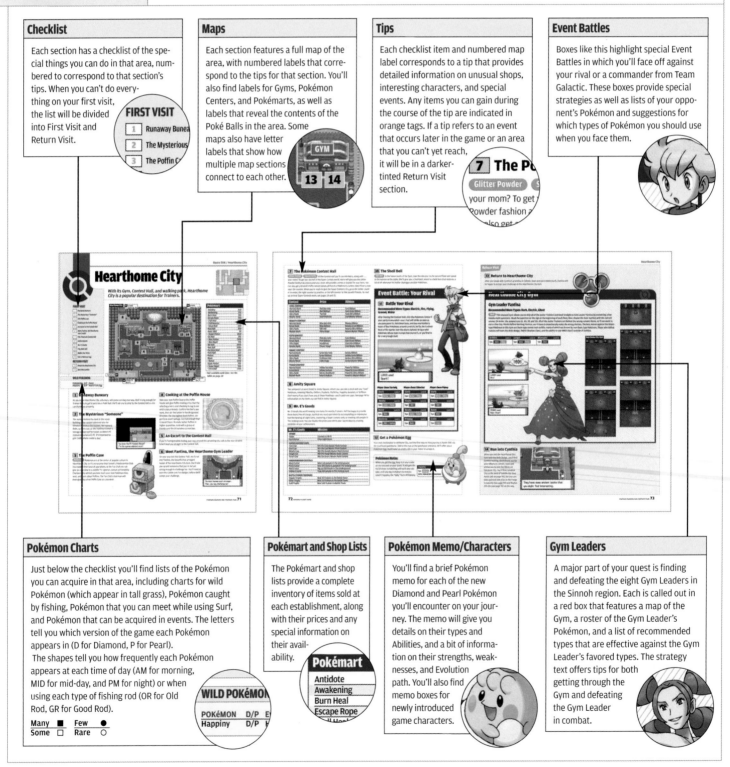

Pokémon Charts

Just below the checklist you'll find lists of the Pokémon you can acquire in that area, including charts for wild Pokémon (which appear in tall grass), Pokémon caught by fishing, Pokémon that you can meet while using Surf, and Pokémon that can be acquired in events. The letters tell you which version of the game each Pokémon appears in (D for Diamond, P for Pearl). The shapes tell you how frequently each Pokémon appears at each time of day (AM for morning, MID for mid-day, and PM for night) or when using each type of fishing rod (OR for Old Rod, GR for Good Rod).

Many ■   Few ●
Some □   Rare ○

Pokémart and Shop Lists

The Pokémart and shop lists provide a complete inventory of items sold at each establishment, along with their prices and any special information on their availability.

Pokémon Memo/Characters

You'll find a brief Pokémon memo for each of the new Diamond and Pearl Pokémon you'll encounter on your journey. The memo will give you details on their types and Abilities, and a bit of information on their strengths, weaknesses, and Evolution path. You'll also find memo boxes for newly introduced game characters.

Gym Leaders

A major part of your quest is finding and defeating the eight Gym Leaders in the Sinnoh region. Each is called out in a red box that features a map of the Gym, a roster of the Gym Leader's Pokémon, and a list of recommended types that are effective against the Gym Leader's favored types. The strategy text offers tips for both getting through the Gym and defeating the Gym Leader in combat.

Walkthrough

Walkthrough Checklist

You'll need to complete many tasks to foil Team Galactic and become League Champion. Use the checklist below to make sure you don't miss any!

Twinleaf Town — pg.46

- [ ] Meet your rival at his home and follow him to Lake Verity.

Lake Verity — pg.48

- [ ] Pick a starter Pokémon and use it to win your first battle.

Twinleaf Town — pg.46

- [ ] Get the Running Shoes from your mom.

Sandgem Town / Route 202 — pg.49

- [ ] Get the Pokédex from the professor.

Twinleaf Town — pg.46

- [ ] Speak with your mom and get a Journal. Also speak with your friend's mom and agree to deliver the Parcel to her son in Jubilife City.

Jubilife City — pg.50

- [ ] Go to the Trainers' School and get a Town Map from your rival.
- [ ] Complete the promotional campaign to earn a free Pokétch.
- [ ] Get the Old Rod from the fisherman in the Route 218 gatehouse.

Oreburgh Gate — pg.53

- [ ] Get HM06 (Rock Smash) from a hiker.

Oreburgh City — pg.54

- [ ] Get a Pal Pad at the Pokémon Center.

Oreburgh Mine — pg.56

- [ ] Speak with the Gym Leader and convince him to return to the Gym.

Oreburgh City — pg.54

- [ ] Defeat the Gym Leader to earn the Coal Badge.
- [ ] Meet your rival at the west exit and discuss your next step.

Jubilife City — pg.50

- [ ] Save the professor from the Galactic Grunts and receive a Fashion Case.

Ravaged Path — pg.57

- [ ] Use HM06 (Rock Smash) to open a path through the cave.

Floaroma Town — pg.57

- [ ] Get the Sprayduck watering can.

Route 205 — pg.59

- [ ] Speak with the little girl to learn about her kidnapped father.

Valley Windworks — pg.60

- [ ] Battle with the Grunt outside the Valley Windworks.

Floaroma Town — pg.57

- [ ] Battle the Galactic Grunts in Floaroma Meadow to obtain the Windworks Keys. Acquire some Honey from the Meadow Keeper.

Valley Windworks — pg.60

- [ ] Unlock the door to the Valley Windworks and battle Commander Mars.

Eterna City — pg.63

- [ ] Meet Cynthia outside of the Team Galactic Building and receive HM01 (Cut).
- [ ] Obtain the Friendship Checker at the Pokémon Center.
- [ ] Visit the cycle shop to find out where the owner is.
- [ ] Defeat the Gym Leader to earn the Forest Badge.

Team Galactic Building — pg.66

- [ ] Defeat Commander Jupiter and rescue the cycle shop's owner.

Eterna City — pg.63

- [ ] Receive a free Bicycle at the cycle shop.
- [ ] Get the Explorer's Kit from the Underground Man.

Route 207 — pg.69

- [ ] Speak with the professor's assistant to obtain a Vs. Seeker and a Dowsing Machine.

Route 208 — pg.70

- [ ] Obtain the Berry Searcher app at the Berry Master's house.
- [ ] Speak to the guy with the headband and get the Odd Keystone.

Hearthome City — pg.71

- [ ] Obtain the Poffin Case at the Pokémon Fan Club.
- [ ] Meet Fantina the Gym Leader at the Contest Hall.
- [ ] Battle your rival.

Route 209 — pg.75

- [ ] Receive the Good Rod.
- [ ] Use the Odd Keystone to restore the Hallowed Tower.

The Lost Tower — pg.76

- ☐ Fight your way to the top of the tower and obtain HM04 (Strength).

Solaceon Town — pg.77

- ☐ Get the Pokémon History app.
- ☐ Get the Seal Case.
- ☐ Leave a Pokémon at the Day-Care Center to get the Day Care Checker app.

Solaceon Ruins — pg.78

- ☐ Meet the son of the woman who gave you the Seal Case.

Solaceon Town — pg.77

- ☐ Bring Unown Pokémon to the boy to receive corresponding letter seals.

Veilstone City — pg.82

- ☐ Get the Coin Case.
- ☐ Defeat the Gym Leader to earn the Cobble Badge.
- ☐ Help the professor's assistant defeat the Galactic Grunts. Get HM02 (Fly) in the warehouse.

Pastoria City — pg.87

- ☐ Defeat the Gym Leader to earn the Fen Badge.
- ☐ Visit the Great Marsh and receive HM05 (Defog).
- ☐ Speak to the Galactic Grunt and then follow him to the east gatehouse.
- ☐ Battle your rival on your way out of town.

Route 213 (Valor Lakefront) — pg.90

- ☐ Catch up to the Galactic Grunt on the outskirts of the resort.
- ☐ Battle the Galactic Grunt at the entrance to Lake Valor.
- ☐ Receive the Secret Potion from Cynthia.

Route 210 — pg.80

- ☐ Give the Secret Potion to the Psyduck and recieve the Old Charm from Cynthia.
- ☐ Use Defog to clear the heavy fog in the foothills.

Celestic Town — pg.93

- ☐ Obtain the Analog Watch app.
- ☐ Defeat the Galactic Grunt that is threatening Celestic Town. Then give the Old Charm to Cynthia's grandma.
- ☐ Examine the ruins and receive HM03 (Surf) from Cynthia's grandma.

Hearthome City — pg.71

- ☐ Defeat the Gym Leader to earn the Relic Badge.
- ☐ Speak with Cynthia outside of the gym.

Route 218 — pg.96

- ☐ Receive the Pokédex upgrade from the professor's assistant.

Canalave City — pg.97

- ☐ Battle your rival on the Canalave City bridge.
- ☐ Defeat the Gym Leader to earn the Mine Badge.
- ☐ Speak with your friends on the third floor of the Canalave City library.

Lake Valor — pg.100

- ☐ Battle Commander Saturn at the Valor Cavern.

Lake Verity — pg.48

- ☐ Battle Commander Mars at the Verity Lakefront.

Route 217 — pg.104

- ☐ Find HM05 (Rock Climb) behind the cabin.

Snowpoint City — pg.105

- ☐ Defeat the Gym Leader to earn the Icicle Badge.

Lake Acuity — pg.107

- ☐ Provide support for your rival.

Veilstone City — pg.82

- ☐ Get the Storage Key at the main entrance to Galactic HQ.

Galactic HQ — pg.108

- ☐ Enter via the warehouse and search for the Galactic Key.
- ☐ Use the Galactic Key to enter through the main entrance.
- ☐ Defeat Cyrus and get the Master Ball.
- ☐ Defeat Commander Saturn.
- ☐ Set the Mirage Pokémon free.

Mt. Coronet — pg.110

- ☐ Traverse the cavern to reach Mt. Coronet's peak.
- ☐ Catch up with Team Galactic at the Hall of Origin.
- ☐ Defeat Commanders Mars and Jupiter in a Double Battle.
- ☐ Defeat Cyrus to end Team Galactic's diabolical plan.
- ☐ Face off against Dialga or Palkia. Pick up the Adamant Orb or Luminous Orb.

Sunyshore City — pg.115

- ☐ Speak to the Gym Leader at the top of the lighthouse.
- ☐ Defeat the Gym Leader to earn the Beacon Badge.
- ☐ Receive HM07 (Waterfall) from Jasmine.

The Pokémon League — pg.119

- ☐ Battle your rival for the last time.
- ☐ Traverse Victory Road to reach the Pokémon League Building.

The Elite Four — pg.121

- ☐ Defeat Aaron of the Elite Four.
- ☐ Defeat Bertha of the Elite Four.
- ☐ Defeat Flint of the Elite Four.
- ☐ Defeat Lucian of the Elite Four.
- ☐ Defeat the League Champion and take your place in the Hall of Fame.

Twinleaf Town

It seems like another quiet day in Twinleaf Town, but a hike to Lake Verity is about to change your life forever.

FIRST VISIT

| 1 | An Urgent Summons |
| 2 | Meet Your Friend |

RETURN VISIT

| 3 | Get a Present from Mom |
| 4 | The Journal |

WILD POKéMON

POKéMON	D/P	OR	GR
Goldeen	D/P		☐
Magikarp	D/P	■	■

POKéMON	D/P	Surf	
Golduck	D/P	☐	
Psyduck	D/P	■	

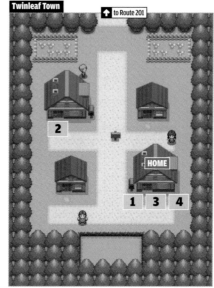

Twinleaf Town — to Route 201

Your Friend . . . and Rival!

Your best friend is a competitive sort, and when you both join the world of Pokémon Trainers, he'll become a passionate rival. He will attempt to beat you to all of Sinnoh's Gym Badges and will often appear suddenly to challenge you to difficult Trainer battles. Choose an appropriate name for this lovable hothead.

▸ New name!
Barry
Damion
Tyson
Markus

What might his name be?

1 | An Urgent Summons

As much as you may like to hang out in your bedroom playing with your Wii, adventure is beckoning! Check out your computer and a note on the wall for basic game info, then head downstairs to talk with Mom. She'll report that your friend has called and asked you to visit him at his home (the building to the northwest). His so-called emergency isn't all that urgent, so feel free to chat with your other neighbors on the way.

Damion came calling for you a little while ago.

2 | Meet Your Friend

You've dawdled too long, and your friend is getting antsy—he's in such a hurry to leave that he forgets his bag and journal. When he returns home to grab them, follow him upstairs. He'll grab his gear and dash out the door, insisting you follow close behind. His mom will point you north toward Route 201, where you'll find him tapping his foot impatiently.

Damion: ...I'd better take my Bag and Journal, too...

Return Visit

3 | Get a Present from Mom

Running Shoes When you return home from Lake Verity, tell your mom what happened at the lakefront. She'll suggest you pay Prof. Rowan a visit in Sandgem Town to explain yourself, and she'll give you a pair of Running Shoes to make the journey easier. The shoes will be equipped automatically, and will let you run at double speed by holding down the B Button. You can reach Sandgem Town by heading east through Route 201.

You need to properly explain why you had no choice but to use his Pokémon.

With those Running Shoes, you can get to faraway places much faster.

4 | The Journal

Journal **Parcel**
Return home after visiting Sandgem Town to tell your mom about your talk with Prof. Rowan. She'll support your quest enthusiastically, and even give you a Journal that will automatically record your experiences. Your friend's mom will also pop in for a visit and ask you to deliver a Parcel to her son in Jubilife City.

Check it, and you'll be able to remember what you did last.

Route 201

You'll take the first steps of your journey on the short stretch of road north of Twinleaf Town.

FIRST VISIT

1. Hike to Lake Verity

RETURN VISIT

2. Run into Prof. Rowan
3. Pokémon in the Tall Grass
4. A Free Potion Sample

WILD POKéMON

POKéMON	D/P	AM	MID	PM
Bidoof	D/P	■	■	■
Starly	D/P	■	■	■

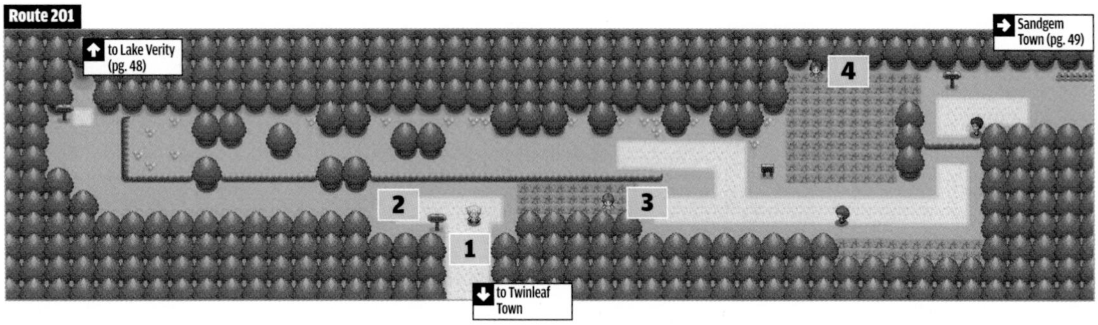

Route 201

to Lake Verity (pg. 48)

Sandgem Town (pg. 49)

to Twinleaf Town

1 Hike to Lake Verity

When your friend meets you at the path outside of town, he'll finally spill the details—you're heading to Lake Verity to search for unique Pokémon. But that news report was about an entirely different lake . . . what are the odds that you'll actually find anything? Head west down Route 201 and enter Lake Verity via the path north through the trees.

Damion: All right! To the lake! Let's find us a red GYARADOS!

Pokémon Notes

The Starly you'll meet here aren't much of a threat—Tackle is their only real attack. But if you can catch a Starly and evolve it twice, its nice speed and array of physical attacks will make it a serious threat to your foes.

Starly
Type: Normal Flying
Ability: Keen Eye

Bidoof is a basic physical attacker that eventually evolves into a Normal-and-Water-type Bibarel. If you want to add a Bidoof to your roster, try to catch one with the Unaware ability, which allows Bidoof to ignore its foe's stat boosts.

Bidoof
Type: Normal
Ability: Simple/Unaware

2 Run into Prof. Rowan

On your way home from Lake Verity you'll run into Prof. Rowan and his assistant. When it becomes clear that you've used his Pokémon, he'll leave in a huff. The assistant will suggest you pay a visit to his lab in Sandgem City, but the first order of business is to return home and report to mom.

I heard from Dawn that you used our Pokémon?

3 Pokémon in the Tall Grass

Your mom wouldn't let you cross the tall grass earlier, but she won't stop you now so long as you have a Pokémon to protect you. The first Pokémon you'll encounter in the tall grass are Level-2 or Level-3 Bidoof and Starly that should be easy for your Level-5 starter to beat. Don't worry about the other people in the grass—they're not Trainers, and they have useful information to share.

BIDOOF   Lv.2

A wild BIDOOF appeared!

4 A Free Potion Sample

Potion Be sure to speak to the woman in the second patch of grass. She'll teach you about Pokémon HP and hand over a free Potion to promote her Pokémart. If your Pokémon is too wounded to make it home for healing, press X to open the menu, select your Bag, and reach into the Medicine pouch to find that Potion.

Here, let me give you a Potion as a free sample. First one's free!

Lake Verity

The Pokémon Professor has left his briefcase at the Lake Verity shore. What would it hurt to take a little peek inside?

FIRST VISIT

1. Prof. Rowan's Lost Briefcase

RETURN VISIT

2. Battle Commander Mars

3. Capture Mesprit

WILD POKéMON

POKéMON	D/P	AM	MID	PM
Bidoof	D/P	■	■	■
Starly	D/P	■	■	■

POKéMON	D/P	OR	GR
Goldeen	D/P		□
Magikarp	D/P	■	■

POKéMON	D/P	Surf
Golduck	D/P	□
Psyduck	D/P	■

POKéMON	D/P	Event
Chimchar	D/P	Event only
Piplup	D/P	Event only
Turtwig	D/P	Event only

POKéMON	D/P	Event
Mesprit	D/P	After event

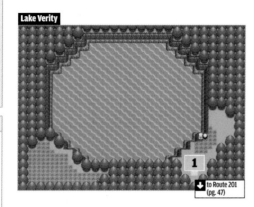

Lake Verity

to Route 201 (pg. 47)

TM38

to Route 201 (pg. 47)

1 Prof. Rowan's Lost Briefcase

Your friend isn't the only one with a sudden interest in Lake Verity. As you enter the lakefront you'll pass Prof. Rowan and his assistant on their way out. But when you investigate the briefcase the professor left behind, a pair of Starly will attack, leaving you no choice but to grab a Poké Ball from the briefcase and defend yourself. When the danger has passed, head home to Twinleaf Town.

Pokémon Notes

Piplup won't learn many powerful moves early in the game, but it will ultimately evolve into a powerful Water-and-Steel-type with resistance to 12 of the 17 Pokémon types! Piplup is an excellent choice for defensively minded players.

Piplup
Type: Water
Ability: Torrent

Chimchar gains its second type earlier than the other starters, as soon as it evolves into Monferno at Level 14. The combination of Fire and Fighting types isn't worth much on defense, but offers a variety of solid attack moves.

Chimchar
Type: Fire
Ability: Blaze

Turtwig
Type: Grass
Ability: Overgrow

Turtwig specializes in HP-draining attacks but will also learn moves with an unusually wide variety of types and effects. Its final form is Grass-and-Ground-type Torterra.

Return Visit

Event Battle: Team Galactic

2 Battle Commander Mars

Recommended Move Types: Electric, Fighting, Fire

After your battle at Lake Valor, return to Lake Verity to help Prof. Rowan and his assistant fight off Commander Mars and her team of Grunts at the lakefront. After you beat them, Prof. Rowan will send you north to Lake Acuity, which you can reach via the Mt. Coronet tunnel between Eterna City and Celestic Town.

MACHOKE used Vital Throw!

Commander Mars's Purugly is packing a Sitrus Berry, so either try to KO the Purugly with one big type-trumping Fighting-type attack, or Pluck it and eat the berry yourself.

Golbat	Level 37	Bronsor	Level 37	Purugly	Level 39
Type: Poison Flying		Type: Steel Psychic		Type: Normal	

3 Capture Mesprit

After defeating Cyrus at Mt. Coronet, visit the cavern at the center of Lake Verity to meet Mesprit. You'll collect its Pokédex data, but it will disappear before you can challenge it. Use the Marking Map (received at the Pokétch Co.) to find its current location. You'll have to pursue it on foot—it will teleport to a new location whenever you use the Fly move.

Sandgem Town / Route 202

If you can summon the courage to speak with gruff Prof. Rowan, he'll make you an offer you can't refuse.

FIRST VISIT

1	An Escort to the Lab
2	Meet the Professor and Get the Sinnoh Pokédex
3	The Pokémon Center
4	The Pokémart

RETURN VISIT

5	The Assistant's Final Lesson
6	The First Trainer Battle

WILD POKÉMON

POKÉMON	D/P	AM	MID	PM
Bidoof	D/P	■	■	■
Kricketot	D/P	□		□
Shinx	D/P	■	■	■
Starly	D/P	■	■	□

1 An Escort to the Lab

Prof. Rowan's assistant will meet you at the entrance to Sandgem Town and escort you straight to the research lab. Once again you'll run into your friend, whose hasty ways keep him one step ahead fo you.

2 Meet the Professor and Get the Sinnoh Pokédex

Pokédex You've treated your Pokémon well, so Prof. Rowan will allow you to keep it and even rename it if you like. Impressed by your Trainer potential, Prof. Rowan will ask a favor in return—travel through Sinnoh and collect information about local Pokémon in a Pokédex. How can you say no?

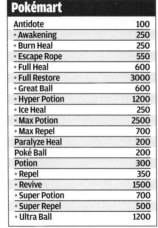

3 The Pokémon Center

When you leave the lab, Prof. Rowan's assistant will take you on a tour of Sandgem's Trainer hotspots. The first stop is the Pokémon Center, where you can receive free healing for your team. Make sure to stop in after the tour!

4 The Pokémart

The next stop on the tour is the Pokémart, where your novice status will limit your selection to only a few items. The tour isn't over, but that's where Prof. Rowan's assistant will send you home to tell mom about your new job. Before you do, buy a few Poké Balls and Potions, then get your Pokémon healed at the Pokémon Center.

Pokémart	
Antidote	100
• Awakening	250
• Burn Heal	250
• Escape Rope	550
• Full Heal	600
• Full Restore	3000
• Great Ball	600
• Hyper Potion	1200
• Ice Heal	250
• Max Potion	2500
• Max Repel	700
Paralyze Heal	200
Poké Ball	200
Potion	300
• Repel	350
• Revive	1500
• Super Potion	700
• Super Repel	500
• Ultra Ball	1200

• Not available until later; see the table on page 28

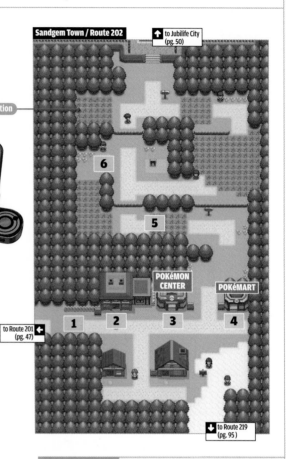

Potion

6

5

to Jubilife City (pg. 50)

to Route 201 (pg. 47)

to Route 219 (pg. 95)

POKéMON CENTER

POKéMART

1 2 3 4

Sandgem Town / Route 202

to Jubilife City (pg. 50)
to Route 201 (pg. 47)
to Route 219 (pg. 95)

The Professor

Prof. Rowan was born in Sinnoh, but has spent most of his professional life studying Pokémon abroad. Now he intends to continue his research in his homeland, and is recruiting willing assistants.

Pokémon Notes

The wild Pokémon of Route 202 include Electric-type Shinx and Bug-type Kricketot. Kricketot can't do much in combat, but it will become a worthy recruit when it evolves into Kricketune at Level 10 and begins to learn attack moves.

Kricketot
Type: **Bug**
Ability: **Shed Skin**

Shinx
Type: **Electric**
Ability: **Rivalry / Intimidate**

Return Visit

5 The Assistant's Final Lesson

5 Poké Balls After you report to Mom, you'll find Prof. Rowan's assistant waiting at the edge of the grass on Route 202. She will teach you how to catch wild Pokémon, and give you five Poké Balls to get you started. Your roster has five empty slots to fill, so start capturing!

6 The First Trainer Battle

If your Pokémon are in bad shape as you're leaving the second grass patch, return to the Sandgem Pokémon Center to get them healed. When you pass that point, the first Trainer will challenge you. He only has a single Level-5 Starly, but it can be a serious threat to wounded Pokémon. There are two more Trainers you won't be able to avoid on the way to Jubilife City, so return to Sandgem Town for healing often.

Jubilife City

Jubilife City is home to such Sinnoh institutions as the Pokétch Co., Jubilife TV, and the Global Trade Station.

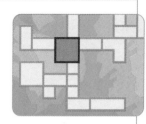

FIRST VISIT

1	Chat with Prof. Rowan's Assistant
2	Enroll in Trainers' School
3	The Pokétch Campaign
4	New Items for Sale
5	Creating a Group
6	A Free Quick Claw
7	Freebies at the Pokétch Co.
8	Your First TV Interview
9	Get the Old Rod

RETURN VISIT

10	GTS (Global Trade Station)
11	Save the Professor
12	The Daily Loto
13	A New Trainer Every Day
14	Dressing Up Your Pokémon
15	The Ranking Rooms

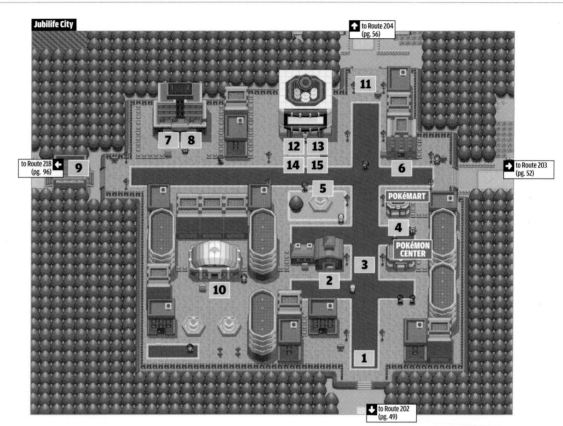

Jubilife City

to Route 204 (pg. 56)

to Route 218 (pg. 96)

to Route 203 (pg. 52)

POKéMART

POKéMON CENTER

to Route 202 (pg. 49)

---

1 Chat with Prof. Rowan's Assistant

When you first enter Jubilife City, Prof. Rowan's assistant will approach you to see how many Pokémon you've caught. Whether she approves or not, she'll suggest you pay a visit to the Trainers' School–the same place that she sent your friend.

2 Enroll in Trainers' School

Town Map **TM10** You'll find your friend at the blackboard of the Trainers' School, where he'll accept the Parcel from his mom. It contains a pair of Town Maps, one of which he'll generously give to you before running off to challenge the Gym in Oreburgh City. That's your next destination too, but there's still plenty to do in Jubilife City, including a pair of Trainer battles right here in the Trainers' School! Defeat both Trainers' Abra to earn TM10 (Hidden Power).

3 The Pokétch Campaign

Pokétch When you head north from the school you'll meet the inventor of the Pokétch, who is conducting a new promotional campaign. He'll send you to search for three clowns in Jubilife City and answer a quiz question from each. You'll find one behind the Pokémon Center, one at the entrance to the Jubilife TV building, and one in front of the Pokétch Co. Answer yes to all of their questions to earn Pokétch Coupons, and bring those to the inventor to win a Pokétch with four free apps!

4 New Items for Sale

The right clerk at this Pokémart sells the usual items, while the left clerk sells Air Mail and Heal Balls. Heal Balls are pricier than Poké Balls, but they completely heal the Pokémon you catch, leaving it ready for immediate use in combat.

5 Creating a Group

Speak to the lady in the small park at point 5; she'll offer to help you create a new group. When you meet other players in a Union Room, you can invite them to join your group, which will allow your copies of the game to share information, leading to special events that happen simultaneously for everyone in the group.

6 A Free Quick Claw

Quick Claw Visit the Jubilife Condominiums and speak with the blonde girl on the ground floor. She'll give you a free Quick Claw, a held item that can give any Pokémon a small shot at striking first in combat.

Pokémart

Item	Price
Air Mail	50
Antidote	100
• Awakening	250
• Burn Heal	250
• Escape Rope	550
• Full Heal	600
• Full Restore	3000
• Great Ball	600
Heal Ball	300
• Hyper Potion	1200
• Ice Heal	250
• Max Potion	2500
• Max Repel	700
Paralyze Heal	200
Poké Ball	200
Potion	300
• Repel	350
• Revive	1500
• Super Potion	700
• Super Repel	500
• Ultra Ball	1200

• Not available until later; see the table on page 28

7 Freebies at the Pokétch Co.

The Pokétch Co. is constantly developing new Pokétch apps, and will happily share their products with you. New apps are made available after you receive every odd-numbered badge, so check back often! You can learn more about the apps you already own by examining the computers in the third-floor cubicles.

There are descriptions of Pokétch apps.

Pokétch Apps

Memo Pad	After 1st badge
Marking Map	After 3rd badge
Link Searcher	After 5th badge
Pedometer	After 7th badge

8 Your First TV Interview

There's a television reporter on the first floor of the Pokémon Co., and she'd be thrilled to interview a Trainer like yourself. You can respond only by selecting a single word from a list, so it may end up being a bit of a non sequitur. Don't worry—it'll sound good when you hear the interview on a TV later in the game.

9 Get the Old Rod

Old Rod Your next destination is to the east, but it pays to poke your head into the small building at the west exit of Jubilife City. There you'll find a fisherman who asks if "an Old Rod is a good thing." Say yes, and your new friend will give you an Old Rod that you can use to fish wherever there's water. Select the item from your Bag's Key Items pocket to cast it into the water, and reel it in by tapping the A Button as soon as the exclamation point appears over your head.

Return Visit

10 GTS (Global Trade Station)

You can visit the GTS at any time after you win the Coal Badge from the Oreburgh City Gym. If you have access to a Wi-Fi connection, you can post your extra Pokémon for trade or scroll through the list of desired trades posted by other players around the world. Don't forget to register your location at the giant globe!

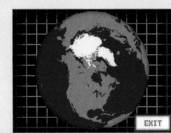

Would you like to do a global Pokémon trade over Nintendo WFC?

Event Battle: Galactic Grunts

11 Save the Professor

Fashion Case On your return trip from Oreburgh City, you'll find strange miscreants hassling Professor Rowan at the entrance to Route 204. Team up with the professor's assistant in a Double Battle that will make short work of the Galactic Grunts. Your Pokémon prowess will impress a Jubilife TV reporter, who will reward you with a Fashion Case.

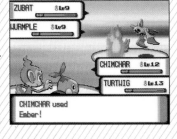

CHIMCHAR used Ember!

Zubat	Level 9	Wurmple	Level 9
Type: Poison Flying		Type: Bug	

12 The Daily Loto

After rescuing the professor, pay a visit to the Jubilife TV building. Speak to the clerk on the ground floor to draw a five-digit Loto number, which will be compared to the ID number of your lead Pokémon. If any digits match, you'll win a prize! You can draw a new number once each day.

Loto Prizes

Jackpot	Master Ball
1st Prize	Max Revive
2nd Prize	Exp. Share
3rd Prize	PP UP
4th Prize	Wallpaper for Pokémon dress-up event

13 A New Trainer Every Day

To the left of the Pokémon Lottery Corner counter you'll meet a Trainer who will politely invite you to duel (you may refuse if you like). You'll find a new Trainer here every day, so visit the Jubilife TV building any time you want to earn experience and a bit of money.

I'm working on a story. Can you battle me?

14 Dressing Up Your Pokémon

A photographer on the second floor of the Jubilife TV building will ask if he can photograph your Pokémon. If you agree, he'll lead you into his studio, where you can dress up your Pokémon by using the stylus to drag accessories onto it.

15 The Ranking Rooms

On the the third floor of the Jubilife TV building you'll find two ranking rooms where you can see how you fare against other Trainers in the categories of Pokémon defeated, Pokémon caught, Pokémon Eggs hatched, and Pokémon encountered while fishing. The Group Ranking room compares you only to the other players in your group (see tip 5), while the Global Ranking Room compares you to Trainers around the world.

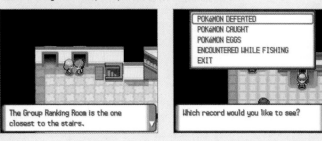

The Group Ranking Room is the one closest to the stairs.

Which record would you like to see?

Route 203

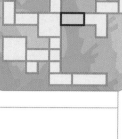

Route 203 connects Jubilife City to Oreburgh Gate, and is a great place to challenge Trainers and hunt wild Pokémon.

| 1 | A Friend Becomes a Rival |
| 2 | Moving on to Oreburgh City |

WILD POKéMON

POKéMON	D/P	AM	MID	PM
Abra	D/P	☐	☐	☐
Bidoof	D/P	☐	☐	☐
Kricketot	D/P	☐	☐	☐
Shinx	D/P	■	■	■
Starly	D/P	■	■	☐
Zubat	D/P			☐

POKéMON	D/P	OR	GR
Goldeen	D/P		☐
Magikarp	D/P	■	■

POKéMON	D/P	Surf
Golduck	D/P	☐
Psyduck	D/P	■

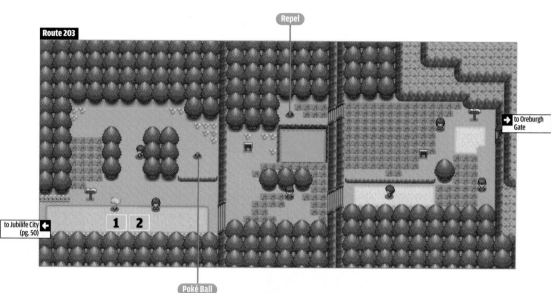

Route 203

Repel

to Oreburgh Gate

to Jubilife City (pg. 50)

1 2

Poké Ball

Event Battle: Your Rival

1 A Friend Becomes a Rival

Recommended Move Types: Electric, Fire, Flying, Grass, Water

Your friend said he was moving on to Oreburgh, but in truth he's been waiting to show off his newly developed skills by challenging you to a battle. He has shrewdly chosen whichever starter Pokémon trumps yours (see the correlations below), and has also caught a Starly. Have your starter battle the Starly, and rely on your newly caught Pokémon to take down his powerful Level-9 starter.

Player chose Turtwig

Starly	Level 7
Type:	Normal Flying

Chimchar	Level 9
Type:	Fire

Player chose Chimchar

Starly	Level 7
Type:	Normal Flying

Piplup	Level 9
Type:	Water

Player chose Piplup

Starly	Level 7
Type:	Normal Flying

Turtwig	Level 9
Type:	Grass

2 Moving on to Oreburgh City

Stung by defeat, your rival will run east to strengthen himself by challenging the Oreburgh City Gym. To reach Oreburgh City you'll have to fight past several Trainers and then pass through a short cave passage. Don't try to do it all at once; beat a few Trainers, try to catch a wild Pokémon or two, then return to Jubilife City for healing.

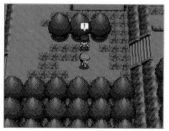

Oreburgh Gate

The tunnel to Oreburgh City is a short one, but experienced explorers can find plenty of treasures there.

FIRST VISIT

| 1 | Get HM06 (Rock Smash) |

RETURN VISIT

| 2 | Bicycle Tricks on B1 |

WILD POKéMON

1F

POKéMON	D/P	AM	MID	PM
Geodude	D/P	■	■	■
Zubat	D/P	□	□	□

B1

POKéMON	D/P	AM	MID	PM
Geodude	D/P	□	□	□
Psyduck	D/P	■	■	■
Zubat	D/P	■	■	■

POKéMON	D/P	OR	GR	
Barboach	D/P		□	
Magikarp	D/P	■		

POKéMON	D/P	Surf	
Golbat	D/P	●	
Golduck	D/P	●	
Psyduck	D/P	■	
Zubat	D/P	■	

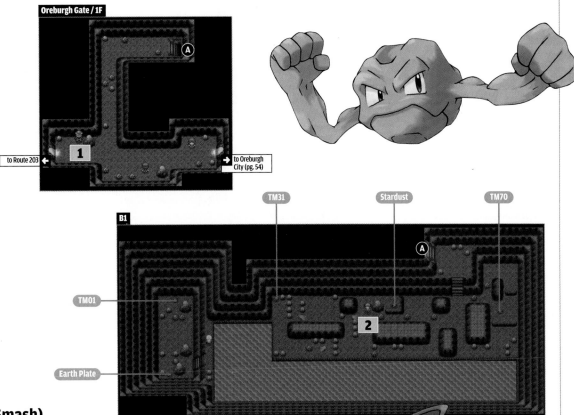

Oreburgh Gate / 1F

to Route 203

to Oreburgh City (pg. 54)

TM31 Stardust TM70

B1

TM01

2

Earth Plate

1 Get HM06 (Rock Smash)

HM06 Weary travelers may be alarmed when the exclamation point pops up over the guy's head at point 1, but there's no need to worry—he just wants to give you a welcoming gift. The present is HM06 (Rock Smash) which lets you smash the cracked boulders you see strewn around the cave. You can't use it for that purpose until you earn Oreburgh City's Gym Badge, but you can use it immediately to teach the Fighting-type Rock Smash move to any Pokémon that would benefit from another solid attack move. Head east to reach the entrance to Oreburgh City, but heal first if you need to—those next two guys aren't there to give you presents.

So, let me make a gift of this
Hidden Machine to you!

Return Visit

2 Bicycle Tricks on B1F

The lower floor of Oreburgh Gate is full of natural rock formations that look a lot like bike ramps. If you have the Bicycle, the Coal Badge, and HM06 (Rock Smash) you can expose the ramps, switch to fourth gear, and use them to leap over indestructible rocks. Pick up TM31 using the bike ramps. Visit later with HM03 (Surf) to reach TM01 and the Earth Plate.

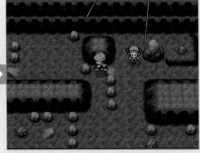

Oreburgh City

This is primarily a mining city, but a visit to the Gym will prove that Oreburgh takes Pokémon training seriously, too.

FIRST VISIT

1	The Missing Gym Leader
2	Choose Your Trainer Identity
3	Learn about the Wi-Fi Club
4	Trade a Machop for an Abra
5	Score a Free Heal Ball
6	Score a Free Dusk Ball
7	Score a Free Great Ball
8	From Fossils to Pokémon

RETURN VISIT

9	Where to Go Next

WILD POKÉMON

POKÉMON	D/P	Event
Abra	D/P	Trade only
Cranidos	D	Fossil
Shieldon	P	Fossil

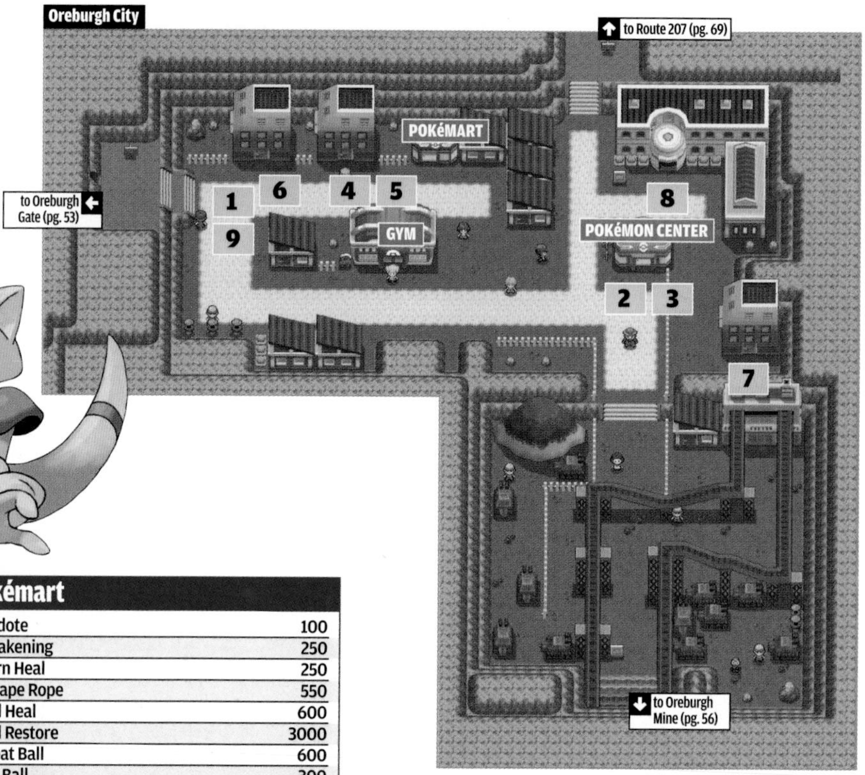

Oreburgh City

to Route 207 (pg. 69)

POKéMART

to Oreburgh Gate (pg. 53)

GYM

POKÉMON CENTER

to Oreburgh Mine (pg. 56)

1 The Missing Gym Leader

A kindly Oreburghian will take you straight to the Gym, where you'll find your rival waiting. He'll report that the Gym Leader has gone into the Oreburgh Mine—find him there if you want to challenge the Gym.

2 Choose Your Trainer Identity

A customer on the ground floor of the Pokémon Center will ask what kind of Trainers you like, and offer you four options from the ten possibilities below. The kinds you choose will determine how your character appears to others in Union Rooms.

Boy Options	Girl Options
Ace Trainer	Ace Trainer
Black Belt	Battle Girl
Bug Catcher	Beauty
Psychic	Cowgirl
Rich Boy	Lady
Roughneck	Lass
Ruin Maniac	Pop Idol
School Kid	Socialite

▶ School Kid
　 Bug Catcher
　 Ace Trainer
　 Roughneck
　 EXIT

Which kind of Trainer would you like to be?

Pokémart

Antidote	100
• Awakening	250
• Burn Heal	250
• Escape Rope	550
• Full Heal	600
• Full Restore	3000
• Great Ball	600
Heal Ball	300
• Hyper Potion	1200
• Ice Heal	250
• Max Potion	2500
• Max Repel	700
Net Ball	1000
Paralyze Heal	200
Poké Ball	200
Potion	300
• Repel	350
• Revive	1500
• Super Potion	700
• Super Repel	500
Tunnel Mail	50
• Ultra Ball	1200

• Not available until later in the game; see the table on page 28

3 Learn About the Wi-Fi Club

Pal Pad The basement floor of every Pokémon Center is devoted to the Wi-Fi Club, but this is the first one that has opened for business. When you first visit, a clerk named Teala will give you a Pal Pad and guide you through the process of registering friends from anywhere in the world. Once you've registered a friend, you may link with that friend over Nintendo WFC to trade or battle with them. Upstairs is the Union Room, where you may connect directly with local friends over DS wireless connection to trade Pokémon, battle one-on-one, or mix records. There's also a Colosseum where you can engage in Single, Double, or Mixed Battles with up to three local players.

4 Trade a Machop for an Abra

The lady on the ground floor of this building is desperate for a Machop, and willing to trade away her Abra. If you're interested, return here when you have one to spare.

▶ YES
　 NO

Would you be willing to trade your MACHOP for my ABRA?

5 Score a Free Heal Ball

Heal Ball A man on the second floor of the same building is interested in a Zubat. He doesn't want to trade—he just wants to see one, and if you bring him a Zubat he'll thank you with a free Heal Ball.

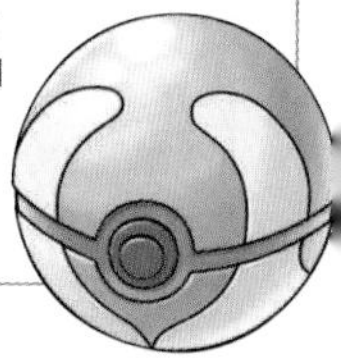

6 Score a Free Dusk Ball

Dusk Ball Pay a visit to the building next door, where a woman on the second floor will hand over a Dusk Ball and ask for nothing in return. The Dusk Ball has a much higher rate of success when used to catch Pokémon at night or in dark places like caves than it does in daylight situations.

7 Score a Free Great Ball

Great Ball You'll find another freebie past the museum on the east side of town. Talk to a boy on the second floor, and he'll happily present you with a Great Ball. Great Balls are one step above Poké Balls, and they improve your odds of success when catching higher-level Pokémon.

8 From Fossils to Pokémon

The scientists at the Oreburgh Mining Museum are on the verge of learning how to transform million-year-old Fossils into living, breathing Pokémon. You won't find any Pokémon Fossils in the Oreburgh Mine, but in the future you may find a fossil of Cranidos or Shieldon in an area known as The Underground. If you do, show it to the scientists and they'll bring your Fossil to life.

Return Visit

Oreburgh City Gym

Gym Leader Roark

Recommended Move Types: Fighting, Grass, Water

TM76 Players who chose Turtwig or Piplup will have an advantage against the Rock-types preferred by Roark and his Junior Trainers, but Chimchar Trainers may want to catch a Machop on Route 207 and level it up a bit before challenging this Gym. When battling Roark, save your best Pokémon for the Cranidos that anchors his team. It's quite a bit tougher than the Pokémon that precede it, and Roark will use a Potion to heal it when its HP gets low.

Geodude	Level 12	Onix	Level 12	Cranidos	Level 14
Type: Rock Ground		Type: Rock Ground		Type: Rock	

Oreburgh City Gym

TURTWIG used Razor Leaf!

Pokémon Notes

This 100-million-year old Pokémon can be revived from a Fossil found only in Pokémon Diamond. Cranidos is a pure Rock-type that enjoys a spectacular Attack score.

Cranidos
Type: Rock
Ability: Mold Breaker

Shieldon, revived from a Fossil found only in Pokémon Pearl, is a defensive powerhouse. The combination of Rock and Steel types gives it incredible resistance to both Physical and Special attacks.

Shieldon
Type: Rock Steel
Ability: Sturdy

9 Where to Go Next

You won't get far on Route 207 without a Bicycle, so your only option is to return the way you came. You'll meet your rival on the road out of town. But before you follow him to Jubilife City, stop in at the Pokémart, where you can now buy all sorts of new items—one of the many perks of holding a Gym Badge. Another is the ability to use Rock Smash, which will allow you to visit the lower floor of Oreburgh Gate.

So, yeah, I went to Route 207, but you can't go there without a Bicycle.

Oreburgh Mine

Oreburgh Trainers often visit the town's cavernous ore mine to hunt for wild Rock-type Pokémon.

| 1 | Find Gym Leader Roark |

WILD POKéMON

1F / 2F

POKéMON	D/P	AM	MID	PM
Geodude	D/P	■	■	■
Onix	D/P	□	□	□
Zubat	D/P	□	□	□

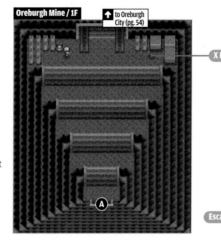

Oreburgh Mine / 1F — to Oreburgh City (pg. 54) — X Defend — A

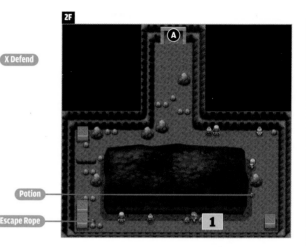

2F — A — Potion — Escape Rope — 1

1 Find Gym Leader Roark

The mine is full of wild Pokémon, providing a great opportunity to level up your Grass- and Water-type Pokémon before you challenge the Gym. Roark will agree to reopen the Gym without a fight, but the other miners will insist on a duel.

Route 204

Your roundabout path to Eterna City begins on the hilly trail that connects Jubilife City to Floaroma Town.

FIRST VISIT

| 1 | Take on the Twins |

RETURN VISIT

| 2 | A Teacher on a Field Trip |

WILD POKéMON

POKéMON	D/P	AM	MID	PM
Bidoof	D/P	□	□	□
Budew	D/P	□	□	□
Kricketot	D/P	□		
Shinx	D/P	■	■	■
Starly	D/P	□	■	□
Zubat	D/P			

POKéMON	D/P	OR	GR
Goldeen	D/P		□
Magikarp	D/P	■	■

POKéMON	D/P	Surf	
Golduck	D/P	□	
Psyduck	D/P	■	

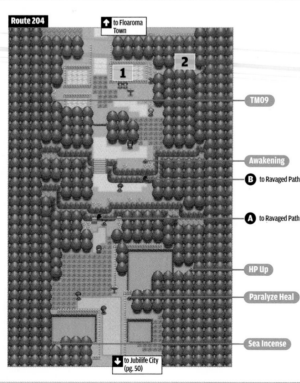

Route 204 — to Floaroma Town — 2 — 1 — TM09 — Awakening — B to Ravaged Path — A to Ravaged Path — HP Up — Paralyze Heal — Sea Incense — to Jubilife City (pg. 50)

1 Take on the Twins

Twins Liv and Liz will attack at the entrance to Floaroma Town, with each throwing a Pachirisu into the battle at the same time. Since you have no other Trainer to help, you'll be allowed to meet their challenge with the top two Pokémon in your roster.

Pokémon Notes

Take good care of your Budew! If you can raise its friendship level high enough, it will reward you by blooming into a Roselia—but only during morning and daytime hours.

Budew

Type: Grass / Poison
Ability: **Natural Cure / Poison Point**

Return Visit

2 A Teacher on a Field Trip

TM78 Once you earn HM01 and the Forest Badge, return to this spot to cut down the tree and speak with a Trainers' School teacher at point 2. She'll give you a quick lesson about Pokémon gender and hand over TM78, which contains Captivate, a move that works only on Pokémon of the opposite gender.

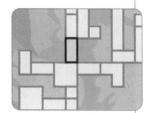

Ravaged Path

Boulders block the small cave at the center of Route 204, so only those with the Coal Badge can proceed.

| 1 | Use HM06 (Rock Smash) |

WILD POKéMON

POKéMON	D/P	AM	MID	PM
Geodude	D/P	□	□	□
Psyduck	D/P	●	●	●
Zubat	D/P	■	■	■

POKéMON	D/P	OR	GR
Barboach	D/P		□
Magikarp	D/P	■	■

POKéMON	D/P	Surf
Golbat	D/P	●
Golduck	D/P	●
Psyduck	D/P	■
Zubat	D/P	■

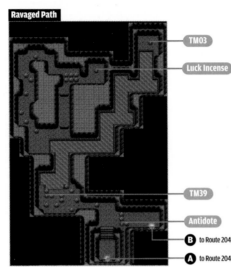

Ravaged Path

- TM03
- Luck Incense
- TM39
- Antidote
- **B** to Route 204
- **A** to Route 204

1 Use HM06 (Rock Smash)

If you've earned the Coal Badge but haven't taught anyone Rock Smash yet, do so now and have your designated rock smasher clear the boulders to the east. You'll need to return with HM03 (Surf) to explore the rest of the cave.

Floaroma Town

Despite the fragrant flower fields, something stinks in Floaroma Town. What is Team Galactic up to?

FIRST VISIT

1	Picking and Planting Berries
2	Freebies from the Florist
3	A Plucky Young Girl
4	Agents from Team Galactic

RETURN VISIT

| 5 | Battle for the Windworks Key |
| 6 | Slather the Scented Tree |

Floaroma Town

- **A** (pg. 58)
- Berry Patch
- 4
- SHOP
- 1 2
- POKéMART
- 3
- POKéMON CENTER
- to Route 205 (pg. 59)
- to Route 204

Flower Shop

Black Specs	20 Wepear Berries
Blue Flower	30 Cornn Berries
Cape	250 Cornn Berries
Carpet	100 Spelon Berries
Colored Parasol	50 Magost Berries
Confetti	30 Razz Berries
Fluffy Bed	150 Watmel Berries
Googly Specs	20 Nomel Berries
Gorgeous Specs	40 Pinap Berries
Mirror Ball	250 Durin Berries
Old Umbrella	50 Pamtre Berries
Orange Flower	15 Magost Berries
Photo Board	200 Belue Berries
Pink Flower	10 Bluk Berries
Red Flower	10 Razz Berries
Retro Pipe	120 Pamtre Berries
Spotlight	80 Nomel Berries
Standing Mike	80 Bluk Berries
Surfboard	180 Wepear Berries
Sweet Candy	30 Nanab Berries
White Flower	10 Nanab Berries
Yellow Flower	15 Rabuta Berries

Pokémart

Antidote	100
Awakening	250
Bloom Mail	50
Burn Heal	250
Escape Rope	550
• Full Heal	600
• Full Restore	3000
• Great Ball	600
Heal Ball	300
• Hyper Potion	1200
Ice Heal	250
• Max Potion	2500
• Max Repel	700
Net Ball	1000
Paralyze Heal	200
Poké Ball	200
Potion	300
Repel	350
• Revive	1500
Super Potion	700
• Super Repel	500
• Ultra Ball	1200

• Not available until later in the game; see the table on page 28

1 Picking and Planting Berries

You'll find a pair of berry bushes at the entrance to the florist's shop. Examine them to pick their fruit, and then plant your newfound berries right where you discovered them. Those berries will grow into healthy plants capable of producing multiple berries, thereby providing you with a limitless berry supply in the long run.

2 Freebies from the Florist

Sprayduck Inside the florist's shop, a lady will give you a free Sprayduck watering can, which you can use to soften the earth wherever you plant your berries. A nearby clerk will hand over a free berry, and the florist herself will show you a list of accessories and furniture that the shop will trade for berries.

Trainer, please water Berries using this Sprayduck watering can.

3 A Plucky Young Girl

TM88 Speak to the little girl with the Clefairy, and answer "Yes" to her question. She'll reward you with TM88, which can teach the Flying-type Pluck move to Pokémon like Starly. Not only does Pluck do respectable damage, but it allows the attacker to eat any berries held by the defending Pokémon!

Do you think it's cute how Pokémon pluck Berries?

4 Agents from Team Galactic

The locals speak highly of Floaroma Meadow, but if you try to visit it you'll find the path blocked by a pair of Team Galactic members. They're too busy talking amongst themselves to even notice you, so you'll have to postpone the meadow trip for now.

Standing around among flowers... This doesn't seem all that cool.

Floaroma Meadow

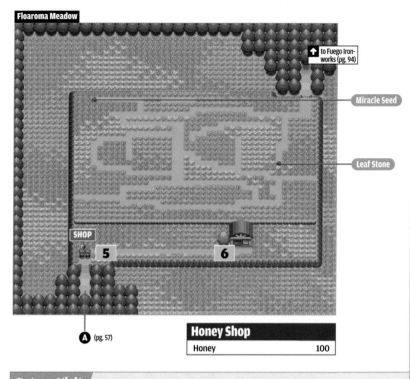

to Fuego Ironworks (pg. 94)

Miracle Seed

Leaf Stone

SHOP

5

6

Ⓐ (pg. 57)

Honey Shop	
Honey	100

Return Visit

5 Battle for the Windworks Key

Works Key **Honey** After battling the guard at the entrance to the Valley Windworks, return to Floaroma Meadow to battle a pair of Galactic Grunts for the second Works Key. You'll have to battle them one at a time with no break in between, but their Wurmple, Silcoon, and Zubat should be no threat for a well-rested team. In addition to the key, the grateful Meadow Keeper will give you a free sample of Honey. Speak to him at any time to buy more.

Money ₽ 6536

▶YES NO

Would you like to buy some Honey for a mere ₽100?

6 Slather the Scented Tree

You can use Honey to attract wild Pokémon to certain sweet-scented trees. You'll find one such tree outside of the Meadow Keeper's home, and another near the Valley Windworks. Slather one or both with Honey, and if you return in 12 to 24 hours, you may find the tree rustling with a wild Pokémon! Honey-slathering is the only way to catch several exclusive Pokémon, so buy plenty of Honey and try it whenever you see a golden tree.

▶YES NO

Slather the bark with Honey?

Route 205 (Floaroma Town Side)

Mountainous Route 205 is home to several must-catch new Pokémon. Too bad Team Galactic is in the way yet again!

FIRST VISIT

1 | Help Rescue Papa

RETURN VISIT

2 | A Rest Stop for Weary Travelers

WILD POKÉMON

POKÉMON	D/P	AM	MID	PM
Bidoof	D/P	□	□	□
Buizel	D/P	■	■	■
Pachirisu	D/P	□	□	□
Shellos	D/P	■		

POKÉMON	D/P	OR	GR
Finneon	D/P		□
Magikarp	D/P	■	■

POKÉMON	D/P	Surf
Pelipper	D/P	●
Tentacool	D/P	■
Tentacruel	D/P	●
Wingull	D/P	■

1 Help Rescue Papa

Not only is Team Galactic blocking Floaroma Meadow and the bridge across the Route 205 river, but they're also holding a poor girl's father in the Valley Windworks! Drive Team Galactic out of the WIndworks—they'll also withdraw from the Route 205 bridge.

Please, Trainer! Get my papa from the Valley Windworks!

Pokémon Notes

Shellos is a hearty Water-type Pokémon whose appearance varies by region. Don't be surprised if Shellos look radically different the next time you encounter it!

Shellos
Type: Water
Ability: Sticky Hold / Storm Drain

Pachirisu
Type: Electric
Ability: Run Away / Pickup

Pachirisu learns useful Electric-type moves much earlier than Shinx does, making it an immediate asset to your team. However, unlike Shinx, Pachirisu is not able to evolve into more-powerful forms.

Finneon
Type: Water
Ability: Swift Swim / Storm Drain

Those with a Great Rod can catch new Finneon in the river that runs through Route 205. Finneon will evolve into a beautiful Lumineon at Level 31.

Buizel and evolved form Floatzel both look like weasels, but they're Water-types through and through. They love moisture so much that their Speed doubles in the rain.

Buizel
Type: Water
Ability: Swift Swim

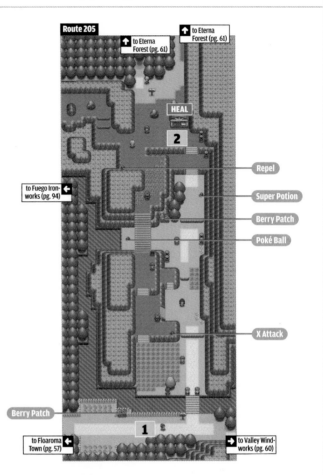

Route 205

↑ to Eterna Forest (pg. 61)

↑ to Eterna Forest (pg. 61)

HEAL

2

Repel
Super Potion
Berry Patch
Poké Ball

X Attack

Berry Patch

← to Fuego Ironworks (pg. 94)

1

← to Floaroma Town (pg. 57)

→ to Valley Windworks (pg. 60)

Return Visit

2 A Rest Stop for Weary Travelers

After driving Team Galactic out of Route 205, you'll be able to travel north to the mysterious Eterna Forest. You'll face several powerful Trainers on the way, so it's fortunate that a friendly couple has set up a free rest stop at point 2. Stop in to heal all your Pokémon before you set foot on the Eterna Forest path.

▶ YES
NO

You seem to be tired...
Rest a while.

Valley Windworks

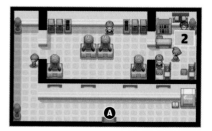

The Valley Windworks provides safe, environmentally friendly power to the entire Sinnoh region.

FIRST VISIT

1 The Windworks Watchman

RETURN VISIT

2 Defeat Commander Mars

WILD POKéMON

POKéMON	D/P	AM	MID	PM
Bidoof	D/P	☐	☐	☐
Buizel	D/P	■	■	■
Pachirisu	D/P	■	■	■
Shellos	D/P	■	■	■

POKéMON	D/P	OR	GR
Finneon	D/P		☐
Magikarp	D/P	■	■

POKéMON	D/P	Surf
Pelipper	D/P	●
Tentacool	D/P	■
Tentacruel	D/P	●
Wingull	D/P	■

POKéMON	D/P	Event
Drifloon	D/P	Friday at windmills

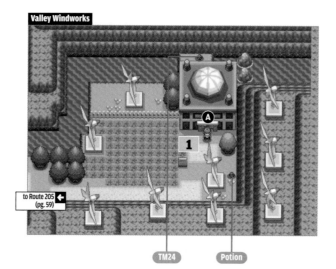

Valley Windworks

to Route 205 (pg. 59)

TM24   Potion

1 The Windworks Watchman

Team Galactic has posted a sentry at the Windworks door, where he'll defend his post with a Level-14 Glameow. If you beat him, he'll run into the Windworks and lock the door behind him, taunting you with the fact that the team's Floaroma Meadow agents have the only other key. Heal up and return to Floaroma Town for another Galactic Grunt fight.

Galactic Grunt sent out GLAMEOW!

But you can't do a thing if I lock myself in with my Works Key!

Pokémon Notes

The Windworks scientist speaks of a Pokémon that appears only on a certain day of the week. He's talking about Drifloon, which hangs around the windmills every Friday. Drifloon has a unique combination of types that is sure to intrigue any serious Pokémon Trainer.

Drifloon

Type: Ghost Flying
Ability: Acrobatic / Detonate

Return Visit

Event Battle: Team Galactic

2 Defeat Commander Mars

Recommended Move Types: Electric, Fighting, Rock

After you win the Works Key in Floaroma Meadow, battle past two Galactic Grunts to reach their leader, Commander Mars. Like her henchmen, she'll attempt to poison your Pokémon, so bring an Antidote or a Cheri Berry. If you've taught a Pokémon Pluck, use it against the Purugly to steal its Oran Berry.

PURUGLY ♀Lv16

STARAVIA ♂Lv14
21/43

STARAVIA stole and ate its foe's Oran Berry!

Zubat	Level 14
Type:	Poison Flying
Purugly	**Level 16**
Type:	Normal

Eterna Forest

As perilous as it is enchanting, Eterna Forest is no place for a young Trainer to travel alone.

FIRST VISIT

1	Team Up with a New Friend
2	A Pleasantly Cool Rock
3	Chansey Is the Cure
4	Part Ways with Cheryl

RETURN VISIT

| 5 | The Old Chateau |
| 6 | The Forest Bypass Route |

WILD POKéMON

POKéMON	D/P	AM	MID	PM
Beautifly	D	●	●	●
Budew	D/P	□	□	□
Buneary	D/P	□	□	□
Cascoon	P	□	□	□
Dustox	P	●	●	●
Misdreavus	P			□
Murkrow	D			□
Silcoon	D	□	□	□
Wurmple	D/P	■	■	□

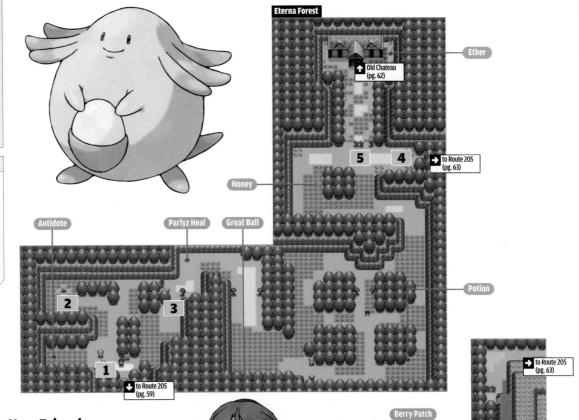

1 Team Up with a New Friend

At the entrance to Eterna Forest, a woman named Cheryl will propose that you travel together. With Cheryl by your side, all of the battles in Eterna Forest will be Double Battles in which your lead Pokémon fights alongside Cheryl's Chansey.

The only downside to teaming up is that it will make it tougher to catch wild Pokémon—they will attack in pairs, and you won't be able to throw a Poké Ball until one of them has been KO'ed. You're then likely to have just one shot before Chansey KO's your intended target.

2 A Pleasantly Cool Rock

In all of Sinnoh, there is no other rock like the pleasantly cool, moss-covered one you'll find in this damp corner of Eterna Forest. Perhaps this mystical stone has some connection to Eevee's new Leafeon form?

3 Chansey Is the Cure

Trainers like the Lass-and-Bug Catcher pair at point 3 use Poison-inducing Pokémon almost exclusively, so you may need to use an Antidote to survive in tough fights. However, you needn't worry about curing and healing wounded Pokémon between battles, because Cheryl's Chansey will take care of that for you. You'll begin each new battle with every Pokémon in good condition and at full HP!

4 Part Ways with Cheryl

It would be great if you could stay with Cheryl and her super-Chansey forever, but alas, all good things must come to an end. At least you can now capture the wild Pokémon of Eterna Forest without Chansey's interference.

Pokémon Notes

It's easy to love the adorable Buneary, and doting on it will pay off in the long run. After hitting the max friendship level, Buneary will evolve into a Lopunny the next time it levels up. If you're lucky, that Lopunny will gain the Cute Charm ability that infatuates physical attackers.

Buneary
Type: Normal
Ability: Run Away / Klutz

5 The Old Chateau

If you have a Pokémon that has learned HM01 (Cut) and the Forest Badge, you can hack open a path to this creepy haunted mansion. Be sure to search the grass to its right, where you can find some Ether in a Poké Ball, and a hidden Insect Plate at a hole in the gate.

6 The Forest Bypass Route

After you earn the Forest Badge and the ability to use Cut, trim the trees here to expose a new area of Route 205 that allows you to travel south without crossing Eterna Forest. You'll find all sorts of great items on the path, including TM82 (Sleep Talk) and a Silver Powder held item that boosts the strength of Bug-type moves. You'll also find a a quartet of berry bushes, a scented tree, and a woman who will give you the Big Tree fashion accessory.

Oh, are you collecting Accessories? I've got something for you.

Old Chateau

This crumbling mansion was abandoned to a pack of Gastly long ago, but a few choice treasures still remain.

1 | Ghostly Phenomena

WILD POKéMON

POKÉMON	D/P	AM	MID	PM
Gastly	D/P	■	■	■

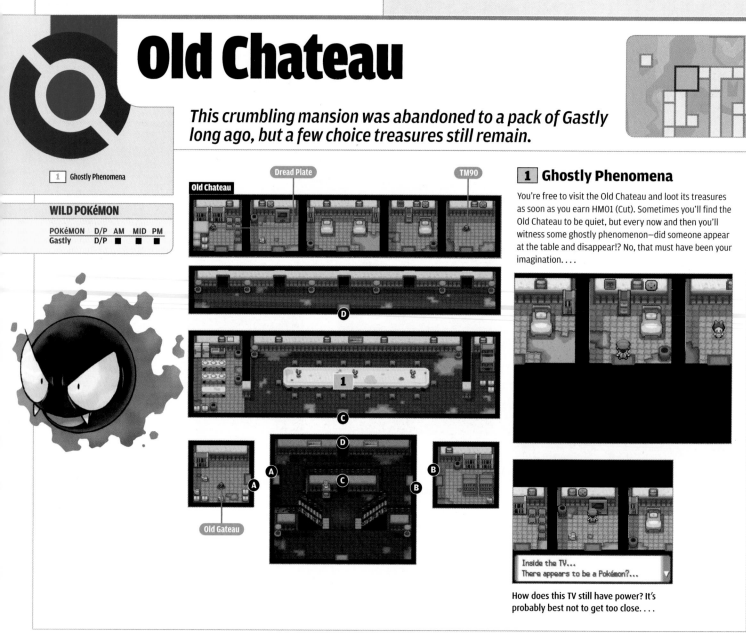

1 Ghostly Phenomena

You're free to visit the Old Chateau and loot its treasures as soon as you earn HM01 (Cut). Sometimes you'll find the Old Chateau to be quiet, but every now and then you'll witness some ghostly phenomenon—did someone appear at the table and disappear!? No, that must have been your imagination. . . .

Inside the TV...
There appears to be a Pokémon?...

How does this TV still have power? It's probably best not to get too close. . . .

Route 205 (Eterna City Side)

The eastern chunk of Route 205 is one of Sinnoh's most popular fishing spots. Eterna City is just ahead!

WILD POKéMON

POKéMON	D/P	AM	MID	PM
Bidoof	D/P	■	■	■
Buizel	D/P	■	■	■
Pachirisu	D/P	☐	☐	☐
Shellos	D/P	☐	☐	☐

POKéMON	D/P	OR	GR	
Barboach	D/P		☐	
Magikarp	D/P	■	■	

POKéMON	D/P	Surf		
Golduck	D/P	☐		
Psyduck	D/P	■		

Route 205 — to Eterna Forest (pg. 61) · Berry Patch · to Eterna Forest (pg. 61) · to Eterna City · Potion

Eterna City

Eterna City is now known as the bicycling capitol of Sinnoh, but its proud history stretches back for centuries.

FIRST VISIT

1	A Gift from a Fellow Trainer
2	The Friendship Checker
3	Rad Rickshaw's Cycle Shop

RETURN VISIT

4	Pick Up Your Reward
5	Learn the Art of Spelunking
6	The Pokémon Name Rater
7	Trade a Buizel for Chatot?
8	TM67 (Recycle)
9	The Herbal Medicine Shop
10	The Vacant House
11	Get the Exp. Share

Eterna City — to Team Galactic Building (pg. 66) · SHOP · POKéMON CENTER · to Route 205 · to Route 211 (pg. 66) · POKéMART · Explorer Kit · TM46 · GYM · Super Potion · to Route 206 (pg. 67)

WILD POKéMON

POKéMON	D/P	OR	GR	
Barboach	D/P		☐	
Magikarp	D/P	■	■	

POKéMON	D/P	Surf		
Golduck	D/P	☐		
Psyduck	D/P	■		

POKéMON	D/P	Event		
Chatot	D/P	Trade only		

Pokémart

Air Mail	50
Antidote	100
Awakening	250
Burn Heal	250
Escape Rope	550
• Full Heal	600
• Full Restore	3000
• Great Ball	600
Heal Ball	300
• Hyper Potion	1200
Ice Heal	250
• Max Potion	2500
• Max Repel	700
Net Ball	1000
Nest Ball	1000
Paralyze Heal	200
Poké Ball	200
Potion	300
Repel	350
• Revive	1500
Super Potion	700
• Super Repel	500
• Ultra Ball	1200

• Not available until later; see the table on page 28

Herb Shop

Energypowder	500
Energy Root	800
Heal Powder	450
Revival Herb	2800

1 | A Gift from a Fellow Trainer

HM01 A friendly Trainer named Cynthia will meet you outside of the Galactic HQ and give you HM01 (Cut), which will allow you to fell small trees after you earn the Forest Badge. She'll also point you east to a mysterious statue that is the pride of Eterna City.

Cynthia: Remember, the hidden move Cut can be used in the field.

2 | The Friendship Checker

Friendship Checker

A woman in the Pokémon Center will give you the Friendship Checker Pokétch app. If you leave the center and return to speak to her, she'll tell you how much your lead Pokémon likes you. If Pokémon such as Buneary and Budew like you enough, they'll evolve into new forms! Select the Friendship Checker app and tap any Pokémon's icon. You can tell how much that Pokémon likes you by the number of hearts that pop up. To boost a Pokémon's friendship level, use it in combat, give it items to hold, and don't let it get KO'ed.

The Friendship Checker app identifies the Pokémon that like you.

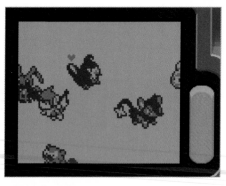

3 | Rad Rickshaw's Cycle Shop

You've finally found the Cycle Shop, but the clerk has gone missing after paying a visit to the Team Galactic building. The only way to follow him is to use Cut on the trees in front of the building, but you can't do that without the Forest Badge. Sounds like it's time to pay a visit to the Eterna City Gym!

The manager's gone off to the Team Galactic building and hasn't returned.

Eterna City Gym

Gym Leader Gardenia
Recommended Move Types: Bug, Fire, Flying

TM86 Flying-types like Starly and Bug-types like Kricketune will do well in this Gym, but anyone who needs a boost can visit the routes to the east to catch a Fire-type Ponyta. (Ponyta is also on the routes to the south, but you'll need the Bicycle to get there.) When your team is ready, scour every nook of this Gym to find the hidden Trainers—you'll need to beat each one to reveal the next. When you battle Gardenia at the end, target her Roserade with Pluck to deal type-trumping damage and eat its life-restoring Sitrus Berry!

Eterna City Gym

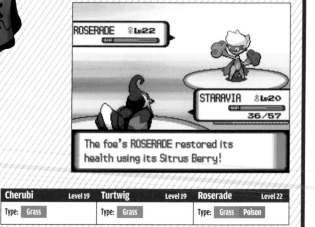

The foe's ROSERADE restored its health using its Sitrus Berry!

Cherubi	Level 19	Turtwig	Level 19	Roserade	Level 22
Type: Grass		Type: Grass		Type: Grass Poison	

Pokémon Notes

Chatot's penchant for mimicry manifests in copying abilities like Mirror Move and Mimic, as well as the Chatot-exclusive Chatter move. Chatter causes confusion, and its odds of success are based on the amount of noise you make into the microphone of your Nintendo DS.

Chatot
Type: Normal Flying
Ability: Keen Eye / Tangled Feet

Return Visit

4 Pick Up Your Reward

Bicycle After you rescue the Cycle Shop clerk (see page 66), return to the shop to accept a free Bicycle. It's a two-speed, and you can press the B Button to shift between third gear (which is slower but more maneuverable) and fourth gear (which sacrifices maneuverability for speed). When you're done practicing, ride into one of the blue bike stands and press the A Button to hop off.

It's the latest model Bicycle! You must take it. I insist!

5 Learn the Art of Spelunking

Explorer's Kit The Underground Man discovered the secret tunnel network beneath Sinnoh, and will give you an Explorer Kit so that you can share in the fun. After accepting the kit, step outside his house and select the kit from your Key Items pouch to be sent straight to The Underground. Explore a bit, then return to the surface and speak to the Underground Man to receive a reward.

Visit the Underground Man whenever you have time to spare—he'll give you a new mission, along with the gear and knowledge you need to engage in activities like digging up rare items and constructing a Secret Base. You'll be a full-fledged spelunker before you know it!

Missions	Rewards
Go underground (1st test)	Move Trap (up), Bubble Trap, Leaf Trap
Dig up an object (2nd test)	Prism Sphere 1, Red Sphere 1, Blue Sphere 1
Bury a sphere (3rd test)	Digger Drill
Dig out a Secret Base (4th test)	Plain Table, Wooden Chair, Small Bookshelf, Buneary Doll
Decorate the Secret Base (5th test)	A doll based on your starter Pokémon
Get Bronze Flag (1 Flag)	Pretty Gem
Get Silver Flag (3 Flags)	Shiny Gem
Get Gold Flag (10 Flags)	Mystic Gem
Get Platinum Flag (50 Flags)	Glitter Gem

6 The Pokémon Name Rater

There are lots of interesting people to meet in the Eterna Condominiums, beginning with the official Name Rater of Sinnoh. Select any Pokémon in your roster, and the Name Rater will offer both his opinion and an opportunity to change the name.

▶ YES
NO

Want me to rate the nicknames of your Pokémon?

7 Trade a Buizel for a Chatot?

On the ground floor of the Eterna Condominiums you'll also meet a young boy who is looking to trade his Chatot for a Buizel. That's a pretty good deal, since wild Buizel are very common in western Sinnoh. Even if you've found your own Chatot elsewhere, you may be interested to hear what the boy has to say about Chatot's trademark Chatter move.

Oh yeah, CHATOT can learn some human speech pretty quickly.

8 TM67 (Recycle)

TM67 Continue your Eterna Condominium tour by speaking to the elderly woman on the second floor. She'll give you TM67, which will teach a Pokémon the Recycle move. If you use this in combat you can return expended items to your inventory, allowing you to get multiple uses out of one-shot items like Potions.

I do hope you'll put it to good use, young Trainer.

9 The Herbal Medicine Shop

You can buy herbal remedies like Energy Root and Heal Powder at this small shop. Herbal medicine is just as effective as the stuff sold at a Pokémart, and quite a bit cheaper. The downside is that Pokémon hate the taste and it will kick their friendship level down a notch. Still, Revive isn't yet available in stores, so it's well worth the drawback to pick up a few Revival Herbs here.

Money	
₽ 15576	

Heal Powder	₽ 450
EnergyPowder	₽ 500
Energy Root	₽ 800
Revival Herb	₽2800
CANCEL	

A very bitter medicine powder. It heals all the status problems of a single Pokémon.

10 The Vacant House

Upgrade You'll find the small home at point 10 empty on your first few trips to Eterna City, but if you visit after you've beaten the game, you'll find that its owner has returned. Celebrate his homecoming by popping in to receive a free Upgrade, which will allow you to evolve Porygon into Porygon2.

11 Get the Exp. Share

Exp. Share Your next destination is Hearthome City, which is due south of Eterna City via the Cycling Road. On the way out of town you'll run into one of Prof. Rowan's assistants, who will check on your progress and reward your continued efforts with the Exp. Share item (if you've seen 35 or more Pokémon). Use it to level up weak Pokémon without exposing them to combat.

I would say an Exp. Share is quite useful for raising weak Pokémon.

Team Galactic Building

Team Galactic has used its ill-gotten wealth to build a spacious headquarters for its Eterna City operations.

| 1 | Battle Commander Jupiter |

Galactic Building 2F

Galactic Building 4F

Galactic Building 1F

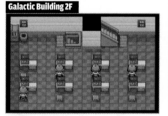

to Eterna City (pg. 63)

Galactic Building 3F

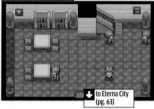

Event Battle: Team Galactic

1 **Battle Commander Jupiter**

Recommended Move Types: Electric, Ground, Psychic, Rock

Bring a few Antidotes with you as you battle to the top of the Team Galactic building—Team Galactic is particularly fond of Poison-type Pokémon. The toughest fight will come on the fourth floor, where you'll need to defeat Commander Jupiter's Level-18 and Level-20 Poison-type Pokémon to free the Cycle Shop manager. Visit him at the shop later to receive your reward.

The foe's SKUNTANK used Poison Gas!

Zubat	Level 18
Type: Poison	Flying

Skuntank	Level 20
Type: Poison	Dark

Route 211 (Eterna City Side)

You'll need HMO4 (Strength) to cross Mt. Coronet's north path, but you can hunt for Pokémon on Route 211 anytime.

| 1 | A Hidden Trainer |

WILD POKéMON

POKéMON	D/P	AM	MID	PM
Bidoof	D/P	■	■	☐
Chingling	D/P	☐	☐	☐
Geodude	D/P	☐	☐	☐
Hoothoot	D/P			☐
Meditite	D/P	■	■	☐
Ponyta	D/P	☐	☐	☐
Zubat	D/P			☐

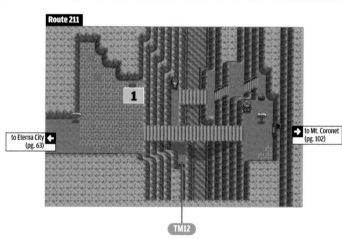

Route 211

to Eterna City (pg. 63)

to Mt. Coronet (pg. 102)

TM12

1 **A Hidden Trainer**

Is that brown spot buried treasure? A berry patch? No—it's a trap! Watch out for Ninja Boy Trainers who suddenly appear when you investigate unfamiliar objects.

Pokémon Notes

Chingling emits jingle-like cries by agitating an orb at the back of its throat. Raise its Friendship level by treating it well, and it will evolve into Chimecho—but only at night.

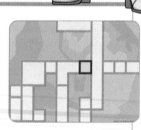

Chingling	
Type:	Psychic
Ability:	Levitate

Route 206

Most travelers use the Cycling Road to zoom through Route 206 so quickly that they never notice the cave in its shadow.

1	Careen Down the Cycling Road
2	Another Free Accessory
3	The Wayward Cave

WILD POKéMON

POKéMON	D/P	AM	MID	PM
Bronzor	D/P	☐	☐	☐
Geodude	D	☐	☐	☐
Geodude	P	■	■	■
Kricketot	D/P	☐		
Kricketune	D/P	☐	☐	■
Ponyta	D/P	■	■	■
Stunky	D	■	■	■
Zubat	D/P			☐

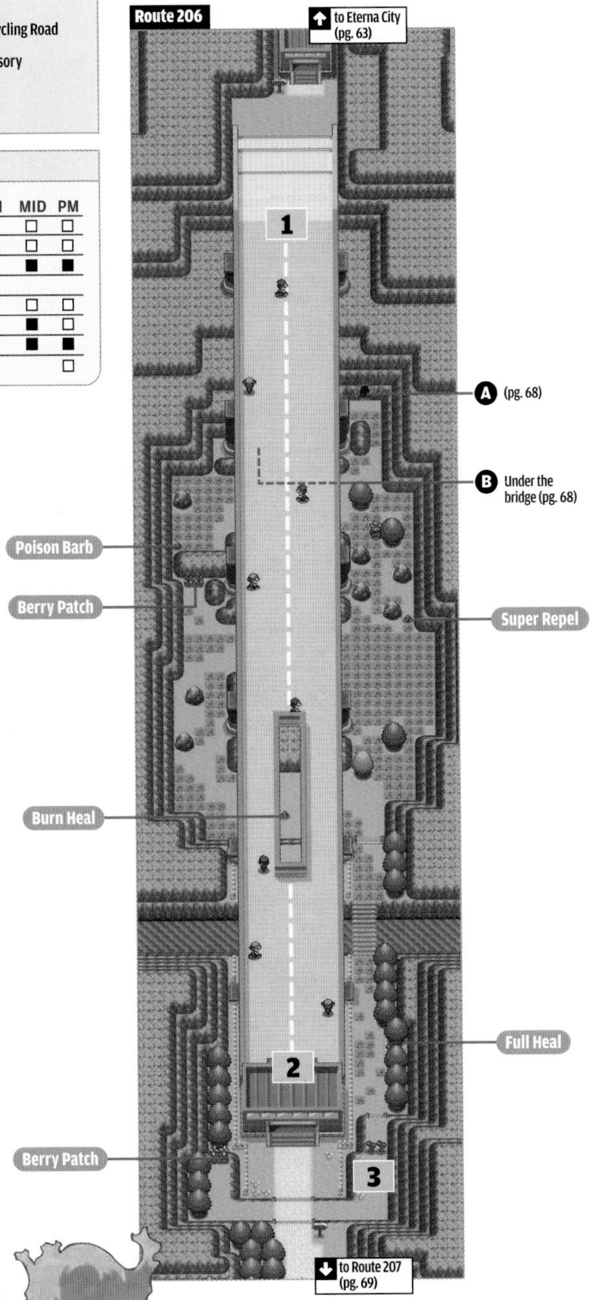

Route 206

to Eterna City (pg. 63)

1

A (pg. 68)

B Under the bridge (pg. 68)

Poison Barb

Berry Patch

Super Repel

Burn Heal

Full Heal

2

Berry Patch

3

to Route 207 (pg. 69)

1 Careen Down the Cycling Road

Route 206's Cycling Road is tilted sharply southward, so use third gear to give yourself the maneuverability you need to evade other Trainers. The slant makes it easy to reach Route 207, but pedaling the other direction can be a chore—finish your business in Eterna City before exploring Route 206.

2 Another Free Accessory

Talk to the blonde girl in the gatehouse at the south end of the road; she'll give you a Flag fashion accessory. You can use it as a prop in the Pokémon Super Contests held in Hearthome City, which she'll direct you to—south to Route 207, then east through Mt. Coronet's south path.

You've got to have a Flag! It's a Pokémon Accessory!

3 The Wayward Cave

Your objective is to the south, but you can Cut the trees to the east of the gatehouse and travel north to the Wayward Cave. The cave has a hidden entrance that is completely obscured by the road above, but you'll need HM04 (Strength) to get past its doorway.

Pokémon Notes

Although Kricketot has no consistent way to deal damage, its evolved form, Kricketune, learns several useful Bug-type attacks as it levels up. They're both good Pokémon to use when battling Psychic-types.

Kricketune
Type: Bug
Ability: Swarm

Stunky is noteworthy for its ability to learn Toxic at Level 20. If you can use this move to poison powerful foes like the Gym Leader's Pokémon, victory will be all but assured.

Stunky
Type: Poison Dark
Ability: Stench / Aftermath

Bronzor specializes in status conditions, and constantly pesters enemy Pokémon with Confuse- and Sleep-inducing moves. It will learn more conventional attacks after evolving at Level 33.

Bronzor
Type: Steel Psychic
Ability: Levitate / Heatproof

Wayward Cave

It's easy to get lost in this dark, labyrinthine cave. Try to keep your bearings so that you can help others in need.

FIRST VISIT

| 1 | A Maze of Darkness |
| 2 | Lead Mira to Safety |

RETURN VISIT

| 3 | The Bike-Jump Course |
| 4 | The Final Jump |

WILD POKéMON

1F

POKéMON	D/P	AM	MID	PM
Bronzor	D/P	■	■	■
Geodude	D/P	□	□	□
Zubat	D/P	■	■	■

2F

POKéMON	D/P	AM	MID	PM
Bronzor	D/P	■	■	■
Geodude	D/P	□	□	□
Gible	D/P	□	□	□
Zubat	D/P	■	■	■

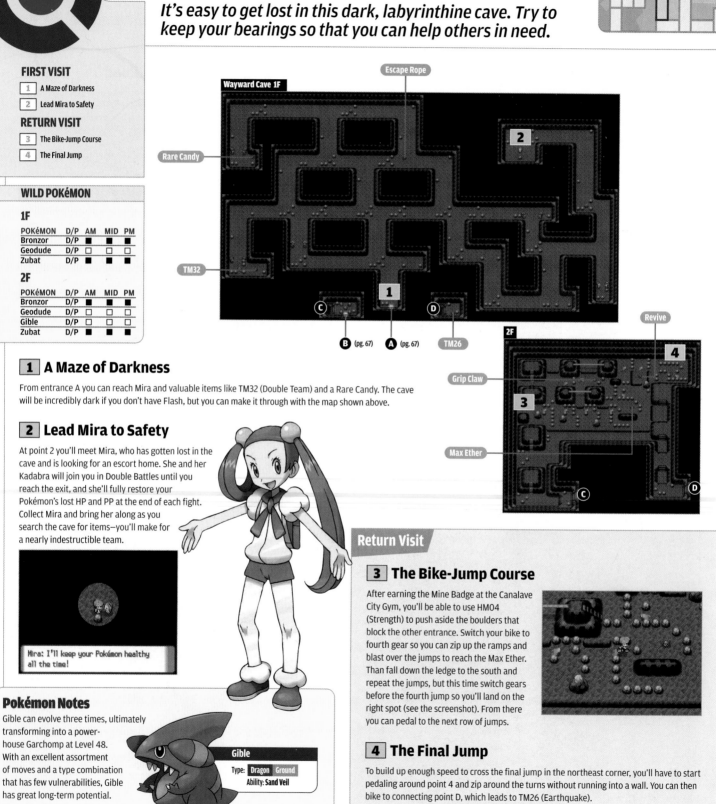

Wayward Cave 1F — Escape Rope, Rare Candy, TM32, 2, 1, B (pg. 67), A (pg. 67), C, D, TM26, 2F, Grip Claw, Max Ether, Revive, 4, 3, C, D

1 A Maze of Darkness

From entrance A you can reach Mira and valuable items like TM32 (Double Team) and a Rare Candy. The cave will be incredibly dark if you don't have Flash, but you can make it through with the map shown above.

2 Lead Mira to Safety

At point 2 you'll meet Mira, who has gotten lost in the cave and is looking for an escort home. She and her Kadabra will join you in Double Battles until you reach the exit, and she'll fully restore your Pokémon's lost HP and PP at the end of each fight. Collect Mira and bring her along as you search the cave for items—you'll make for a nearly indestructible team.

Mira: I'll keep your Pokémon healthy all the time!

Pokémon Notes

Gible can evolve three times, ultimately transforming into a power-house Garchomp at Level 48. With an excellent assortment of moves and a type combination that has few vulnerabilities, Gible has great long-term potential.

Gible
Type: **Dragon Ground**
Ability: **Sand Veil**

Return Visit

3 The Bike-Jump Course

After earning the Mine Badge at the Canalave City Gym, you'll be able to use HM04 (Strength) to push aside the boulders that block the other entrance. Switch your bike to fourth gear so you can zip up the ramps and blast over the jumps to reach the Max Ether. Than fall down the ledge to the south and repeat the jumps, but this time switch gears before the fourth jump so you'll land on the right spot (see the screenshot). From there you can pedal to the next row of jumps.

4 The Final Jump

To build up enough speed to cross the final jump in the northeast corner, you'll have to start pedaling around point 4 and zip around the turns without running into a wall. You can then bike to connecting point D, which leads to TM26 (Earthquake).

Route 207

Route 207's mountain valley connects Route 206 and Oreburgh City to the shortest tunnel through Mt. Coronet.

FIRST VISIT

1. Pick a Hand
2. The Bike Ramp to Oreburgh
3. The Mt. Coronet Traveler

RETURN VISIT

4. Climbing to the Iron

WILD POKéMON

POKéMON	D/P	AM	MID	PM
Geodude	D/P	■	■	■
Kricketot	D/P	□		□
Machop	D/P	■	■	□
Zubat	D/P			□

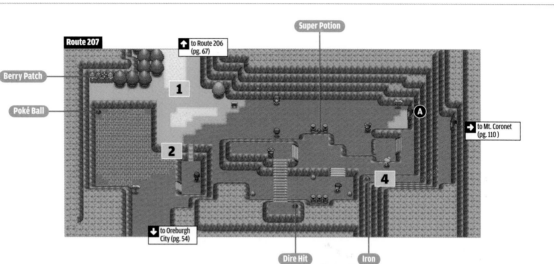

Route 207

Berry Patch · Poké Ball · to Route 206 (pg. 67) · Super Potion · A · to Mt. Coronet (pg. 110) · to Oreburgh City (pg. 54) · Dire Hit · Iron

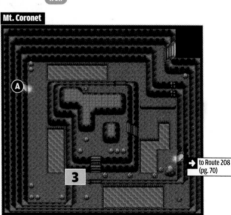

Mt. Coronet

A · to Route 208 (pg. 70)

1 Pick a Hand

VS. Seeker **Dowsing Machine** As you enter Route 207 from the north, the professor's assistant will approach and ask you to pick a hand. It doesn't really matter which one you choose, because you'll get the contents of both either way. One holds a Vs. Seeker that will help you find Trainers who are ready for a rematch, and the other holds the Dowsing Machine Pokétch app, which allows you to locate hidden items on the field by tapping the lower screen.

▶ RIGHT
  LEFT

Chris, choose which hand you want.

2 The Bike Ramp to Oreburgh

If you slide down the hill at point 2, you can return to Oreburgh for healing and supplies. To get back on track, switch your bike to fourth gear and blast up the hill with a full head of steam. Then hang a right and head into Mt. Coronet's southern tunnel, which is the gateway to Route 208 and, beyond that, Hearthome City.

3 The Mt. Coronet Traveler

As you pass beneath the stairs at point 3, a mysterious man will appear, launch into a bizarre speech about the history of Mt. Coronet and the Sinnoh region, and then leave abruptly. From this point you can Rock Smash your way east, or Cut through the upper ledge to reach the exit. If you choose the latter route, try out your new Dowsing Machine to reveal a hidden Ether.

Because the human spirit is weak and incomplete, strife has spread...

Return Visit

4 Climbing to the Iron

Reaching this dose of Iron won't be easy. You'll need to use HM08 (Rock Climb)— you can do so after earning the Icicle Badge—to climb up the handholds in the northeast part of the Mt. Coronet cave, and take the stairs to reach an upper level of Mt. Coronet (see the map on page 110). Take the second exit to Route 207, and then Rock Climb down to the Iron.

Route 208

On the outskirts of Hearthome City, Route 208 is best
known as the home of Sinnoh's legendary Berry Master.

FIRST VISIT

1	The Berry Master's House
2	Get the Berry Searcher App
3	Get the Odd Keystone

RETURN VISIT

| 4 | Traveling Upstream |

WILD POKéMON

POKéMON	D/P	AM	MID	PM
Bibarel	D/P	☐	☐	☐
Bidoof	D/P	☐	☐	☐
Machop	D/P	☐	☐	☐
Meditite	D/P	☐	☐	☐
Psyduck	D/P	■	■	■
Zubat	D/P			☐

POKéMON	D/P	OR	GR
Barboach	D/P		
Magikarp	D/P	■	■

POKéMON	D/P	Surf
Golduck	D/P	☐
Psyduck	D/P	■

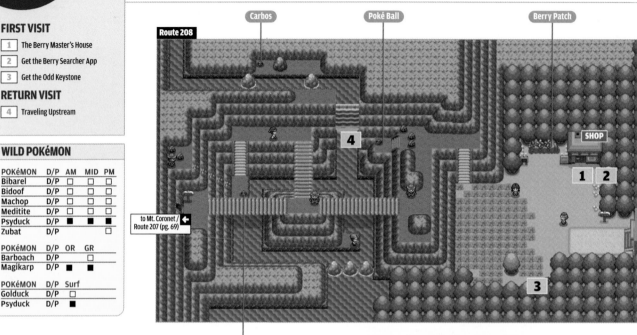

Carbos · Poké Ball · Berry Patch

Route 208

SHOP

to Mt. Coronet / Route 207 (pg. 69)

to Hearthome City

X Speed

1 The Berry Master's House

The Berry Master hands out free berries to visitors (once per day per customer) and may
give you new varieties long before you can find them in the wild. You can also buy mulch
from his daughter, who sells four different mixtures: Growth Mulch will promote faster
growth, but dry out the soil. Damp Mulch slows the growth of berries and causes the soil to
stay moist. Stable mulch extends the time ripened berries remain on their plant before
falling. Gooey mulch restores soil where plants have withered.

Berries Given by the Berry Master

Aguav Berry	Hondew Berry	Oran Berry	Razz Berry
Aspear Berry	Iapapa Berry	Pecha Berry	Sitrus Berry
Bluk Berry	Kelpsy Berry	Persim Berry	Tamato Berry
Cheri Berry	Leppa Berry	Pinap Berry	Wepear Berry
Chesto Berry	Lum Berry	Pomeg Berry	Wiki Berry
Figy Berry	Mago Berry	Qualot Berry	
Grepa Berry	Nanab Berry	Rawst Berry	

2 The Berry Searcher App

Berry Searcher Can't remember where you planted all those berries? The little girl in the
Berry Master's house has a solution. Her Berry Searcher Pokétch app will display all of your
planted berry bushes that have pickable fruit.

3 Get the Odd Keystone

Odd Keystone Don't miss the guy with the headband who is hiding in a wooded corner. He
doesn't want to challenge you—he just wants to give you an item known as the Odd
Keystone. He's short on details, but you're apparently supposed to take it to Route 209, "go
underground, listen to the stone pillar, and talk to the people underground." We'll figure
out what he's talking about on page 75.

Mulch Shop

Damp Mulch	200
Gooey Mulch	200
Growth Mulch	200
Stable Mulch	200

Pokémon Notes

Bibarel, the Evolved form of Bidoof, resides in
areas that have easy access to streams, trees,
and mud. Those are the ingredients it needs to
dam rivers and construct its
intricate nest.

Bibarel

Type: **Normal** **Water**
Ability: **Simple / Unaware**

Return Visit

4 Traveling Upstream

To reach the item in Route 208's
upstream area, you'll need a Pokémon
who knows both HM03 (Surf) and HM07
(Waterfall). Surf up the river from the
spot where the X Speed is, and use
Waterfall to climb up the rapids.
Maneuver around the rock to get a valuable bottle of Carbos.

Hearthome City

With its Gym, Contest Hall, and walking park, Hearthome City is a popular destination for Trainers.

FIRST VISIT

1	Runaway Buneary
2	The Mysterious "Someone"
3	The Poffin Case
4	Cooking at the Poffin House
5	An Escort to the Contest Hall
6	Meet Fantina, the Hearthome Gym Leader
7	The Pokémon Contest Hall
8	Amity Square
9	Mr. E's Goods
10	The Shell Bell
11	Battle Your Rival
12	Get a Pokémon Egg

RETURN VISIT

13	Return to Hearthome City
14	Run into Cynthia

WILD POKÉMON

POKÉMON	D/P	Event
Happiny	D/P	Hatch from Egg

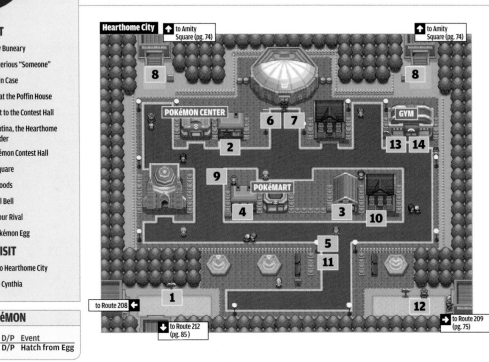

Hearthome City — to Amity Square (pg. 74) / to Amity Square (pg. 74) / POKÉMON CENTER / GYM / POKéMART / to Route 208 / to Route 212 (pg. 85) / to Route 209 (pg. 75)

Pokémart

Antidote	100
Awakening	250
Burn Heal	250
Escape Rope	550
• Full Heal	600
• Full Restore	3000
• Great Ball	600
Heal Ball	300
Heart Mail	50
• Hyper Potion	1200
Ice Heal	250
• Max Potion	2500
• Max Repel	700
Net Ball	1000
Nest Ball	1000
Paralyze Heal	200
Poké Ball	200
Potion	300
Repel	350
• Revive	1500
Super Potion	700
• Super Repel	500
• Ultra Ball	1200

• Not available until later; see the table on page 28

1 Runaway Buneary

As you enter Hearthome City, a Buneary will come running your way. Stall it long enough for Trainer Keira to get it back into a Poké Ball; she'll ask you to drop by the Contest Hall so she can thank you properly.

2 The Mysterious "Someone"

The woman behind the desk in this small building is the system administrator for Sinnoh's Pokémon Box system. Her name is Bebe, so from now on the Pokémon Center's storage system will be known as Bebe's PC instead of Someone's PC. It's important to give credit where credit is due!

You know the PC Pokémon Boxes? I'm the system administrator!

3 The Poffin Case

Poffin Case Pokémon are at the center of popular culture in Hearthome City, so it's no surprise that Sinnoh's Pokémon Fan Club has made it their base of operations. At the Fan Club you can give an interview to a Jubilife TV reporter, consult a Friendship Checker (who will tell you how much your lead Pokémon likes you), and learn about Poffins. The Fan Club's chairman will even give you a free Poffin Case as a souvenir.

4 Cooking at the Poffin House

Take your new Poffin Case to the Poffin House and give Poffin-making a try. Start by selecting a berry and checking its tag to see which stats it boosts. Confirm the berry you want, then stir the batter in the designated direction. For the highest-level Poffins, stir gently to avoid spillage, but fast enough that it doesn't burn. To make better Poffins in higher quantities, cook with a group of friends over the DS wireless connection.

5 An Escort to the Contest Hall

If you're having trouble finding your way around this sprawling city, talk to the man at point 5; he'll lead you straight to the Contest Hall.

6 Meet Fantina, the Hearthome Gym Leader

On your way into the Contest Hall, you'll run into Fantina, the beautiful but arrogant leader of the Hearthome City Gym. She'll size you up and announce that you're not yet strong enough to challenge her. You'll need to earn the Cobble and Fen Badges before she'll accept your challenge.

You must become much stronger. Then, you may challenge me!

7 The Pokémon Contest Hall

(Glitter Powder) (Smooth Poffin) At the Contest Hall you'll run into Keira, along with . . . your mom? To get you started in the Super Contest world, Keira will give you the Glitter Powder fashion accessory and your mom will provide a dress or tuxedo for your hero. You can also get a Smooth Poffin (which boosts all five of a Pokémon's contest stats) from a man near the counter. When you're ready to give the Super Contest a try, go to the center counter to enter, the right counter to practice, or the left counter to link up with friends. To read up on how Super Contests work, see pages 34 and 35.

Contest	Prize	Ribbon
COOL CONTEST		
Normal Rank	Red Barrette	Cool Ribbon
Great Rank	Red Balloon	Cool Great Ribbon
Ultra Rank	Top Hat	Cool Ultra Ribbon
Master Rank	Gold Pedestal	Cool Master Ribbon
BEAUTY CONTEST		
Normal Rank	Blue Barrette	Beauty Ribbon
Great Rank	Blue Balloon	Beauty Great Ribbon
Ultra Rank	Silk Veil	Beauty Ultra Ribbon
Master Rank	Glass Stage	Beauty Master Ribbon
CUTE CONTEST		
Normal Rank	Pink Barrette	Cute Ribbon
Great Rank	Pink Balloon	Cute Great Ribbon
Ultra Rank	Headdress	Cute Ultra Ribbon
Master Rank	Flower Stage	Cute Master Ribbon
SMART CONTEST		
Normal Rank	Green Barrette	Genius Ribbon
Great Rank	Green Balloon	Genius Great Ribbon
Ultra Rank	Professor Hat	Genius Ultra Ribbon
Master Rank	Cube Stage	Genius Master Ribbon
TOUGH CONTEST		
Normal Rank	Yellow Barrette	Powerful Ribbon
Great Rank	Yellow Balloon	Powerful Great Ribbon
Ultra Rank	Heroic Headband	Powerful Ultra Ribbon
Master Rank	Award Podium	Powerful Master Ribbon

8 Amity Square

Two entrances at point 8 lead to Amity Square, where you can take a stroll with any "cute" Pokémon, meaning Pikachu, Clefairy, Psyduck, Pachirisu, Happiny, Buneary, or Drifloon. Don't worry if you don't have any of those Pokémon—you'll catch one soon. See page 74 for information on the items you can find in Amity Square.

9 Mr. E's Goods

Mr. E travels the world seeking rare items for worthy Trainers. He'll be happy to provide these items free of charge, but first you must earn them by accomplishing an impressive feat like beating all eight Gyms, mastering a Super Contest rank, or meeting 100 people in The Underground. You can display the prizes you win in your Secret Base as a lasting reminder of your achievement.

Mr. E's Goods	Mission
OTHER	
Globe	Connect to Wi-Fi
Gym Statue	Clear eight Gyms
SUPER CONTEST CUPS	
Cute Cup	Win the Cute Master Rank Contest
Cool Cup	Win the Cool Master Rank Contest
Beauty Cup	Win the Beauty Master Rank Contest
Tough Cup	Win the Tough Master Rank Contest
Smart Cup	Win the Smart Master Rank Contest
UNDERGROUND CRYSTALS	
Blue Crystal	Meet 100 people in The Underground
Pink Crystal	Give 100 items to people in The Underground
Red Crystal	Dig up 100 Fossils in The Underground
Yellow Crystal	Trap 100 people in The Underground
BATTLE TOWER TROPHIES	
Copper Trophy	Beat 10 Trainers in the Battle Tower
Silver Trophy	Beat 50 Trainers in the Battle Tower
Gold Trophy	Beat 100 Trainers in Battle Tower

10 The Shell Bell

(Shell Bell) In the home south of the Gym, take the elevator to the second floor and speak to the woman at the table. She'll give you a Shell Bell, which is a held item that restores a bit of HP whenever its holder damages another Pokémon.

Event Battle: Your Rival

11 Battle Your Rival

Recommended Move Types: Electric, Fire, Flying, Ground, Water

After leaving the Contest Hall, visit the Pokémon Center if your party is wounded—your rival will strike as soon as you pass point 11. He's been busy, and has marshalled a team of four Pokémon around Level 20, led by the evolved form of his starter (see the charts below). Bring a wild Pokémon whose type trumps that starter's, or you'll be in for a very tough duel.

LUXIO used Spark!

Player chose Turtwig		
Starly		Level 19
Type:	Normal	Flying
Roselia		Level 20
Type:	Grass	Poison
Buizel		Level 20
Type:	Water	
Monferno		Level 21
Type:	Fire	Fighting

Player chose Chimchar		
Starly		Level 19
Type:	Normal	Flying
Ponyta		Level 20
Type:	Fire	
Roselia		Level 20
Type:	Grass	Poison
Prinplup		Level 21
Type:	Water	

Player chose Piplup		
Starly		Level 19
Type:	Normal	Flying
Ponyta		Level 20
Type:	Fire	
Buizel		Level 20
Type:	Water	
Grotle		Level 21
Type:	Grass	

12 Get a Pokémon Egg

Your next destination is Veilstone City, and the first step on that journey is Route 209, via the southeast gatehouse. Talk to the man at the gatehouse entrance. He'll offer you a Pokémon Egg. You'll need an empty slot in your roster to accept it.

Pokémon Notes

When you get the Egg, keep it in your roster as you proceed on your quest. It will get a little bit closer to hatching with each step you take, until one day it shatters to reveal a Level-1 Happiny, the "baby" form of Chansey.

Happiny
Type: Normal
Ability: Natural Cure /Serene Grace

13 Return to Hearthome City

After you speak with Cynthia's grandma in Celestic Town and earn HMO3 (Surf), Fantina will be happy to accept your challenge at the Hearthome City Gym.

Hearthome City Gym

Gym Leader Fantina

Recommended Move Types: Dark, Electric, Ghost

TM65 This unusual Gym allows you to skip all of the Junior Trainers and head straight to Gym Leader Fantina by answering a few simple math questions. Read the question on the sign at the beginning of each floor, then choose the door marked with the correct answer (in order, the answers are 15, 40, 39, and 15). All of the Junior Trainers are behind the wrong-answer doors, so if you want to earn a few Exp. Points before battling Fantina, you'll have to intentionally make the wrong choices. The best moves against the Ghost-type Pokémon in this Gym are Dark-type moves such as Bite, many of which are known by non-Dark-type Pokémon. Those who defeat Fantina will earn the Relic Badge, TM65 (Shadow Claw), and the ability to use HMO3 (Surf) outside of combat.

Drifblim	Level 32	Gengar	Level 34	Mismagius	Level 36
Type: Ghost Flying		Type: Ghost Poison		Type: Ghost	

LUXRAY used
Bite!

STUNKY used
Night Slash!

Hearthome City Gym

14 Run into Cynthia

When you exit the Hearthome City Gym with the Relic Badge, you'll find Cynthia waiting. She'll thank you for your efforts in Celestic Town and advise you to visit the library in Canalave City. You'll find Canalave City to the west of Jubilife City (see Route 218 on page 96), but you can take optional side trips to the Fuego Ironworks (see page 94) and Routes 219-221 (see page 95) on the way.

They have some ancient books that
you might find interesting.

Amity Square

Hearthome City's Amity Square is a lovely spot where Trainers can frolick with certain cute Pokémon.

1 Walking Is Worth It
2 Secrets of Amity Square

Amity Square

Spooky Plate

TM45

2

1

TM43

to Hearthome City (pg. 71)

to Hearthome City (pg. 71)

---

1 Walking Is Worth It

You can enter Amity Square if you have Pikachu, Clefairy, Psyduck, Pachirisu, Happiny, Buneary, or Drifloon in your roster. Once inside you can stroll to your heart's content, giving your companion exercise, fresh air, and a chance to dig up small items. Your Pokémon will discover an item roughly every 200 steps, so speak to it often to see what it has found. The items are primarily fashion accessories, but there are several rare berries to be found as well.

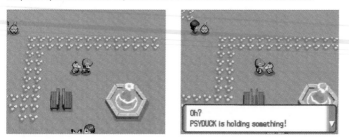

Oh?
PSYDUCK is holding something!

2 Secrets of Amity Square

Amulet Coin Amity Square is also full of standard treasures, including two TMs (Secret Power and Attract) and a Ghost-type-boosting Spooky Plate. Additionally, you can find an Amulet Coin inside one of the rock huts by facing its left wall and pressing the A Button. This held item doubles the money you earn in Trainer battles whenever the holder participates.

Chris found an Amulet Coin!

Pokémon and the Accessories They Will Find

Clefairy	Drifloon	Pachirisu / Psyduck	Pikachu	Buneary / Happiny	How Often
White Fluff	Pink Fluff	Jagged Stone	Orange Fluff	Pink Scale	Sometimes
Orange Fluff	Red Feather	Snaggy Stone	Brown Fluff	Shed Horn	Sometimes
White Feather	Yellow Feather	Brown Fluff	Small Leaf	Pink Fluff	Sometimes
Round Stone	Black Beard	Round Stone	Red Feather	Yellow Feather	Sometimes
Small Leaf	Narrow Scale	Black Moustache	Yellow Feather	Shed Claw	Sometimes
Blue Scale	White Fluff	Shed Horn	Yelllow Fluff	Black Fluff	Sometimes
White Beard	White Moustache	Narrow Scale	Glitter Stone	Jagged Stone	Rarely
Thin Mushroom	Shed Claw	Mini Stone	Big Scale	Big Leaf	Rarely
Big Scale	Narrow Leaf	Green Scale	Black Moustache	Green Scale	Rarely
Stump	Purple Scale	Thick Mushroom	Purple Scale	Black Stone	Very Rarely

Clefairy, Drifloon, Pachirisu, Psyduck, Pikachu, Buneary, and Happiny	How Often
Cornn Berry, Magost Berry, Nomel Berry, Rabuta Berry	Rarely
Belue Berry, Durin Berry, Pamtre Berry, Spelon Berry, Watmel Berry	Very Rarely

Route 209

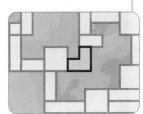

A series of excavations on Route 209 has unearthed two ancient towers. One is intact, but the other lies in ruin.

1 Upgrade Your Fishing Rod
2 Challenge the Jogger
3 The Secret of the Odd Keystone

WILD POKéMON

POKéMON	D/P	AM	MID	PM
Bibarel	D/P	■	■	■
Bonsly	P	□	●	●
Chansey	D/P	●	●	●
Gastly	D/P			□
Mime Jr.	D	□	●	●
Staravia	D/P	□	□	□
Starly	D/P	□	□	□
Zubat	D/P			□

POKéMON	D/P	OR	GR
Goldeen	D/P		□
Magikarp	D/P	■	■

POKéMON	D/P	Surf
Golduck	D/P	□
Psyduck	D/P	■

POKéMON	D/P	Event
Spiritomb	D/P	Event only

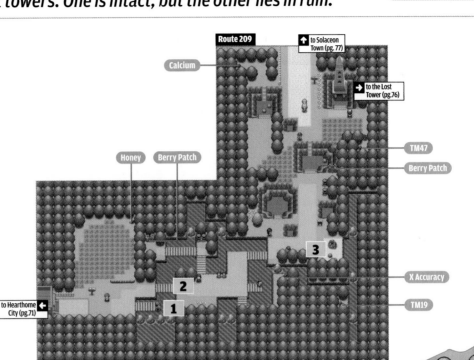

Route 209

Calcium

↑ to Solaceon Town (pg. 77)

→ to the Lost Tower (pg.76)

TM47

Berry Patch

Honey · Berry Patch

3

X Accuracy

2

TM19

← to Hearthome City (pg.71)

1

1 Upgrade Your Fishing Rod

Good Rod Speak to a fisherman and agree that a Good Rod is, indeed, good. He'll reward your depth of insight by giving you a Good Rod of your own, which you can use—finally—to fish up Pokémon other than Magikarp.

2 Challenge the Jogger

The jogger here wants to fight only in the morning, so if you want to challege him, you'll need to speak to him between 4 and 10 am. There isn't any particular prize for beating him, but it's worth the trouble just to teach him a lesson about being so darn perky in the morning.

I jog every morning to keep my Pokémon fit.

3 The Secret of the Odd Keystone

Route 209's small beach has a broken, crumbling tower with a spot that exactly matches the Odd Keystone you received on Route 208. Using the Odd Keystone will restore the Hallowed Tower, but the tower won't do anything unless you've met at least 32 players in The Underground. (Check your progress by using the Explorer Kit to go to The Underground and selecting your name from the menu.) When you hit 32, return to the Hallowed Tower to battle a rare Spiritomb.

The stone tower has been restored! "Hallowed Tower" is written on it.

Pokémon Notes

Spiritomb is a mysterious Pokémon born from the union of 108 fallen souls. It can learn both parts of the Hypnosis / Dream Eater combo, a fact that surely haunts its foes.

Spiritomb
Type: Ghost | Dark
Ability: Pressure

Bonsly made its debut in Pokémon XD: Gale of Darkness, and you can finally capture it for yourself—if you're playing the Pearl version of the game. Diamond players will instead find Mime Jr., a "baby" version of the classic Mr. Mime.

Bonsly
Type: Rock
Ability: Sturdy / Rock Head

Mime Jr.
Type: Psychic
Ability: Soundproof / Filter

Staravia
Type: Normal | Flying
Ability: Intimidate

Staravia is the evolved form of Starly, and has higher stats and more-powerful attacks. If you don't want to take the time to evolve Starly, catch a wild Staravia to fill out its Pokédex page.

The Lost Tower

The good people of Sinnoh pay tribute to their fallen Pokémon at Route 209's Lost Tower.

1	Pay your Respects at the Lost Tower

WILD POKéMON

1F / 2F

POKéMON	D/P	AM	MID	PM
Gastly	D/P	■	■	■
Misdreavus	P			□
Murkrow	D			□
Zubat	D/P	■	■	■

3F

POKéMON	D/P	AM	MID	PM
Gastly	D/P	■	■	■
Golbat	D/P	○	○	○
Misdreavus	P			□
Murkrow	D			□
Zubat	D/P	■	■	■

4F

POKéMON	D/P	AM	MID	PM
Gastly	D/P	■	■	■
Golbat	D/P	●	●	●
Misdreavus	P			□
Murkrow	D			□
Zubat	D/P	■	■	■

5F

POKéMON	D/P	AM	MID	PM
Gastly	D/P	■	■	■
Golbat	D/P	□	□	□
Misdreavus	P			□
Murkrow	D			□
Zubat	D/P	■	■	■

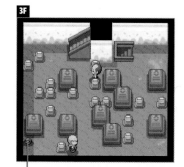

3F

Revive

4F — TM27

5F

1

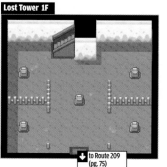

Lost Tower 1F

2F — Oval Stone

to Route 209 (pg. 75)

1 Pay Your Respects at the Lost Tower

HM04 You'll face wild Ghost-type Pokémon and antsy Trainers in the Lost Tower, but those who persevere will earn the respect of the elderly ladies on the top floor. They'll reward you with a Cleanse Tag held item that drives wild Pokémon away, and HM04 (Strength). You can fire it up now to learn the battle move, but you won't be able to use it to push rocks until after you earn the Mine Badge in Canalave City, which is several Gyms away.

It is good of you to have visited. Here, take this Hidden Machine.

Solaceon Town

Solaceon Town is home to Sinnoh's Day Care Center, as well as the entrance to the mysterious Solaceon Ruins.

FIRST VISIT

1 Another Free Pokétch App
2 A Pokémon Research Job
3 Pokémon Day Care
4 The Day Care Checker
5 Using Poké Ball Seals

RETURN VISIT

6 Earning Alphabet Seals

Solaceon Town

to Route 210 (pg. 80)

to Solaceon Ruins (pg.78)

to Solaceon Ruins (pg.78)

POKéMON CENTER

Berry Patch

POKéMART

to Route 209 (pg. 75)

Pokémart	
Air Mail	50
Antidote	100
Awakening	250
Burn Heal	250
Dusk Ball	1000
Escape Rope	550
• Full Heal	600
• Full Restore	3000
• Great Ball	600
• Hyper Potion	1200
Ice Heal	250
• Max Potion	2500
• Max Repel	700
Net Ball	1000
Nest Ball	1000
Paralyze Heal	200
Poké Ball	200
Potion	300
Repel	350
• Revive	1500
Super Potion	700
• Super Repel	500
• Ultra Ball	1200

• Not available until later; see the table on page 28

1 Another Free Pokétch App

Pokémon History The first man you meet in Solaceon Town will update your Pokétch with a new Pokémon History app. This one shows the last 12 Pokémon you've acquired, and you can tap any Pokémon on the display to hear its call.

2 A Pokémon Research Job

Sinnoh's daily newspaper is made in a small building at point 2, and the reporter on the Pokémon beat is always looking for help meeting his deadlines. Every day he'll ask you to bring him a specific Pokémon (just to see, not to keep), and if you do he'll thank you by handing over three Poké Balls selected at random from the list below. Check back every day—it's an easy prize to win if the Pokémon he needs is already in your box.

Research Job Rewards
Dive Ball
Dusk Ball
Great Ball
Heal Ball
Luxury Ball
Nest Ball
Net Ball
Poké Ball
Quick Ball
Repeat Ball
Timer Ball
Ultra Ball

3 Pokémon Day Care

You can leave up to two Pokémon at the Pokémon Day Care, where they'll gradually level up based on the number of steps you walk (you'll have to pay a small fee for this service when you pick them up). If you leave two Pokémon of opposite genders who are in the same Egg Group, the two just might produce an Egg—see page 32 for more details on Pokémon breeding. After dropping off a breeding pair, step outside to ask the Day Care Lady's husband how they're getting along.

4 The Day Care Checker

Day-Care Checker After dropping off at least one Pokémon at the Day Care Center, leave and return. Speak to the man who is now sitting at the table near the entrance; he'll update your Pokétch with the Day Care Checker app. The nifty app lets you keep tabs on the levels of the Pokémon you've left behind, so you'll know when they're ready to be picked up and returned to active duty.

Since you're a fellow fan of the Day Care, I'm compelled to share this!

5 Using Poké Ball Seals

Seal Case To visit the secluded home at point 5, travel to the north end of town and leap down the second series of ledges. Speak to the lady of the house to receive a Seal Case and a lesson on how to use your computer to customize Poké Balls by sticking Seals on them. Speak to her again, and she'll tell you how her son gathers new Seals by visiting the Solaceon Ruins. You can buy Seals at some shops, but if you want to expand your Seal selection to include letters, you'll have to pay a visit to the Solaceon Ruins yourself (see tip 6).

Return Visit

6 Earning Alphabet Seals

After you speak to the Seal Lady's son in the Solaceon Ruins, he'll return home to manage his Seal collection. Visit him with an Unown in the top spot of your roster, and the boy will give you 10 free Seals of the corresponding letter!

I'll give you a bunch of Seals that look like it.

Keep catching Unown and bringing them to the boy to earn more and more letters. Soon you'll be able to spell names, words, and phrases on your Poké Balls!

Solaceon Ruins

The Solaceon Ruins are an elaborate riddle left by an enigmatic species of Pokémon. Can you crack the code?

FIRST VISIT

1. The Unown Alphabet
2. The Seal Lady's Son

RETURN VISIT

3. Punctuating the Unown

WILD POKÉMON

POKéMON	D/P	AM	MID	PM
Unown	D/P	■	■	■

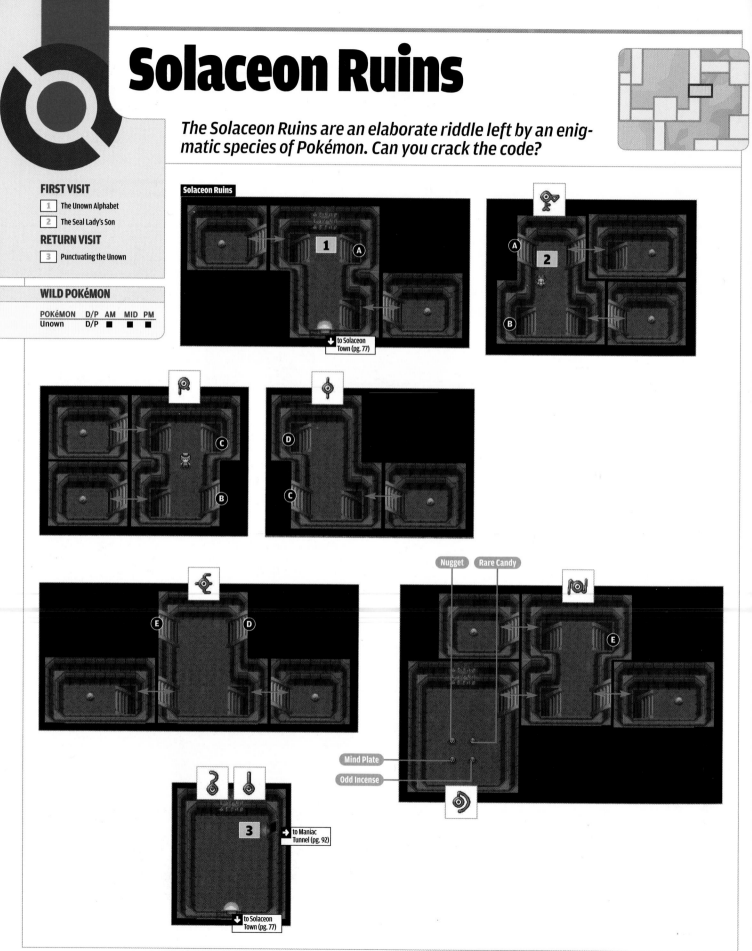

Solaceon Ruins

to Solaceon Town (pg. 77)

Nugget · Rare Candy

Mind Plate · Odd Incense

to Maniac Tunnel (pg. 92)

to Solaceon Town (pg. 77)

1 The Unown Alphabet

You'll find mysterious symbols scrawled across the north wall in the first room of the ruins. If you can decode the Unown-shaped letters (see the chart below if you need help), you'll see that the message is actually a series of directions that tell you which staircases to take on your travels through the ruins. Follow the directions to end up in a room with the Unowns' message of peace and several rare treasures.

2 The Seal Lady's Son

Seals You'll find the Solaceon Seal Lady's little boy in the "F" chamber of the ruins. He'll return to his Solaceon Town home, where you can visit him when you finish exploring the ruins. Put an Unown at the top slot of your roster when you speak to him, and he'll give you 10 Seals of the corresponding letter. If you can catch a variety of Unown and convert them to seals, you'll be able to spell whole phrases on your Poké Balls!

Pokémon Notes

There are 28 different Unown, all of which you can capture in the Solaceon Ruins. If you follow the directions at point 1, you'll pass through six rooms whose labels spell F-R-I-E-N-D. In each of those rooms you'll find only the Unown that matches the room's letter. Unown corresponding to the other 20 letters appear randomly in the dead-end rooms that you'll reach when you ignore the instructions. The "!" and "?" Unown appear only in the room at point 3, which can be reached via the Maniac Tunnel (see page page 92).

Unown
Type: **Psychic**
Ability: **Levitate**

Unown take the shape of 28 letters and punctuation marks. It isn't clear if they're based on the alphabet or if the alphabet is based on them.

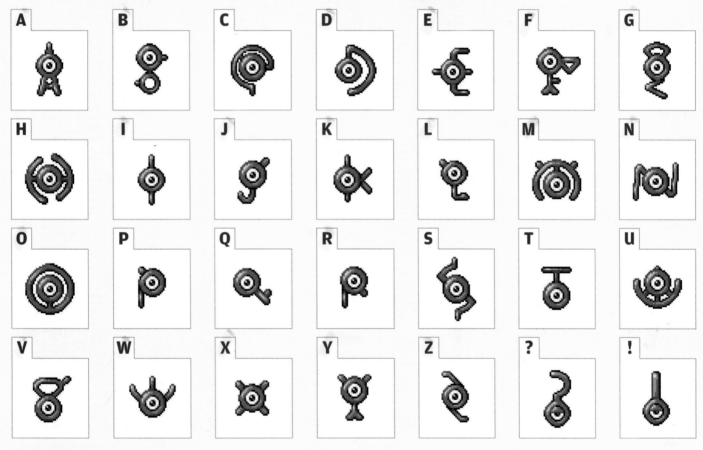

Return Visit

3 Punctuating the Unown

You'll meet the Maniac Digger on Route 214 (page 92), where he'll hatch a mad plan of tunneling west through the mountains into the Solaceon Ruins. The more Unown you catch, the farther his tunnel will extend, and it won't break through to the ruins until you've caught every last one of the 26 lettered Unown. You can then enter the tunnel at Route 214 and follow it west into a special Solaceon Ruins chamber that contains the "!" and "?" Unown, as well as a new message for Unown code-crackers to decipher.

Route 210

The fog in the northern half of Route 210 is sometimes too thick for even the native Psyduck population to bear.

WILD POKéMON

ROUTE 210 A

POKéMON	D/P	AM	MID	PM
Bonsly	P	□	●	●
Chansey	D/P	●	●	●
Geodude	D/P	■	■	■
Kricketune	D/P	□	□	■
Mime Jr.	D	□	●	●
Ponyta	D/P	■	■	■

ROUTE 210 B

POKéMON	D/P	AM	MID	PM
Bibarel	D/P	■	■	■
Hoothoot	D/P			□
Machoke	D/P	□	□	□
Machop	D/P	□	□	□
Meditite	D/P	■	■	□
Noctowl	D/P			□
Psyduck	D/P	□	□	□

POKéMON	D/P	OR	GR
Barboach	D/P		□
Magikarp	D/P	■	■

POKéMON	D/P	Surf	
Golduck	D/P	□	
Psyduck	D/P	■	

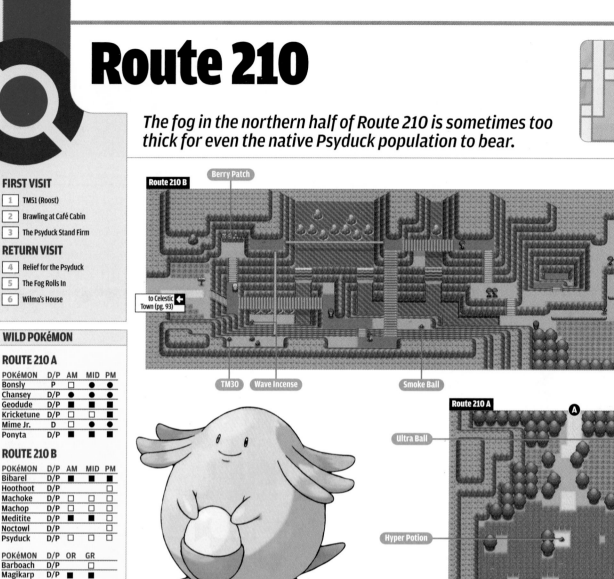

Route 210 B · Berry Patch · TM30 · Wave Incense · Smoke Ball · to Celestic Town (pg. 93) · Route 210 A · Ultra Ball · Hyper Potion · Super Repel · SHOP · Great Ball · to Route 215 · Berry Patch · to Solaceon Town (pg. 77)

Shop

MooMoo Milk	500

1 TM51 (Roost)

TM51 Not all of the Trainers on Route 210 are hoping for a fight. The woman on the ledge at point 1 just wants to talk, and will hand over TM51 (Roost) if you listen to what she has to say. The TM contains Roost, a wonderful Flying-type healing move for winged Pokémon.

2 Brawling at Café Cabin

The Café Cabin sells bottles of MooMoo Milk that can restore 100 of a Pokémon's lost HP. But don't consider the cabin a rest stop—you can't even approach the counter without being challenged by a waitress. Most of the customers are eager for a fight too, but at least they have some information to share about the Psyduck outside.

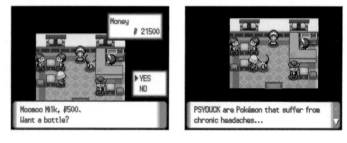

Money ₱ 21500

▶ YES
NO

Moomoo Milk, ₱500.
Want a bottle?

PSYDUCK are Pokémon that suffer from chronic headaches...

3 The Psyduck Stand Firm

The northern path through Route 210 is blocked by a pack of Psyduck that are suffering from debilitating headaches. You'll find a cure for their malady later, but there's nothing you can do for them now. Abandon the northern path and head east to Route 215 instead.

The PSYDUCK are standing firm. They aren't inclined to move at all.

Return Visit

4 Relief for the Psyduck

Old Charm After you receive the Secret Potion from Cynthia in Route 213, you can return to Route 210 and cure those achin' Psyduck. As soon as they disperse, Cynthia will appear behind you and ask you to deliver the Old Charm to her grandma in Celestic Town. You can reach Celestic Town by crossing a series of bridges in the deep canyon that dominates the northern half of Route 210.

Would you like to use the SecretPotion?

▶YES
NO

I want you to deliver this Old Charm to my grandma in Celestic Town.

5 The Fog Rolls In

A thick fog will roll into Route 210 when you reach this point. In addition to making the route hard to see, the fog will cut the Accuracy of all Pokémon attacks in combat. You can clear it with HM05 (Defog), but it isn't strictly necessary. In fact, if you use moves like Swift (which always hit) you can turn the fog into an asset in combat!

6 Wilma's House

To reach the house at point 6 you'll have to use HM08 (Rock Climb) from the east edge of the ledge at the top of the second staircase. Inside you'll find a Dragon-type Trainer named Wilma, who will offer to teach the powerful Draco Meteor attack to any Dragon-type Pokémon.

Route 215

The shadow of Mt. Coronet keeps Route 215 rainy and damp. At least travelers can dry out in nearby Veilstone City.

| 1 | A Sudden Downpour |
| 2 | TM66 (Payback) |

WILD POKéMON

POKéMON	D/P	AM	MID	PM
Abra	D/P	□	□	□
Geodude	D/P	■	■	■
Kadabra	D/P	□	□	□
Kricketune	D/P	□	□	□
Ponyta	D/P	■	■	□

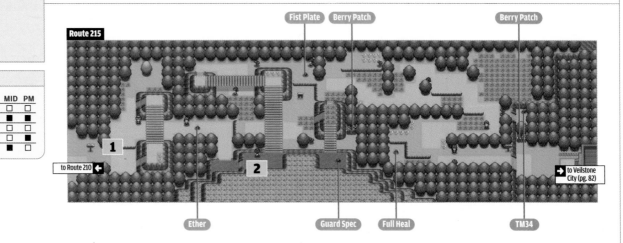

Route 215

Fist Plate Berry Patch Berry Patch

1

2

to Route 210 ◀

to Veilstone City (pg. 82) ▶

Ether Guard Spec Full Heal TM34

1 A Sudden Downpour

A heavy rain will begin to fall when you cross from Route 210 to Route 215, and every battle you fight on Route 215 will be affected by it; Water-type moves will do extra damage, Fire-type moves will do reduced damage, and the Thunder move will always hit.

2 TM66 (Payback)

TM66 As a general rule, the Trainers who are staring away from the path aren't interested in challenging you. The guy at point 2 is no exception—if you chat him up he'll give you TM66 (Payback) instead of a fight.

Veilstone City

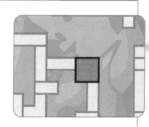

Veilstone City is a shopper's paradise. You'll have a great time here, but it will take a toll on your pocketbook.

FIRST VISIT

1	The Veilstone Department Store
2	The Galactic Veilstone Building
3	Win a Free Coin Case
4	The Game Corner
5	The Coin Exchange
6	TM63 (Embargo)
7	Free Pokémon Massages
8	Help the Professor's Assistant
9	Battle Galactic Grunts for HM02 (Fly)

RETURN VISIT

10	Pick up the Storage Key

Veilstone City

PP Up

to Galactic HQ (pg.108)

to Route 215 (pg. 81)

VEILSTONE DPT. STORE

POKéMON CENTER

GYM

Full Incense

HM02

to Route 214 (pg. 92)

Veilstone Department Store / 1F	
Antidote	100
Awakening	250
Bubble Mail	50
Burn Heal	250
Escape Rope	550
Flame Mail	50
Full Heal	600
Grass Mail	50
Great Ball	600
Hyper Potion	1200
Ice Heal	250
Max Potion	2500
Max Repel	700
Parlyz Heal	200
Poké Ball	200
Poké Doll	1000
Potion	300
Repel	350
Revive	1500
Space Mail	50
Super Potion	700
Super Repel	500
Ultra Ball	1200

2F	
Calcium	9800
Carbos	9800
Dire Hit	650
Guard Spec	700
HP Up	9800
Iron	9800
Protein	9800
X Accuracy	950
X Attack	500
X Defend	550
X Sp. Def	350
X Special	350
X Speed	350
Zinc	9800

3F	
TM14 Blizzard	5500
TM15 Hyper Beam	7500
TM16 Light Screen	2000
TM17 Protect	2000
TM20 Safeguard	2000
TM22 Solarbeam	3000
TM25 Thunder	5500
TM33 Reflect	2000
TM38 Fire Blast	5500
TM52 Focus Blast	5500
TM54 False Swipe	2000
TM70 Flash	1000
TM83 Natural Gift	2000

4F	
Bonsly Doll	2000
Buizel Doll	3000
Chatot Doll	3000
Cupboard	1000
Mantyke Doll	3000
Mime Jr. Doll	2000
Munchlax Doll	2000
Pretty Sink	3000
Refrigerator	1000
TV	4500
Yellow Cushion	500

5F / Vending Machine	
Fresh Water	200
Lemonade	350
Soda Pop	300

1 The Veilstone Department Store

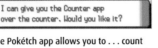 The Veilstone Department Store sells a stunning variety of goods, and there are plenty of free items to be found as well. The old lady on the first floor will give you a fashionable mask of the starter chosen by the professor's assistant, a woman on the second floor will give you the free Counter Pokéch app, and a man on the fifth floor will give you the Sticky Barb held item. When you're done collecting freebies, open up your wallet and buy some TMs, Ultra Balls, and stat-boosters. If you buy five items, you'll be considered a regular and the clerks will call you by name.

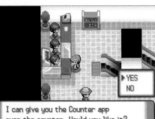

The Pokémon masks let you dress up one Pokémon to resemble another.

The Pokétch app allows you to . . . count things? Hey, what do you expect for free?

The damaging Sticky Barb will stick to enemies who physically attack the holder.

2 The Galactic Veilstone Building

Something fishy is clearly going on at the Veilstone Galactic Building, but it's locked up tight and the receptionist isn't talking. You'll have an opportunity to take a closer look after earning the Icicle Badge.

3 Win a Free Coin Case

Coin Case The clown at this home is constantly performing magic tricks with a coin. If you can guess which hand it's in, he'll give you a Coin Case as a prize. The hand it lands in is random, so keep trying until you get it right—you'll need that Coin Case to play at the Game Corner.

4 The Game Corner

After winning a Coin Case, you'll be able to play the slots at the Game Corner. Two men near the entrance will give you a total of 70 free coins, and you can buy more at the counter in increments of 50 or 500 coins. After sitting down at a machine, press X to insert three coins, and push down on the Control Pad to get the slots rolling. Press the Y, B, and A Buttons to stop the left, center, and right reels, respectively. Keep your eye on the bottom screen, where you can match the movements of a wiggling Poké Ball to earn 15-payoff replays.

When Clefairy appears, hit three 7s or Team Galactic symbols (this will be easier than usual). The bonus round will begin!

During the bonus round, Clefairy will point to the reel to stop. If you follow its gestures, you'll earn replays every time.

When the moon turns red, intentionally pick the wrong reel, or the bonus round will end prematurely.

If you can complete the bonus round 10 times in a row, you'll earn TM62 (Explosion) from the girl at the counter.

5 The Coin Exchange

You can't sell your coins for money, but you can exchange them for prizes at the building next door.

Game Corner Prizes			
Metronome	1000	TM44 (Rest)	6000
Silk Scarf	1000	TM58 (Endure)	2000
TM10 (Hidden Power)	6000	TM68 (Giga Impact)	20000
TM13 (Ice Beam)	10000	TM74 (Gyro Ball)	15000
TM21 (Frustration)	8000	TM75 (Swords Dance)	4000
TM24 (Thunderbolt)	10000	TM89 (U-turn)	6000
TM27 (Return)	8000	TM90 (Substitute)	2000
TM29 (Psychic)	10000	Wide Lens	1000
TM32 (Double Team)	4000	Zoom Lens	1000
TM35 (Flamethrower)	10000		

6 TM63 (Embargo)

TM63 There's no need to spend hours at the slots to earn this TM. Just listen as the man at point 6 boasts about his town a bit, and he'll hand over TM63.

7 Free Pokémon Massages

You can visit this building once a day to get a free massage for a Pokémon of your choice. Not only will the massage raise the friendship status of your Pokémon, but sometimes the masseuse will find a fashion accessory buried in the Pokémon's fur!

Massage Fashion Accessories	
Eerie Thing	Puffy Smoke
Glitter Powder	Seashell
Gutsy Determination	Shimmering Fire
Humming Note	Shiny Powder
Mystic Fire	Snow Crystal
Peculiar Spoon	Sparks
Poison Extract	Spring
Pretty Dewdrop	Wealthy Coin

Veilstone City Gym

Gym Leader Maylene

Recommended Move Types: Psychic, Flying, Ground

TM60 You don't need to jump through any hoops to earn the right to challenge the Veilstone Gym, but you'll find tough mental and physical challenges waiting inside. The first order of business is to defeat all four Junior Trainers; try to level up your Psychic- and Flying-type Pokémon in the process.

When you've bested the Junior Trainers, push the sliding panels on either side of the paths so you can travel up to the northwest and northeast corners of the Gym. From there you can push aside the final sliding panels that block the path to Maylene.

Use your Psychic-types to beat Maylene's Meditite and Machoke, then switch to a Flying-type so you can Pluck Lucario before it can eat its Sitrus Berry. Victory will earn you the Cobble Badge, TM60, and the right to use HM02 (Fly) outside of combat.

Veilstone City Gym

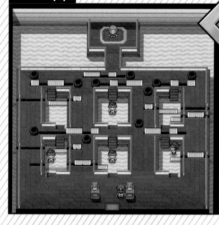

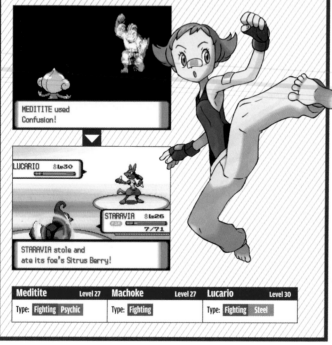

MEDITITE used Confusion!

LUCARIO ♂Lv30

STARAVIA ♀Lv26
PAR
7/71

STARAVIA stole and ate its foe's Sitrus Berry!

Meditite	Level 27	Machoke	Level 27	Lucario	Level 30
Type: Fighting Psychic		Type: Fighting		Type: Fighting Steel	

---

8 Help the Professor's Assistant

After beating Maylene you'll run into the professor's assistant outside the Gym. Apparently the assistant has misplaced a Pokédex, and Team Galactic has gotten their hands on it. You can't leave the assistant to take on Team Galactic alone, so run directly to the Team Galactic warehouse to provide some much-needed backup.

I dropped my Pokédex by accident, and Team Galactic found it.

Please, I need your help. Team up and battle with me!

▶ YES
NO

9 Battle Galactic Grunts for HM02 (Fly)

HM02 Meet the professor's assistant outside of the Team Galactic warehouse and agree to team up. The assistant's Clefairy will join your top Pokémon in a battle with the Grunts' team of four Level-25 Poison-type Pokémon. If you can beat them, they'll return the Pokédex and allow you into the warehouse, where you'll find HM02 (Fly). Teach that move to a Pokémon and use it to fly to Hearthome City, which is the closest point to Pastoria City.

CLEFAIRY used Gravity!

Return Visit

10 Pick Up the Storage Key

Storage Key After visiting all three lakes, return to Veilstone City and approach the Galactic HQ. Near the satellite dish you'll meet a Galactic Grunt that you've defeated before, and he'll become so flustered that he'll drop the Storage Key when he runs off. You can use that key to unlock the rusty door in the Galactic warehouse, where you'll find a Dusk Stone and a secret entrance to the Galactic HQ. (See page 108 for more details.)

I don't know anything about any Storage Key!

You must speak with this Galactic Grunt before he'll drop the Storage Key.

The rusty door creaked open!

The Storage Key fits the lock in the warehouse where you originally found HM02 (Fly). Save and heal before you head into the heart of Team Galactic's headquarters!

Route 212

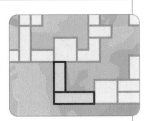

Team Galactic is moving to Pastoria City, and you must follow. Fly to Hearthome City and head south to Route 212.

1 Officer on Patrol
2 Bike across the Logs
3 Trade Shards for TMs
4 Stuck in the Mud

WILD POKéMON

ROUTE 212 A

POKéMON	D/P	AM	MID	PM
Budew	D/P	■	■	■
Kricketune	D/P	□	□	■
Roselia	D/P	□	□	□
Staravia	D/P	□	□	●
Starly	D/P	□	□	□

POKéMON	D/P	OR	GR
Goldeen	D/P		□
Magikarp	D/P	■	■

POKéMON	D/P	Surf
Golduck	D/P	□
Psyduck	D/P	■

ROUTE 212 B

POKéMON	D/P	AM	MID	PM
Bibarel	D/P	■	■	□
Kricketune	D/P	□	□	■
Roselia	D/P	□	□	□
Wooper	D/P	■	■	■

POKéMON	D/P	OR	GR
Barboach	D/P		□
Magikarp	D/P	■	■

POKéMON	D/P	Surf
Quagsire	D/P	□
Wooper	D/P	■

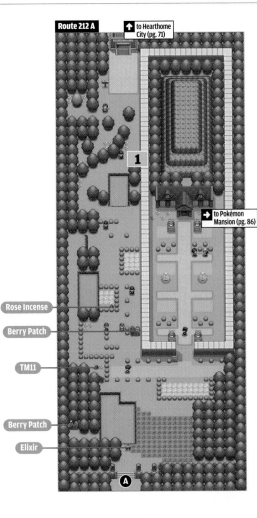

Route 212 A

to Hearthome City (pg. 71)

to Pokémon Mansion (pg. 86)

Rose Incense
Berry Patch
TM11
Berry Patch
Elixir

1 Officer on Patrol

The patrolman at point 1 is a friendly enough fellow during the day, but he isn't taking any chances at night. If you speak to him between the hours of 8 pm and 4 am, he'll challenge you to a duel.

2 Bike across the Logs

The rickety logs that connect island to island are too thin for feet, but you can cross them on a bicycle. It's a scary ride, but the prize at the end is worth it—the Silver Wind move in TM62 will both deal damage and boost the stats of a Bug-type Pokémon.

3 Trade Shards for TMs

The woman in the small hut at point 3 collects the colored shards that you can dig up in The Underground. When you collect 10 of a color, bring them to the hut to earn a valuable TM.

TMs for Shards

10 Blue Shards	TM18
10 Green Shards	TM07
10 Red Shards	TM11
10 Yellow Shards	TM37

4 Stuck in the Mud

You'll sink deeper into the mud with every step that you take, but you can free yourself by pressing left and right on the Control Pad. When you get to the other side, ride your bike across the log bridge to reach a free dose of Zinc.

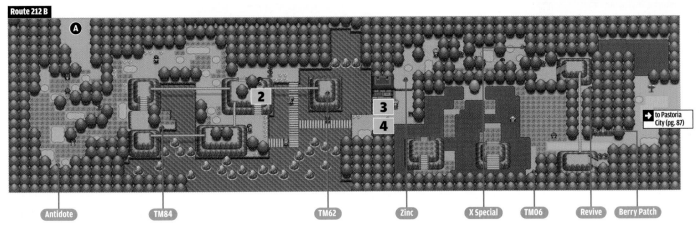

Route 212 B

to Pastoria City (pg. 87)

Antidote   TM84   TM62   Zinc   X Special   TM06   Revive   Berry Patch

Pokémon Mansion

An army of guards defends Mr. Backlot's mansion, but Trainers are free to visit the Trophy Garden in back.

WILD POKéMON

POKéMON	D/P	AM	MID	PM
Kricketune	D/P	□	□	■
Pichu	D/P	■	□	□
Pikachu	D/P	□	□	□
Roselia	D/P	■	■	■
Staravia	D/P	□	■	□

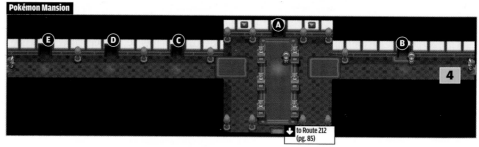

Trophy Garden

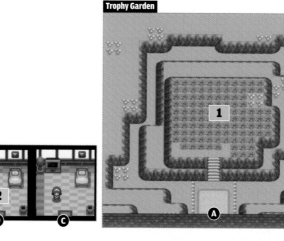

Pokémon Mansion

to Route 212 (pg. 85)

1 Poaching in the Trophy Garden

Mr. Backlot maintains a private Trophy Garden behind his house just to attract rare Pokémon. At the moment you won't find anything you couldn't catch elsewhere, but it is the easiest place to catch a Pichu or a Pikachu. Return here after you beat the Elite Four, and you may find several new Pokémon playing in the garden.

2 A Gift from the Maid

Soothe Bell The maid in the room at point 2 will give you the Soothe Bell, a held item that will relax any Pokémon who holds it. Giving the bell to a skittish Pokémon is a great way to raise its friendship level!

3 The Master of the House

Mr. Backlot tolerates visitors, but there are some lines guests are not allowed to cross. That's why he employs a full-time guard to make sure that no one touches his beloved Pokémon statue. If that just makes you want to touch it all the more, sneak back between the hours of 2 am and 6 am, when the guard is on break. Then you can touch the statue to your heart's content! Bwahahahahaha!!!

4 Mr. Backlot's Secrets

No one is sure what's behind the doors at either end of the hallway, but apparently it's even more important to Mr. Backlot than his statue is. Maids block the entrance 24 hours a day so, alas, we may never know.

Pastoria City

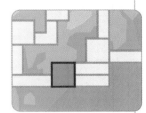

Verdant Pastoria City sits at the foot of the Great Marsh, a muddy wetland that teems with rare Pokémon.

1 Another Daily Berry
2 The Burmy Fan Club
3 The Pokémon Move Tutor
4 Your Rival's Mask
5 Free Pokémon Scarves
6 Follow the Galactic Grunt
7 Battle Your Rival

WILD POKéMON

POKéMON	D/P	OR	GR
Magikarp	D/P	■	□
Remoraid	D/P		□

POKéMON	D/P	Surf
Pelipper	D/P	●
Tentacool	D/P	■
Tentacruel	D/P	●
Wingull	D/P	■

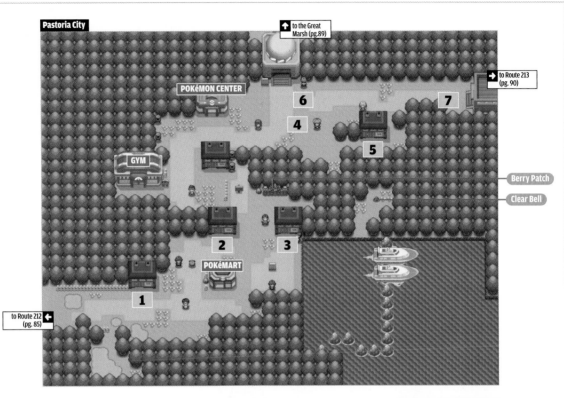

Pastoria City

to the Great Marsh (pg.89)

POKéMON CENTER

to Route 213 (pg. 90)

GYM

Berry Patch

Clear Bell

POKéMART

to Route 212 (pg. 85)

---

1 Another Daily Berry

Like the Berry Master, the woman at point 1 will provide one free berry a day to visiting Trainers. However, the berries she provides are of completely different varieties, and many of them can protect a holder against type-trumping attacks of a specific type.

Berries Given

Babiri Berry	Haban Berry	Rindo Berry
Charti Berry	Kasib Berry	Shuca Berry
Chilan Berry	Kebia Berry	Tanga Berry
Chople Berry	Occa Berry	Wacan Berry
Coba Berry	Passho Berry	Yache Berry
Colbur Berry	Payapa Berry	

2 The Burmy Fan Club

Macho Brace The people in this house adore Burmy, which are among the most common Pokémon to appear at honey-slathered trees. A Burmy can change its "cloak" to reflect its environment and will do so after each battle, leaving you with a leaf-cloaked Burmy if you fought in a forest area, a sand-cloaked Burmy if you fought in a cave, and a garbage-cloaked Burmy if you fought in a town or a building. Show all three to the man in this house, and he'll reward you with a Macho Brace held item. Assembling all three Burmy will take some work, but the Macho Brace is a fantastic item that increases the amount by which stats grow when a Pokémon levels up—it's well worth the trouble (although it lowers a Pokémon's Speed while it holds it).

3 The Pokémon Move Tutor

The Pokémon Move Tutor can reteach a Pokémon any move it has learned but since forgotten. This service isn't free, however; you'll have to give him a Heart Scale (which you can find in The Underground) each time you want to teach a Pokémon a lost move.

If any of your Pokémon needs to learn a move, come back with a Heart Scale.

4 Your Rival's Mask

Pokémon Mask The woman at point 4 saw your rival recently, and was so impressed by his starter Pokémon that she made a mask of it. She'll be happy to provide a copy for your Fashion Case.

Pokémart

Air Mail	50
Antidote	100
Awakening	250
Burn Heal	250
Dusk Ball	1000
Escape Rope	550
• Full Heal	600
• Full Restore	3000
Great Ball	600
• Hyper Potion	1200
Ice Heal	250
• Max Potion	2500
• Max Repel	700
Nest Ball	1000
Paralyze Heal	200
Poké Ball	200
Potion	300
Quick Ball	1000
Repel	350
Revive	1500
• Super Potion	700
Super Repel	500
• Ultra Ball	1200

• Not available until later; see the table on page 28

5 | Free Pokémon Scarves

Super Contest fans should put their favorite entrant at the lead of their party before visiting this house. If that Pokémon is beautiful, smart, cute, cool, or tough enough, you'll receive a free scarf that will further boost that trait.

Scarves	Receive When
Blue Scarf	Pokémon's beauty is 200 or more
Green Scarf	Pokémon's smartness is 200 or more
Pink Scarf	Pokémon's cuteness is 200 or more
Red Scarf	Pokémon's coolness is 200 or more
Yellow Scarf	Pokémon's toughness is 200 or more

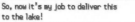

Pastoria City Gym

Gym Leader Crasher Wake

Recommended Move Types: Electric, Grass

TM55 Electric-type Pokémon are great against the Water-types in this Gym, but you'll need at least one Grass-type to deal with half-Ground-types like Barbroach and Quagsire. As you defeat each Trainer, hit a nearby switch to raise or lower the water level and allow you to reach the next one. After six Junior Trainer battles, you'll be ready to battle Wake for the Fen Badge, TM55 (Brine), and the right to use the HM05 (Defog) outside of combat.

ROSELIA used
Giga Drain!

Pastoria City Gym

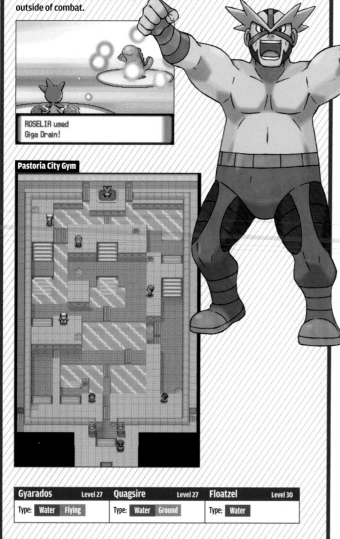

Gyarados	Level 27	Quagsire	Level 27	Floatzel	Level 30
Type: Water Flying		Type: Water Ground		Type: Water	

6 | Follow the Galactic Grunt

The warehouse package from Veilstone City has found its way into the hands of the Galactic Grunt at point 6. Speak to him after claiming the Fen Badge; he'll run off to the Route 213 gatehouse. Follow him there and speak to him again—but only if your team is in fighting shape. Your rival is about to appear, and he's always eager for a duel.

So, now it's my job to deliver this to the lake!

I'm telling you now, don't you come chasing after me!

Event Battle: Your Rival

7 | Battle Your Rival

Recommended Move Types: Electric, Fire, Grass, Water

Although your rival's Pokémon have gotten stronger, his roster hasn't changed since you last fought in Hearthome City. Use a diverse party so that you can swap in a type-trumping Pokémon whenever one of your rival's Pokémon is knocked out.

BIBAREL used
Water Gun!

MONFERNO used
Flame Wheel!

Player Chose Turtwig

Starly	Level 26
Type: Normal Flying	
Roselia	Level 25
Type: Grass Poison	
Buizel	Level 25
Type: Water	
Monferno	Level 28
Type: Fire Fighting	

Player Chose Chimchar

Starly	Level 19
Type: Normal Flying	
Ponyta	Level 25
Type: Fire	
Roselia	Level 25
Type: Grass Poison	
Prinplup	Level 28
Type: Water	

Player Chose Piplup

Starly	Level 19
Type: Normal Flying	
Ponyta	Level 25
Type: Fire	
Buizel	Level 25
Type: Water	
Grotle	Level 28
Type: Grass	

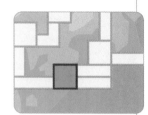

The Great Marsh

To protect this fragile ecosystem, visitors are given special Poké Balls and limited to only 500 steps per visit.

1	The Observatory
2	The Safari Game
3	Get HM05 (Defog)
4	The Quick Trams

WILD POKÉMON

AREAS 1 & 2

POKéMON	D/P	AM	MID	PM
Azurill	D/P	○	○	○
Bibarel	D/P	□	□	□
Bidoof	D/P	○	○	○
Budew	D/P	□	□	
Hoothoot	D/P			□
Marill	D/P	□	□	□
Noctowl	D/P			□
Psyduck	D/P	●	●	●
Quagsire	D/P	□	□	□
Starly	D/P	□	□	
Wooper	D/P	□	□	□

AREAS 3, 4, & 6

POKéMON	D/P	AM	MID	PM
Azurill	D/P	○	○	○
Bibarel	D/P	□	□	□
Bidoof	D/P	○	○	○
Budew	D/P	□	□	
Hoothoot	D/P			□
Marill	D/P	□	□	□
Psyduck	D/P	●	●	●
Quagsire	D/P	□	□	□
Starly	D/P	□	□	
Wooper	D/P	□	□	□

AREA 5

POKéMON	D/P	AM	MID	PM
Azurill	D/P	●	●	●
Bibarel	D/P	□	□	□
Bidoof	D/P	●	●	●
Budew	D/P	□	□	
Hoothoot	D/P			□
Marill	D/P	□	□	□
Quagsire	D/P	□	□	□
Starly	D/P	□	□	
Wooper	D/P	□	□	□

ALL AREAS

POKéMON	D/P	OR	GR
Barboach	D/P		□
Gyarados	D/P		●
Magikarp	D/P	■	■

POKéMON	D/P	Surf
Marill	D/P	■
Psyduck	D/P	●
Quagsire	D/P	●
Wooper	D/P	■

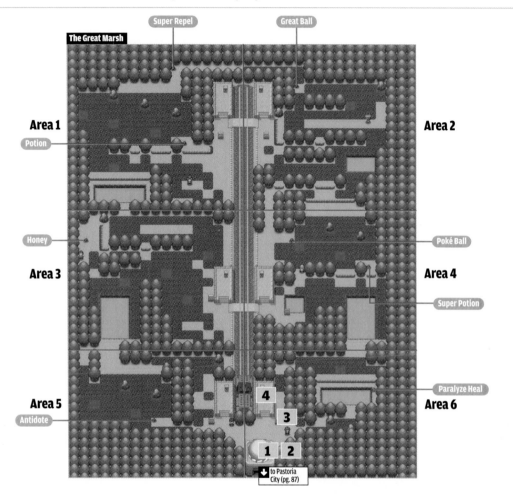

Super Repel • Great Ball

The Great Marsh

Area 1 — Potion
Area 2
Honey — Area 3 — Area 4 — Poké Ball
Super Potion
Area 5 — Antidote — Area 6 — Paralyze Heal
4
3
1 2
↓ to Pastoria City (pg. 87)

1 The Observatory

Before you pay the entrance fee to the Great Marsh, visit the upstairs observatory. The locals there can tell you how the Great Marsh works, and the binoculars lined up against the window will give you a preview of the marsh by providing a quick glimpse of the Pokémon you can catch. The areas aren't shown in any set order, so pay special attention to the terrain (particularly the number and shape of the lakes) so you know where to look when you enter the marsh. The Binoculars will usually reveal the random daily Pokémon (listed on the table to the right) that appear in addition to the Pokémon listed in the charts to the left.

Daily Pokémon

Azurill
Bibarel
Bidoof
Carnivine
Croagunk
Golduck
Marill
Quagsire
Roselia
Skorupi
Staravia
Wooper

The Binoculars provide a preview of the Pokémon you'll find in each area.

Head straight to the area of the Pokémon you want most!

2 | The Safari Game

The clerk at the entrance to the Great Marsh will explain the rules: For 500 Poké Dollars, you're allowed to travel 500 steps and throw up to 30 Safari Balls. You can't fight with Pokémon here, so the only way to make capturing easier is to throw mud or bait. Sometimes this will drive the target away, but a successful baiting or mud splattering will make the Safari Balls much easier to use.

3 | Get HM05 (Defog)

HM05 Speak to the Safari Game player who hangs out near the gate. She has found HM05 (Defog) in the mud, and would be happy to hand it over. You'll need Defog later, so be sure to challenge the Safari Game at least once!

4 | The Quick Trams

Your number of steps is limited and travel through mud can be difficult (you'll get stuck often—move the Control Pad around to escape). Fortunately, the Great Marsh has a tram system that will take you directly to any of the six areas. To summon the tram, approach one of the yellow boxes and press the A Button.

Pokémon Notes

Croagunk and its Evolved form, Toxicroak, excel at mixing poison with damage. Most of their strikes have a 30% chance of inflicting Poison.

Croagunk
Type: Poison Fighting
Ability: Anticipate / Dry Skin

Carnivine is a pure Grass-type that attracts prey with its sweet-smelling saliva. It has strong offensive stats but cannot evolve.

Carnivine
Type: Grass
Ability: Levitate

Skorupi
Type: Poison Bug
Ability: Battle Armor / Sniper

Skorupi is a conventional Bug-and-Poison-type until it evolves into Drapion at Level 40. Then it swaps its Bug-type for a Dark-type and grows fivefold.

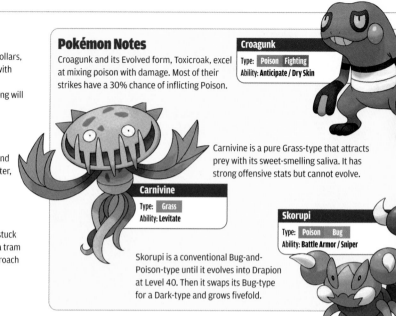

Route 213 (Valor Lakefront)

Nestled between the beach and scenic Lake Valor, Route 213 is one of Sinnoh's most popular resort destinations.

FIRST VISIT

1	Dr. Footstep's House
2	Catch Up to the Galactic Grunt
3	TM92 (Trick Room)
4	A Battle and a Meal
5	Hot on the Grunt's Trail
6	Find the Suite Key
7	Beat Down the Galactic Grunt
8	Medicine for the Psyduck
9	Protectors of the Lake

RETURN VISIT

10	Climb for the Coin Toss

WILD POKéMON

ROUTE 213

POKéMON	D/P	AM	MID	PM
Buizel	D/P	■	■	■
Floatzel	D/P	□	□	□
Shellos	D/P	■	■	■
Wingull	D/P	□	□	□

POKéMON	D/P	OR	GR
Magikarp	D/P	■	
Remoraid	D/P		□

POKéMON	D/P	Surf
Pelipper	D/P	●
Tentacool	D/P	■
Tentacruel	D/P	●
Wingull	D/P	■

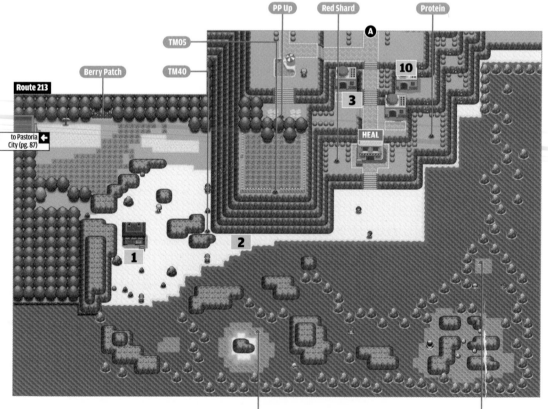

Route 213
to Pastoria City (pg. 87)
Berry Patch
TM40
TM05
PP Up
Red Shard
Protein
HEAL
Max Revive
Water Stone

WILD POKéMON (CONTINUED)

VALOR LAKEFRONT

POKéMON	D/P	AM	MID	PM
Bibarel	D/P	□	□	□
Geodude	D/P	□	□	□
Girafarig	D/P	■	■	■
Graveler	D/P	□	□	●
Kricketune	D/P	●	●	□
Staravia	D/P	□	□	●

↑ to Route 214 (pg. 92)

9 8

← to Lake Valor (pg.100)

TM85   Paralyze Heal

7

Valor Lakefront

6

4

5

Ⓐ

→ to Route 222 (pg. 114)

1 Dr. Footstep's House

Dr. Footstep claims to be able to read the thoughts of the top Pokémon in your roster by examining its footsteps. His words are based on the Pokémon's friendship status, but differ greatly from the usual Friendship Checker script. If you show him a Pokémon whose friendship has reached the max level, he'll attach a Footprint Ribbon that you can view on the Ribbons page of the Pokémon's Summary screen.

2 Catch Up to the Galactic Grunt

Once again, you'll catch the Galactic Grunt babbling to himself about Team Galactic's plans. When he catches you eavesdropping, he'll flee to the entrance to Lake Valor, northeast of the small resort town.

3 TM92 (Trick Room)

TM92 The Valor Lakefront is a resort community where you can find free healing and speak with vacationing Sinnoh residents. Among the guests are a traveling circus troupe, and one of its members will give you TM92 (Trick Room). This strange move reverses the usual intiative rules to allow slower Pokémon to act first.

In place of a formal introduction, please take this!

4 A Battle and a Meal

The Seven Stars Restaurant encourages Pokémon duels, and if you arrive during business hours (9 am to 11 pm) you can challenge any couple in the restaurant to a Double Battle. The customers change daily, making this a great place to earn money and Exp. Points.

It's way more fun for me to battle than go eat fancy dinners!

School Kid Esteban and Pokéfan Meredith!

5 Hot on the Grunt's Trail

You'll next meet the babbling Galactic Grunt at point 5, where he'll turn and flee to the north. You have no choice but to follow; if you attempt to continue east a man will block your path and tell you that the road to Route 222 is closed.

6 Find the Suite key

Lava Cookie The woman outside this bunga-low has lost her Suite Key somewhere north of the Hotel Grand Lake reception desk. Switch your Pokétch to the Dowsing Machine and search the small stretch of path north of the reception building but south of the first stair-case. The Dowsing Machine should pick it up right away. Bring the key to the woman and she'll head inside her room, where she'll offer you a status-condition-healing Lava Cookie.

Chris found a Suite Key!

7 Beat Down the Galactic Grunt

The Galactic Grunt is tiring quickly, and he'll be just about spent by the time you catch him at point 7. He'll finally stand and fight, summoning his lone Pokémon—a Level-25 Glameow. When you beat him, he'll run past the guards at point 9, where you won't be able to follow.

8 Medicine for the Psyduck

Secret Potion Just when you start to lose hope, you'll run into Cynthia. She can't help you reach Lake Valor, but she can give you some medicine that will cure the suffering Psyduck on Route 210.

9 Protectors of the Lake

Two men block the entrance at Lake Valor, having been asked to protect it by someone named Cyrus. They've clearly been tricked by Team Galactic, but there's no way to talk them down now. Instead, use HM02 (Fly) to return to Solaceon Town, which is just south of Psyduck-blocked Route 210. (See page 80.)

Pokémon Notes

Buizel's Evolved form of Floatzel prowls the coastline here, using its floatation sac to rescue drowning swimmers. It doesn't have access to many powerful attacks, but Floatzel has an unusually high Speed stat, which is very rare for Water-type Pokémon.

Floatzel	
Type:	Water
Ability:	Swift Swim

Return Visit

10 Climb for the Coin Toss

Coin Toss After earning the Icicle Badge, use HM08 (Rock Climb) to descend the cliff at point 10. You'll land on a ledge where there's a small bunga-low; a man inside will give you the Coin Toss Pokétch app, which can be used to flip a vir-tual coin. If you were hoping for a more significant reward, check the trash can—you'll find a rare Max Revive .

This is something we don't need anymore. Will you take it?

Route 214

Route 214 is an alternate route that connects the Valor Lakefront to Veilstone City.

1 The Maniac Digger's Tunnel

WILD POKéMON

ROUTE 214

POKéMON	D/P	AM	MID	PM
Geodude	D/P	☐	☐	☐
Girafarig	D/P	☐	☐	☐
Graveler	D/P	☐	☐	●
Kricketune	D/P	●	●	☐
Ponyta	D/P	■	■	☐
Stunky	D	☐	☐	☐
Sudowoodo	P	☐	☐	☐

POKéMON	D/P	OR	GR
Goldeen	D/P		☐
Magikarp	D/P	■	■

POKéMON	D/P	Surf
Golduck	D/P	☐
Psyduck	D/P	■

MANIAC CAVE

POKéMON	D/P	AM	MID	PM
Geodude	D/P	■	■	■
Hippopotas	D/P	●	●	●

MANIAC TUNNEL

POKéMON	D/P	AM	MID	PM
Geodude	D/P	■	■	■
Hippopotas	D/P	☐	☐	☐

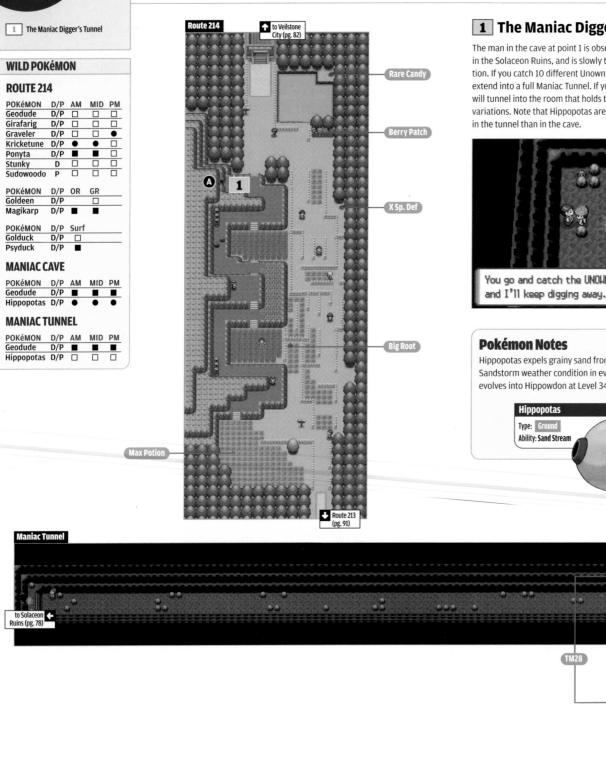

Route 214

to Veilstone City (pg. 82)

Rare Candy

Berry Patch

X Sp. Def

Big Root

Max Potion

Route 213 (pg. 91)

1 The Maniac Digger's Tunnel

The man in the cave at point 1 is obsessed with the Unown in the Solaceon Ruins, and is slowly tunneling in that direction. If you catch 10 different Unown, the Maniac Cave will extend into a full Maniac Tunnel. If you catch all 26, the man will tunnel into the room that holds the "!" and "?" Unown variations. Note that Hippopotas are much more common in the tunnel than in the cave.

You go and catch the UNOWN, and I'll keep digging away.

Pokémon Notes

Hippopotas expels grainy sand from its body, causing the Sandstorm weather condition in every battle it joins. It evolves into Hippowdon at Level 34.

Hippopotas

Type: Ground
Ability: Sand Stream

Maniac Tunnel

to Solaceon Ruins (pg. 78)

A

TM28

Maniac Cave

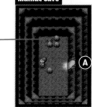

A

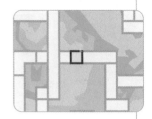

Celestic Town

Visions of the past live on in Celestic Town, a tiny village that is said to be as old as Sinnoh itself.

FIRST VISIT

1. A Bonus for Kind Trainers
2. The Analog Watch App
3. A Spectacle Blowout
4. Visit Cynthia's Grandma
5. Stop the Galactic Grunt
6. Get HM03 (Surf)
7. Cyrus Introduces Himself

RETURN VISIT

8. Filling Out Your Pokédex

WILD POKéMON

POKéMON	D/P	OR	GR
Barboach	D/P		☐
Magikarp	D/P	■	■

POKéMON	D/P	Surf
Golduck	D/P	☐
Psyduck	D/P	■

Celestic Town

SHOP

3 8

5 6 7

to Route 211 (pg.101)

to Route 210 (pg. 80)

POKéMON CENTER

2 4 1

Shop

Air Mail	50
Antidote	100
Awakening	250
Burn Heal	250
Dusk Ball	1000
Escape Rope	550
• Full Heal	600
• Full Restore	3000
Great Ball	600
• Hyper Potion	1200
Ice Heal	250
• Max Potion	2500
• Max Repel	700
Paralyze Heal	200
Poké Ball	200
Potion	300
Quick Ball	1000
Repel	350
Revive	1500
Super Potion	700
Super Repel	500
Timer Ball	1000
• Ultra Ball	1200

• Not available until later; see the table on page 28

1 A Bonus for Kind Trainers

Great Ball Put your friendliest Pokémon in the lead spot in your roster and speak to the balding man in the Celestic Town Pokémon Center. If the Pokémon's friendship level is high enough, the man will give you a free Great Ball.

2 The Analog Watch App

Analog Watch The young man in the home at point 2 has no further need for his Analog Watch Pokétch app, and will happily pass it on to you. Now your Pokétch can tell time in both digital and analog. Hurrah!

3 A Spectacle Blowout

There isn't a Pokémart in Celestic Town, but you can pick up anything you need in this small house. You'll also find a man giving away free eyewear for Pokémon—visit him at each time of day to get all three freebies!

Free Glasses

Choice Specs	4 am - 10 am
Blackglasses	10 am - 8 pm
Wise Specs	8 pm - 4 am

4 Visit Cynthia's Grandma

You'll meet Cynthia's grandma at point 4, but she's not in a mood to talk about Cynthia since some crazy Galactic Grunt is in her town, ranting and raving about blowing up Galactic Bombs and such. Heal your Pokémon at the Pokémon Center so you can help grandma bring peace back to Celestic Town.

5 Stop the Galactic Grunt

The troublesome Galactic Grunt can be found at point 5, where he'll attack you with a Level-25 Beautifly and a Level-27 Croagunk. Knock out both to foil the Grunt's plans, and he'll leave Celestic Town forever. Cynthia's grateful grandma will come to thank you and will finally notice Cynthia's Old Charm. Take Grandma's advice and pay a quick visit to the ruins that the Galactic Grunt was blocking.

6 Get HM03 (Surf)

HM03 When you examine the cave painting inside the ruins, Grandma will appear to give you a quick lesson about Sinnoh's history and hand over HM03 (Surf). This powerful move allows you to cross any body of water, but you won't be able to use it until you earn the Hearthome City Gym Badge.

7 Cyrus Introduces Himself

When you leave the ruins, you'll run into that babbling weirdo from Mt. Coronet. This time he'll formally introduce himself before saying strange things and disappearing again. You don't have time to decipher his unique brand of crazy talk—you have pressing business with Gym Leader Fantina in Hearthome City.

Cyrus

Cyrus views the world on "a galactic scale" and seeks to create a new world that's free of strife and pain. It all sounds fairly noble, but the "G" on his vest suggest that he's involved with some pretty shady characters.

Return Visit

8 Filling Out Your Pokédex

Although you can't *capture* every Pokémon with only a single version of the game, owners of either Diamond or Pearl can *see* every Pokémon in the Sinnoh Pokédex by battling enemy Trainers. The exceptions are Dialga and Palkia, only one of which appears in each version. Fortunately, Cynthia's grandma is on the case—visit her after you earn the Legendary Pokémon at the Spear Pillar—she'll give you the Pokédex data on the other.

Fuego Ironworks

Surf from the bridge at Route 205 (east of Floaroma Town) and follow the river west to reach this foundry.

| 1 | Using the Arrow Tiles |
| 2 | Speak to Mr. Fuego |

WILD POKéMON

POKéMON	D/P	AM	MID	PM
Floatzel	D/P	■	■	■
Gastrodon	D/P	□	□	□
Luxio	D/P	□	□	□
Pachirisu	D/P	□	□	□
Shellos	D/P	□	□	□
Shinx	D/P	■	■	■
Wingull	D/P	□	□	□

POKéMON	D/P	OR	GR
Finneon	D/P		□
Magikarp	D/P	■	■

POKéMON	D/P	Surf
Pelipper	D/P	●
Tentacool	D/P	■
Tentacruel	D/P	●
Wingull	D/P	■

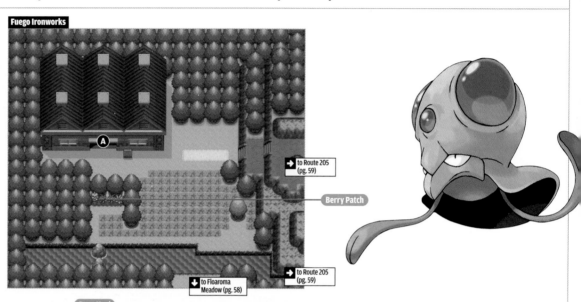

Fuego Ironworks

A

to Route 205 (pg. 59)

Berry Patch

to Route 205 (pg. 59)

to Floaroma Meadow (pg. 58)

Burn Heal

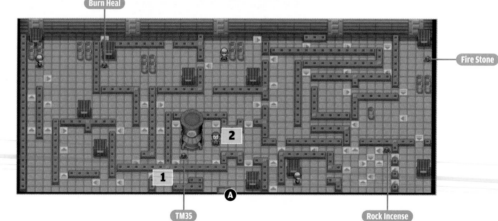

Fire Stone

2

1

A

TM35

Rock Incense

1 Using the Arrow Tiles

Your goal in the ironworks is to reach Mr. Fuego at point 2. To do so, you'll need to circle the ironworks using arrow-printed tiles that will hurl you in the designated direction until you hit a wall. When you have a choice of multiple tiles, use the map to see which leads where. For example, in the southeast corner of the map, only the highest of the three tiles will keep you on your westward course.

2 Speak to Mr. Fuego

Fire Stone Mr. Fuego runs the ironworks, and if you listen to him complain about his job for a bit, he'll reward you with a Fire Stone that you can use to evolve Pokémon like Growlithe and Eevee. Don't miss TM35 (Flamethrower) on the floor nearby!

Pokémon Notes

Shinx gains a hearty stat boost each time it evolves, but its Luxio and Luxray forms learn moves up to eight levels later than the form that precedes them. Wait to evolve members of the Shinx family for as long as you can!

Luxio

Type: Electric
Ability: Rivalry / Intimidate

Gastrodon

Type: Water Ground
Ability: Sticky Hold / Storm Drain

Shellos evolves into Gastrodon at Level 30. Gastrodon gains the Electric-resistant Ground type but maintains its distinctive coloring pattern.

Routes 219-221

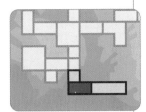

HMO3 (Surf) allows you to explore the three routes that extend southeast from Sandgem Town.

1 Match the Level and Win
2 Pal Park under Construction

WILD POKéMON

ROUTE 219/220

POKéMON	D/P	OR	GR
Finneon	D/P		☐
Magikarp	D/P	■	■

POKéMON	D/P	Surf	
Pelipper	D/P	●	
Tentacool	D/P	■	
Tentacruel	D/P	●	
Wingull	D/P	■	

ROUTE 221

POKéMON	D/P	AM	MID	PM
Floatzel	D/P	☐	☐	☐
Gastrodon	D	☐	☐	☐
Gastrodon	P	■	■	■
Roselia	D/P	☐	☐	☐
Shellos	D/P	☐	☐	☐
Skuntank	D	☐	☐	☐
Stunky	D	☐	☐	☐
Sudowoodo	P	☐	☐	☐
Wingull	D/P	☐	☐	☐

POKéMON	D/P	OR	GR
Finneon	D/P		☐
Magikarp	D/P	■	■

POKéMON	D/P	Surf	
Pelipper	D/P	●	
Tentacool	D/P	■	
Tentacruel	D/P	●	
Wingull	D/P	■	

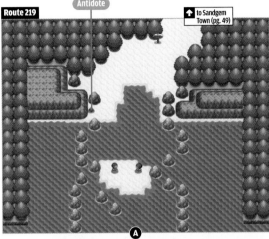

Route 219

Antidote

to Sandgem Town (pg. 49)

A

1 Match the Level and Win

I'll thank you for that visual treat with this Black Belt.

The man in the home at point 1 runs his own private lottery. Every day he chooses a two-digit number, and if you can show him a Pokémon of that level, you win! The first time you win you'll earn a Black Belt, the second time you'll earn an Expert Belt, and the third time you'll earn a Focus Band. If you continue to win, the prizes will repeat from Black Belt again. You may enter once per day.

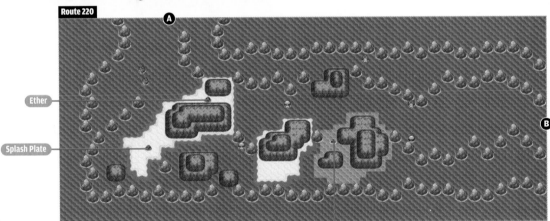

Route 220

A

Ether

Splash Plate

B

Carbos

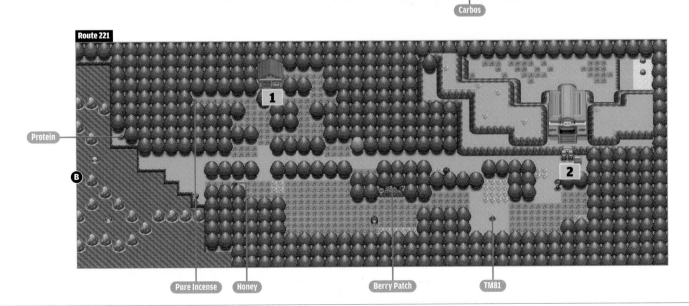

Route 221

Protein

1

B

2

Pure Incense   Honey   Berry Patch   TM81

2 Pal Park under Construction

Pal Park is still under construction, and won't be completed until you beat the Elite Four. Return at that point and you'll be able to use Pal Park to transfer Pokémon from Game Boy Adance Pokémon titles into your Diamond or Pearl version.

Pal Park isn't open yet.
We're still setting up.

Pokémon Notes

Stunky evolves to Skuntank at Level 34. Don't delay this Evolution, or your new Skuntank won't be able to earn the Flamethrower move at level 34!

Skuntank		
Type:	Poison	Dark
Ability: Stench / Aftermath		

Route 218

Fly to Jubilife City and swim west from the end of the pier in Route 218's fishing pond. Canalave City is just ahead!

1 Pokédex Upgrade

WILD POKéMON

POKéMON	D/P	AM	MID	PM
Floatzel	D/P	■	■	■
Glameow	P	□	□	□
Gastrodon	D/P	□	□	□
Mr. Mime	D	□	□	□
Shellos	D/P	□	□	□
Wingull	D/P	□	□	□

POKéMON	D/P	OR	GR
Finneon	D/P		□
Magikarp	D/P	■	■

POKéMON	D/P	Surf
Pelipper	D/P	●
Tentacool	D/P	■
Tentacruel	D/P	●
Wingull	D/P	■

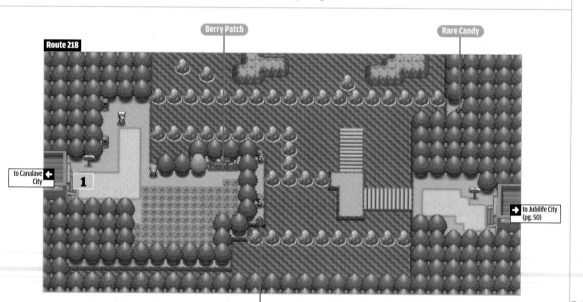

Berry Patch

Rare Candy

Route 218

to Canalave City

1

to Jubilife City (pg. 50)

Honey

1 Pokédex Upgrade

In the gatehouse you'll again run into Prof. Rowan's other assistant. This time his gift is a Pokédex upgrade that allows you to view both the male and female versions of each Pokémon, but only if you've seen both genders in your travels. To use it, press the Forms button on a Pokédex entry and then press See Another Form to toggle between the genders.

It can now display images of male and female Pokémon.

Pokémon Notes

Owners of Pokémon Pearl can catch their own Glameow in Route 218's patch of tall grass. Glameow evolves into Purugly at Level 38.

Glameow	
Type:	Normal
Ability: Limber / Own Tempo	

Canalave City

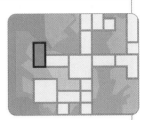

Canalave City is Sinnoh's only western port. Ships sail daily from here to a number of small offshore islands.

1	TM48 (Skill Swap)
2	The Move Deleter
3	Battle on the Bridge
4	Your Next Interview
5	Canalave Docks
6	Meet Your Team at the Library

WILD POKéMON

POKéMON	D/P	OR	GR
Finneon	D/P		☐
Magikarp	D/P	■	■

POKéMON	D/P	Surf
Pelipper	D/P	●
Tentacool	D/P	■
Tentacruel	D/P	●
Wingull	D/P	■

Pokémart

Air Mail	50
Antidote	100
Awakening	250
Burn Heal	250
Escape Rope	550
Full Heal	600
• Full Restore	3000
Great Ball	600
Hyper Potion	1200
Ice Heal	250
• Max Potion	2500
Max Repel	700
Paralyze Heal	200
Poké Ball	200
Potion	300
Quick Ball	1000
Repeat Ball	1000
Repel	350
Revive	1500
Super Potion	700
Super Repel	500
Timer Ball	1000
Utra Ball	1200

• Not available until later; see the table on page 28

to Iron Island (pg. 99)

POKéMON CENTER

GYM

POKéMART

to Route 218

TM89

1 TM48 (Skill Swap)

TM48 The woman in the home at point 1 found TM48 (Skill Swap) in a crate of cargo from another land. It allows a Pokémon to swap abilities with its opponent in combat.

2 The Move Deleter

The Move Deleter in the home at point 2 can help a Pokémon in your roster forget a move, which is a fine service for Pokémon who are wasting move slots with obsolete HM moves like Defog.

You've come to make me force your Pokémon to forget some moves?
▶ YES
NO

Event Battle: Your Rival

3 Battle on the Bridge

Recommended Move Types: Electric, Fire, Flying, Ground, Water

Heal at the Pokémon Center—your rival is waiting to ambush you on the bridge across the canal. Your rival has added a Level-30 Heracross to his roster, so bring a Flying-type Pokémon (or at least a Pokémon with Flying-type moves) so you can trump both its types for quadruple damage.

HERACROSS ♂Lv30

STARAVIA ♂Lv32
86/86

STARAVIA used Wing Attack!

Player Chose Turtwig

Staravia	Level 31
Type: Normal Flying	

Heracross	Level 30
Type: Bug Fighting	

Buizel	Level 32
Type: Water	

Roselia	Level 32
Type: Grass Poison	

Infernape	Level 35
Type: Fire Fighting	

Player Chose Chimchar

Staravia	Level 31
Type: Normal Flying	

Heracross	Level 30
Type: Bug Fighting	

Roselia	Level 32
Type: Grass Poison	

Ponyta	Level 32
Type: Fire	

Prinplup	Level 35
Type: Water	

Player Chose Piplup

Staravia	Level 31
Type: Normal Flying	

Heracross	Level 30
Type: Bug Fighting	

Buizel	Level 32
Type: Water	

Ponyta	Level 32
Type: Fire	

Grotle	Level 35
Type: Grass	

Canalave City Gym

Gym Leader Byron
Recommended Move Types: Fire, Fighting, Ground, Water

The Canalave City Gym is full of rising and sliding lifts that are guarded by Junior Trainers. Take the fourth of the four lifts lined up on the ground floor—the route should be clear from that point on. Against the mostly Onix-packing Junior Trainers, a Water-type Pokémon will make for an ideal leader, but swap it out for a good Fire-type when you challenge Byron. After your Fire-type dispenses with Bronzor and Steelix, use Water-, Ground-, and Fighting-types to take down the Bastiodon. You'll win the Mine Badge, TM91 (Flash Cannon), and the ability to use Strength outside of combat.

MACHOKE used
Seismic Toss!

Bronzor	Level 36	Steelix	Level 36	Bastiodon	Level 39
Type: Steel Psychic		Type: Steel Ground		Type: Rock Steel	

Canalave City Gym

4 Your Next Interview

You'll run into another Jubilife TV reporter in the small home at point 4. This time the interview topic is your favorite type of Pokémon. Look for this thrilling broadcast on a TV in the near future!

▶ Normal
Fire
Water
Electric
Grass
Ice
Fighting
Poison

Please select your favorite Pokémon type from this list.

5 Canalave Docks

The ship that you'll find waiting at the Canalave Docks can take you to a number of nearby islands. At the moment, Iron Island is your only option, but after future game events (which occur after you beat the Elite Four) you'll be able to select other destinations. Iron Island is an optional area, but it's a great place to earn a rare Pokémon and gather Exp. Points.

▶ IRON ISLAND
EXIT

Do you wanna set sail?

6 Meet your Team at the Library

After claiming victory in the Canalave City Gym, you'll run into your rival outside. Follow him north to the Canalave Library, where you'll find him waiting on the third floor, along with Prof. Rowan and his assistant. The professor is interested in the Mirage Pokémon that are said to live in the three lakes of Sinnoh, and will suggest the three Trainers split up so each can investigate one lake. The professor's assistant will take Lake Verity, your rival will handle Lake Acuity, and that leaves Lake Valor for you. You can't Fly there directly, so you'll have to travel on foot from Pastoria City.

The professor's mission is an urgent one, but he'd understand if you wanted to take a few minutes off to do some research. There isn't much on the lower floors, but the bookcases on the third floor are full of tomes about Sinnoh's history and mythology.

▶ YES
NO

This book is titled "Sinnoh Region's Mythology." Want to read it?

Iron Island

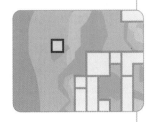

Bring no more than five Pokémon to Iron Island—you can earn a rare Pokémon Egg for your efforts here.

| 1 | Team Up with Riley |
| 2 | Take Home a Riolu Egg |

WILD POKéMON

IRON ISLAND DOCKS

POKéMON	D/P	OR	GR
Finneon	D/P		☐
Magikarp	D/P	■	■

POKéMON	D/P	Surf
Pelipper	D/P	●
Tentacool	D/P	■
Tentacruel	D/P	●
Wingull	D/P	■

1F

POKéMON	D/P	AM	MID	PM
Geodude	D/P	■	■	■
Golbat	D/P	☐	☐	☐
Graveler	D/P	■	■	■
Onix	D/P	☐	☐	☐
Zubat	D/P	☐	☐	☐

B1/A & B1/B

POKéMON	D/P	AM	MID	PM
Geodude	D/P	○	○	○
Golbat	D/P	☐	☐	☐
Graveler	D/P	■	■	■
Onix	D/P	☐	☐	☐

B2/A

POKéMON	D/P	AM	MID	PM
Geodude	D/P	○	○	○
Golbat	D/P	☐	☐	☐
Graveler	D/P	■	■	■
Onix	D/P	■	■	■

B2/B

POKéMON	D/P	AM	MID	PM
Geodude	D/P	○	○	○
Golbat	D/P	☐	☐	☐
Graveler	D/P	■	■	■
Onix	D/P	■	■	■
Steelix	D/P	☐	☐	☐

POKéMON	D/P	Event
Riolu	D/P	Reward

B3

POKéMON	D/P	AM	MID	PM
Geodude	D/P	○	○	○
Golbat	D/P	☐	☐	☐
Graveler	D/P	■	■	■
Onix	D/P	■	■	■
Steelix	D/P	☐	☐	☐

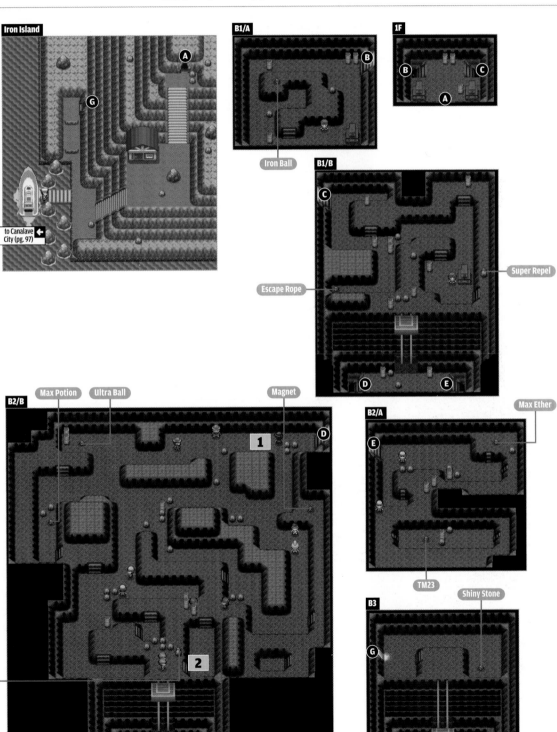

Iron Island

to Canalave City (pg. 97)

B1/A

Iron Ball

1F

B1/B

Super Repel

Escape Rope

Max Potion   Ultra Ball   Magnet   Max Ether

B2/B

B2/A

TM23   Shiny Stone

B3

HP Up

1 Team up with Riley

The Iron Island cave contains a massive central cavern that is packed with treasure but heavily guarded by wild Pokémon and enemy Trainers. Fortunately, you won't have to slog through it alone—a Trainer named Riley will meet you at the entrance and his Lucario will fight by your side for the entire floor. Like past partners, Riley will heal all of your Pokémon completely between fights.

If you'd like, we could team up. The wild Pokémon here are restless.

2 Take Home a Riolu Egg

You'll find two Galactic Grunts waiting at the southern exit to the main chamber. Defeat them with Riley's help, and he'll send you off with a parting gift of a Riolu Egg. If you don't have room for it, you'll have to walk all the way back to this point, so be sure to enter the Iron Island cave with only five Pokémon in your roster!

Would you take it with you?

▶ YES
   NO

Pokémon Notes

Riolu is a solid Fighting-type that can evolve into the excellent Fighting-and-Steel-type Lucario. Its Evolution is based on its friendship level, so give it items to hold, treat it to massages, and use it frequently in combat. When its friendship level is at a high enough stage, it will evolve—but only during morning or daytime hours.

Riolu

Type: Fighting
Ability: Steadfast / Inner Focus

Lake Valor

Team Galactic has drained Lake Valor in the search for Mirage Pokémon. Don't let this crime go unpunished!

FIRST VISIT

1	The Remains of Lake Valor
2	Battle Commander Saturn

RETURN VISIT

3	Capture Azelf

WILD POKéMON

POKéMON	D/P	AM	MID	PM
Bibarel	D/P	■	■	■
Chingling	D/P	□	□	□
Noctowl	D/P			□
Psyduck	D/P	□	□	□
Staravia	D/P	□	□	●

POKéMON	D/P	OR	GR
Goldeen	D/P		□
Magikarp	D/P	■	■

POKéMON	D/P	Surf	
Golduck	D/P	□	
Psyduck	D/P	■	

POKéMON	D/P	EVENT	
Azelf	D/P	After event	

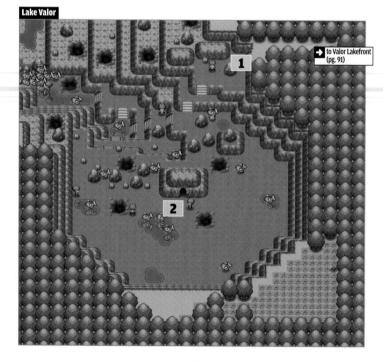

Lake Valor

→ to Valor Lakefront (pg. 91)

1

2

1 The Remains of Lake Valor

Fly to Pastoria City and travel east to the Lake Valor entrance that was previously blocked by Cyrus's stooges. You'll find the lake in terrible shape, and the Galactic Grunt at point 1 couldn't be more proud. He'll announce his intent to move on to Twinleaf Town's Lake Verity, but don't run off to defend your hometown yet—you have to find his commander and teach him a lesson first.

The closest civilization is that hick town called Twinleaf!

Event Battle: Team Galactic

2 Battle Commander Saturn

Recommended Move Types: Dark, Fire, Ground, Psychic

Make your way past a series of Galactic Grunts to the cave at the center of the lakebed, where you'll find Commander Saturn surveying his vile handiwork. Put a Pokémon with good Dark-type attacks at the front of your roster so you can defeat his Kadabra with ease, then switch to a Psychic-type of your own when he sends out Toxicroak. The defeated Commander Saturn will spill some beans about Commander Mars's team at Lake Verity before fleeing with his team. Turn to page 48 for more details on the battle that awaits you there.

The foe's TOXICROAK used Revenge!

Kadabra	Level 35	Bronzor	Level 35	Toxicroak	Level 37
Type: **Psychic**		Type: **Steel** **Psychic**		Type: **Poison** **Fighting**	

Lake Valor after Galactic Battle

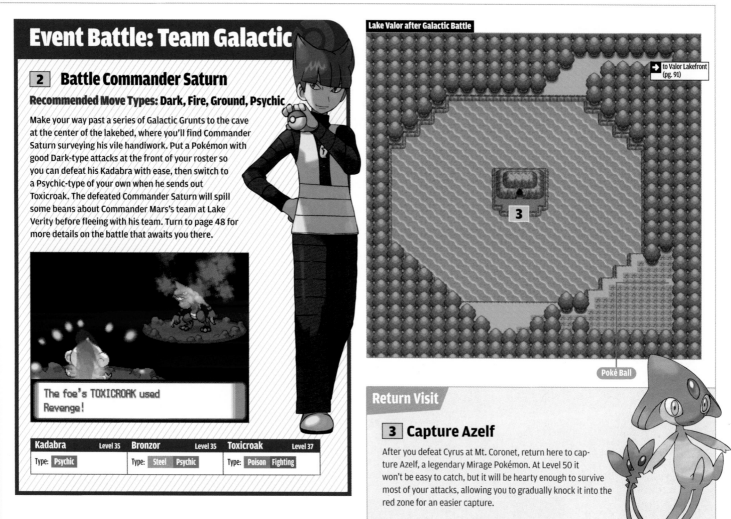

→ to Valor Lakefront (pg. 91)

3

Poké Ball

Return Visit

3 Capture Azelf

After you defeat Cyrus at Mt. Coronet, return here to capture Azelf, a legendary Mirage Pokémon. At Level 50 it won't be easy to catch, but it will be hearty enough to survive most of your attacks, allowing you to gradually knock it into the red zone for an easier capture.

Route 211 (Celestic Town Side)

Route 211 is divided in half by Mt. Coronet. Both segments contain entrances to Mt. Coronet's northern pass.

1 TM77 (Psych Up)

WILD POKÉMON

POKÉMON	D/P	AM	MID	PM
Chingling	D/P	☐	☐	☐
Graveler	D/P	■	■	■
Machoke	D/P	☐	☐	☐
Meditite	D/P	■	☐	☐
Noctowl	D/P			☐
Ponyta	D/P	☐	☐	●
Zubat	D/P			☐

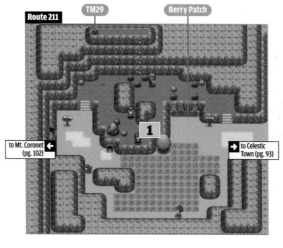

Route 211 TM29 Berry Patch

1

→ to Mt. Coronet (pg. 102)   → to Celestic Town (pg. 93)

1 TM77 (Psych Up)

TM77 To reach this chunk of Route 211, fly to Celestic Town and travel west. You'll face a few Trainers on the hilly northern part of the map, but heading that way allows you to pick up TM77 (Psych Up) at point 1.

Your Pokémon can use Psych Up to get the same Defense boost as its foe.

Mt. Coronet (North)

Whichever entrance you take to enter Mt. Coronet, you'll need HMO4 (Strength) to proceed north toward Lake Acuity.

WILD POKéMON

1F/A

POKéMON	D/P	AM	MID	PM
Chingling	D/P	□	□	□
Cleffa	D/P	□	●	●
Geodude	D/P	□	■	■
Machop	D/P	■	■	■
Meditite	D/P	□	□	□
Zubat	D/P	□	□	□

1F/B

POKéMON	D/P	AM	MID	PM
Chingling	D/P	□	□	□
Clefairy	D/P	□	□	□
Golbat	D/P	□	□	□
Graveler	D/P	□	□	□
Machoke	D/P	□	□	□
Meditite	D/P	□	□	□

B1

POKéMON	D/P	AM	MID	PM
Chingling	D/P	□	□	□
Clefairy	D/P	□	□	□
Golbat	D/P	□	□	□
Graveler	D/P	□	□	□
Machoke	D/P	□	□	□
Meditite	D/P	□	□	□

POKéMON	D/P	OR	GR
Barboach	D/P		□
Feebas	D/P	■	■
Magikarp	D/P	■	■

POKéMON	D/P	Surf
Golbat	D/P	□
Zubat	D/P	■

1 Catching a Feebas

This underground lake is the only place in Sinnoh where you can catch a Feebas. Doing so won't be easy, however; at any given point there are only four spots in the whole lake where you can catch one, and those spots are different every day and in every copy of the game. (These spots are not necessarily along the shore–you can fish at the center of the lake while using Surf.) If you don't want to try every spot, get together with other players who are in your group, since the fishing spots will be set in the same places for every member of the group. Note that even at the right spots, the chance of catching a Feebas is only 50%.

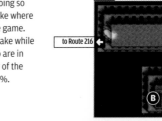

1F/B

to Route 216

B

B1

B

Revive

Soft Sand

Max Elixir

Full Restore

Light Clay

1

A

Stardust

Mt. Coronet 1F/A

A

Rare Candy

TM69

to Route 211 (pg. 101)

to Route 211 (pg. 66)

Escape Rope

TM02

to Mt. Coronet (pg. 113)

Route 216

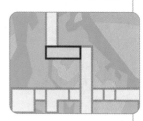

The north exit of Mt. Coronet will take you to the first of two snowy routes that lead to Lake Acuity and Snowpoint City.

1	A Warm Bed for Travelers

WILD POKéMON

POKéMON	D/P	AM	MID	PM
Graveler	D/P	●	●	●
Machoke	D/P	□	□	□
Meditite	D/P	□	□	□
Noctowl	D/P			□
Sneasel	D/P	□	□	□
Snover	D/P	□	□	□
Zubat	D/P			□

1 A Warm Bed for Travelers

It's a long, cold walk from Mt. Coronet to the Acuity Lakefront. Even the most talented of Trainers will end up with injured Pokémon, since the constant hail will hurt every non-Ice-type Pokémon in each turn of combat. Thankfully you can heal at any time at the small home at point 1–just get into the bed, face forward, and press the A Button to drift off to sleep.

It's a bed...
Want to take a rest?

▶ YES
NO

to Route 217
(pg. 104)

Ice Heal   Mental Herb   HP Up   TM13

HEAL

1

to Mt. Coronet

Pokémon Notes

Ice and Grass is a strange combination of types that leaves Snover (and its Evolved form, Abomasnow) with several vulnerabilities. But its combination of powerful Grass- and Ice-type attacks gives it the ability to trump a wide variety of types.

Snover
Type: Grass Ice
Ability: **Snow Warning**

Route 217

Route 217 is a vast snowfield buffeted by an endless blizzard. Wrap yourself tight and trudge north to Lake Acuity.

FIRST VISIT

1 Get HM08 (Rock Climb)

2 Desperate for Visitors

RETURN VISIT

3 Evolving Glaceon

WILD POKéMON

POKéMON	D/P	AM	MID	PM
Machoke	D/P	☐	☐	☐
Medicham	D/P	☐	☐	☐
Meditite	D/P	☐	☐	
Noctowl	D/P			☐
Sneasel	D/P	☐	☐	☐
Snover	D/P	☐	☐	☐
Zubat	D/P			☐

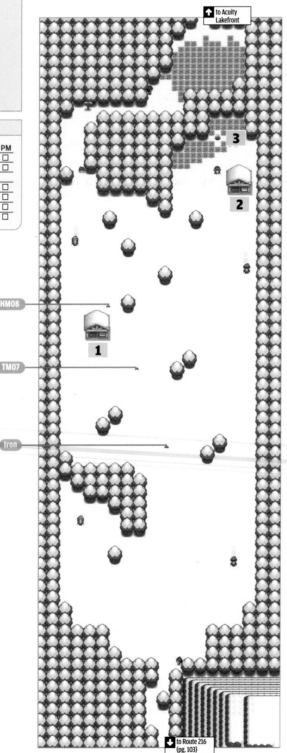

1 Get HM08 (Rock Climb)

`HM08` `Icicle Plate` The man inside the house at point 1 has lost his HM in the snowfield. You can find it directly behind the house, and if you then attempt to return it, the man will let you keep it, and reward your honesty with a free Icicle Plate as well.

I like your honesty, though.
Let me reward you with this.

2 Desperate for Visitors

`Spell Tag`

The woman in this home is so grateful for a visit that she'll immediately hand over a Spell Tag. Brightening her day is a small price to pay for this Ghost-type-enhancing held item.

...Thank you for visiting...
...A gift...

Return Visit

3 Evolving Glaceon

Just as the moss-covered rock in the Eterna Forest can evolve Eevee into Leafeon, this icy rock can evolve Eevee into an Ice-type Glaceon. All you need to do is bring Eevee to this route and level it up in combat.

Congratulations! Your EEVEE evolved into GLACEON!

Acuity Lakefront

This small strip of snow and grass connects Route 217 to Lake Acuity and Sinnoh's northern port, Snowpoint City.

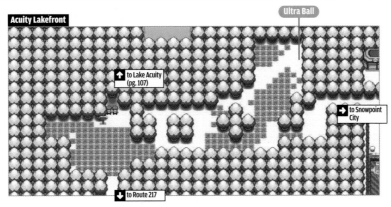

1 The Lakefront Path

WILD POKéMON

POKéMON	D/P	AM	MID	PM
Machoke	D/P	☐	☐	☐
Medicham	D/P	☐	☐	☐
Meditite	D/P	☐	☐	
Noctowl	D/P			☐
Sneasel	D/P	☐	☐	☐
Snover	D/P	☐	☐	☐
Zubat	D/P			☐

1 The Lakefront Path

You've reached the entrance to Lake Acuity, but a pair of Galactic Grunts won't let you pass. For now, head east to Snowpoint City and battle Gym Leader Candice to earn the Icicle Badge. Once you have that, the Grunts will allow you through.

Snowpoint City

The remote city of Snowpoint doesn't get a lot of tourists, but Trainers often visit to compete for the Icicle Badge.

FIRST VISIT

1 The Word of the Day

2 Trade for a Haunter

RETURN VISIT

3 Snowpoint Temple

4 Snowpoint Harbor

WILD POKéMON

POKéMON	D/P	Event
Haunter	D/P	Trade

Pokémart

Antidote	100
Awakening	250
Burn Heal	250
Dusk Ball	1000
Escape Rope	550
Full Heal	600
• Full Restore	3000
Great Ball	600
Hyper Potion	1200
Ice Heal	250
• Max Potion	2500
Max Repel	700
Paralyze Heal	200
Poké Ball	200
Potion	300
Quick Ball	1000
Repel	350
Revive	1500
Snow Mail	50
Super Potion	700
Super Repel	500
Timer Ball	1000
Ultra Ball	1200

• Not available until later; see the table on page 28

Snowpoint City Gym

Gym Leader Candice

Recommended Move Types: Fighting, Fire, Flying

TM72 The icy floor of this Gym forces you to skid around the room, aiming for snowballs and snowdrifts to break your slide. From the snowdrifts, slide down the ledges and into the snowballs in the lower ledges to destroy them and create a path to the Gym Leader. When battling Junior Trainers, bring along an Electric- or Grass-type—they're terrible against Ice-types but you'll face a lot of Water-types here too. Switch to Fire-type moves against Candice, which will make short work of her Snover and Abomasnow.

Snowpoint City Gym

The foe's ABOMASNOW used Avalanche!

Snover	Level 38	Sneasel	Level 38	Medicham	Level 40
Type: Ice Grass		Type: Dark Ice		Type: Fighting Psychic	

Abomasnow	Level 42
Type: Ice Grass	

1 The Word of the Day

The man in this house will offer up a new "trendy saying" every day. This word will be added to the game's vocabulary system, so you can use it in interviews and conversations for the remainder of your journey.

I hope you'll use trendy sayings in a trendy way.

2 Trade for a Haunter

The Trainer in the home at point 2 wants to swap her Haunter for a Medicham. But won't Haunter evolve into a Gengar as soon as it's traded? Not this time, because the Haunter is holding a free bonus—an Everstone that prevents Evolution. If you're interested, you can catch a Medicham at the Acuity Lakefront.

If you do, would you like to trade your MEDICHAM for my HAUNTER?

Return Visit

3 Snowpoint Temple

When you receive the National Pokédex after becoming League Champion, you can enter the mysterious dungeon inside Snowpoint Temple. Import Regirock, Regice, and Registeel from a Pokémon Ruby, Sapphire, or Emerald game and bring them with you to make Regigigas emerge.

4 Snowpoint Harbor

After defeating the Elite Four and becoming League Champion, your rival will ask you to meet him in Snowpoint City. He will have already moved on by the time you get there, but you can follow him to the game's final continent by catching a ship in Snowpoint Harbor.

What is it? Do you want to sail to the Battle Zone?

Lake Acuity

Sinnoh's northernmost lake is Team Galactic's next target.
Help your rival protect the third and final Mirage Pokémon.

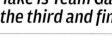

WILD POKÉMON

POKéMON	D/P	AM	MID	PM
Bibarel	D/P	■	■	□
Chingling	D/P	□	□	□
Noctowl	D/P			□
Psyduck	D/P	■	■	□
Sneasel	D/P		□	□

POKéMON	D/P	OR	GR
Goldeen	D/P		□
Magikarp	D/P	■	■

POKéMON	D/P	Surf	
Golduck	D/P	□	
Psyduck	D/P	■	

POKéMON	D/P	Event
Uxie	D/P	After event

Lake Acuity

1 to Acuity Lakefront (pg. 105)

TM14

Lake Acuity After Team Galactic

1 Back Up Your Rival

After earning the Icicle Badge, you'll find that the guards at Lake Acuity have stepped out of the way, allowing you to approach the lakefront. There your rival is sparring with Commander Jupiter, who will escape with the third legendary Mirage Pokémon. At least she'll tell you exactly where she's going—Galactic HQ at Veilstone City. Console your rival, then Fly to Veilstone City to put a stop to Team Galactic's nefarious plan (see page 82).

Don't waste your time coming to our HQ in Veilstone.

I couldn't do anything against Team Galactic!

2 to Acuity Lakefront (pg. 105)

Return Visit

2 Capture Uxie

After you foil Team Galactic's plans on Mt. Coronet, the water level at Lake Acuity will rise. You can then Surf across the lake to reach the other shore and the Acuity Cavern. Like Azelf, Uxie will happily stay and fight, giving you a chance to catch another powerful Level-50 Psychic-type.

Kyouuuun!

Galactic Headquarters

Team Galactic has taken the Mirage Pokémon to their Veilstone City headquarters. Save them before it's too late!

1. Search for the Galactic Key
2. March through the Front Door
3. Battle Galactic Boss Cyrus
4. Battle Commander Saturn
5. Set the Mirage Pokémon Free

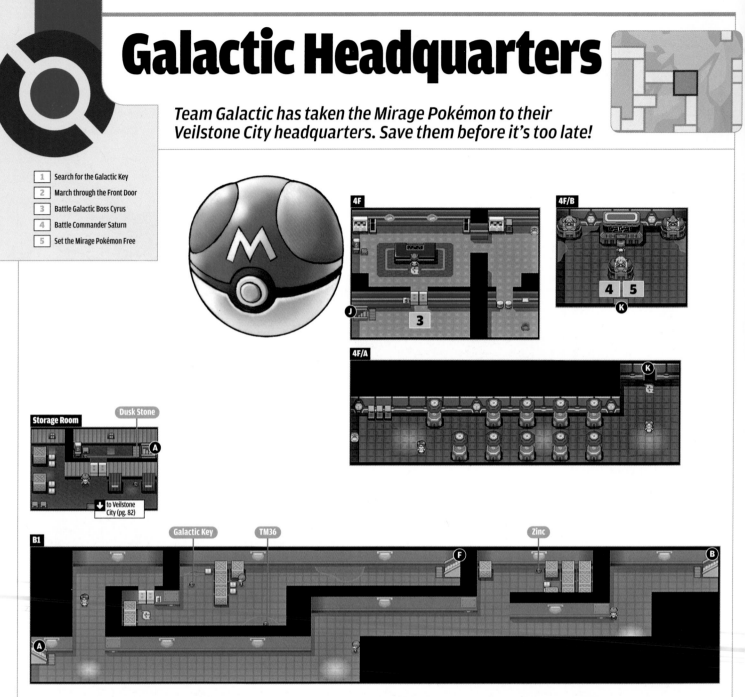

4F — **J** — **3**

4F/B — **4 5** — **K**

4F/A — **K**

Storage Room — **Dusk Stone** — **A** — to Veilstone City (pg. 82)

B1 — Galactic Key — TM36 — Zinc — **F** — **B** — **A**

1 Search for the Galactic Key

Upon entering Galactic HQ from Veilstone City's Galactic Warehouse, the first priority is to find the Galactic Key, which can open any door in the building. To reach it, follow the staircases in order from A to C. That will put you in a room with two warps; take the right one to find TM49 (Snatch) then backtrack and take the left warp to reach staircase D. Use the warp at point 1, then follow staircases E and F to reach the room with the Galactic Key.

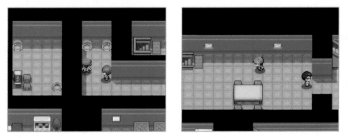

2 March through the Front Door

Leave through the warehouse and walk through Veilstone City to reach the main entrance of Galactic HQ. Unlock the door in the lobby and take staircase G to the room at point 2. Here you'll find three warps; the one in the southeast corner leads to a Max Revive, the one in the northeast leads to a dead end, and the one in the TV room leads to the nap room. Catch some sleep in the nap room, then take staircase H.

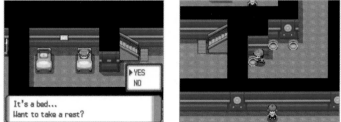

It's a bed...
Want to take a rest?
▶ YES
NO

3F

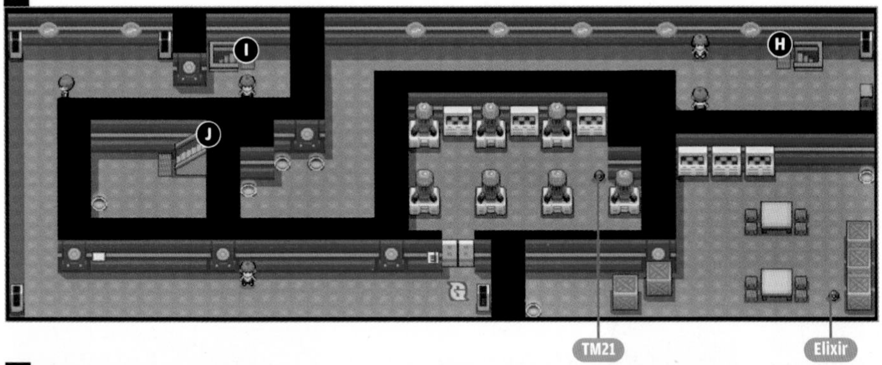

TM21 **Elixir**

2F

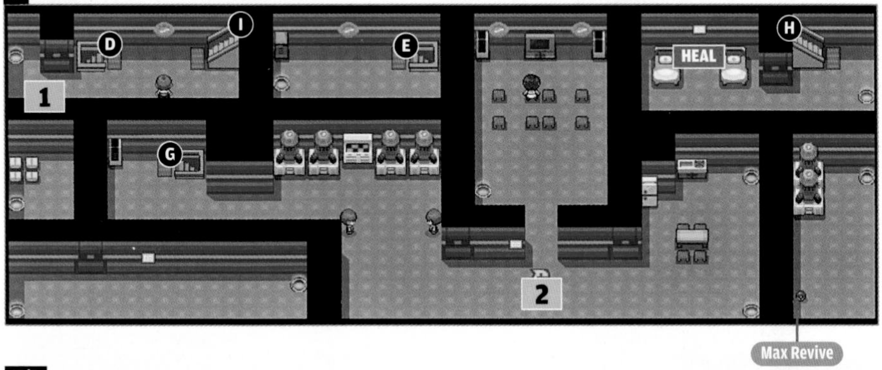

1 **HEAL** **H**

2

Max Revive

1F/B

TM49

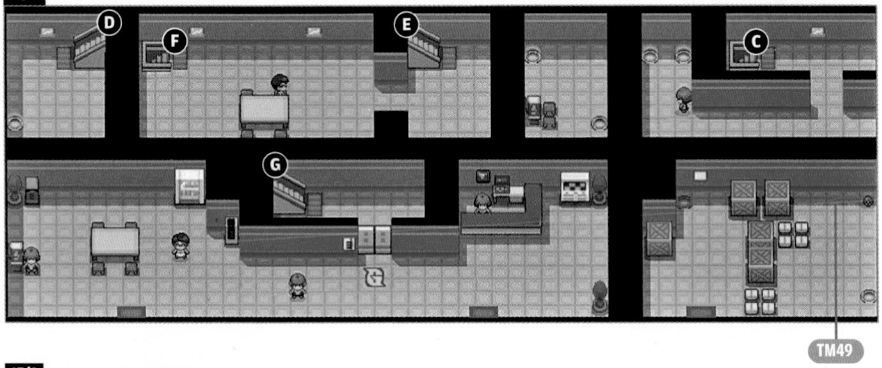

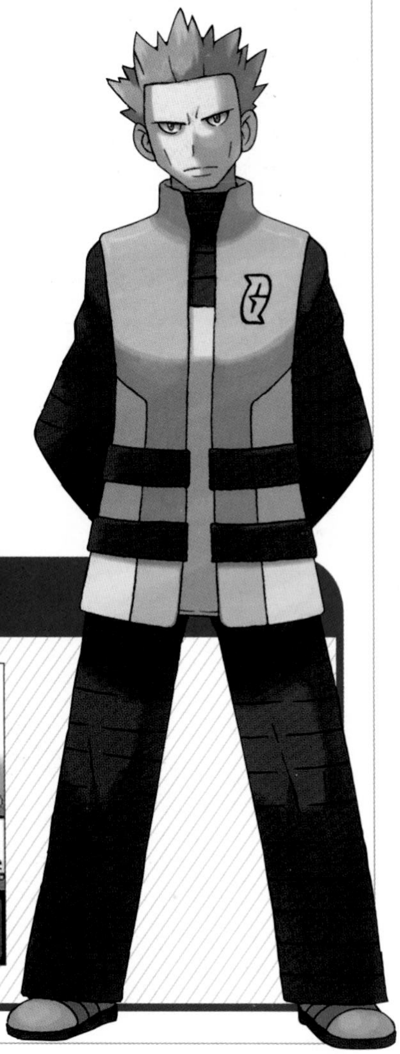

1F/A

Event Battle: Team Galactic

3 Battle Galactic Boss Cyrus

Recommended Move Types: Electric, Fighting, Ice, Rock,

Master Ball Cyrus doesn't mind letting you free the Mirage Pokémon, but he wants a fight all the same. Lead off with an Electric-type Pokémon that can make short work of his Murkrow and Golbat, then use Fire-type attacks to melt Sneasel's cold heart. Use your strongest moves even when Cyrus's Pokémon seem seriously wounded, because Cyrus has several Super Potions and Sneasel is holding a Sitrus Berry. Once he's defeated, Cyrus will give you a Master Ball.

Murkrow		Level 40	Golbat		Level 40	Sneasel		Level 43
Type:	Dark	Flying	Type:	Poison	Flying	Type:	Dark	Ice

SNEASEL Lv43

INFERNAPE Lv39
112/112

INFERNAPE used
Mach Punch!

Event Battle: Team Galactic

4 Battle Commander Saturn

Recommended Move Types: Dark, Fire, Flying, Psychic

Commander Saturn hasn't forgotten the beating you gave him at Lake Valor, and is eager for revenge. Lead off with a Bug- or Dark-type to take down Kadabra, then be ready to switch to a user of Fire-type moves to battle Bronzor. Psychic-types are strongest against Toxicroak, but a Flying-type can both damage it and swipe its Sitrus Berry with the Pluck move.

SKUNTANK used
Flamethrower!

Kadabra	Level 38	Bronzor	Level 38	Toxicroak	Level 40
Type: Psychic		Type: Steel Psychic		Type: Poison Fighting	

5 Set the Mirage Pokémon Free

After besting Commander Saturn, press the red button on the glowing green machine to free Mesprit, Azelf, and Uxie. Commander Saturn will give you more information about Cyrus's current plan, then leave himself. On your way out, you'll notice the gate that previously blocked the green warp is gone, and you can now use the warp to teleport directly to the building's lobby. You can't yet capture the Mirage Pokémon, so your course is clear: Warp to Oreburgh City and head northwest to Mt. Coronet.

Press the button and set the Pokémon free?

▶ YES
NO

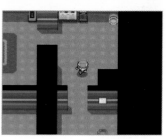

Mt. Coronet

After your battle, Cyrus will announce that he is returning to the site of your first meeting. What is he up to now?

1	Reach the Upper Ledge
2	Hot on Cyrus's Trail
3	To the Spear Pillar
4	Cyrus's Endgame Begins
5	Commanders Mars and Jupiter
6	Boss Cyrus
7	Capture Dialga or Palkia
8	On to New Challenges

WILD POKéMON

1F/A

POKéMON	D/P	AM	MID	PM
Chingling	D/P	☐	☐	☐
Cleffa	D/P	☐	●	●
Geodude	D/P	☐	■	■
Machop	D/P	■	■	■
Meditite	D/P	☐	☐	☐
Zubat	D/P	☐	☐	☐

POKéMON	D/P	OR	GR
Barboach	D/P		☐
Magikarp	D/P	■	■

POKéMON	D/P	Surf
Golbat	D/P	☐
Zubat	D/P	■

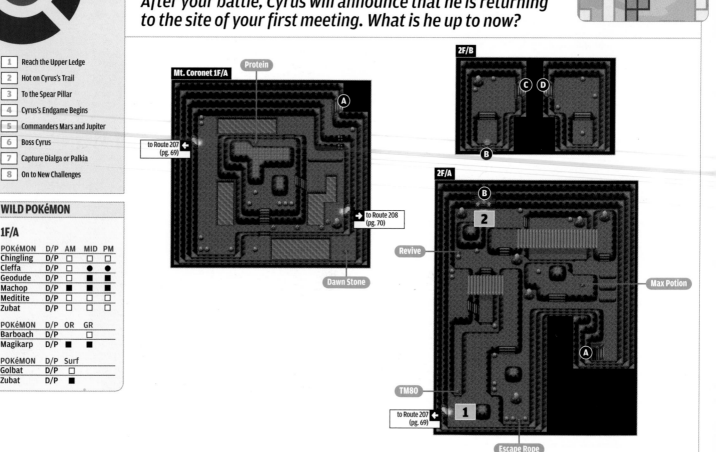

Mt. Coronet 1F/A
Protein
A
to Route 207 (pg. 69)
to Route 208 (pg. 70)
Dawn Stone

2F/B
C D
B

2F/A
B
2
Revive
Max Potion
A
TM80
1
to Route 207 (pg. 69)
Escape Rope

WILD POKéMON

1F/B

POKéMON	D/P	AM	MID	PM
Bronzong	D/P	●	●	●
Chingling	D/P	☐	☐	☐
Clefairy	D/P	☐	☐	☐
Golbat	D/P	☐	☐	☐
Graveler	D/P	■	■	■
Machoke	D/P	☐	☐	☐
Medicham	D/P	☐	☐	☐

2F/A & 2F/B, 3F

POKéMON	D/P	AM	MID	PM
Bronzong	D/P	☐	☐	☐
Bronzor	D/P	●	●	●
Chingling	D/P	☐	☐	☐
Clefairy	D/P	☐	☐	☐
Golbat	D/P	☐	☐	☐
Graveler	D/P	☐	☐	☐
Machoke	D/P	☐	☐	☐
Medicham	D/P	☐	☐	☐

4F/A

POKéMON	D/P	AM	MID	PM
Bronzong	D/P	☐	☐	☐
Chingling	D/P	☐	☐	☐
Clefairy	D/P	☐	☐	☐
Golbat	D/P	☐	☐	☐
Graveler	D/P	☐	☐	☐
Machoke	D/P	☐	☐	☐
Medicham	D/P	☐	☐	☐

POKéMON	D/P	OR	GR
Barboach	D/P		☐
Magikarp	D/P	■	■

POKéMON	D/P	Surf
Golbat	D/P	☐
Zubat	D/P	■

4F/B

POKéMON	D/P	AM	MID	PM
Bronzong	D/P	☐	☐	☐
Chimecho	D/P	●	●	●
Chingling	D/P	●	●	●
Clefairy	D/P	☐	☐	☐
Golbat	D/P	☐	☐	☐
Graveler	D/P	☐	☐	☐
Machoke	D/P	☐	☐	☐
Medicham	D/P	☐	☐	☐

5 & 6F

POKéMON	D/P	AM	MID	PM
Bronzong	D/P	☐	☐	☐
Chimecho	D/P	☐	☐	☐
Clefairy	D/P	☐	☐	☐
Golbat	D/P	☐	☐	☐
Graveler	D/P	☐	☐	☐
Machoke	D/P	☐	☐	☐
Medicham	D/P	☐	☐	☐

MT. CORONET PEAK

POKéMON	D/P	AM	MID	PM
Abomasnow	D/P	☐	☐	☐
Bronzong	D/P	●	●	●
Chingling	D/P	☐	☐	☐
Clefairy	D/P	●	●	●
Golbat	D/P	☐	☐	☐
Machoke	D/P	☐	☐	☐
Medicham	D/P	☐	☐	☐
Noctowl	D/P	☐	☐	☐
Snover	D/P	☐	☐	☐

SPEAR PILLAR

POKéMON	D/P	Event
Dialga	D	Event only
Palkia	P	Event only

1 Reach the Upper Ledge

From the ground floor, use Rock Climb to reach the stairs to level 2F. If you exit that floor via the door at point 1, you'll reach an upper ledge on Route 207. From there you can use Rock Climb to get you to another valuable dose of Iron.

2 Hot on Cyrus's Trail

If you're visiting this region before the battle at Galactic Headquarters, you'll find a wall with a cave painting here. But if you visit after first defeating Cyrus, you'll find a path has been blasted open—surely Team Galactic's handiwork.

3 To the Spear Pillar

When you pass through door E, you'll find yourself on the cold and misty peak of Mt. Coronet. Follow the grass to a spot where you can use Rock Climb, and then head west through another patch of grass to enter the cavern at door H. Use Rock Climb to reach door I, then maneuver to the north end of the peak and enter a second cavern through door K. From door K you can travel directly to the Spear Pillar, although you'll have to battle several Grunts on the way.

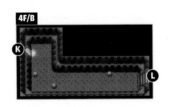

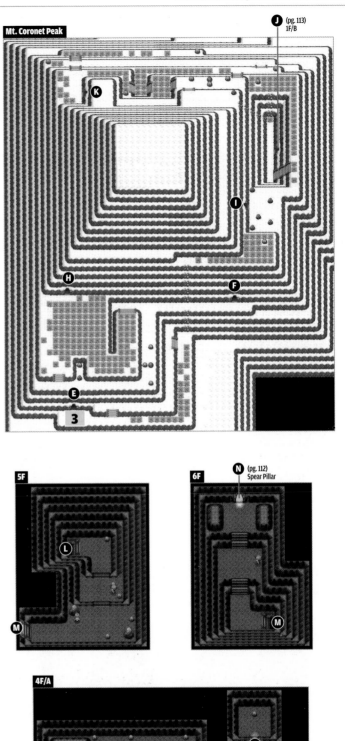

Mt. Coronet Peak

J (pg. 113) 1F/B

N (pg. 112) Spear Pillar

5F

6F

4F/B

4F/A

3F

4 Cyrus's Endgame Begins

After battling a pair of Galactic Grunts, you'll find Commander Mars, Commander Jupiter, and Cyrus at the center of the map. Watch the event that introduces Dialga (in the Diamond version) or Palkia (in the Pearl version), then heal your wounded Pokémon and save your game. You're going to face two challenging battles in a row, but at least you won't have to tackle the first one alone—when you approach Commanders Mars and Jupiter, your rival will run up to join you for a two-on-two brawl. Don't worry about keeping your Pokémon alive during that battle, because your rival will fully heal your Pokémon before you go head-to-head with Cyrus.

Spear Pillar

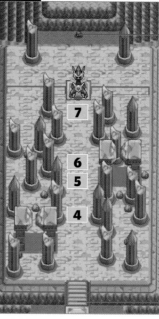

Adamant or Lustrous Orb

Note: This map is taken from the Diamond version. Palkia will appear instead of Dialga in the Pearl version of the game. Additionally, this map is flipped in the Pearl version.

N (pg. 111) 6F

Event Battle: Team Galactic

5 Battle Commanders Mars and Jupiter

Recommended Move Types: Electric, Fighting, Fire, Rock

Your rival will lead off with a Munchlax, which has a lot of stat-boosting moves but won't contribute much to your offense. Lead off with a Fire-type Pokémon so you can take out a Bronzor quickly, then focus on knocking out the two Pokémon that replace it. Once you reduce the battle to a two-on-one fight, your victory will be all but assured.

PONYTA used Fire Blast!

STARAPTOR used Close Combat!

Commander Mars Team	
Bronzor	Level 41
Type: Steel Psychic	
Golbat	Level 42
Type: Poison Flying	
Purugly	Level 45
Type: Normal	

Commander Jupiter Team	
Bronzor	Level 41
Type: Steel Psychic	
Golbat	Level 41
Type: Poison Flying	
Skuntank	Level 46
Type: Poison Dark	

Event Battle: Team Galactic

6 Battle Boss Cyrus

Recommended Move Types: Electric, Rock, Fighting, Fire

Cyrus uses some powerful Pokémon but hasn't done a great job of arranging his team—with three Flying-types he is extremely vulnerable to Electric-type moves (and to a lesser extent, Rock-type moves). Figure out which Pokémon is best able to exploit this weakness, and keep it healthy at all costs. As always when battling Cyrus, use your best moves against even heavily wounded Pokémon, since Cyrus has Super Potions and even Full Restores.

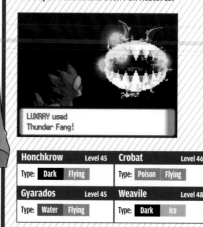

LUXRAY used Thunder Fang!

Honchkrow	Level 45	Crobat	Level 46
Type: Dark Flying		Type: Poison Flying	
Gyarados	Level 45	Weavile	Level 48
Type: Water Flying		Type: Dark Ice	

7 Capture Dialga or Palkia

After you beat the Team Galactic Commanders and Cyrus, Prof. Rowan and his assistant will show up. They'll urge you to challenge Dialga and Palkia—save your game first, just in case. This is the best time to use the Master Ball you received from Cyrus, because you have only one chance to catch this Pokémon and it won't be easy to do using conventional means.

The Legendary Pokémon

The Steel-and-Dragon-type Dialga is vulnerable to Fighting- and Ground-type moves and resistant to almost everything else. It differs from the Water-and-Dragon-type Palkia in its ability to learn a few Steel-type moves (instead of Palkia's Water-type moves) and its higher Defense score.

While Dialga's types complement each other, Palkia's mostly cancel each other out. Palkia is vulnerable only to rare Dragon-type moves, but has very few resistances. Palkia has a higher Special Defense score than Dialga.

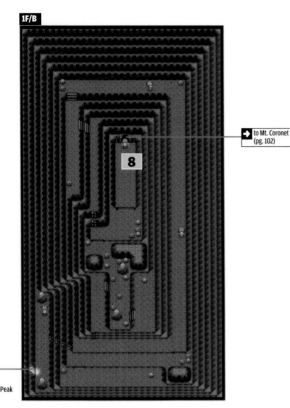

1F/B

8

to Mt. Coronet (pg. 102)

J (pg. 111) Mt. Coronet Peak

8 | On to New Challenges

Prof. Rowan will usher you out of the hall—be sure to head back in to pick up the Adamant Orb (in Pokémon Diamond) or the Lustrous Orb (in Pokémon Pearl), held items made especially for Dialga and Palkia. Once you leave the hall, you can use the Dig move or an Escape Rope to flee; if you have neither, take door J on the peak for the quickest route out.

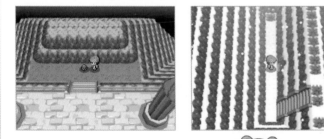

Dialga
Type: Steel Dragon
Ability: **Pressure**

Pokémon Notes

Among the wild Pokémon in this area are the Evolved forms of Bronzor and Snover. Bronzong offers spectacular stats in both the Defense and Special Defense categories, but a limited selection of damage-dealing moves. Abomasnow can learn Grass-type Wood Hammer and Ice-type Blizzard, both of which have eye-popping Power stats of 120. Be very wary when battling these dangerous foes!

Bronzong
Type: Steel Psychic
Ability: **Levitate / Heat Proof**

Abomasnow
Type: Grass Ice
Ability: **Snow Warning**

Palkia
Type: Water Dragon
Ability: **Pressure**

Route 222

*Team Galactic has been foiled, but your quest continues.
The passage west of Valor Lakefront is now open.*

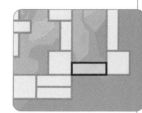

1. TM56 (Fling)
2. Pikachu Fan Club
3. Pokémon Size Contest

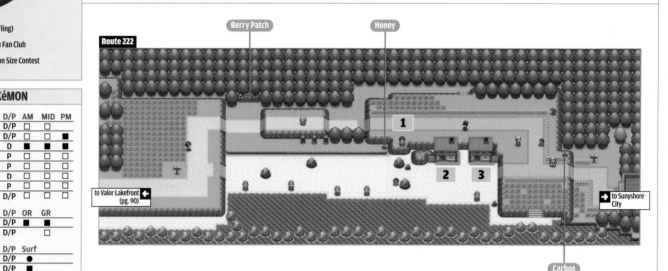

WILD POKéMON

POKéMON	D/P	AM	MID	PM
Chatot	D/P	□	□	
Floatzel	D/P	□	□	■
Gastrodon	D	■	■	■
Gastrodon	P	□	□	□
Glameow	P	□	□	□
Mr. Mime	D	□	□	□
Purugly	P	□	□	□
Wingull	D/P	□	□	□

POKéMON	D/P	OR	GR
Magikarp	D/P	□	□
Remoraid	D/P		□

POKéMON	D/P	Surf
Pelipper	D/P	●
Tentacool	D/P	■
Tentacruel	D/P	●
Wingull	D/P	■

1 TM56 (Fling)

TM56 The man at point 1 will give you the TM for the move Fling, which allows a Pokémon to hurl whatever item it is currently holding. The move's effects vary based on which item is thrown.

Using that move, the Pokémon hurls whatever item it's holding at the foe.

3 Pokémon Size Contest

Net Ball The man at this home dreams of giant Remoraid, and will reward you with a Net Ball whenever you catch a Remoraid of record size. Catching one shouldn't be difficult—they're the most common Pokémon you'll encounter if you use a Good Rod at the Route 222 shore.

H-how big of a REMORAID did you bring me?!

2 Pikachu Fan Club

The guy who lives at point 2 really loves Pikachu, and you'll find six of the critters in his home. Actually, make that five—if you speak to each of the Pokémon, you'll discover that one isn't a Pikachu at all—it's Poké Kid Janet, who will challenge you to a duel if you find her out. Her roster consists, of course, entirely of Pikachu.

You can spot the imposter by the sound she makes. That's not what a Pikachu sounds like!

Bika bikabika!
Pigachu!

Sunyshore City

The "Sunshine City" has an elevated pathway made entirely out of solar panels that power the Sunyshore City Gym.

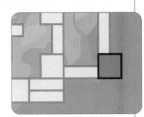

1 Meet Flint, of the Elite Four
2 Vista Lighthouse
3 HM07 (Waterfall)
4 The Seals of the Day
5 A Reward for Good Effort
6 Julia's Delightful Ribbons
7 Pokémon Nature Apps

WILD POKéMON

POKéMON	D/P	OR	GR
Magikarp	D/P	■	■
Remoraid	D/P		□

POKéMON	D/P	Surf
Mantyke	D/P	□
Pelipper	D/P	■
Tentacruel	D/P	■

Pokémart

Antidote	100
Awakening	250
Burn Heal	250
Escape Rope	550
Full Heal	600
• Full Restore	3000
Great Ball	600
Hyper Potion	1200
Ice Heal	250
Luxury Ball	1000
Max Potion	2500
Max Repel	700
Paralyze Heal	200
Poké Ball	200
Potion	300
Repel	350
Revive	1500
Steel Mail	50
Super Potion	700
Super Repel	500
Ultra Ball	1200

• Not available until later; see the table on page 28

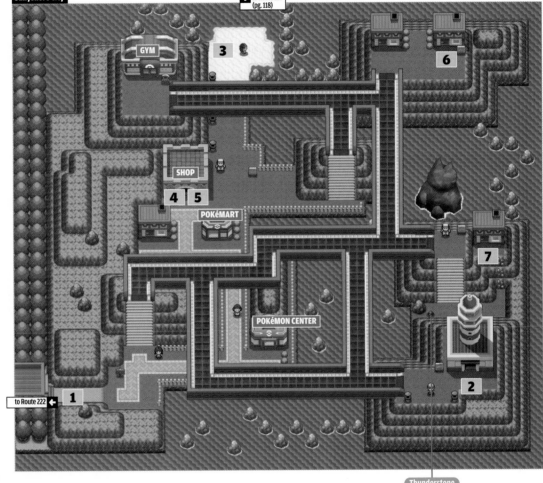

Sunyshore City

to Route 223 (pg. 118)

GYM

3

6

SHOP

4 5

POKéMART

7

POKéMON CENTER

to Route 222

1

2

Thunderstone

Shop

MONDAY		WEDNESDAY		FRIDAY		SUNDAY	
Fire Seal A	50	Fire Seal C	50	Flora Seal D	50	Flora Seal F	50
Heart Seal A	50	Flora Seal B	50	Foamy Seal B	50	Foamy Seal D	50
Song Seal A	50	Heart Seal C	50	Party Seal A	50	Song Seal G	50
Star Seal B	50	Song Seal C	50	Song Seal E	50	Star Seal A	50
Ele-Seal B	100	Star Seal D	50	Heart Scale E	100	Ele-Seal A	100
Line Seal C	100	Ele-Seal D	100	Smoke Seal C	100	Line Seal B	100
Party Seal D	100	Smoke Seal A	100	Star Seal F	100	Party Seal C	100
TUESDAY		**THURSDAY**		**SATURDAY**			
Fire Seal B	50	Fire Seal D	50	Flora Seal E	50		
Flora Seal A	50	Flora Seal C	50	Foamy Seal C	50		
Heart Seal B	50	Foamy Seal A	50	Party Seal B	50		
Song Seal B	50	Heart Seal D	50	Song Seal F	50		
Star Seal C	50	Song Seal D	50	Heart Seal F	100		
Ele-Seal C	100	Smoke Seal B	100	Line Seal A	100		
Line Seal D	100	Star Seal E	100	Smoke Seal D	100		

1 Meet Flint, of the Elite Four

At the entrance to Sunyshore you'll meet Flint, a member of the Elite Four. He'll ask you to give Gym Leader Volkner the challenge of his life to reignite his passion for battle. However, you won't find Volkner at the Gym—he's at the Vista Lighthouse in the southwest corner of town.

He's been so bored, he spends all his time renovating the Gym.

2 Vista Lighthouse

You'll find Volkner using the Binoculars at the top floor of the lighthouse. He was considering a League Challenge, but is perfectly happy to shelve that plan to challenge you. Before you follow him out, use his Binoculars to get your first look at the Pokémon League building, where the Elite Four and the League Champion await all challengers.

If I find you to be weak, I'm going to challenge the Pokémon League.

Sunyshore City Gym

Gym Leader Volkner

Recommended Move Types: Ground, Fighting, Electric

TM57 To traverse the Sunyshore City Gym you'll need to rotate the gears by stepping on the colored dots at their center. If you get confused, simply head for the nearest Junior Trainer to put yourself back on track. On the final map, you'll have to pass Volkner, battle the Trainer at the northeast staircase, and head south to step on one of the red dots before the bridges line up correctly. When you do reach Volkner, use a team of Ground- and Grass-types backed up by your new Legendary Pokémon to win the Beacon Badge, TM57 (Charge Beam), and the ability to use the HM07 (Waterfall) outside of battle.

Raichu	Level 46	Ambipom	Level 47	Octillery	Level 47	Luxray	Level 49
Type: Electric		Type: Normal		Type: Water		Type: Electric	

Sunyshore City Gym

ROSELIA used Giga Drain!

DIALGA used Roar of Time!

Now that you've earned the final Gym Badge, Pokémon of any level will obey you. If you need some help in the challenges to come, go ahead and borrow a high-level Pokémon from a friend!

Against you, even the Elite Four will be pushed to fend off your challenge!

3 HM07 (Waterfall)

HM07 On this small beach you'll run into Jasmine from Johto, making a cameo from Pokémon Gold and Pokémon Silver. If you show her your Beacon Badge, she'll give you HM07 (Waterfall), which you'll need to reach the Pokémon League building.

If you use it, you can get to the Pokémon League.

4 The Seals of the Day

Sunyshore Market sells a wide selection of Poké Ball Seals, and the selection changes every day of the week. Many of the Seals have cool special effects like confetti bursts and puffs of smoke, so read their descriptions instead of judging them by their names alone.

Ah, please, allow me a little of your time, if you will. You won't regret it.

Money		
₽105224		
Heart Seal D	₽	50
Foamy Seal A	₽	50
Fire Seal D	₽	50
Flora Seal C	₽	50
Song Seal D	₽	50
Star Seal E	₽	100
Smoke Seal B	₽	100

This Seal releases a cloud of big black hearts.

5 A Reward for Good Effort

Another woman in the Sunyshore Market will examine your lead Pokémon and pass judgment on its level of effort. If she finds it acceptable, you'll earn an Effort Ribbon for the Ribbons page of your Pokémon's Summary screen. To increase a Pokémon's level of effort, you'll have to use it in combat a lot, so you probably won't be able to earn an Effort Ribbon on your first visit to Sunyshore City.

It needs to work a little harder.

6 Julia's Delightful Ribbons

Julia's husband is off at sea, and she gets terribly bored in his absence. She'll ask you to visit from time to time and tell her stories of your travels by using the vocabulary system to answer her questions. If you do, she'll thank you by attaching a ribbon to your lead Pokémon. If you want to earn every ribbon for a Pokémon, you'll have to bring it to Julia's story time every day of the week.

You can't tell Julia a story the first time you visit her. You'll have to return the next day to earn your first ribbon.

Starting tomorrow, please visit and tell me stories about your travels.

Julia's Ribbons

Monday	Alert Ribbon
Tuesday	Shock Ribbon
Wednesday	Downcast Ribbon
Thursday	Careless Ribbon
Friday	Relax Ribbon
Saturday	Snooze Ribbon
Sunday	Smile Ribbon

7 Pokémon Nature Apps

Use Rock Climb to reach a small home where you'll find a man who has developed three new Pokétch apps. He'll give you the apps if you let him see Pokémon with three specific Natures. Check the Trainer Memo page of the Pokémon Summary screen to learn a Pokémon's Nature, and pull the needed Pokémon out of your box to get all three apps.

I got OK'd by the Pokétch Company to develop original Pokétch apps.

Pokémon Natures and Related Apps

Serious	Calendar app
Naive	Dot Artist app
Quirky	Roulette app

Pokémon Memo

You can finally catch a Mantyke by surfing in Sunyshore Bay. Mantyke evolves into Mantine in a very unique way: You simply need to level it up while Remoraid is in your roster.

Mantyke
Type: Water Flying
Ability: Swift Swim / Water Absorb

Route 223

The final stage of your quest to become League Champion begins when you surf north from Sunyshore City.

1 A Tricky Path
2 Using Waterfall

WILD POKéMON

POKéMON	D/P	OR	GR
Magikarp	D/P	■	■
Remoraid	D/P		☐

POKéMON	D/P	Surf
Mantyke	D/P	☐
Pelipper	D/P	■
Tentacruel	D/P	■

Route 223

↑ to the Pokémon League

2

Pearl

TM18

1

↓ to Sunyshore City (pg. 115)

1 A Tricky Path

To reach TM18 (Rain Dance), you'll need to plot a careful course between the rocks by using the map to find the spaces that are wide enough to surf through. You'll encounter more rocks to the north, in the formation where the Pearl is, so plan a route well in advance, especially if you're trying to avoid Trainers.

2 Using Waterfall

The north end of the map is blocked by a giant waterfall. To cross it, you'll need to have won the Beacon Badge in Sunyshore City and shown that badge to Jasmine to get HM07 (Waterfall). Teach Waterfall to a Water-type Pokémon and use it here to reach the entrance to Victory Road.

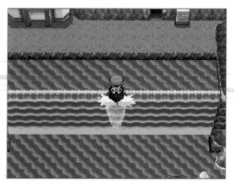

Pokémon League

Reaching the Pokémon League's entrance is almost as great a challenge as beating the Trainers who reside there.

FIRST VISIT

1 Victory Road Preparations

RETURN VISIT

2 Your Rival's Final Duel

3 Challenge the Elite Four

WILD POKéMON

POKéMON	D/P	OR	GR
Magikarp	D/P	■	■
Remoraid	D/P		□

POKéMON	D/P	Surf	
Pelipper	D/P	■	
Tentacruel	D/P	■	

1 Victory Road Preparations

The cave at point 1 is the entrance to Victory Road, the longest and most challenging dungeon area yet. The proper preparations are crucial. Bring your best team of Pokémon, but make sure they have (or can learn) all five of the following HM moves: Strength, Rock Smash, Surf, Waterfall, and Rock Climb. You can't pass through Victory Road without using all five moves.

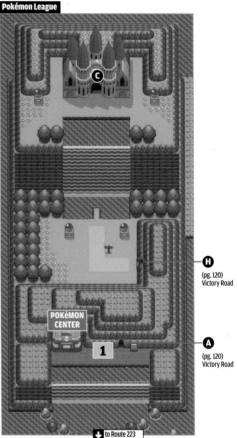

Pokémon League

H (pg. 120) Victory Road

A (pg. 120) Victory Road

POKéMON CENTER

to Route 223

Return Visit

Event Battle: Your Rival

2 Your Rival's Final Duel

Recommended Move Types: Electric, Fighting, Fire, Flying, Ground, Water

Your rival has been very busy. He has filled out his roster with new Pokémon, evolved most of his current ones to their ultimate forms, and boosted them all to an average of Level 50. Put your Electric-type at the head of your roster when you talk to the clerk at the door; that way you'll be ready to get the jump on Staraptor. If Dialga or Palkia has the new Heal Block move, use it against Snorlax to cut off its Rest move (unless you have a strong Fighting-type that can beat it outright). Your rival has grown more canny about switching Pokémon to type-trump you, so be ready to zig when he zags.

Rival Chose Turtwig

Staraptor	Level 48
Type: Normal Flying	

Heracross	Level 50
Type: Bug Fighting	

Snorlax	Level 51
Type: Normal	

Floatzel	Level 49
Type: Water	

Roserade	Level 49
Type: Grass Poison	

Infernape	Level 53
Type: Fire Fighting	

Rival Chose Chimchar

Staraptor	Level 48
Type: Normal Flying	

Heracross	Level 50
Type: Bug Fighting	

Snorlax	Level 51
Type: Normal	

Roserade	Level 49
Type: Grass Poison	

Rapidash	Level 49
Type: Fire	

Empoleon	Level 53
Type: Water Steel	

Rival Chose Piplup

Staraptor	Level 48
Type: Normal Flying	

Heracross	Level 50
Type: Bug Fighting	

Snorlax	Level 51
Type: Normal	

Floatzel	Level 49
Type: Water	

Rapidash	Level 49
Type: Fire	

Torterra	Level 53
Type: Grass Ground	

3 Challenge the Elite Four

After besting your rival, heal and do some shopping. The clerk at the right counter sells Full Restores, which combine a Full Heal and a Max Potion into one handy item—buy several if you can afford it. Then show your badges to the clerk at the door and prepare for the fight of your life!

Pokémart

Antidote	100
Awakening	250
Burn Heal	250
Dusk Ball	1000
Escape Rope	550
Full Heal	600
Full Restore	3000
Great Ball	600
Heal Ball	300
Hyper Potion	1200
Ice Heal	250
Luxury Ball	1000
Max Potion	2500
Max Repel	700
Nest Ball	1000
Net Ball	1000
Paralyze Heal	200
Poké Ball	200
Potion	300
Quick Ball	1000
Repeat Ball	1000
Repel	350
Revive	1500
Super Potion	700
Super Repel	500
Timer Ball	1000
Ultra Ball	1200

Victory Road

Before you can challenge the Elite Four, you must prove your worth as a Pokémon Trainer in this challenging cave.

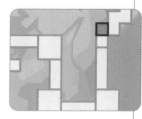

1. The Long Road to the Surface
2. Solve the Rock Puzzles
3. A Path for Champions Only

WILD POKÉMON

B1/A

POKÉMON	D/P	AM	MID	PM
Floatzel	D/P	■	■	■
Golbat	D/P	☐	☐	☐
Machoke	D/P	■	■	■
Medicham	D/P	☐	☐	☐
Steelix	D/P	☐	☐	☐

POKÉMON	D/P	OR	GR
Magikarp	D/P	■	■

POKÉMON	D/P	Surf
Golbat	D/P	■

1F

POKÉMON	D/P	AM	MID	PM
Golbat	D/P	☐	☐	☐
Graveler	D/P	■	■	■
Machoke	D/P	■	■	■
Medicham	D/P	☐	☐	☐
Onix	D/P	☐	☐	☐
Steelix	D/P	☐	☐	☐

2F

POKÉMON	D/P	AM	MID	PM
Golbat	D/P	☐	☐	☐
Graveler	D/P	■	■	■
Kadabra	D/P	■	■	■
Medicham	D/P	☐	☐	☐
Onix	D/P	☐	☐	☐
Steelix	D/P	☐	☐	☐

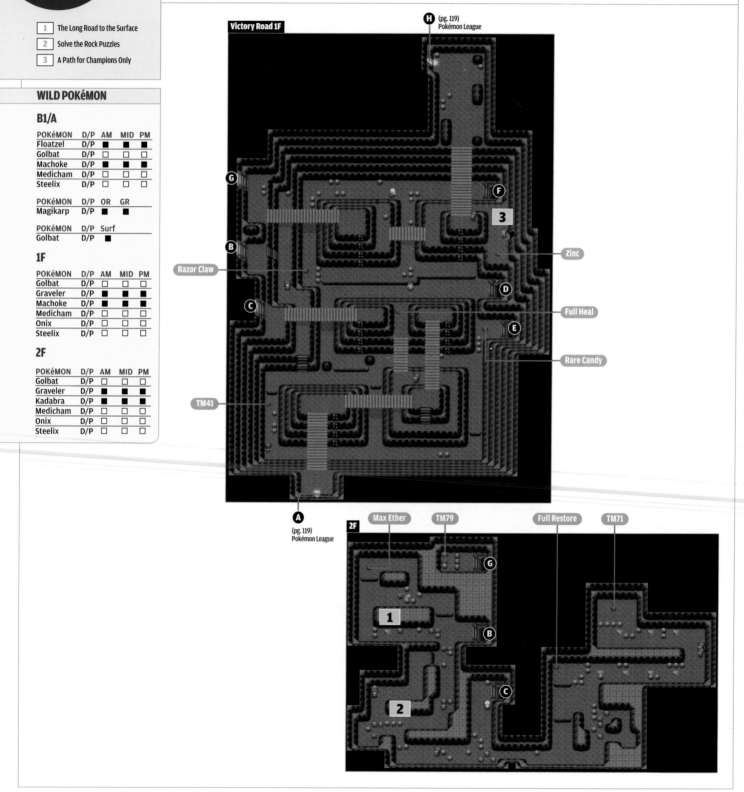

Victory Road 1F

H (pg. 119) Pokémon League

Razor Claw

Zinc

Full Heal

Rare Candy

TM41

A (pg. 119) Pokémon League

2F Max Ether · TM79 · Full Restore · TM71

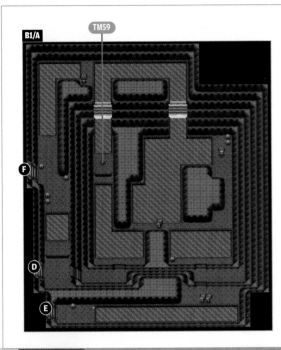

B1/A

TM59

F

D

E

1 The Long Road to the Surface

To reach the end of Victory Road, follow the letters on the maps in alphebetical order. Enter at doorway A, then make your way up stairway B. In the next cavern you'll find optional areas in the northwest and east where you can use bike jumps to earn rare items, but the only path to progress is through stairway C, then D. Stairway E is optional but worth it, since it requires only a short side trip to find a piece of Rare Candy. Continue to stairway F, from which you can attempt another side trip to obtain TM79 (through G), or head straight for the exit (door H).

2 Solve the Rock Puzzles

This path is full of puzzles that you can solve only by using the Strength move to push rocks in a certain order. Consider each push very carefully, or you may have to retreat to the stairs to reset their placements and start over. At point 2, push the left rock down without touching the right one, then smash the boulder with Rock Smash so you can push the left rock back to its original position. To get past the next formation and head east, you'll need to descend the stairway to the north and then climb back up the same stairway. This will reset the rock positions so that you can push the top rock south. Returning to continue your exploration of this floor is entirely optional, but you can find a TM and a Full Restore beyond a series of bike jumps to the east.

3 A Path for Champions Only

As large as Victory Road may seem, you've only scratched its surface. Beyond the door at point 3 you'll find more maps full of puzzles and tough battles—and beyond that, the exit to Route 224. But that route is not for beginners, and the man guarding the door won't let you through until you become the Pokémon League Champion.

The Elite Four

The Elite Four is composed of Sinnoh's most accomplished Trainers, and led by the Pokémon League Champion. Do you have what it takes to beat them?

Preparing for Battle

Once you step through that door, there's no backing out until you've defeated each of the Elite Four and the Pokémon League Champion. Proper preparation is essential!

Rules of the Elite Four

You'll have all the time you need to heal or rearrange your roster between Trainers, but you cannot return to the Pokémon Center—all of your healing will have to come from your Bag. Buy lots of cheap Revives and Hyper Potions for between-battle healing, and save the best stuff (Max Revives, Full Restores) for in-battle use.

Money		
₽110524	Poké Ball	₽ 200
	Great Ball	₽ 600
	Ultra Ball	₽1200
	Potion	₽ 300
	Super Potion	₽ 700
	Hyper Potion	₽1200
	Max Potion	₽2500

A device for catching wild Pokémon. It is thrown like a ball at the target. It is designed as a capsule system.

Boosting Your Troops

Now that you've reached the building that houses the Elite Four, you're free to use Fly to return here at any time. After you buy all the medicine you'll need, Fly to Veilstone City and spend the rest of your cash on stat-boosters like Calcium and Iron, and TMs that teach powerful moves. If your team still isn't strong enough, spend some time battling foes on Victory Road to level up your troops.

Money		
₽110524	Protein	₽9800
	Iron	₽9800
	Calcium	₽9800
	Zinc	₽9800
	Carbos	₽9800
	HP Up	₽9800
	CANCEL	

A nutritious drink for Pokémon. It raises the base Attack stat of a single Pokémon.

Picking the Right Team

Picking the right team is essential to beating the Elite Four. Your best Pokémon will surely include your starter and Dialgia or Palkia, but a few common Pokémon can also be very effective partners. Select the ones that add the most type variety to your team.

Luxray	Level 50+
Type:	Electric

Luxray can lower an opponent's Speed with moves or Paralyze, then use Electric- or Dark-type Flinch-inducing attacks.

Staraptor	Level 50+
Type:	Normal Flying

When Staraptor enters the battlefield, it will lower the opponent's Attack stat. Staraptor also has lots of quick-hitting moves.

Lucario	Level 50+
Type:	Fighting Steel

Lucario is great against foes who use Flinch attacks, since its ability will either protect it or boost its Speed when it Flinches.

Gastrodon	Level 50+
Type:	Water Ground

Gastrodon's Ground-type will protect it from Electric-type attacks. Use a TM to teach it a good Ground-type move like Earthquake.

Roserade	Level 50+
Type:	Grass Poison

Roserade has a Special Attack score high enough to KO foes in one shot, and the Speed necessary to strike first.

Rapidash	Level 50+
Type:	Fire

Fire-type Pokémon are rare in Sinnoh—if you didn't pick Chimchar as your starter you can't do much better than a trusty Rapidash.

Elite Four: Battle 1

Aaron

Recommended Move Types: Fire, Flying, Rock, Electric, Ground

Put a Fire-, Flying-, or Rock-type Pokémon at the head of your roster before you speak to Aaron. Even if that Pokémon is at a much lower level than Aaron's, it may manage to take down the first four Pokémon in his roster. The wild card is Drapion, whose Poison-and-Dark- type combo leaves it weak to only one thing: Ground-type attacks. If your starter is Torterra (Turtwig's Evolved form), don't send it out, or you'll walk into a bunch of Drapion's Ice- and Bug-type attacks. Gastrodon is much better at exploiting Drapion's weakness to Ground without exposing itself to dangerous attacks.

> The foe's DRAPION used Aerial Ace!

Dustox	Level 53	Flying-, Fire-, Rock-, and Psychic-type attacks should be able to take out Dustox in a single hit.
Type: Bug Poison		

Beautifly	Level 53	Rock-type attacks will deal quadruple damage to Bug-and-Flying-type Pokémon.
Type: Bug Flying		

Vespiquen	Level 54	Vespiquen's Pressure Ability will knock off an extra 2 PP each time you hit Vespiquen with a move, so don't waste any low-PP moves on this fight.
Type: Bug Flying		

Heracross	Level 54	Your Fire-type will do well against Heracross, but a Flying-type attack will deal the maximum possible damage.
Type: Bug Fighting		

Drapion	Level 57	A selection of Ice-, Bug-, and even Flying-type attacks gives Drapion many ways to trump its enemies.
Type: Poison Dark		

Elite Four: Battle 2

Bertha

Recommended Move Types: Grass, Water

This is a wonderful time to have a Grass-type at the head of your roster, since it can type-trump anything Bertha sends out. If your access to Grass-type attacks is limited, use Water-types against the part-Rock-type Pokémon, and Flying-types against Quagsire and Whiscash—they won't have a type advantage, but they'll at least be immune to Ground-type attacks like Earthquake. One of these foes will certainly kick up a sandstorm, so remember—your Pokémon will be immune to the damage if they're at least partially Rock-, Steel-, or Ground-types.

> The foe's HIPPOWDON used Stone Edge!

Quagsire	Level 55	Quagsire's strategy seems to be summoning a sandstorm and then stalling with defensive maneuvers.
Type: Water Ground		

Sudowoodo	Level 56	Sudowoodo's Special Defense is much lower than its Physical Defense, so choose your attack accordingly.
Type: Rock		

Golem	Level 56	A Grass- or Water-type attack can deal quadruple damage against Golem, so aim for a one-hit KO.
Type: Rock Ground		

Whiscash	Level 55	Whiscash has a move that can KO in one hit, but its accuracy is only 30%. Beat it quickly, just in case.
Type: Water Ground		

Hippowdon	Level 59	This can be a long fight—Hippowdon has good defensive stats that it can boost with moves, and it holds a Sitrus Berry.
Type: Ground		

Elite Four: Battle 3

Flint

Recommended Move Types: Electric, Fighting, Ground, Water

Water is usually the go-to type when you're facing Fire-type Pokémon, but not this time. Flint often begins the battle by using the Sunny Day move to switch the weather to sunlight for five turns, which will cut the power of Water-type moves in half for the duration of the battle. It also boosts the power of Fire-type moves, something you can turn to your own advantage by using Fire-type moves against Steelix, Drifblim, and Lopunny. When the sun is shining, rely on Rock- and Ground-type attacks to take down Rapidash, and Ground-, Flying-, or Psychic-type moves against Infernape.

The foe's RAPIDASH used Sunny Day!

| Rapidash | Level 58 | Rapidash uses the Sunny Day and Solarbeam combo for heavy damage; KO it before it can use the second move. |
| Type: | Fire | |

| Steelix | Level 57 | If the sun is shining, your Fire-type moves should do triple damage to Steelix. |
| Type: | Steel Ground | |

| Drifblim | Level 58 | Electric-, Ice-, Rock-, Ghost-, and Dark-type moves are effective against Drifblim's unique combination of types. |
| Type: | Ghost Flying | |

| Lopunny | Level 57 | Lopunny can defend itself from Special Attacks, which is all the more reason to attack with Fighting-type moves. |
| Type: | Normal | |

| Infernape | Level 61 | With Water-types weakened by the sun, rely on Ground-, Flying-, and Psychic-type attacks against Infernape. |
| Type: | Fire Fighting | |

Elite Four: Battle 4

Lucian

Recommended Move Types: Bug, Dark, Fire, Flying, Ghost

Lucian isn't being boastful—he really is the toughest of the four by far. Your Bug- and Dark-type moves are very effective against his Psychic-type roster, and fortunately, a lot of Pokémon know Dark-type moves, so non-Dark-type Pokémon like Luxray can also be very effective here. However, your best Fire-type will be equally important, since Lucian's Bronzong is the strongest Pokémon you've fought yet. If your Fire-type-user faints, bring it back with a Max Revive—no other type can put a dent in Bronzong. Use the moves that have the highest chance of causing a Burn condition, because Lucian will use plenty of items to restore Bronzong's HP.

The foe's BRONZONG used Psychic!

| Mr. Mime | Level 59 | Mr. Mime will set up long-term defensive moves like Light Screen, giving a boost to the Pokémon that follow. |
| Type: | Psychic | |

| Girafarig | Level 59 | Girafarig uses both Psychic- and Dark-type moves, so a Dark-type Pokémon will be a resilient defender. |
| Type: | Normal Psychic | |

| Medicham | Level 60 | Put your Dark-type away, because only Ghost- and Flying-type moves can trump Medicham. |
| Type: | Fighting Psychic | |

| Alakazam | Level 60 | Alakazam can restore HP with the Recover move, so keep it on the ropes with powerful physical attacks. |
| Type: | Psychic | |

| Bronzong | Level 63 | Bronzong levitates, leaving Fire as the only type that can trump it. With its high defensive stats, you'll need an edge. |
| Type: | Steel Psychic | |

Pokémon League Champion

Cynthia

Recommended Move Types: Electric, Fire, Flying, Grass, Ground, Ice

Your battle with Cynthia will begin as soon as you enter her room, so do all of your healing and saving in Lucian's room. She starts out strong with a Spiritomb, which is weak to absolutely nothing—just use your best moves from your strongest Pokémon (as long as they're not Normal-, Fighting-, or Psychic-types) or take the Spiritomb down gradually with Toxic. Most of Cynthia's Pokémon have only one or two weaknesses and know moves that trump the types that should theoretically trump them. When possible, surprise Cynthia by using type-trumping moves from a Pokémon that is not of the same type as the move it's using.

The foe's GARCHOMP used Giga Impact!

Spiritomb	Level 61	Spiritomb is weak to nothing and immune to Normal-, Fighting-, and Psychic-type attacks.
Type: Ghost Dark		

Roserade	Level 60	Unlike Cynthia's other Pokémon, Roserade has weaknesses to several types: Fire, Ice, Poison, Flying, Bug, Ghost, and Dark.
Type: Grass Poison		

Gastrodon	Level 60	Gastrodon's lone weakness is Grass, but it can deal heavy damage to Grass-types with the Poison-type Sludge Bomb.
Type: Water Ground		

Lucario	Level 63	Use Physical attacks of the Fire, Fighting, or Ground types to get around Lucario's high Special Defense.
Type: Fighting Steel		

Milotic	Level 63	Milotic will blast a Grass-type attacker with Ice Beam, so exploit its weakness to Electric-type moves instead.
Type: Water		

Garchomp	Level 66	Garchomp is weak to Ice- and Dragon-type moves. Dragons are also weak to it, so focus on Ice-type attacks if you can.
Type: Dragon Ground		

After the Elite Four and the Pokémon League Champion

Defeating Cynthia and becoming Pokémon League Champion isn't the end of your quest—it's a new beginning. As Pokémon League Champion you'll gain access to several new areas, and you'll find major changes and new Pokémon in several old areas. There's still so much to do!

The National Pokédex

So, since you're here, let me upgrade your Pokédex with the National Mode.

Load your game after winning the Pokémon League Championship, and you'll find yourself back home in Twinleaf Town. If you've battled every Trainer in the game, visited every optional area, and attempted to capture the three Mirage Pokémon, you will have at least partial entries for 149 Sinnoh Pokémon. Visit Cynthia's grandmother in Celestic Town to earn the final Sinnoh Pokédex entry (Palkia or Dialga—whichever isn't in your version of the game), then show your completed Pokédex to Prof. Rowan in Sandgem Town. When you do, a surprise visitor at Prof. Rowan's lab will upgrade your Sinnoh Pokédex to the National Pokédex, which has over 300 new entries to fill! To help you find these new Pokémon, Prof. Rowan will give you a Poké Radar that will reveal their positions in the tall grass.

Chris obtained the Poké Radar!

Battle Park

Hop on a ship in Snowpoint City to reach the as-yet-unexplored northeast landmass. There you can battle skilled Trainers to earn Battle Points that can be redeemed for prizes.

Pal Park

When you earn the National Pokédex, the Pal Park at the end of Route 221 will open for business. You can import Pokémon from your GBA games and capture them there.

Stark Mountain

The Battle Zone landmass is dominated by a huge volcano that puts Victory Road to shame. Battle Master Trainers and meet the Legendary Pokémon that lives at its heart!

Fullmoon Island

Visit Sailor Eldritch's home near his boat in Canalave City and speak to his family to trigger a new quest. Sailor Eldritch will then sail you to the new Fullmoon Island area.

Snowpoint Temple

The Snowpoint Temple offers a series of sliding ice puzzles. You may find a surprise at the end.

The Turnback Cave

You'll find the new Sendoff Spring area on the east side of Route 214 (south of Veilstone City). Search for a new Pokémon in the Turnback Cave at the spring's basin.

Sinnoh Pokédex and Data

Sinnoh Pokédex

Prof. Rowan is counting on you to collect data on all of Sinnoh's native Pokémon. Catch a glimpse of all 150 to unlock the National Pokédex.

Reading the Sinnoh Pokédex

The Sinnoh Pokédex List that follows will show you each of Sinnoh's 150 native Pokémon (plus optional #151, Manaphy) with all the information you need to find, evolve, or breed each one.

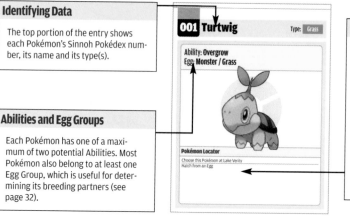

Identifying Data

The top portion of the entry shows each Pokémon's Sinnoh Pokédex number, its name and its type(s).

Abilities and Egg Groups

Each Pokémon has one of a maximum of two potential Abilities. Most Pokémon also belong to at least one Egg Group, which is useful for determining its breeding partners (see page 32).

Pokémon Locator

The Pokémon Locator displays information on how to acquire each Pokémon. If that Pokémon is available through Evolution, you'll find information about its pre-evolved form and conditions of Evolution. If it can be caught in the wild, its habitats will be listed along with which versions it appears in and at what times of day it appears— (M)orning, (D)ay, and (N)ight.

Sinnoh Pokédex vs. National Pokédex

When you've completed the entire Sinnoh Pokédex and become Pokémon League Champion, bring your Pokédex to Prof. Rowan in Sandgem Town. He will upgrade it to a National Pokédex that has room for every known Pokémon, many of which will begin to appear in the Sinnoh region. Your Sinnoh Pokémon will be renumbered in the National Pokédex, but if you prefer the Sinnoh Pokédex you can switch back to it with the tap of a button.

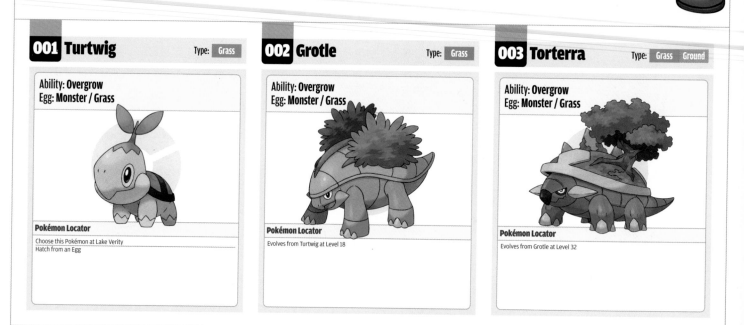

001 Turtwig — Type: Grass

Ability: **Overgrow**
Egg: **Monster / Grass**

Pokémon Locator
Choose this Pokémon at Lake Verity
Hatch from an Egg

002 Grotle — Type: Grass

Ability: **Overgrow**
Egg: **Monster / Grass**

Pokémon Locator
Evolves from Turtwig at Level 18

003 Torterra — Type: Grass Ground

Ability: **Overgrow**
Egg: **Monster / Grass**

Pokémon Locator
Evolves from Grotle at Level 32

004 Chimchar — Type: Fire

Ability: **Blaze**
Egg: **Field / Human-Like**

Pokémon Locator

Choose this Pokémon at Lake Verity
Hatch from an Egg

005 Monferno — Type: Fire Fighting

Ability: **Blaze**
Egg: **Field / Human-Like**

Pokémon Locator

Evolves from Chimchar at Level 14

006 Infernape — Type: Fire Fighting

Ability: **Blaze**
Egg: **Field / Human-Like**

Pokémon Locator

Evolves from Monferno at Level 36

007 Piplup — Type: Water

Ability: **Torrent**
Egg: **Water 1 / Field**

Pokémon Locator

Choose this Pokémon at Lake Verity
Hatch from an Egg

008 Prinplup — Type: Water

Ability: **Torrent**
Egg: **Water 1 / Field**

Pokémon Locator

Evolves from Piplup at Level 16

009 Empoleon — Type: Water Steel

Ability: **Torrent**
Egg: **Water 1 / Field**

Pokémon Locator

Evolves from Prinplup at Level 36

010 Starly — Type: Normal Flying

Ability: **Keen Eye**
Egg: **Flying**

Pokémon Locator

Route 201, Lake Verity—M: many / D: many / N: many
Routes 202 and 203—M: many / D: many / N: some
Route 204—M: some / D: many / N: some
Routes 209 and 212—M: some / D: some / N: some
Great Marsh (Areas 1-6)—M: some / D: some / N: none
Hatch from an Egg

011 Staravia — Type: Normal Flying

Ability: **Intimidate**
Egg: **Flying**

Pokémon Locator

Pokémon Mansion (Trophy Garden)—M: some / D: many / N: some
Route 209—M: some / D: some / N: some
Route 212, Sendoff Spring, Lake Valor, Valor Lakefront—M: some / D: some / N: few
Dual Slot (FR, LG, E)—Lake Verity: few
Great Marsh: varies day to day
Evolves from Starly at Level 14

012 Staraptor — Type: Normal Flying

Ability: **Intimidate**
Egg: **Flying**

Pokémon Locator

Evolves from Staravia at Level 34

013 Bidoof

Type: Normal

Ability: Simple / Unaware
Egg: Water 1 / Field

Pokémon Locator

Routes 201, 202, 205 (Eterna City Side), Lake Verity—M: many / D: many / N: many
Route 211 (Eterna City Side)—M: many / D: many / N: some
Routes 203, 204, 205 (Floaroma Town Side), 208, Valley Windworks—
M: some / D: some / N: some
Great Marsh (Area 5)—M: few / D: few / N: few
Great Marsh (Areas 1, 2, 3, 4, 6)—M: rare / D: rare / N: rare
Hatch from an Egg

014 Bibarel

Type: Normal Water

Ability: Simple / Unaware
Egg: Water 1 / Field

Pokémon Locator

Route 209, 210 (mist) Sendoff Spring, Lake Valor—many / D: many / N: many
Route 212 (rain), Lake Acuity—M: many / D: many / N: many
Routes 208, Great Marsh (Areas 1-6), Valor Lakefront—
M: some / D: some / N: some
Dual slot (FR, LG, E)—Lake Verity: few
Evolves from Bidoof at Level 15

015 Kricketot

Type: Bug

Ability: Shed Skin
Egg: Bug

Pokémon Locator

Route 206—M: some / D: none / N: none
Routes 202, 203, 204, 207—M: some / D: none / N: some
Hatch from an Egg

016 Kricketune

Type: Bug

Ability: Swarm
Egg: Bug

Pokémon Locator

Routes 210, 212, 212 (rain), 215, Pokémon Mansion (Trophy Garden)—M: some /
D: some / N: many
Route 206—M: some / D: some / N: some
Route 214, Valor Lakefront—M: few / D: few / N: some
Evolves from Kricketot at Level 10

017 Shinx

Type: Electric

Ability: Rivalry / Intimidate
Egg: Field

Pokémon Locator

Routes 202, 203, 204, Fuego Ironworks—M: many / D: many / N: many
Hatch from an Egg

018 Luxio

Type: Electric

Ability: Rivalry / Intimidate
Egg: Field

Pokémon Locator

Fuego Ironworks—M: some / D: some / N: some
Evolves from Shinx at Level 15

019 Luxray

Type: Electric

Ability: Rivalry / Intimidate
Egg: Field

Pokémon Locator

Evolves from Luxio at Level 30

020 Abra

Type: Psychic

Ability: Synchronize / Inner Focus
Egg: Human-Like

Pokémon Locator

Routes 203 and 215—M: some / D: some / N: some
Trade for Machop in Oreburgh City
Hatch from an Egg

021 Kadabra

Type: Psychic

Ability: Synchronize / Inner Focus
Egg: Human-Like

Pokémon Locator

Route 215—M: some / D: some / N: some
Victory Road (2F)—M: many / D: many / N: many
Evolves from Abra at Level 16

022 Alakazam
Type: Psychic

Ability: Synchronize / Inner Focus
Egg: Human-Like

Pokémon Locator

Evolves from Kadabra (trade Evolution)

023 Magikarp
Type: Water

Ability: Swift Swim
Egg: Water 2 / Dragon

Pokémon Locator

Routes 203, 204, 205 (Eterna City Side and Floaroma Town Side), 208, 209, 210 (mist), 212, 212 (rain), 213, 214, 218, 219, 220, 221, 222, 223, Ravaged Path, Lake Acuity, Celestic Town, Oreburgh Gate (B1), Iron Island, Lake Verity, Great Marsh (Areas 1, 2, 3, 4, 6), Fuego Ironworks, Valley Windworks, Victory Road (B1), Mt. Coronet (1F, 4F waterfall), Mt. Coronet (North–B1), Sunyshore City, Pastoria City, Eterna City, Twinleaf Town, Pokémon League, Canalave City, Lake Valor–
Old Rod: many / Good Rod: many
Trade for a Finneon on Route 226
Hatch from an Egg

024 Gyarados
Type: Water Flying

Ability: Intimidate
Egg: Water 2 / Dragon

Pokémon Locator

Routes 203, 204, 205 (Eterna City Side and Floaroma Town Side), 208, 209, 210 (mist), 212, 212 (rain), 213, 214, 218, 219, 220, 221, 222, 223, 224, 225, 226, 227, 229, 230, Ravaged Path, Lake Acuity, Sendoff Spring, Celestic Town, Oreburgh Gate (B1), Iron Island, Lake Verity, Fuego Ironworks, Valley Windworks, Victory Road (B1A, B2), Mt. Coronet (1F, 4F waterfall), Mt. Coronet (North–B1), Sunyshore City, Pastoria City, Eterna City, Twinleaf Town, Pokémon League, Canalave City, Resort Area, Lake Valor–Super Rod: many
Great Marsh (Areas 1, 2, 3, 4, 6)–Good Rod–few / Super Rod:few
Evolves from Magikarp at Level 20

025 Budew
Type: Grass Poison

Ability: Natural Cure / Poison Point
Egg: None

Pokémon Locator

Route 212–M: many / D: many / N: many
Route 204, Eterna Forest–M: some / D: some / N: some
Great Marsh (Areas 1-6)–M: some / D: some / N: none
Hatch from an Egg

026 Roselia
Type: Grass Poison

Ability: Natural Cure / Poison Point
Egg: Fairy / Grass

Pokémon Locator

Pokémon Mansion (Trophy Garden)–M: many / D: many / N: many
Routes 212, 212 (rain), 221, 224–M: some / D: some / N: some
Pearl Version–Route 224–M: some / D: some / N: some
Diamond Version–Route 229–M: some / D: some / N: some
Great Marsh: varies day to day
Evolves from Budew (Friendship Evolution between 4:00am and 8:00pm)
Hatch from an Egg

027 Roserade
Type: Grass Poison

Ability: Natural Cure / Poison Point
Egg: Fairy / Grass

Pokémon Locator

Evolves from Roselia (Shiny Stone)

028 Zubat
Type: Poison Flying

Ability: Inner Focus
Egg: Flying

Pokémon Locator

Ravaged Path, Oreburgh Gate (B1), Wayward Cave (1F, B1), Lost Tower (1F-5F)–M: many / D: many / N: many
Oreburgh Gate (1F), Oreburgh Mine (1F, B1), Iron Island (1F), Mt. Coronet (1F), Mt. Coronet (North–1F)–M: some / D: some / N: some
Routes 203, 204 (under and upper), 206, 207, 208, 209, 211 (Celestic Town Side and Eterna City Side), 216, 217, Acuity Lakefront–M: none / D: none / N: some
Ravaged Path, Oreburgh Gate (B1), Mt. Coronet (1F, 4F waterfall), Mt. Coronet (North–B1)–Surf: many

029 Golbat
Type: Poison Flying

Ability: Inner Focus
Egg: Flying

Pokémon Locator

Snowpoint Temple (1F, B1-B5), Turnback Cave–M: many / D: many / N: many
Iron Island (1F, B1/A, B1/B, B2/A, B2/B, B3), Victory Road (1F passage, B1/A, B1/B, B1/C, B2, 2F), Mt. Coronet (1F entrance, 2F, 3F, 4F, 4F small room, 4F waterfall, 5F, 6F), Mt. Coronet (North–1F passage, B1), Stark Mountain, Lost Tower (5F)–M: some / D: some/ N: some
Lost Tower (4F)–M: few / D: few / N: few
Lost Tower (3F)–M: rare / D: rare / N: rare
Route 227, Mt. Coronet (top), Stark Mountain–M: none / D: none / N: some
Victory Road (B1/A, B2)–Surf: many
Mt. Coronet (1F, 4F waterfall), Mt. Coronet (North–B1)–Surf: some
Oreburgh Gate (B1), Ravaged Path–Surf: few
Evolves from Zubat at Level 22

030 Crobat
Type: Poison Flying

Ability: Inner Focus
Egg: Flying

Pokémon Locator

Evolves from Golbat (Friendship Evolution)

031 Geodude
Type: Rock Ground

Ability: Rock Head / Sturdy
Egg: Mineral

Pokémon Locator

Pearl Version—Route 206—M: many / D: many / N: many
Routes 207 and 210, Ruin Maniac Cave, Oreburgh Gate (1F), Oreburgh Mine (1F, B1), Iron Island (1F), Maniac Tunnel—M: many / D: many / N: many
Route 215—M: many / D: many / N: many
Mt. Coronet (1F), Mt. Coronet (North—1F)—M: some / D: many / N: many
Diamond Version—Route 206—M: some / D: some / N: some
Route 211 (Eterna City Side), Route 214, Ravaged Path, Oreburgh Gate (B1), Wayward Cave (1F, B1), Valor Lakefront—M: some / D-some / N: some
Stark Mountain—M: few / D: few / N: few
Iron Island (B1/A, B1/B, B2/A, B2/B, B3)—M: rare / D: rare / N: rare
Hatch from an Egg

032 Graveler
Type: Rock Ground

Ability: Rock Head / Sturdy
Egg: Mineral

Pokémon Locator

Route 211 (Celestic Town Side), Iron Island (1F, B1/A, B1/B, B2/A, B2/B, B3), Mt. Coronet (1F entrance), Victory Road (1F, 1F passage, 2F)—M: many / D: many / N: many
Snowpoint Temple (1F, B1, B2, B3, B4, B5), Mt. Coronet (2F, 3F, 4F, 4F small room, 4F waterfall, 5F, 6F), Mt. Coronet (North—1F passage, B1)—M: some, / D: some / N: some
Route 216—M: few / D: few / N: few
Routes 214 and 227, Stark Mountain (outside), Valor Lakefront—M: some / D: some / N: few
Evolves from Geodude at Level 25

033 Golem
Type: Rock Ground

Ability: Rock Head / Sturdy
Egg: Mineral

Pokémon Locator

Evolves from Graveler (trade Evolution)

034 Onix
Type: Rock Ground

Ability: Rock Head / Sturdy
Egg: Mineral

Pokémon Locator

Iron Island (B2/A, B2/B, B3)—M: many / D: many / N: many
Snowpoint Temple (1F), Oreburgh Mine (1F, B1), Iron Island (1F, B1/A, B1/B), Victory Road (1F, 1F passage, 2F)—M: some / D: some / N: some
Snowpoint Temple (B1, B2, B3), Stark Mountain—M: few / D: few / N: few
Hatch from an Egg

035 Steelix
Type: Steel Ground

Ability: Rock Head / Sturdy
Egg: Mineral

Pokémon Locator

Iron Island (B2/B, B3), Victory Road (1F, 1F passage, 2F, B1, B1/A, B1/B, B1/C)—M: some / D: some / N: some
Snowpoint Temple (1F)—M: few / D: few / N: few
Evolves from Onix (trade Evolution while holding Metal Coat)

036 Cranidos
Type: Rock

Ability: Mold Breaker
Egg: Monster

Pokémon Locator

Diamond Version—turn in Skull Fossil at Oreburgh Mine Museum
Hatch from an Egg

037 Rampardos
Type: Rock

Ability: Mold Breaker
Egg: Monster

Pokémon Locator

Evolves from Cranidos at Level 30

038 Shieldon
Type: Rock Steel

Ability: Sturdy
Egg: Monster

Pokémon Locator

Pearl Version—turn in Armor Fossil at the Oreburgh Mine Museum
Hatch from an Egg

039 Bastiodon
Type: Rock Steel

Ability: Sturdy
Egg: Monster

Pokémon Locator

Evolves from Shieldon at Level 30

040 Machop — Type: Fighting

Ability: Guts / No Guard
Egg: Human-Like

Pokémon Locator

Route 207–M: many / D: many / N: some
Routes 208 and 210 (mist)–M: some / D: some / N: some
Mt. Coronet (1F), Mt. Coronet (North–1F)–M: many / D: many / N: many
Hatch from an Egg

041 Machoke — Type: Fighting

Ability: Guts / No Guard
Egg: Human-Like

Pokémon Locator

Routes 210 (mist), 211, 216, 217, 226, Acuity Lakefront, Mt. Coronet (1F entrance, 2F, 3F, 4F, 4F small room, 4F waterfall, 5F, 6F, top), Mt. Coronet (North–1F passage, B1), Stark Mountain–M: some / D: some / N: some
Victory Road (1F, 1F passage, B1, B1/A, B1/B, B1/C)–M: many / D: many / N: many
Route 225–M: few / D: few / N: few
Evolves from Machop at Level 28

042 Machamp — Type: Fighting

Ability: Guts / No Guard
Egg: Human-Like

Pokémon Locator

...es from Machoke (trade Evolution)

043 Psyduck — Type: Water

Ability: Damp / Cloud Nine
Egg: Water 1 / Field

Pokémon Locator

Route 208, Oreburgh Gate (B1)–M: many / D: many / N: many
Lake Acuity–M: many / D: many / N: many
Route 210 (mist), Lake Valor–M: some / D: some / N: some
Ravaged Path, Great Marsh (Areas 1, 2, 3, 4, 6)–M: few / D: few / N: few
Routes 203, 204, 205 (Eterna City Side), 208, 209, 210 (mist), 21...
Path, Lake Acuity, Celestic Town, Oreburgh Gate (B1), Lake Val...
Twinleaf Town, Lake Valor–Surf: many
Great Marsh (Areas 1, 2, 3, 4, 6)–Surf: few

044 Golduck — Type: Water

Ability: Damp / Cloud Nine
Egg: Water 1 / Field

Pokémon Locator

Routes 226, 230, Sendoff Spring–M: some / D: some / N: some
Route 225, Sendoff Spring, Resort Area–Surf–M: many / D: many / N: many
Routes 203, 204, 205 (Eterna City Side), 208, 209, 210 (mist), 212, 214, Lake Acuity, Celestic Town, Lake Verity, Eterna City, Twinleaf Town, Lake Valor–Surf: some
Oreburgh Gate (B1), Ravaged Path–Surf: few
Great Marsh: varies day to day
Evolves from Psyduck at Level 33

045 Burmy — Type: Bug

Ability: Shed Skin
Egg: Bug

Pokémon Locator

Honey Tree: Routes 205 (Eterna City Side and Floaroma Town Side), 206, 207, 208, 209, 210 (mist), 211 (Celestic Town Side), 212, 212 (rain), 213, 214, 215, 218, 221, 222, Floaroma Meadow, Fuego Ironworks, Valley Windworks, Eterna Forest
Hatch from an Egg

046 Wormadam — Type: Bug Grass

Ability: Anticipate
Egg: Bug

Pokémon Locator

Evolves from Burmy at Level 20 (Plant Cloak–female only)

046 Wormadam — Type: Bug Ground

Ability: Anticipate
Egg: Bug

Pokémon Locator

Evolves from Burmy at Level 20 (Sand Cloak–female only)

046 Wormadam — Type: Bug Steel

Ability: Anticipate
Egg: Bug

Pokémon Locator

Evolves from Burmy at Level 20 (Trash Cloak–female only)

047 Mothim
Type: Bug | Flying

Ability: Swarm
Egg: Bug

Pokémon Locator
Evolves from Burmy at Level 20 (male only)

048 Wurmple
Type: Bug

Ability: Shield Dust
Egg: Bug

Pokémon Locator
Eterna Forest—M; many / D: many / N: some
Honey Tree: Routes 205 (Eterna City Side and Floaroma Town Side), 206, 207, 208, 209, 210, 210 (mist), 211 (Celestic Town Side), 212, 212 (rain), 213, 214, 215, 218, 221, 222, Floaroma Meadow, Fuego Ironworks, Valley Windworks, Eterna Forest
Hatch from an Egg

049 Silcoon
Type: Bug

Ability: Shed Skin
Egg: Bug

Pokémon Locator
Diamond Version—Eterna Forest—M: some / D: some / N: some
Diamond Version—Honey Tree: Routes 205 (Eterna City Side and Floaroma Town Side), 206, 207, 208, 209, 210, 210 (mist), 211 (Celestic Town Side), 212, 212 (rain), 213, 214, 215, 218, 221, 222, Floaroma Meadow, Fuego Ironworks, Valley Windworks, Eterna Forest
Evolves from Wurmple at Level 7 (sometimes Evolves into Cascoon)

050 Beautifly
Type: Bug | Flying

Ability: Swarm
Egg: Bug

Pokémon Locator
Diamond Version—Route 230—M: some / D: some / N: some
Diamond Version—Route 244, Eterna Forest—M: few / D: few / N: few
Evolves from Silcoon at Level 10

051 Cascoon
Type: Bug

Ability: Shed Skin
Egg: Bug

Pokémon Locator
Pearl Version—Eterna Forest—M: some / D: some / N: some
Pearl Version—Honey Tree: Floaroma Meadow, Fuego Ironworks, Valley Windworks, Eterna Forest, Routes 205 (Eterna City Side and Floaroma Town Side), 206, 207, 208, 209, 210, 210 (mist), 211 (Celestic Town Side), 212, 212 (rain), 213, 214, 215, 218, 221, 222
Evolves from Wurmple at Level 7 (sometimes Evolves into Silcoon)

052 Dustox
Type: Bug | Poison

Ability: Shield Dust
Egg: Bug

Pokémon Locator
Pearl Version—Route 230—M: some / D: some / N: some
Pearl Version—Eterna Forest—M: few / D: few / N: few
Evolves from Cascoon at Level 10

053 Combee
Type: Bug | Flying

Ability: Honey Gather
Egg: Bug

Pokémon Locator
Honey Tree: Floaroma Meadow, Fuego Ironworks, Valley Windworks, Eterna Forest, Routes 205 (Eterna City Side and Floaroma Town Side), 206, 207, 208, 209, 210, 210 (mist), 211 (Celestic Town Side), 212, 212 (rain), 213, 214, 215, 218, 221, 222
Hatch from an Egg

054 Vespiquen
Type: Bug | Flying

Ability: Pressure
Egg: Bug

Pokémon Locator
Evolves from Combee at Level 21 (female only)

055 Pachirisu
Type: Electric

Ability: Run Away / Pickup
Egg: Field / Fairy

Pokémon Locator
Route 205 (Eterna City Side and Floaroma Town Side), Fuego Ironworks—M: some / D: some / N: some
Valley Windworks—M: many / D: many / N: many
Hatch from an Egg

056 Buizel Type: **Water**

Ability: Swift Swim
Egg: **Water 1 / Field**

Pokémon Locator

Routes 205 (Eterna City Side and Floaroma Town Side), 213, Valley Windworks−
M: many / D: many / N: many
Route 224−M: few / D: few / N: few
Hatch from an Egg

057 Floatzel Type: **Water**

Ability: Swift Swim
Egg: **Water 1 / Field**

Pokémon Locator

Route 218, Victory Road (B1/A), Fuego Ironworks−M: many / D: many / N: many
Routes 222, 224−M: some / D: some / N: many
Routes 213, 221, 230−M: some / D-some / N: some
Evolves from Buizel at Level 26

058 Cherubi Type: **Grass**

Ability: Chlorophyll
Egg: **Fairy / Grass**

Pokémon Locator

Honey Tree: Floaroma Meadow, Fuego Ironworks, Valley Windworks, Eterna
Forest, Routes 205 (Eterna City Side and Floaroma Town Side), 206, 207, 208, 209,
210, 210 (mist), 211 (Celestic Town Side), 212, 212 (rain), 213, 214, 215, 218, 221, 222
Hatch from an Egg

059 Cherrim Type: **Grass**

Ability: Flower Gift
Egg: **Fairy / Grass**

Pokémon Locator

Evolves from Cherubi at Level 25

060 Shellos Type: **Water**

Ability: Sticky Hold / Storm Drain
Egg: **Water 1 / Amorphous**

Pokémon Locator

Routes 205 (Floaroma Town Side), 213, Fuego Ironworks−
M: many / D: many / N: many
Routes 205 (Floaroma Town Side), 218, 221, Valley Windworks−
M: some / D: some / N: some
Route 224−M: rare / D: rare / N: rare
Hatch from an Egg

061 Gastrodon Type: **Water** **Ground**

Ability: Sticky Hold / Storm Drain
Egg: **Water 1 / Amorphous**

Pokémon Locator

Pearl Version−Route 221−M: many / D: many / N: many
Diamond Version−Route 222−M: many / D:many / N: many
Route 224−M: some / D: some / N: many
Route 218, Fuego Ironworks−M: some / D: some / N: some
Diamond Version−Route 221−M: some / D-some / N: some
Route 230−M: few / D: few / N: few
Evolves from Shellos at Level 30

062 Heracross Type: **Bug** **Fighting**

Ability: Swarm / Guts
Egg: **Bug**

Pokémon Locator

Honey Tree: Routes 205 (Eterna City Side and Floaroma Town Side), 206, 207, 208,
209, 210, 210 (mist), 211 (Celestic Town Side), 212, 212 (rain), 213, 214, 215, 218, 221,
222, Floaroma Meadow, Fuego Ironworks, Valley Windworks, Eterna Forest
Hatch from an Egg

063 Aipom Type: **Normal**

Ability: Run Away / Pickup
Egg: **Field**

Pokémon Locator

Honey Tree: Routes 205 (Eterna City Side and Floaroma Town Side), 206, 207,
208, 209, 210, 210 (mist), 211 (Celestic Town Side), 212, 212 (rain), 213, 214, 215,
218, 222, Floaroma Meadow, Fuego Ironworks, Valley Windworks, Eterna Forest
Hatch from an Egg

064 Ambipom Type: **Normal**

Ability: Technician / Pickup
Egg: **Field**

Pokémon Locator

Evolves from Aipom (learn Double Attack)

065 Drifloon   Type: Ghost Flying

Ability: **Aftermath / Unburden**
Egg: **Amorphous**

Pokémon Locator
Valley Windworks (Fridays only)
Hatch from an Egg

066 Drifblim   Type: Ghost Flying

Ability: **Aftermath / Unburden**
Egg: **Amorphous**

Pokémon Locator
Evolves from Drifloon at Level 28

067 Buneary   Type: Normal

Ability: **Run Away / Klutz**
Egg: **Field / Human-Like**

Pokémon Locator
Eterna Forest—M: some / D: some / N: some
Hatch from an Egg

068 Lopunny   Type: Normal

Ability: **Cute Charm / Klutz**
Egg: **Field / Human-Like**

Pokémon Locator
Evolves from Buneary (Friendship Evolution)

069 Gastly   Type: Ghost Poison

Ability: **Levitate**
Egg: **Amorphous**

Pokémon Locator
Old Chateau, Lost Tower (1F-5F)—M: many / D:many / N: many
Route 209—M: none / D-none / N: some
Hatch from an Egg

070 Haunter   Type: Ghost Poison

Ability: **Levitate**
Egg: **Amorphous**

Pokémon Locator
Turnback Cave—M: many / D: many / N: many
Dual Slot (R, S, E, FR, LG)—Old Chateau: few
Trade for Medicham in Snowpoint City
Evolves from Gastly at Level 25

071 Gengar   Type: Ghost Poison

Ability: **Levitate**
Egg: **Amorphous**

Pokémon Locator
Dual Slot (R, S, E, FR, LG)—Old Chateau (2F second room from the right): few
Evolves from Haunter (trade)

072 Misdreavus   Type: Ghost

Ability: **Levitate**
Egg: **Amorphous**

Pokémon Locator
Pearl Version—Eterna Forest, Lost Tower (1F-5F)—M: none / D: none / N: some
Hatch from an Egg

073 Mismagius   Type: Ghost

Ability: **Levitate**
Egg: **Amorphous**

Pokémon Locator
Evolves from Misdreavus (Dusk Stone)

074 Murkrow Type: Dark Flying

Ability: **Insomnia / Super Luck**
Egg: **Flying**

Pokémon Locator

Diamond Version—Eterna Forest, Lost Tower (1F-5F)—M: none / D: none / N: some
Hatch from an Egg

---

075 Honchkrow Type: Dark Flying

Ability: **Insomnia / Super Luck**
Egg: **Flying**

Pokémon Locator

Evolves from Murkrow (Dusk Stone)

---

076 Glameow Type: Normal

Ability: **Limber / Own Tempo**
Egg: **Field**

Pokémon Locator

Pearl Version—Routes 218 and 222—M: some / D: some / N: some
Hatch from an Egg

---

077 Purugly Type: Normal

Ability: **Thick Fat / Own Tempo**
Egg: **Field**

Pokémon Locator

Pearl Version—Routes 222 and 229—M: some / D: some / N: some
Evolves from Glameow at Level 38

---

078 Goldeen Type: Water

Ability: **Swift Swim / Water Veil**
Egg: **Water 2**

Pokémon Locator

Routes 203, 204, 209, 212, 214, Lake Acuity, Lake Verity, Twinleaf Town, Lake
Valor, Sendoff Spring—Good Rod: some
Hatch from an Egg

---

079 Seaking Type: Water

Ability: **Swift Swim / Water Veil**
Egg: **Water 2**

Pokémon Locator

Routes 203, 204, 209, 212, 214, Lake Acuity, Sendoff Spring, Lake Verity, Twinleaf
Town, Resort Area, Lake Valor—Super Rod: some
Evolves from Goldeen at Level 33

---

080 Barboach Type: Water Ground

Ability: **Oblivious / Anticipate**
Egg: **Water 2**

Pokémon Locator

Routes 205 (Eterna City Side), 208, 210 (mist), 212 (rain), 227, 228, Ravaged Path,
Celestic Town, Oreburgh Gate (B1), Great Marsh (Areas 1, 2, 3, 4, 6), Mt Coronet
(1F, 4F Waterfall), Mt. Coronet (North—B1), Eterna City—Good Rod: some

---

081 Whiscash Type: Water Ground

Ability: **Oblivious / Anticipate**
Egg: **Water 2**

Pokémon Locator

Great Marsh (Areas 1, 2, 3, 4, 6)—Super Rod: many
Routes 205 (Eterna City Side), 208, 210 (mist), 212 (rain), 227, 228, Ravaged Path,
Oreburgh Gate (B1), Mt. Coronet (1F), Mt. Coronet (North—B1), Eterna City—
Super Rod: some
Celestic Town—Super Rod: few
Evolves from Barboach at Level 30

---

082 Chingling Type: Psychic

Ability: **Levitate**
Egg: **None**

Pokémon Locator

Route 211 (Eterna City Side and Celestic Town Side), Lake Acuity, Mt. Coronet (1F,
1F entrance, 2F, 3F, 4F small room, 4F waterfall, top), Mt. Coronet (North—1F, 1F
passage, B1), Lake Valor—M: some / D: some / N: some
Mt. Coronet (4F)—M: few / D: few / N: few
Hatch from an Egg

083 Chimecho — Type: Psychic

Ability: Levitate
Egg: Amorphous

Pokémon Locator

Sendoff Spring, Mt. Coronet (5F, 6F)—M: some / D: some / N: some
Mt. Coronet (4F)—M: few / D: few / N: few
Evolves from Chingling (Friendship Evolution between 8:00pm and 4:00am)
Hatch from an Egg

084 Stunky — Type: Poison Dark

Ability: Stench / Aftermath
Egg: Field

Pokémon Locator

Diamond Version—Route 206—M: many / D: many / N: many
Diamond Version—Routes 214 and 221—M: some / D: some / N: some
Hatch from an Egg

085 Skuntank — Type: Poison Dark

Ability: Stench / Aftermath
Egg: Field

Pokémon Locator

Diamond Version—Routes 221 and 225—M: some / D: some / N: some
Evolves from Stunky at Level 34

086 Meditite — Type: Fighting Psychic

Ability: Pure Power
Egg: Human-Like

Pokémon Locator

Route 211 (Celestic Town Side)—M: many / D: many / N: many
Routes 210 (mist), 211 (Eterna City Side)—M: many / D: many / N: some
Routes 208 and 216, Mt. Coronet (1F), Mt. Coronet (North—1F passage, B1)—M: some / D: some / N: some
Route 217, Acuity Lakefront—M: some / D: some / N: none
Hatch from an Egg

087 Medicham — Type: Fighting Psychic

Ability: Pure Power
Egg: Human-Like

Pokémon Locator

Route 217, Acuity Lakefront, Victory Road (1F, 1F passage, 2F, B1/A, B1/B, B1/C), Mt. Coronet (1F entrance, 2F, 3F, 4F, 4F small room, 4F waterfall, 5F, 6F, top)—M: some / D: some / N: some
Evolves from Meditite at Level 37

088 Bronzor — Type: Steel Psychic

Ability: Levitate / Heat Proof
Egg: Mineral

Pokémon Locator

Wayward Cave (1F, B1)—M: many / D: many / N: many
Route 206—M: some / D: some / N: some
Mt Coronet (2F, 3F), Turnback Cave—M: few / D: few / N: few
Hatch from an Egg

089 Bronzong — Type: Steel Psychic

Ability: Levitate / Heat Proof
Egg: Mineral

Pokémon Locator

Turnback Cave—M: many, D: many, N: many)
Mt Coronet (2F, 3F, 4F, 4F small room, 4F waterfall, 5F, 6F)—M: some / D: some / N: some
Mt. Coronet (1F entrance, top)—M: few / D: few / N: few
Evolves from Bronzor at Level 33

090 Ponyta — Type: Fire

Ability: Run Away / Flash Fire
Egg: Field

Pokémon Locator

Route 210—M: many / D: many / N: many
Routes 206, 214, 215—M: many / D: many / N: some
Route 211 (Eterna City Side)—M: some / D: some / N: some
Route 211 (Celestic Town Side)—M: some / D: some / N: few
Hatch from an Egg

091 Rapidash — Type: Fire

Ability: Run Away / Flash Fire
Egg: Field

Pokémon Locator

Evolves from Ponyta at Level 40

092 Bonsly
Type: **Rock**

Ability: Sturdy / Rock Head
Egg: None

Pokémon Locator

Pearl Version–Routes 209, 210–M: some / D: few / N: few
Diamond Version–Appears randomly when you talk to the master of the Pokémon Mansion on Route 212: some
Hatch from an Egg

093 Sudowoodo
Type: **Rock**

Ability: Sturdy / Rock Head
Egg: Mineral

Pokémon Locator

Pearl Version–Routes 214 and 221–M: some / D: some / N: some
Evolves from Bonsly (learn Mimic)
Hatch from an Egg

094 Mime Jr.
Type: **Psychic**

Ability: Soundproof / Filter
Egg: None

Pokémon Locator

Diamond Version–Routes 209 and 210–M: some / D: few / N: few
Pearl Version–Appears randomly if you talk to the master of the Pokémon Mansion on Route 212: some
Hatch from an Egg

095 Mr. Mime
Type: **Psychic**

Ability: Soundproof / Filter
Egg: Human-Like

Pokémon Locator

Diamond Version–Routes 218 and 222–M: some / D: some / N: some
Evolves from Mime Jr. (learn Mimic)
Hatch from an Egg

096 Happiny
Type: **Normal**

Ability: Natural Cure / Serene Grace
Egg: None

Pokémon Locator

Appears randomly when you talk to the master of the Pokémon Mansion on Route 212: some
Hearthome City (receive an Egg)
Hatch from an Egg

097 Chansey
Type: **Normal**

Ability: Natural Cure / Serene Grace
Egg: Fairy

Pokémon Locator

Routes 209, 210–M: few / D: few / N: few
Appears randomly when you talk to the master of the Pokémon Mansion on Route 212: some
Evolves from Happiny (level-up with Oval Stone between 4:00am and 8:00pm)
Hatch from an Egg

098 Blissey
Type: **Normal**

Ability: Natural Cure / Serene Grace
Egg: Fairy

Pokémon Locator

Evolves from Chansey (Friendship Evolution)

099 Cleffa
Type: **Normal**

Ability: Cute Charm / Magic Guard
Egg: None

Pokémon Locator

Mt. Coronet (1F), Mt. Coronet (North–1F)–M: some / D: few / N: few
Appears randomly when you talk to the master of the Pokémon Mansion on Route 212: some
Hatch from an Egg

100 Clefairy
Type: **Normal**

Ability: Cute Charm / Magic Guard
Egg: Fairy

Pokémon Locator

Mt Coronet (1F entrance, 2F, 3F, 4F, 4F small room, 4F waterfall, 5F, 6F), Mt Coronet (North–1F passage, B1)–M: some / D: some / N: some
Mt Coronet (top)–M: few / D: few / N: few
Appears randomly when you talk to the master of the Pokémon Mansion on Route 212: some
Evolves from Cleffa (Friendship Evolution)

101 Clefable
Type: Normal

Ability: Cute Charm / Magic Guard
Egg: Fairy

Pokémon Locator
Evolves from Clefairy (Moon Stone)

102 Chatot
Type: Normal Flying

Ability: Keen Eye / Tangled Feet
Egg: Flying

Pokémon Locator
Routes 222 and 224—M: some / D: some / N: none
Trade for Buizel in Eterna City
Hatch from an Egg

103 Pichu
Type: Electric

Ability: Static
Egg: None

Pokémon Locator
Pokémon Mansion (Trophy Garden)—M: many / D: some / N: some
Hatch from an Egg

104 Pikachu
Type: Electric

Ability: Static
Egg: Field / Fairy

Pokémon Locator
Pokémon Mansion (Trophy Garden)—M: some D: some / N: some
Evolves from Pichu (Friendship Evolution)

105 Raichu
Type: Electric

Ability: Static
Egg: Field / Fairy

Pokémon Locator
Evolves from Pikachu (Thunderstone)

106 Hoothoot
Type: Normal Flying

Ability: Insomnia / Keen Eye
Egg: Flying

Pokémon Locator
Route 210 (mist), 211 (Eterna City Side), Great Marsh (Areas 1-6)—
M: none / D: none / N: some
Hatch from an Egg

107 Noctowl
Type: Normal Flying

Ability: Insomnia / Keen Eye
Egg: Flying

Pokémon Locator
Routes, 210 (mist), 211 (Celestic Town Side), 216, 217, Sendoff Spring, Lake Acuity,
Acuity Lakefront, Great Marsh (Areas 1 and 2), Mt. Coronet (top), Lake Valor—
M: none / D: none / N: some
Evolves from Hoothoot at Level 20

108 Spiritomb
Type: Ghost Dark

Ability: Pressure
Egg: Amorphous

Pokémon Locator
Route 209 (use Old Keystone at Route 209 after talking to 32 people in The
Underground)
Hatch from an Egg

109 Gible
Type: Dragon Ground

Ability: Sand Veil
Egg: Monster / Dragon

Pokémon Locator
Wayward Cave (B1)—M: some / D: some / N: some
Hatch from an Egg

110 Gabite — Type: Dragon Ground

Ability: **Sand Veil**
Egg: **Monster / Dragon**

Pokémon Locator

Evolves from Gible at Level 24

111 Garchomp — Type: Dragon Ground

Ability: **Sand Veil**
Egg: **Monster / Dragon**

Pokémon Locator

Evolves from Gabite at Level 48

112 Munchlax — Type: Normal

Ability: **Pickup / Thick Fat**
Egg: **None**

Pokémon Locator

Honey Tree: Routes 205 (Floaroma Town Side), 206, 207, 208, 209, 210, 210 (mist), 211 (Celestic Town Side), 212, 212 (rain), 213, 214, 215, 218, 221, 222, Floaroma Meadow, Valley Windworks, Eterna Forest
Hatch from an Egg

113 Snorlax — Type: Normal

Ability: **Immunity / Thick Fat**
Egg: **Monster**

Pokémon Locator

Evolves from Munchlax (Friendship Evolution)
Hatch from an Egg

114 Unown — Type: Psychic

Ability: **Levitate**
Egg: **None**

Pokémon Locator

Solaceon Ruins—M: many / D: many / N: many

115 Riolu — Type: Fighting

Ability: **Steadfast / Inner Focus**
Egg: **None**

Pokémon Locator

Receive an Egg at Iron Island (B2/B)
Hatch from an Egg

116 Lucario — Type: Fighting Steel

Ability: **Steadfast / Inner Focus**
Egg: **Field / Human-Like**

Pokémon Locator

Evolves from Riolu (Friendship Evolution between 4:00am and 8:00pm)

117 Wooper — Type: Water Ground

Ability: **Damp / Water Absorb**
Egg: **Water 1 / Field**

Pokémon Locator

Route 212 (rain)—M: many / D: Many / N: many
Great Marsh (Areas 1-6)—M: some / D: some / N: some
Route 212 (rain), Great Marsh (Areas 1, 2, 3, 4, 6)—Surf: many
Hatch from an Egg

118 Quagsire — Type: Water Ground

Ability: **Damp / Water Absorb**
Egg: **Water 1 / Field**

Pokémon Locator

Great Marsh (Areas 1-6)—M: some / D: some / N: some
Route 212 (rain)—Surf: some
Great Marsh (Areas 1, 2, 3, 4, 6)—Surf: few
Evolves from Wooper at Level 20

119 Wingull
Type: Water Flying

Ability: Keen Eye
Egg: Water 1 / Flying

Pokémon Locator

Routes 213, 218, 221, 222, Fuego Ironworks—M: some / D: some / N: some
Routes 205 (Floaroma Town Side), 213, 218, 219, 220, 221, 222, 229, Iron Island,
Fuego Ironworks, Valley Windworks, Pastoria City, Canalave City—Surf: many

120 Pelipper
Type: Water Flying

Ability: Keen Eye
Egg: Water 1 / Flying

Pokémon Locator

Routes 223, 224, 226, 229, 230, Canalave City, Sunyshore City, Pokémon League—
Surf: many
Routes 205 (Floaroma Town Side), 213, 218, 219, 220, 221, 222, Iron Island, Fuego
Ironworks, Valley Windworks, Pastoria City, Canalave City—Surf: few
Evolves from Wingull at Level 25

121 Girafarig
Type: Normal Psychic

Ability: Inner Focus / Early Bird
Egg: Field

Pokémon Locator

Valor Lakefront—M: many / D: many / N: many
Route 214—M: some / D: some / N: some
Hatch from an Egg

122 Hippopotas
Type: Ground

Ability: Sand Stream
Egg: Field

Pokémon Locator

Ruin Maniac Cave—M: few / D: few / N: few
Maniac Tunnel—M: some / D: some / N: some
Hatch from an Egg

123 Hippowdon
Type: Ground

Ability: Sand Stream
Egg: Field

Pokémon Locator

Route 228—M: some / D: some / N: some
Evolves from Hippopotas at Level 34

124 Azurill
Type: Normal

Ability: Thick Fat / Huge Power
Egg: None

Pokémon Locator

Great Marsh (Area 5)—M: few / D: few / N: few
Great Marsh (Areas 1, 2, 3, 4, 6)—M: rare / D: rare / N: rare
Appears randomly when you talk to the master of the Pokémon Mansion on
Route 212—some
Hatch from an Egg

125 Marill
Type: Water

Ability: Thick Fat / Huge Power
Egg: Water 1 / Fairy

Pokémon Locator

Great Marsh (Areas 1-6)—M: some / D: some / N: some
Great Marsh (Areas 1, 2, 3, 4, 6)—Surf: many
Appears randomly when you talk to the master of the Pokémon Mansion on
Route 212—some
Evolves from Azurill (Friendship Evolution)
Hatch from an Egg

126 Azumarill
Type: Water

Ability: Thick Fat / Huge Power
Egg: Water 1 / Fairy

Pokémon Locator

Evolves from Marill at Level 18

127 Skorupi
Type: Poison Bug

Ability: Battle Armor / Sniper
Egg: Bug / Water 3

Pokémon Locator

Great Marsh: varies day to day
Hatch from an Egg

128 Drapion　　Type: Poison Dark

Ability: Battle Armor / Sniper
Egg: Bug / Water 3

Pokémon Locator

Great Marsh (varies day to day)
Evolves from Skorupi at Level 40

129 Croagunk　　Type: Poison Fighting

Ability: Anticipate / Dry Skin
Egg: Human-Like

Pokémon Locator

Great Marsh: varies day to day
Hatch from an Egg

130 Toxicroak　　Type: Poison Fighting

Ability: Anticipate / Dry Skin
Egg: Human-Like

Pokémon Locator

Great Marsh: varies day to day
Evolves from Croagunk at Level 37

131 Carnivine　　Type: Grass

Ability: Levitate
Egg: Grass

Pokémon Locator

Great Marsh (varies day to day)
Hatch from an Egg

132 Remoraid　　Type: Water

Ability: Hustle / Sniper
Egg: Water 1 / Water 2

Pokémon Locator

Routes 213, 222, 223, Sunyshore City, Pastoria City, Pokémon League–
Good Rod: some
Hatch from an Egg

133 Octillery　　Type: Water

Ability: Suction Cups / Sniper
Egg: Water 1 / Water 2

Pokémon Locator

Routes 213, 222, 224, Sunyshore City, Pastoria City, Pokémon League–
Super Rod: some
Routes 223 and 230–Super Rod: few
Evolves from Remoraid at Level 25

134 Finneon　　Type: Water

Ability: Swift Swim / Storm Drain
Egg: Water 2

Pokémon Locator

Routes 205 (Floaroma Town Side), 218, 219, 220, 221, Iron Island, Fuego
Ironworks, Valley Windworks, Canalave City–Good Rod: some

135 Lumineon　　Type: Water

Ability: Swift Swim / Storm Drain
Egg: Water 2

Pokémon Locator

Routes 205 (Floaroma Town Side), 218, 219, 221, Iron Island, Fuego Ironworks,
Valley Windworks, Canalave City–Super Rod: some
Route 220–Super Rod: few
Evolves from Finneon at Level 31

136 Tentacool　　Type: Water Poison

Ability: Clear Body / Liquid Ooze
Egg: Water 3

Pokémon Locator

Routes 205 (Floaroma Town Side), 213, 218, 219, 220, 221, 222, Iron Island, Fuego
Ironworks, Valley Windworks, Pastoria City, Canalave City–Surf: many
Hatch from an Egg

137 Tentacruel
Type: Water | Poison

Ability: Clear Body / Liquid Ooze
Egg: Water 3

Pokémon Locator

Routes 223, 224, Sunyshore City, Pokémon League–Surf: many
Routes 205 (Floaroma Town Side), 213, 218, 219, 220, 221, 222, 226, 230, Iron Island, Fuego Ironworks, Valley Windworks, Pastoria City, Canalave City–Surf: few
Evolves from Tentacool at Level 30

138 Feebas
Type: Water

Ability: Swift Swim
Egg: Water 1 / Dragon

Pokémon Locator

Mt. Coronet (North–B1): there are four places to fish, use any Rod to catch
Hatch from an Egg

139 Milotic
Type: Water

Ability: Marvel Scale
Egg: Water 1 / Dragon

Pokémon Locator

Evolves from Feebas (high beauty)

140 Mantyke
Type: Water | Flying

Ability: Swift Swim / Water Absorb
Egg: None

Pokémon Locator

Route 223, Sunyshore City–Surf: some
Hatch from an Egg

141 Mantine
Type: Water | Flying

Ability: Swift Swim / Water Absorb
Egg: Water 1

Pokémon Locator

Evolves from Mantyke (Level-up when Remoraid is in your party)
Hatch from an Egg

142 Snover
Type: Grass | Ice

Ability: Snow Warning
Egg: Monster / Grass

Pokémon Locator

Routes 216, 217, Acuity Lakefront, Mt. Coronet (top)–M: some / D: some / N: some
Hatch from an Egg

143 Abomasnow
Type: Grass | Ice

Ability: Snow Warning
Egg: Monster / Grass

Pokémon Locator

Mt. Coronet (top)–M: some / D: some / N: some
Evolves from Snover at Level 40

144 Sneasel
Type: Dark | Ice

Ability: Inner Focus / Keen Eye
Egg: Field

Pokémon Locator

Snowpoint Temple (1F, B1, B2, B3, B4, B5)–M: many / D: many / N: many
Routes 216, 217, Lake Acuity, Acuity Lakefront–M: some / D: some / N: some
Hatch from an Egg

145 Weavile
Type: Dark | Ice

Ability: Pressure
Egg: Field

Pokémon Locator

Evolves from Sneasel (level-up between 8:00pm and 4:00am while holding Razor Claw)

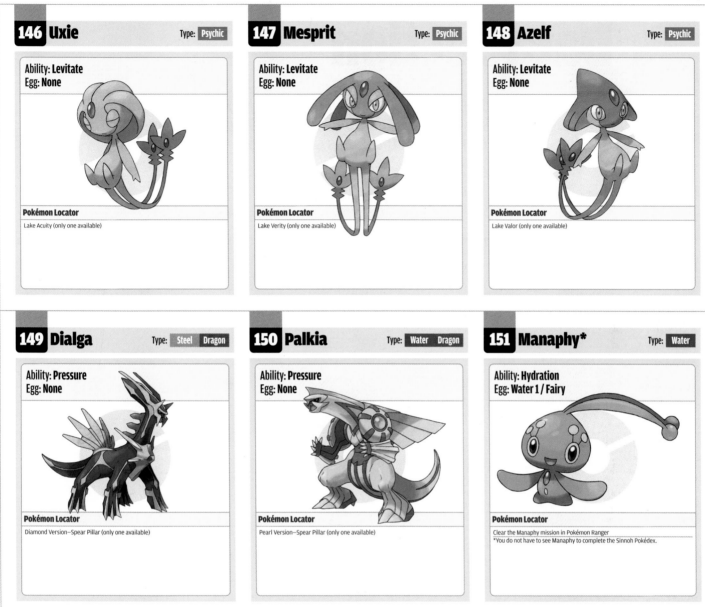

146 Uxie
Type: **Psychic**

Ability: Levitate
Egg: None

Pokémon Locator

Lake Acuity (only one available)

147 Mesprit
Type: **Psychic**

Ability: Levitate
Egg: None

Pokémon Locator

Lake Verity (only one available)

148 Azelf
Type: **Psychic**

Ability: Levitate
Egg: None

Pokémon Locator

Lake Valor (only one available)

149 Dialga
Type: **Steel** **Dragon**

Ability: Pressure
Egg: None

Pokémon Locator

Diamond Version–Spear Pillar (only one available)

150 Palkia
Type: **Water** **Dragon**

Ability: Pressure
Egg: None

Pokémon Locator

Pearl Version–Spear Pillar (only one available)

151 Manaphy*
Type: **Water**

Ability: Hydration
Egg: Water 1 / Fairy

Pokémon Locator

Clear the Manaphy mission in Pokémon Ranger
*You do not have to see Manaphy to complete the Sinnoh Pokédex.

Data Section

Having trouble keep tracking of the several thousand items, moves, and abilities in Pokémon Diamond and Pearl? You'll find complete data on every one of them on the pages that follow.

Items Adamant Orb – Green Scarf

The letters following an item's price denote the following: c=coins, bp=Battle Points. An asterisk (*) indicates a hidden item that can be detected with the Dowsing Machine app.

Item	Description	Location	Price
Adamant Orb	Boosts the power of Dialga's Dragon- and Steel-type moves	Spear Pillar (Diamond version only)	–
Amulet Coin	Doubles a battle's prize money if the holding Pokémon joins in	Amity Square	–
Armor Fossil	Can be changed into Shieldon at the Oreburgh Mining Museum	The Underground (Pearl version only)	–
Big Mushroom	A large and rare mushroom; sells for a high price	Wild Paras*	2500
Big Pearl	A quite-large pearl that sparkles in a pretty silver color; sells for a high price	Victory Road/Wild Gulpin, Shellder, Clamperl*	3750
Big Root	Boosts the power of HP-stealing moves to let the holder recover more HP	Route 214	–
Black Belt	A belt that boosts determination and Fighting-type moves	Route 221	–
Black Flute	Its melody makes wild Pokémon less likely to appear	Trade from Ruby, Sapphire, or Emerald version	–
Black Sludge	Gradually restores the HP of Poison-type Pokémon during battle; it inflicts damage on all other types	Wild Croagunk, Toxicroak	–
Blackglasses	A shady-looking pair of glasses that boosts Dark-type moves	Celestic Town (10:00am-7:59pm)	–
Blue Scarf	Boosts the "Beauty" aspect of the holder in a Super Contest	Pastoria City	–
Blue Shard	A small blue shard; 10 can be exchanged for TM18 (Rain Dance) on Route 212	The Underground	–
Bright Powder	Casts a tricky glare that raises Evasiveness	Battle Park	48bp
Charcoal	A combustible fuel that boosts the power of Fire-type moves	Route 227	–
Choice Band	Boosts Attack x1.5, but allows the use of only one kind of move	Battle Park	48bp
Choice Scarf	Boosts Speed x1.5, but allows the use of only one kind of move	Battle Park	48bp
Choice Specs	Boost Special Attack x1.5, but allows the use of only one kind of move	Celestic Town (4:00am-9:59pm)	–
Claw Fossil	Can be changed into Anorith at the Oreburgh Mining Museum	The Underground	–
Cleanse Tag	Helps keep wild Pokémon away if the holder is the first one in the party	Lost Tower	–
Damp Mulch	Causes the soil to dry slower; slows the growth of berries	Route 208	200
Damp Rock	Extends the duration of the move Rain Dance used by the holder	The Underground	–
Dawn Stone	A peculiar stone that makes certain species of Pokémon evolve	Mt. Coronet/Pickup	–
Deepseascale	Raises Clamperl's Special Defense stat x2; evolves Clamperl to Gorebyss (during trade)	Wild Relicanth, Chinchou, Lanturn	–
Deepseatooth	Raises Clamperl's Special Attack stat x2; evolves Clamperl to Huntail (during trade)	Wild Carvanha, Sharpedo	–
Destiny Knot	A long, thin, bright red string; if the holder becomes infatuated, the foe does too	Route 224	–
Dome Fossil	Can be changed into Kabuto at the Oreburgh Mining Museum	The Underground	–
Draco Plate	A stone tablet that boosts the power of Dragon-type moves	The Underground*	–
Dragon Fang	A hard and sharp fang that ups the power of Dragon-type moves	Wild Bagon	–
Dragon Scale	A thick and tough scale; evolves Seadra during a trade	Wild Dratini, Dragonair, Seadra, Horsea	–
Dread Plate	A stone tablet that boosts the power of Dark-type moves	Old Chateau, The Underground	–
Dubious Disc	A transparent device overflowing with dubious data; evolves Porygon2 during a trade	Route 225	–
Dusk Stone	A peculiar stone that makes certain species of Pokémon evolve	Galactic Warehouse, Victory Road/Pickup	–
Earth Plate	A stone tablet that boosts the power of Ground-type moves	Oreburgh Gate, The Underground	–
Electirizer	Packed with a tremendous amount of electric energy; evolves Electabuzz during a trade	Wild Elekid (more common in Pearl version)	–
Escape Rope	Use it to escape instantly from a cave or a dungeon.	Pokémart (once you have one badge), Oreburgh Mine, Wayward Cave, Iron Island, Mt. Coronet, Stark Mountain/Pickup*	550
Everstone	The Pokémon holding this peculiar stone is prevented from evolving	Snowpoint City, The Underground/Wild Geodude, Graveler	–
Exp. Share	The holder gets a share of a battle's Exp. Points without battling	Eterna City	–
Expert Belt	A well-worn belt that slightly boosts the power of supereffective moves	Route 221	–
Fire Stone	A peculiar stone that makes certain species of Pokémon evolve	Fuego Ironworks, The Underground	–
Fist Plate	A stone tablet that boosts the power of Fighting-type moves	Route 215, The Underground	–
Flame Orb	A bizarre orb that inflicts a burn on the holder in battle	Battle Park	16bp
Flame Plate	A stone tablet that boosts the power of Fire-type moves	The Underground*	–
Focus Band	The holder may endure one potential KO attack, leaving 1 HP	Battle Park	48bp
Focus Sash	Prevents a Pokémon from Fainting when HP is full	Route 221, Battle Park	48bp
Full Incense	Holder always attacks after foe	Veilstone City	–
Gooey Mulch	Put on soft soil to up the number of times new plants can grow where mature plants withered	Route 208	200
Green Scarf	Boosts the "Smart" aspect of the holder in a Super Contest	Pastoria City	–

Items (continued) Green Shard – Quick Powder

The letters following an item's price denote the following: c=coins, bp=Battle Points. An asterisk (*) indicates a hidden item that can be detected with the Dowsing Machine app.

Item	Description	Location	Price
Green Shard	A small green shard; 10 can be exchanged for TM07 (Hail) on Route 212	The Underground	–
Grip Claw	Extends the duration of multiturn attacks like Bind and Wrap	Wayward Cave/Wild Sneasel	–
Growth Mulch	Speeds up the growth of berries; it also dries the soil faster	Route 208	200
Hard Stone	An unbreakable stone that ups the power of Rock-type moves	The Underground/Wild Aron, Corsola, Nosepass	–
Heart Scale	Give to the Move Tutor in Pastoria City to teach a Pokémon a move	The Underground/Wild Luvdisc*	–
Heat Rock	Extends the duration of the move Sunny Day used by the holder	The Underground	–
Helix Fossil	Can be changed into Omanyte at the Oreburgh Mining Museum	The Underground	–
Honey	Attracts wild Pokémon when used in tall grass or caves; lures special Pokémon when spread on golden trees	Floaroma Town, Route 209, 218, 221, 222, Eterna Forest, Great Marsh/Wild Combee*	100
Icicle Plate	A stone tablet that boosts the power of Ice-type moves	Route 217, The Underground	–
Icy Rock	Extends the duration of the move Hail used by the holder	The Underground	–
Insect Plate	A stone tablet that boosts the power of Bug-type moves	The Underground*	–
Iron Ball	Cuts Speed; makes Flying-type and levitating holders susceptible to Ground-type moves	Iron Island, The Underground	–
Iron Plate	A stone tablet that boosts the power of Steel-type moves	The Underground*	–
King's Rock	May cause the foe to flinch when the holder inflicts damage	Wild Poliwhirl/Pickup	–
Lagging Tail	Holder always attacks after foe	Route 226/Wild Lickitung, Slowpoke	–
Lax Incense	The tricky aroma of this incense lowers the foe's chances of landing a critical hit	Route 225	–
Leaf Stone	A peculiar stone that makes certain species of Pokémon evolve	Floaroma Meadow, The Underground	–
Leftovers	The holder's HP is gradually restored during battle	Victory Road/Wild Munchlax/Pickup	–
Life Orb	Boosts the power of moves, but at the cost of some HP on each hit	Stark Mountain	–
Light Ball	A puzzling orb that raises Pikachu's Special Attack stat	Wild Pikachu	–
Light Clay	Extends time duration of barrier moves like Light Screen and Reflect used by the holder	The Underground, Mt. Coronet	–
Luck Incense	Doubles a battle's prize money if the holding Pokémon joins in	Ravaged Path	–
Lucky Egg	An egg filled with happiness that earns extra Exp. Points in battle	Wild Chansey	–
Lucky Punch	A pair of gloves that boosts Chansey's critical-hit ratio	Wild Happiny	–
Lustrous Orb	Boosts the power of Palkia's Dragon- and Water-type moves	Spear Pillar (Pearl version only)	–
Macho Brace	A stiff and heavy brace that increases stat growth but reduces Speed by half	Pastoria City (show three varieties of Burmy)	–
Magmarizer	Packed with a tremendous amount of magma energy; evolves Magmar during a trade	Wild Magby (more common in Diamond version)	–
Magnet	A powerful magnet that boosts the power of Electric-type moves	Iron Island	–
Max Repel	Prevents weak wild Pokémon from appearing for 250 steps after its use	Pokémart (once you have five badges)*	700
Meadow Plate	A stone tablet that boosts the power of Grass-type moves	The Underground*	–
Mental Herb	Snaps the holder out of infatuation; it can be used only once	Route 216	–
Metal Coat	A special metallic film that ups the power of Steel-type moves	Iron Island/Wild Steelix, Bronzor, Bronzong, Beldum, Magnemite	–
Metal Powder	Odd powder that doubles Ditto's Defense stat	Wild Ditto	–
Metronome	Boosts a move used consecutively; its effect is reset if another move is used	Veilstone Game Corner/Wild Kricketune, Kricketot, Chatot	1,000c
Mind Plate	A stone tablet that boosts the power of Psychic-type moves	Solaceon Ruins, The Underground	–
Miracle Seed	A seed imbued with life that ups the power of Grass-type moves	Floaroma Meadow/Wild Cherubi	–
Moon Stone	A peculiar stone that makes certain species of Pokémon evolve	The Underground/Wild Cleffa, Clefairy, Lunastone	–
Muscle Band	A headband that slightly boosts the power of physical moves	Battle Park	48bp
Mystic Water	A teardrop-shaped gem that ups the power of Water-type moves	Pastoria City/Wild Castform	–
Nevermelt Ice	A piece of ice that repels heat and boosts the power of Ice-type moves	Snowpoint Temple, Wild Snove, Abomasnow	–
Nugget	A nugget of pure gold that gives off a lustrous gleam; sells for a high price	Solaceon Ruins, Stark Mountain, Resort Area/Wild Grimer/Pickup*	5,000
Odd Incense	Exotic-smelling incense that boosts the power of Psychic-type moves	Solaceon Ruins	–
Odd Keystone	A vital item that is needed to keep a stone from collapsing; used to catch Spiritomb	Route 208, The Underground*	–
Old Amber	Can be changed into Aerodactyl at the Oreburgh Mining Museum	The Underground	–
Oval Stone	A peculiar stone that makes Happiny evolve (between 4:00am and 7:59pm)	Lost Tower/Wild Happiny, Chansey	–
Pearl	A somewhat-small pearl that sparkles in a pretty silver color; sells for a high price	Route 223 / Wild Shellder*	700
Pink Scarf	Boosts the "Cute" aspect of the holder in a Super Contest	Pastoria City	–
Poison Barb	A small, poisonous barb that ups the power of Poison-type moves	Route 206/Wild Skorupi, Budew, Tentacool, Tentacruel, Drapion, Roselia, Qwilfish	–
Power Anklet	Promotes Speed gain on leveling up, but reduces the Speed stat	Battle Park	16bp
Power Band	Promotes Special Defense gain on leveling up, but reduces the Speed stat	Battle Park	16bp
Power Belt	Promotes Defense gain on leveling up, but reduces the Speed stat	Battle Park	16bp
Power Bracer	Promotes Attack gain on leveling up, but reduces the Speed stat	Battle Park	16bp
Power Herb	Allows immediate use of a move that requires charging, but disappears after one use	Battle Park	32bp
Power Lens	Promotes Special Attack gain on leveling up, but reduces the Speed stat	Battle Park	16bp
Power Weight	Promotes HP gain on leveling up, but reduces the Speed stat	Battle Park	16bp
Protector	Extremely stiff and heavy; evolves Rhydon during a trade	Route 228	–
Pure Incense	Helps keep wild Pokémon away if the holder is the first one in the party	Route 221	–
Quick Claw	A light, sharp claw that lets the bearer move first occasionally	Jubilife City	–
Quick Powder	This odd powder boosts Ditto's Speed stat	Wild Ditto	–

Items (continued) Rare Bone – Zoom Lens

The letters following an item's price denote the following: c=coins, bp=Battle Points. An asterisk (*) indicates a hidden item that can be detected with the Dowsing Machine app.

Item	Description	Location	Price
Rare Bone	A bone that is extremely valuable for Pokémon archeology; sells for a high price	The Underground, Turnback Cave	5,000
Razor Claw	A sharply hooked claw that ups the holder's critical-hit ratio; evolves Sneasel	Route 224, Victory Road, Battle Park	–
Razor Fang	May cause the foe to flinch when the holder inflicts damage; evolves Gligar	Battle Park	–
Reaper Cloth	A cloth imbued with horrifyingly strong spiritual energy; evolves Dusclops during a trade	Route 229, Turnback Cave	–
Red Scarf	Boosts the "Cool" aspect of the holder in a Super Contest	Pastoria City	–
Red Shard	A small red shard; 10 can be exchanged for TM11 (Sunny Day) on Route 212	Route 213, The Underground	–
Repel	Prevents weak Pokémon from appearing for 100 steps after use	Pokémart (once you have one badge), Route 203, 205/Pickup*	350
Rock Incense	Exotic-smelling incense that boosts the power of Rock-type moves	Fuego Ironworks	–
Root Fossil	Can be changed into Lileep at the Oreburgh Mining Museum	The Underground	–
Rose Incense	Exotic-smelling incense that boosts the power of Grass-type moves	Route 212	–
Scope Lens	A lens that boosts the holder's critical-hit ratio	Battle Park	48bp
Sea Incense	Incense with a curious aroma that boosts the power of Water-type moves	Route 204	–
Sharp Beak	A long, sharp beak that boosts the power of Flying-type moves	Wild Fearow, Doduo	–
Shed Shell	Enables the holder to switch with a waiting Pokémon in battle	Route 228/Wild Beautifly, Dustox, Venomoth	–
Shell Bell	The holder's HP is restored by 1/8 of maximum HP every time it inflicts damage	Hearthome City	–
Shiny Stone	A peculiar stone that makes certain species of Pokémon evolve	Route 228, Iron Island/Pickup	–
Shoal Salt	Pure salt that was found deep inside Shoal Cave; if held by a Pokémon, it restores a small amount of HP each turn in battle	Trade from Ruby, Sapphire, or Emerald version	–
Shoal Shell	A pretty seashell that was found deep inside Shoal Cave	Trade from Ruby, Sapphire, or Emerald version	–
Silk Scarf	A sumptuous scarf that boosts the power of Normal-type moves	Veilstone Game Corner	1,000c
Silver Powder	A shiny, silver powder that ups the power of Bug-type moves	Eterna Forest	–
Skull Fossil	Can be changed into Cranidos at the Oreburgh Mining Museum	The Underground (Diamond version only)	–
Sky Plate	A stone tablet that boosts the power of Flying-type moves	Pokémon League, The Underground	–
Smoke Ball	Enables the holder to flee from any wild Pokémon without fail	Route 210/Wild Weezing	–
Smooth Rock	Extends the duration of the move Sandstorm used by the holder	The Underground	–
Soft Sand	A loose, silky sand that boosts the power of Ground-type moves	Mt. Coronet/Wild Diglett, Dugtrio, Trapinch	–
Soothe Bell	A bell with a comforting chime that calms the holder and makes it friendly	Pokémon Mansion	–
Soul Dew	A wondrous orb to be held by Latios or Latias; raises both Special Attack and Special Defense stats	Trade from Ruby, Sapphire, or Emerald version	–
Spell Tag	A sinister, eerie tag that boosts the power of Ghost-type moves	Route 217, Wild Banette	–
Splash Plate	A stone tablet that boosts the power of Water-type moves	Route 219, The Underground	–
Spooky Plate	A stone tablet that boosts the power of Ghost-type moves	Amity Square, The Underground	–
Stable Mulch	Extends the time ripened Berries remain on their plants before falling	Route 208	200
Star Piece	A shard of a pretty gem that sparkles in a red color; sells for a high price	The Underground/Wild Staryu	4,900
Stardust	Lovely, red-colored sand with a loose, silky feel; sells for a high price	Route 203, Mt. Coronet, Turnback Cave/Wild Staryu*	1,000
Stick	A very long and stiff stalk of leek that boosts Farfetch'd's critical-hit ratio	Wild Farfetch'd	–
Sticky Barb	A hold item that damages the holder on every turn; it may latch onto foes that touch the holder	Veilstone Dept. Store/Wild Cacnea, Cacturne	–
Stone Plate	A stone tablet that boosts the power of Rock-type moves	The Underground*	–
Sun Stone	A peculiar stone that makes certain species of Pokémon evolve	The Underground/Wild Solrock	–
Super Repel	Prevents wild Pokémon from appearing for 200 steps after its use	Pokémart (once you have three badges), Route 206, 210, Great Marsh, Iron Island*	500
Thick Club	A hard bone of some sort that boosts Cubone and Marowak's Attack stat	Wild Cubone	–
Thunderstone	A peculiar stone that makes certain species of Pokémon evolve	Sunyshore City, The Underground	–
Tinymushroom	A small and rare mushroom; sells for a low price	Wild Paras*	250
Toxic Orb	A bizarre orb that badly poisons the holder in battle	Battle Park	16bp
Toxic Plate	A stone tablet that boosts the power of Poison-type moves	Great Marsh, The Underground	–
Twistedspoon	A spoon imbued with telekinetic power that boosts Psychic-type moves	Wild Abra, Kadabra	–
Up-Grade	Evolves Porygon during a trade	Eterna City (after you visit Pal Park)	–
Water Stone	A peculiar stone that makes certain species of Pokémon evolve	Route 213, The Underground	–
Wave Incense	Exotic-smelling incense that boosts the power of Water-type moves	Route 210	–
White Flute	Its melody makes wild Pokémon more likely to appear	Trade from Ruby, Sapphire, or Emerald version	–
White Herb	Restores any lowered stat in battle; it can be used only once	Battle Park/Pickup	32bp
Wide Lens	A magnifying lens that slightly boosts the Accuracy of moves	Veilstone Game Corner/Wild Yanma	1,000c
Wise Glasses	A thick pair of glasses that slightly boosts the power of Special moves	Celestic Town (8:00am–3:59pm)	–
Yellow Scarf	Boosts the "Tough" aspect of the holder in a Super Contest	Pastoria City	–
Yellow Shard	A small yellow shard; 10 can be exchanged for TM37 (Sandstorm) on Route 212	The Underground	–
Zap Plate	A stone tablet that boosts the power of Electric-type moves	The Underground*	–
Zoom Lens	If the holder moves after the foe, its critical-hit ratio will be boosted	Veilstone Game Corner	1,000c

Health Items

The letters following an item's price denote the following: c=coins, bp=Battle Points. An asterisk (*) indicates a hidden item that can be detected with the Dowsing Machine app.

Item	Description	Location	Price
Antidote	Lifts the effect of poison from one Pokémon	Pokémart, Route 206, 212, 219, Ravaged Path, Eterna Forest, Great Marsh/Pickup*	100
Awakening	Awakens a Pokémon from the clutches of sleep	Pokémart (once you have one badge), Route 204*	250
Burn Heal	Heals a single Pokémon that is suffering from a burn	Pokémart (once you have one badge), Route 206, Fuego Ironworks, Stark Mountain*	250
Calcium	Raises the base Special Attack stat of a single Pokémon	Veilstone Dept. Store, Route 209, Snowpoint Temple, Stark Mountain, Battle Park*	9,800 or 1bp
Carbos	Raises the base Speed stat of a single Pokémon	Veilstone Dept. Store, Route 208, 220, 222, 226, Battle Park*	9,800 or 1bp
Elixir	Restores the PP of all the moves learned by the targeted Pokémon by 10 points each	Route 212, Galactic HQ, Victory Road/Pickup	—
Energy Root	Restores the HP of one Pokémon by 200 points; tastes bitter	Eterna City Herb Shop	800
Energypowder	Restores the HP of one Pokémon by 50 points; tastes bitter	Eterna City Herb Shop	500
Ether	Restores the PP of a Pokémon's selected move by a maximum of 10 points	Eterna Forest, Route 215, 220, Stark Mountain/Pickup*	—
Fresh Water	Restores the HP of one Pokémon by 50 points	Veilstone Dept. Store	200
Full Heal	Heals all the status problems of a single Pokémon	Pokémart (once you have five badges), Route 206, 215, Victory Road/Pickup*	600
Full Restore	Fully restores the HP and heals any status problems of a single Pokémon	Pokémart (once you have eight badges), Route 229, Mt. Coronet, Victory Road, Stark Mountain/Pickup*	3,000
Heal Powder	Heals all status problems of a single Pokémon; tastes bitter	Eterna City Herb Shop	450
HP Up	Raises the base HP of a single Pokémon	Veilstone Dept. Store, Route 204, 216, 225, Iron Island, Battle Park*	9,800 or 1bp
Hyper Potion	Restores the HP of one Pokémon by 200 points	Pokémart (once you have five badges), Route 210/Pickup*	1,200
Ice Heal	Defrosts a Pokémon that has been frozen solid	Pokémart (once you have one badge), Route 216	250
Iron	Raises the base Defense stat of a single Pokémon	Veilstone Dept. Store, Route 207, 217, 228, Battle Park*	9,800 or 1bp
Lava Cookie	Heals all the status problems of one Pokémon	Valor Lakefront	—
Lemonade	Restores the HP of one Pokémon by 80 points	Veilstone Dept. Store	350
Max Elixir	Fully restores the PP of all the moves learned by the targeted Pokémon	Mt. Coronet, Stark Mountain/Pickup*	—
Max Ether	Fully restores the PP of a single selected move that has been learned by the target Pokémon	Wayward Cave, Iron Island, Victory Road*	—
Max Potion	Completely restores the HP of a single Pokémon	Pokémart (once you have seven badges), Route 214, Iron Island, Mt. Coronet*	2,500
Max Revive	Revives a fainted Pokémon; fully restores the Pokémon's HP	Route 213, Galactic HQ, Stark Mountain, The Underground/Pickup*	—
MooMoo Milk	Restores the HP of one Pokémon by 100 points	Route 210/Wild Miltank	500
Old Gateau	Heals all the status problems of a single Pokémon	Old Chateau	—
Paralyze Heal	Eliminates paralysis from a single Pokémon	Pokémart, Route 204, Eterna Forest, Great Marsh, Valor Lakefront*	200
Potion	Restores the HP of one Pokémon by just 20 points	Pokémart, Route 201, 202, 205, Oreburgh Mine, Valley Windworks, Eterna Forest, Great Marsh/Pickup	300
PP Max	Maximally raises the top PP of a selected move that has been learned by the target Pokémon	*	—
PP Up	Raises the level of the maximum PP of a selected move that has been learned by the target Pokémon	Route 213, Veilstone City, Stark Mountain/Pickup*	—
Protein	Raises the base Attack stat of a single Pokémon	Veilstone Dept. Store, Route 213, 221, 229, Mt. Coronet, Battle Park*	9,800 or 1bp
Rare Candy	Raises the level of a single Pokémon by one	Route 214, 218, 224, 225, 230, Wayward Cave, Solaceon Ruins, Mt. Coronet, Victory Road, Stark Mountain, Battle Park/Pickup*	48bp
Revival Herb	Revives a fainted Pokémon, fully restoring its HP; tastes bitter	Eterna City Herb Shop	2,800
Revive	Revives a fainted Pokémon; restores half the Pokémon's maximum HP	Pokémart (once you have three badges), Route 212, 225, Wayward Cave, Lost Tower, Mt. Coronet, The Underground/Pickup*	1,500
Sacred Ash	Revives all fainted Pokémon; in doing so, it also fully restores their HP	Trade from Pokémon XD to GBA cartridge and into D/P	—
Soda Pop	Restores the HP of one Pokémon by 60 points	Veilstone Dept.	300
Super Potion	Restores the HP of one Pokémon by 50 points	Pokémart (once you have one badge), Route 205, 207, Eterna City, Great Marsh*	700
Zinc	Raises the base Special Defense stat of a single Pokémon	Veilstone Dept. Store, Route 212, 227, Galactic HQ, Victory Road, Battle Park*	9,800 or 1bp

Poké Balls

Ball type	Description	Location	Price
Dive Ball	Works especially well on Pokémon that live in the sea	Solaceon Town	—
Dusk Ball	Makes it easier to catch wild Pokémon at night or in dark places like caves	Oreburgh City, Solaceon Town, Pokémart (some)	1,000
Great Ball	Provides a higher Pokémon catch rate than a standard Poké Ball	Pokémart (once you have three badges), Route 210, Eterna Forest, Pokémon Mansion, Great Marsh*	600
Heal Ball	Restores the captured Pokémon's HP and eliminates any status problem	Oreburgh City, Solaceon Town, Pokémart (some)	300
Luxury Ball	Makes a captured wild Pokémon quickly grow friendly	Pokémart (some), Solaceon Town	1,000
Master Ball	Catch any wild Pokémon without fail	Galactic HQ	—
Nest Ball	Works especially well on weaker Pokémon in the wild	Pokémart (some), Solaceon Town	1,000
Net Ball	Works especially well on Water-and Bug-type Pokémon	Pokémart, Solaceon Town, Route 222	1,000
Poké Ball	A device for catching wild Pokémon	Pokémart, Route 203, 205, 207, 208, Great Marsh*	200
Premier Ball	A Poké Ball specially made to commemorate an event of some sort	Received when you buy 10 Poké Balls at once	—
Quick Ball	Provides a better capture rate if it is used at the start of a wild encounter	Pokémart (some), Solaceon Town	1,000
Repeat Ball	Works especially well on Pokémon species that were previously caught	Pokémart (some), Solaceon Town	1,000
Safari Ball	A special Poké Ball that is used only in the Great Marsh	Great Marsh	—
Timer Ball	Becomes progressively better the more turns there are in a battle	Pokémart (some), Solaceon Town	1,000
Ultra Ball	Provides a higher Pokémon catch rate than a standard Great Ball	Pokémart (once you have five badges), Route 210, 225, Iron Island, Acuity Lakefront, Stark Mountain*	1,200

Technical Machines (TMs)

The letters following an item's price denote the following: c=coins, bp=Battle Points.

No.	Move	Location	Price
01	Focus Punch	Oreburgh Gate/Pickup	–
02	Dragon Claw	Mt. Coronet	–
03	Water Pulse	Ravaged Path	–
04	Calm Mind	Battle Park	48bp
05	Roar	Route 213	–
06	Toxic	Route 212, Battle Park	32bp
07	Hail	Route 212. Route 217	–
08	Bulk Up	Battle Park	48bp
09	Bullet Seed	Route 204	–
10	Hidden Power	Jubilife City, Veilstone Game Corner	6,000c
11	Sunny Day	Route 212	–
12	Taunt	Route 211	–
13	Ice Beam	Route 216, Veilstone Game Corner	10,000c
14	Blizzard	Veilstone Dept. Store, Lake Acuity	5,500
15	Hyper Beam	Veilstone Dept. Store	7,500
16	Light Screen	Veilstone Dept. Store	2,000
17	Protect	Veilstone Dept. Store	2,000
18	Rain Dance	Route 223, Route 212	–
19	Giga Drain	Route 209	–
20	Safeguard	Veilstone Dept. Store	2,000
21	Frustration	Galactic HQ, Veilstone Game Corner	8,000c
22	Solarbeam	Veilstone Dept. Store	3,000
23	Iron Tail	Iron Island	–
24	Thunderbolt	Valley Windworks, Veilstone Game Corner	10,000c
25	Thunder	Lake Valor, Veilstone Dept. Store	5,500
26	Earthquake	Wayward Cave, Battle Park/Pickup	80bp
27	Return	Lost Tower, Veilstone Game Corner	8,000c
28	Dig	Ruin Maniac Cave	–
29	Psychic	Route 211, Veilstone Game Corner	10,000c
30	Shadow Ball	Route 210, Battle Park	64bp
31	Brick Break	Oreburgh Gate, Battle Park	40bp
32	Double Team	Wayward Cave, Veilstone Game Corner	4,000c
33	Reflect	Veilstone Dept. Store	2,000
34	Shock Wave	Route 215	–
35	Flamethrower	Fuego Ironworks, Veilstone Game Corner	10,000c
36	Sludge Bomb	Galactic HQ, Battle Park	80bp
37	Sandstorm	Route 228, Route 212	–
38	Fire Blast	Lake Verity, Veilstone Dept. Store	5,500
39	Rock Tomb	Ravaged Path	–
40	Aerial Ace	Route 213, Battle Park	40bp
41	Torment	Victory Road	–
42	Facade	Survival Area	–
43	Secret Power	Amity Square	–
44	Rest	Veilstone Game Corner	6,000c
45	Attract	Amity Square, Battle Park	32bp
46	Thief	Eterna City	–

No.	Move	Location	Price
47	Steel Wing	Route 209	–
48	Skill Swap	Canalave City	–
49	Snatch	Galactic HQ	–
50	Overheat	Stark Mountain	–
51	Roost	Route 210	–
52	Focus Blast	Veilstone Dept. Store Store	5,500
53	Energy Ball	Route 226, Battle Park	64bp
54	False Swipe	Veilstone Dept. Store	2,000
55	Brine	Pastoria Gym	–
56	Fling	Route 222	–
57	Charge Beam	Sunyshore Gym	–
58	Endure	Veilstone Game Corner	2,000c
59	Dragon Pulse	Victory Road, Battle Park	80bp
60	Drain Punch	Veilstone Gym	–
61	Will-O-Wisp	Battle Park	32bp
62	Silver Wind	Route 212	–
63	Embargo	Veilstone City	–
64	Explosion	Game Corner	–
65	Shadow Claw	Hearthome Gym	–
66	Payback	Route 215	–
67	Recycle	Eterna City	–
68	Giga Impact	Veilstone Game Corner	20,000c
69	Rock Polish	Mt. Coronet	–
70	Flash	Oreburgh Gate, Veilstone Dept. Store	1,000
71	Stone Edge	Victory Road, Battle Park	80bp
72	Avalanche	Snowpoint Gym	–
73	Thunder Wave	Battle Park	32bp
74	Gyro Ball	Game Corner	15,000c
75	Swords Dance	Game Corner	4,000c
76	Stealth Rock	Oreburgh Gym	–
77	Psych Up	Route 211	–
78	Captivate	Route 204	–
79	Dark Pulse	Victory Road	–
80	Rock Slide	Mt. Coronet	–
81	X-Scissor	Route 221, Battle Park	64bp
82	Sleep Talk	Eterna Forest	–
83	Natural Gift	Veilstone Dept. Store	2,000
84	Poison Jab	Route 212	–
85	Dream Eater	Valor Lakefront	–
86	Grass Knot	Eterna Gym	–
87	Swagger	Pokémon Mansion	–
88	Pluck	Floaroma Town	–
89	U-Turn	Canalave City, Veilstone Game Corner	6,000c
90	Substitute	Old Chateau, Veilstone Game Corner	2,000c
91	Flash Cannon	Canalave City	–
92	Trick Room	Valor Lakefront	–

Hidden Machines (HMs)

No.	Move	Location	Price
01	Cut	Eterna City	–
02	Fly	Galactic Warehouse	–
03	Surf	Celestic Town	–
04	Strength	Lost Tower	–

No.	Move	Location	Price
05	Defog	Great Marsh	–
06	Rock Smash	Oreburgh Gate	–
07	Waterfall	Sunyshore City	–
08	Rock Climb	Route 217	–

Berries

Berry Type	Description	Location	Flavor
Aguav Berry	If held by a Pokémon, it restores the user's HP in a pinch, but may also cause confusion	Route 210	Bitter
Apicot Berry	If held by a Pokémon, it raises its Special Defense stat in a pinch	Trade from Ruby, Sapphire, or Emerald version	Sour, Dry, Spicy
Aspear Berry	Used or held by a Pokémon to defrost it	Route 210	Sour
Babiri Berry	If held by a Pokémon, it weakens a foe's supereffective Steel-type attack	Pastoria City/Wild Snorunt	Spicy, Dry
Belue Berry	Bury it in soft soil to grow a Belue Plant	Amity Square	Spicy, Sour
Bluk Berry	Bury it in soft soil to grow a Bluk Plant	Route 215	Dry, Sweet
Charti Berry	If held by a Pokémon, it weakens a foe's supereffective Rock-type attack	Pastoria City/Wild Swellow, Taillow	Spicy, Dry
Cheri Berry	Used or held by a Pokémon to recover from paralysis	Floaroma Town	Spicy
Chesto Berry	Used or held by a Pokémon to recover from sleep	Route 205	Dry
Chilan Berry	If held by a Pokémon, it weakens a foe's supereffective Normal-type attack	Pastoria City/Wild Rattata, Raticate	Dry, Sweet
Chople Berry	If held by a Pokémon, it weakens a foe's supereffective Fighting-type attack	Pastoria City/Wild Buneary	Spicy, Bitter
Coba Berry	If held by a Pokémon, it weakens a foe's supereffective Flying-type attack	Pastoria City/Wild Sunkern	Dry, Bitter
Colbur Berry	If held by a Pokémon, it weakens a foe's supereffective Dark-type attack	Pastoria City/Wild Chimecho, Chingling	Bitter, Sour
Cornn Berry	Bury it in soft soil to grow a Cornn Plant	Amity Square	Dry, Sweet
Cutsap Berry	If held by a Pokémon, it gets to move first just once in a pinch	Trade from Ruby, Sapphire, or Emerald version	Bitter, Sweet
Durin Berry	Bury it in soft soil to grow a Durin Plant	Amity Square	Sour, Bitter
Enigma Berry	If held by a Pokémon, it restores its HP if it is hit by a foe's supereffective attack	–	Spicy, Dry
Figy Berry	If held by a Pokémon, it restores the user's HP in a pinch, but may also cause confusion	Solaceon Town	Spicy
Ganlon Berry	If held by a Pokémon, it raises its Defense stat in a pinch	Trade from Ruby, Sapphire, or Emerald version	Bitter, Sweet, Dry
Grepa Berry	Using it on a Pokémon makes it more friendly, but it also lowers its base Special Defense stat	Route 208	Dry, Sweet, Sour
Haban Berry	If held by a Pokémon, it weakens a foe's supereffective Dragon-type attack	Pastoria City/Wild Gible	Sweet, Bitter
Hondew Berry	Using it on a Pokémon makes it more friendly, but it also lowers its base Special Attack stat	Route 221	Dry, Spicy, Bitter
Iapapa Berry	If held by a Pokémon, it restores the user's HP in a pinch, but may also cause confusion	Route 213	Sour
Jaboca Berry	If held by a Pokémon, and if the foe's Physical attack lands, the foes also takes damage	Trade from Ruby, Sapphire, or Emerald version	Bitter, Sour
Kasib Berry	If held by a Pokémon, it weakens a foe's supereffective Ghost-type attack	Pastoria City/Wild Dusclops, Duskull	Dry, Sweet
Kebia Berry	If held by a Pokémon, it weakens a foe's supereffective Poison-type attack	Pastoria City/Wild Shroomish	Dry, Sour
Kelpsy Berry	Using it on a Pokémon makes it more friendly, but it also lowers its base Attack stat	Fuego Ironworks	Dry, Sour, Bitter
Lansat Berry	If held by a Pokémon, it raises its critical hit ratio in a pinch	Trade from Emerald version	All Flavors
Leppa Berry	Used or held by a Pokémon to restore a move's PP by 10	Route 209	Sweet, Spicy, Sour, Bitter
Liechi Berry	If held by a Pokémon, it raises its Attack stat in a pinch	Trade from Ruby, Sapphire, or Emerald version	Sweet, Spicy, Sour
Lum Berry	Used or held by a Pokémon to recover from any status problem	Route 212	All Flavors
Mago Berry	If held by a Pokémon, it restores the user's HP in a pinch, but may also cause confusion	Route 215	Sweet
Magost Berry	Bury it in soft soil to grow a Magost Plant	Amity Square	Sweet, Bitter
Micle Berry	If held by a Pokémon, it raises the Accuracy of a move just once in a pinch	Trade from Ruby, Sapphire, or Emerald version	Dry, Sweet
Nanab Berry	Bury it in soft soil to grow a Nanab Plant	Route 208	Sweet, Bitter
Nomel Berry	Bury it in soft soil to grow a Nomel Plant	Amity Square	Spicy, Sour
Occa Berry	If held by a Pokémon, it weakens a foe's supereffective Fire-type attack	Pastoria City/Wild Mawile	Spicy, Sweet
Oran Berry	Used or held by a Pokémon to heal the user by just 10 HP	Floaroma Town	All Flavors
Pamtre Berry	Bury it in soft soil to grow a Pamtre Plant	Amity Square	Dry, Sweet
Passho Berry	If held by a Pokémon, it weakens a foe's supereffective Water-type attack	Pastoria City/Wild Phanpy	Dry, Bitter
Payapa Berry	If held by a Pokémon, it weakens a foe's supereffective Psychic-type attack	Pastoria City/Wild Primeape, Mankey	Sweet, Sour
Pecha Berry	Used or held by a Pokémon to recover from poison	Route 205	Sweet
Persim Berry	Used or held by a Pokémon to recover from confusion	Solaceon Town	All Flavors
Petaya Berry	If held by a Pokémon, it raises its Special Attack stat in a pinch	Trade from Ruby, Sapphire, or Emerald version	Spicy, Bitter, Sour
Pinap Berry	Bury it in soft soil to grow a Pinap Plant	Route 208	Spicy, Sour
Pomeg Berry	Using it on a Pokémon makes it more friendly, but it also lowers its base HP	Route 214	Sweet, Spicy, Bitter
Qualot Berry	Using it on a Pokémon makes it more friendly, but it also lowers its base Defense stat	Route 222	Sweet, Spicy, Sour
Rabuta Berry	Bury it in soft soil to grow a Rabuta Plant	Amity Square	Sour, Bitter
Rawst Berry	Used or held by a Pokémon to recover from a burn	Route 206	Bitter
Razz Berry	Bury it in soft soil to grow a Razz Plant	Route 206	Dry, Spicy
Rindo Berry	If held by a Pokémon, it weakens a foe's supereffective Grass-type attack	Pastoria City/Wild Finneo, Lumineon	Spicy, Bitter
Rowap Berry	If held by a Pokémon, and if the foe's Special attack lands, the foe also takes damage	Trade from Ruby, Sapphire, or Emerald version	Sour, Spicy
Salac Berry	If held by a Pokémon, it raises its Speed stat in a pinch	Trade from Ruby, Sapphire, or Emerald version	Sour, Sweet, Bitter
Shuca Berry	If held by a Pokémon, it weakens a foe's supereffective Ground-type attack	Pastoria City/Wild Ponyta	Spicy, Sweet
Sitrus Berry	Used or held by a Pokémon to heal the user's HP a little	Route 210	All Flavors
Spelon Berry	Bury it in soft soil to grow a Spelon Plant	Amity Square	Dry, Spicy
Starf Berry	If held by a Pokémon, it raises one of its stats in a pinch	Trade from Emerald version	All Flavors
Tamato Berry	Using it on a Pokémon makes it more friendly, but it also lowers its base Speed stat	Route 212	Dry, Spicy
Tanga Berry	If held by a Pokémon, it weakens a foe's supereffective Bug-type attack	Pastoria City/Wild Spoink	Dry, Sour
Wacan Berry	If held by a Pokémon, it weakens a foe's supereffective Electric-type attack	Pastoria City/Wild Buizel, Floatzel	Sweet, Sour
Watmel Berry	Bury it in soft soil to grow a Watmel Plant	Amity Square	Sweet, Bitter
Wepear Berry	Bury it in soft soil to grow a Wepear Plant	Fuego Ironworks	Sour, Bitter
Wiki Berry	If held by a Pokémon, it restores the user's HP in a pinch, but may also cause confusion	Route 210	Dry
Yache Berry	If held by a Pokémon, it weakens a foe's supereffective Ice-type attack	Pastoria City/Wild Staravia, Starly	Dry, Sour

Mail

Mail Type	Description	Location	Price
Air Mail	Stationery featuring a print of colorful letter sets	Jubilife City, Eterna City, Solaceon Town, Pastoria City, Celestic Town, Canalave City	50
Bloom Mail	Stationery featuring a print of pretty floral patterns	Floaroma Town	50
Bubble Mail	Stationery featuring a print of a blue world underwater	Veilstone Dept. Store	50
Flame Mail	Stationery featuring a print of flames in blazing red	Veilstone Dept. Store	50
Grass Mail	Stationery featuring a print of a refreshingly green field	Veilstone Dept. Store	50
Heart Mail	Stationery featuring a print of giant heart patterns	Hearthome City	50
Snow Mail	Stationery featuring a print of a chilly, snow-covered world	Snowpoint City	50
Space Mail	Stationery featuring a print depicting the huge expanse of space	Veilstone Dept. Store	50
Steel Mail	Stationery featuring a print of cool mechanical designs	Sunyshore City	50
Tunnel Mail	Stationery featuring a print of a dimly lit coal mine	Oreburgh City	50

Battle Items

Item	Description	Location	Price
Blue Flute	Its melody awakens a single Pokémon from sleep	Trade from Ruby, Sapphire, or Emerald version	–
Dire Hit	An item that raises the critical-hit ratio of a Pokémon in battle	Veilstone Dept. Store, Route 207	650
Fluffy Tail	An item that attracts Pokémon; use it to flee from any battle with a wild Pokémon	Trade from Ruby, Sapphire, or Emerald version	–
Guard Spec.	An item that prevents stat reduction among the Trainer's party Pokémon for 5 turns	Veilstone Dept. Store, Route 215	700
Poké Doll	A doll that attracts Pokémon; use it to flee from any battle with a wild Pokémon	Veilstone Dept. Store	1,000
Red Flute	It's melody snaps a single Pokémon out of infatuation	Trade from Ruby, Sapphire, or Emerald version	–
X Accuracy	An item that raises the Defense stat of a Pokémon in battle	Veilstone Dept. Store, Route 209	950
X Attack	An item that raises the Accuracy of a Pokémon in battle	Veilstone Dept. Store, Route 205	500
X Defend	An item that raises the Defense stat of a Pokémon in battle	Veilstone Dept. Store, Oreburgh Mine	550
X Sp. Def	An item that raises the Special Defense stat of a Pokémon in battle	Veilstone Dept. Store, Route 214	350
X Special	An item that raises the Special Attack stat of a Pokémon in battle	Veilstone Dept. Store, Route 212	350
X Speed	An item that raises the Speed stat of a Pokémon in battle	Veilstone Dept. Store, Route 208	350
Yellow Flute	It's melody snaps a single Pokémon out of confusion	Trade from Ruby, Sapphire, or Emerald version	–

Key Items

Item	Description	Location
Bicycle	A folding Bicycle that enables much faster movement than the Running Shoes	Eterna City
Coin Case	A case for holding Coins obtained at the Game Corner; it holds up to 50,000 Coins	Veilstone City
Coupon 1	A coupon to be exchanged for a Pokémon Watch (Pokétch for short); one of three	Jubilife City
Coupon 2	A coupon to be exchanged for a Pokémon Watch (Pokétch for short); two of three	Jubilife City
Coupon 3	A coupon to be exchanged for a Pokémon Watch (Pokétch for short); three of three	Jubilife City
Explorer Kit	A bag filled with convenient tools for exploring; it provides access to the Underground	Eterna City
Fashion Case	A fancy case for the tidy and organized storage of colorful Pokémon Accessories	Jubilife City
Galactic Key	A card key for disengaging security systems in the Galactic HQ	Galactic HQ (Veilstone City)
Good Rod	A new, good-quality fishing rod; use it near bodies of water to fish for wild aquatic Pokémon	Route 209
Journal	A notebook that keeps a day-today record of your adventure so far	Twinleaf Town
Lunar Wing	A feather that glows like the moon; it is said to possess the power to dispel nightmares	Fullmoon Island
Old Charm	An ancient good-luck charm mode from Pokémon bones to be taken to the elder of Celestic Town	Route 210
Old Rod	An old and beat-up fishing rod; use it near bodies of water to fish for wild aquatic Pokémon	Jubilife City
Pal Pad	A convenient notepad that is used for registering your friends and keeping record of game play	Oreburgh City
Parcel	A parcel entrusted in your care; deliver it to your childhood friend who left Twinleaf Town	Twinleaf Town
Poffin Case	A case for storing Poffin cooked from Berries	Hearthome City
Point Card	A card that lists the Battle Points you have earned	Battle Park
Poké Radar	A tool that can search out Pokémon that are hiding in grass; its battery is recharged as you walk	Sandgem Town
Seal Case	A case for storing Seals that can be applied to the capsule cases of Poké Balls	Solaceon Town
Secret Potion	A fantastic medicine dispersed by the pharmacy in Cianwood City; it fully heals a Pokémon of an ailment	Valor Lakefront
Sprayduck	A watering can shaped like a Psyduck; it helps promote healthy growth of Berries planted in soft soil	Floaroma Town
Storage Key	The key to Team Galactic's sinister warehouse located at the edge of Veilstone City	Veilstone City
Suite Key	A key to one of the suites at the luxury hotel by the lake	Route 213
Super Rod	An awesome, high-tech fishing rod; use near bodies of water to fish for wild aquatic Pokémon	Fight Area
Town Map	A map of Sinnoh that shows your present location	Jubilife City
Vs Seeker	A device that indicates Trainers who want to battle; its battery charges while you walk	Route 207
Works Key	A large key for operating the doors of the Valley Windworks in the canyon	Floaroma Meadow

Wild Pokémon Held Items

Some held items are rare (R) or very rare (VR).

Pokémon Number and Name	Item
010 Starly	Yache Berry (VR)
011 Staravia	Yache Berry (VR)
014 Bibarel	Oran Berry (R)/Sitrus Berry (VR)
015 Kricketot	Metronome (VR)
016 Kricketune	Metronome (VR)
020 Abra	Twisted Spoon (VR)
021 Kadabra	Twisted Spoon (VR)
025 Budew	Poison Barb (VR)
026 Roselia	Poison Barb (VR)
031 Geodude	Everstone (VR)
032 Graveler	Everstone (VR)
035 Steelix	Metal Coat (VR)
050 Beautifly	Shed Shell (VR)
052 Dustox	Shed Shell (VR)
053 Combee	Honey
056 Buizel	Wacan Berry (VR)
057 Floatzel	Wacan Berry (VR)
058 Cherubi	Miracle Seed (VR)
067 Buneary	Chople Berry (VR)
076 Glameow	Cheri Berry (VR)
077 Purugly	Cheri Berry (VR)
082 Chingling	Colbur Berry (VR)
083 Chimecho	Colbur Berry (VR)
084 Stunky	Pecha Berry (VR)
085 Skuntank	Pecha Berry (VR)
088 Bronzor	Metal Coat (VR)
089 Bronzong	Metal Coat (VR)
090 Slowpoke	Lagging Tail (VR)
094 Mime Jr.	Leppa Berry (VR)
095 Mr. Mime	Leppa Berry (VR)
097 Chansey	Oval Stone (R)/Lucky Egg (VR)
099 Cleffa	Leppa Berry (R)/Moon Stone (VR)
100 Clefairy	Leppa Berry (R)/Moon Stone (VR)
102 Chatot	Metronome (VR)
103 Pichu	Oran Berry (VR)
104 Pikachu	Oran Berry (R)/Light Ball (VR)
109 Gible	Haban Berry (VR)
112 Munchlax	Leftovers
121 Girafarig	Persim Berry (VR)
127 Skorupi	Poison Barb (VR)
128 Drapion	Poison Barb (VR)
129 Croagunk	Black Sludge (VR)
130 Toxicroak	Black Sludge (VR)
134 Finneon	Rindo Berry (VR)
135 Lumineon	Rindo Berry (VR)
136 Tentacool	Poison Barb (VR)
137 Tentacruel	Poison Barb (VR)
142 Snover	Nevermeltice (VR)
143 Abomasnow	Nevermeltice (VR)
144 Sneasel	Grip Claw (R)/Quick Claw (VR)

Contest Accessories Award Podium – Photo Board

The chart below shows how well each fashion accessory matches each contest theme. The letters refer to (H)igh, (M)edium, and (L)ow.

Item	Shapely	Sharpness	The Created	Nature	The Colorful	The Solid	Brightness	The Gaudy	Flexibility	The Festive	The Intangible	Relaxation	Location
Award Podium	H	M	H	L	M	H	H	H	L	M	L	M	Win 1st place in the Toughness Master Rank Contest
Big Leaf	H	M	L	H	M	M	M	M	M	H	L	M	Amity Square
Big Scale	M	H	L	H	M	H	H	H	M	M	M	L	Amity Square
Big Tree	H	M	L	H	M	H	M	M	M	M	L	M	Eterna Forest
Black Beard	M	H	H	L	H	M	L	H	H	L	M	H	Amity Square
Black Fluff	M	L	L	H	H	M	L	M	H	M	M	H	Amity Square
Black Moustache	M	M	H	L	H	M	L	H	H	H	M	H	Amity Square
Black Specs	H	M	H	L	H	H	L	H	L	L	M	H	Flower Shop in Floaroma Town
Black Stone	H	L	M	M	H	H	L	H	L	M	L	H	Amity Square
Blue Balloon	M	L	H	L	H	L	M	H	H	M	H	M	Win 1st place in the Beauty Great Rank Contest
Blue Barrette	M	M	H	L	H	M	M	H	M	M	M	M	Win 1st place in the Beauty Normal Rank Contest
Blue Feather	M	H	L	H	H	M	M	H	M	M	M	M	Amity Square
Blue Flower	H	M	L	H	H	M	M	M	M	M	M	M	Flower Shop in Floaroma Town
Blue Scale	M	H	L	H	H	M	H	M	H	M	M	H	Amity Square
Brown Fluff	M	L	L	H	H	M	M	M	H	M	M	H	Amity Square
Cape	H	H	H	L	H	M	L	H	H	M	M	H	Flower Shop in Floaroma Town
Carpet	H	L	H	L	H	H	H	H	H	H	H	M	Flower Shop in Floaroma Town
Chimchar Mask	H	L	H	L	M	M	M	H	M	M	M	M	Jubilife TV 2F: player's initial Pokémon / Pastoria City: rival's initial Pokémon / Veilstone City Dept. Store 1F: Prof Rowan's assistant's initial Pokémon
Colored Parasol	H	H	H	L	H	H	H	H	M	H	M	M	Flower Shop in Floaroma Town
Confetti	M	M	H	L	H	M	M	H	H	M	H	M	Flower Shop in Floaroma Town
Crown	H	H	H	L	M	H	H	M	M	H	M	L	Insert FireRed cartridge into Nintendo DS and go to northwest corner on the 2nd floor of Pal Park
Cube Stage	H	M	H	L	M	H	H	H	L	M	L	M	Win 1st place in the Smartness Master Rank Contest
Determination	L	M	M	M	M	L	H	H	H	M	H	M	Massage House in Veilstone City
Eerie Thing	M	L	M	H	H	L	L	L	H	L	H	H	Massage House in Veilstone City
Flag	H	H	H	L	H	H	H	M	H	M	H	M	Cycling Road Southern Gate
Flower Stage	H	M	H	L	M	H	M	H	L	H	L	M	Win 1st place in the Cuteness Master Rank Contest
Fluffy Bed	H	L	H	L	M	M	M	M	H	M	M	M	Flower Shop in Floaroma Town
Glass Stage	H	M	H	L	M	H	H	H	L	H	L	M	Win 1st place in the Beauty Master Rank Contest
Glitter Powder	M	L	H	M	M	M	H	H	H	H	H	L	Massage House in Veilstone City
Glitter Stone	H	L	M	M	M	H	H	H	L	H	L	L	Amity Square
Gold Pedestal	H	M	H	L	M	H	M	H	H	L	L	L	Win 1st place in the Coolness Master Rank Contest
Googly Specs	H	M	H	L	M	H	M	M	L	L	M	H	Flower Shop in Floaroma Town
Gorgeous Specs	H	M	H	L	H	H	L	H	L	H	M	M	Flower Shop in Floaroma Town
Green Balloon	M	L	H	L	H	L	M	H	M	H	M	M	Win 1st place in the Smartness Great Rank Contest
Green Barrette	M	M	H	L	H	M	M	H	M	M	H	M	Win 1st place in the Smartness Normal Rank Contest
Green Scale	M	L	L	H	H	H	M	H	M	M	M	M	Amity Square
Heroic Headband	H	M	H	L	M	M	H	H	M	M	M	M	Win 1st place in the Toughness Ultra Rank Contest
Humming Note	L	M	H	M	M	H	H	H	H	H	H	M	Massage House in Veilstone City
Jagged Boulder	H	L	L	L	H	M	M	L	L	L	L	H	Amity Square
Lace Headdress	H	H	H	L	L	M	H	H	H	M	M	M	Win 1st place in the Cuteness Ultra Rank Contest
Mini Stone	H	L	M	M	M	M	M	H	L	M	L	M	Amity Square
Mirror Ball	H	L	H	L	M	H	H	H	L	H	M	L	Flower Shop in Floaroma Town
Mystic Fire	L	L	M	H	M	L	H	H	H	H	H	M	Massage House in Veilstone City
Narrow Leaf	M	H	L	H	M	M	M	M	H	L	M	M	Amity Square
Narrow Scale	M	L	H	M	H	L	H	M	M	M	M	H	Amity Square
Old Umbrella	H	H	H	L	M	M	H	M	M	L	M	H	Flower Shop in Floaroma Town
Orange Flower	H	M	L	H	H	M	M	M	M	M	M	M	Flower Shop in Floaroma Town
Orange Fluff	M	L	L	H	H	M	M	M	H	M	M	M	Amity Square
Peculiar Spoon	H	M	H	L	L	H	M	M	M	M	L	M	Massage House in Veilstone City
Photo Board	H	M	H	L	M	H	M	H	M	M	H	M	Flower Shop in Floaroma Town

Contest Accessories (continued) Pink Balloon – Yellow Fluff

Item	Shapely	Sharpness	The Created	Nature	The Colorful	The Solid	Brightness	The Gaudy	Flexibility	The Festive	The Intangible	Relaxation	Location
Pink Balloon	M	L	H	L	H	L	M	H	H	M	H	M	Win 1st place in the Cuteness Great Rank Contest
Pink Barrette	M	M	H	L	H	M	M	H	M	M	M	M	Win 1st place in the Cuteness Normal Rank Contest
Pink Flower	H	M	L	H	H	M	M	M	M	M	M	M	Flower Shop in Floaroma Town
Pink Fluff	M	L	L	H	H	M	M	M	H	M	M	M	Amity Square
Pink Scale	M	M	L	H	H	H	M	H	M	M	M	M	Amity Square
Piplup Mask	H	L	H	L	M	M	M	M	H	M	M	M	Jubilife TV 2F: player's initial Pokémon / Pastoria City: rival's initial Pokémon / Veilstone City Dept. Store 1F: Prof Rowan's assistant's initial Pokémon
Poison Extract	L	L	M	H	H	L	L	L	H	L	H	H	Massage House in Veilstone City
Pretty Dewdrop	M	L	L	H	M	L	M	M	H	H	H	L	Massage House in Veilstone City
Professor Hat	H	H	H	L	H	H	M	H	M	M	M	M	Win 1st place in the Smartness Ultra Rank Contest
Puffy Smoke	L	L	L	H	M	L	M	M	H	L	H	M	Massage House in Veilstone City
Purple Scale	M	H	L	H	H	H	M	H	M	M	M	M	Amity Square
Red Balloon	M	L	H	L	H	L	M	H	H	M	H	M	Win 1st place in the Coolness Great Rank Contest
Red Barrette	M	M	H	L	H	M	M	H	M	M	M	M	Win 1st place in the Coolness Normal Rank Contest
Red Feather	M	H	L	H	H	M	M	H	M	M	M	M	Amity Square
Red Flower	H	M	L	H	H	M	M	M	M	M	M	M	Flower Shop in Floaroma Town
Retro Pipe	H	M	H	L	M	H	M	M	L	L	L	M	Flower Shop in Floaroma Town
Round Stone	H	L	M	M	M	H	M	H	L	M	L	M	Amity Square
Seashell Shard	H	M	L	H	L	H	H	M	L	M	M	M	Massage House in Veilstone City
Shed Claw	H	H	M	H	L	H	H	M	L	M	M	L	Amity Square
Shed Horn	H	H	M	H	L	H	H	M	L	M	M	L	Amity Square
Shimmering Fire	L	L	M	H	M	L	H	H	H	H	H	M	Massage House in Veilstone City
Shiny Powder	M	L	H	M	M	M	H	H	H	H	H	L	Massage House in Veilstone City
Silk Veil	H	M	H	L	M	M	H	H	H	H	H	L	Win 1st place in the Beauty Ultra Rank Contest
Small Leaf	M	M	L	H	M	M	M	M	H	L	M	M	Amity Square
Snaggy Pebble	H	L	L	H	L	H	M	M	L	L	L	M	Amity Square
Snow Crystal	M	M	L	H	M	L	H	M	H	H	H	L	Massage House in Veilstone City
Sparks	L	L	M	H	M	L	H	M	H	H	H	M	Massage House in Veilstone City
Spotlight	H	M	H	L	L	H	H	H	M	H	H	L	Flower Shop in Floaroma Town
Spring	H	H	H	L	M	H	M	H	H	M	M	M	Massage House in Veilstone City
Standing Mike	H	H	H	L	M	M	M	H	H	M	M	M	Flower Shop in Floaroma Town
Stump	H	M	M	H	L	M	M	L	L	M	M	M	Amity Square
Surfboard	H	H	H	L	M	H	M	H	L	M	M	M	Flower Shop in Floaroma Town
Sweet Candy	H	M	H	L	M	H	M	H	M	M	M	M	Flower Shop in Floaroma Town
Thick Mushroom	H	M	M	H	M	M	M	M	M	M	M	L	Amity Square
Thin Mushroom	M	H	M	H	M	M	H	M	M	M	M	L	Amity Square
Tiara	H	H	H	L	M	H	H	H	M	H	M	L	Insert LeafGreen cartridge into Nintendo DS and go to northwest corner on the 3nd floor of Pal Park
Top Hat	H	M	H	L	H	M	L	H	M	H	M	H	Win 1st place in the Coolness/Ultra Rank Contest
Turtwig Mask	H	L	H	L	M	M	M	M	H	M	M	M	Jubilife TV 2F: player's initial Pokémon / Pastoria City: rival's initial Pokémon / Veilstone City Dept. Store 1F: Prof Rowan's assistant's initial Pokémon
Wealthy Coin	H	L	H	L	M	H	M	H	L	H	L	L	Massage House in Veilstone City
White Beard	M	H	H	L	M	M	H	H	H	L	M	L	Amity Square
White Feather	M	H	L	H	H	M	H	H	M	M	M	L	Amity Square
White Flower	H	M	L	H	M	M	H	M	M	M	M	L	Flower Shop in Floaroma Town
White Fluff	M	L	L	H	M	M	H	M	H	M	M	L	Amity Square
White Moustache	M	M	H	L	M	M	H	H	L	M	M	L	Amity Square
Yellow Balloon	M	L	H	L	H	L	H	H	H	M	H	M	Win 1st place in the Toughness Great Rank Contest
Yellow Barrette	M	M	H	L	H	M	H	H	M	M	H	M	Win 1st place in the Toughness Normal Rank Contest
Yellow Feather	M	H	L	H	H	M	H	H	M	M	M	M	Amity Square
Yellow Flower	H	M	L	H	H	M	H	M	M	M	M	M	Flower Shop in Floaroma Town
Yellow Fluff	M	L	L	H	H	M	H	M	H	M	M	M	Amity Square

Abilities Adaptability – Magnet Pull

Item	Description
Adaptability	Doubles power of a move when it is the same type as the Pokémon
Aftermath	When Pokémon faints, HP of the opponent who dealt the final blow is reduced by 1/4 of maximum
Air Lock	Prevents Pokémon from being affected by weather during battle
Anger Point	Increases Attack to maximum level when attacked with a critical hit
Anticipation	Warns when opponent Pokémon has supereffective moves or one-hit KO moves
Arena Trap	Prevents foe from switching Pokémon or escaping; not effective against Flying-types and Pokémon with Levitate/ Increases chances of meeting wild Pokémon when the Pokémon is in the team's lead position
Battle Armor	Helps Pokémon avoid critical hits
Blaze	Multiplies power of Pokémon's Fire-type attacks by 1.5 when its HP falls below 1/3 its maximum
Chlorophyll	Doubles a Pokémon's Speed during strong sunlight
Clear Body	Prevents an opponent's move from lowering your Pokémon's stats
Cloud Nine	Eliminates all weather effects in battle
Color Change	Changes Pokémon's type to match the type of a move that hits it
Compoundeyes	Increases accuracy 30%/Increases chances of meeting wild Pokémon with held items when the Pokémon is in the team's lead position
Cute Charm	Attracts opponent Pokémon 30% of the time when opponent strikes Pokémon/ Increases chances of meeting wild Pokémon of opposite gender when the Pokémon is in the team's lead position
Damp	Prevents all Pokémon in battle from using Selfdestruct and Explosion
Download	Increases Attack when foe's Defense is less than its Special Defense; increases Special Attack when foe's Special Defense is less than its Defense
Drizzle	Changes weather to rain when user is sent into battle
Drought	Changes weather to strong sunlight when user is sent into battle
Dry Skin	Restores HP when hit by Water-type moves or when it's raining; weak against Fire-type moves and lowers HP during strong sunlight
Early Bird	Causes Pokémon to wake earlier from Sleep conditions
Effect Spore	Afflicts opponent Pokémon with a Poison, Paralyze or Sleep condition 10% of the time when it attacks Pokémon directly
Filter	Decreases damage Pokémon takes when hit by supereffective move
Flame Body	Afflicts opponent Pokémon with a Burn condition 30% of the time when it attacks Pokémon directly/ Increases chances of hatching the Pokémon's Egg when the Pokémon is in the team
Flash Fire	When hit by Fire-type attack prevents all damage and enhances power of own Fire-type attacks by 50%
Flower Gift	Multiplies ally Pokémon's Attack and Special Attack by 1.5 during strong sunlight
Forecast	Changes Pokémon to a form and type that's connected to weather (strong sunlight=Fire-type, rain=Water-type, hail=Ice-type)
Forewarn	Learn opponent Pokémon's strongest move
Frisk	Learn opponent Pokémon's held item
Gluttony	When HP is low, eats a held berry earlier than usual
Guts	Multiplies power of Pokémon's attacks by 1.5 when it has a status condition
Heatproof	Halves damage caused by Fire-type moves and Burn condition
Honey Gather	Picks up Honey after battle; likelihood depends on Pokémon's level
Huge Power	Increases power of Pokémon's attacks, but the effect is reduced by half if the Ability is changed (e.g., Skill Swap)
Hustle	Multiplies power of Pokémon's attacks by 1.5, but its Accuracy is reduced to 80%/ Increases chances of meeting wild Pokémon of a higher level when the Pokémon is in the team's lead position
Hydration	Cures status conditions when it's raining
Hyper Cutter	Prevents effects that reduce the Pokémon's attack power
Ice Body	Recovers HP every turn when it's hailing
Illuminate	Increases chances of meeting wild Pokémon when the Pokémon is in the team's lead position
Immunity	Prevents Pokémon from getting a Poison condition
Inner Focus	Prevents Pokémon from flinching
Insomnia	Prevents Pokémon from getting a Sleep condition
Intimidate	Reduces the opponent's attack power/ Decreases chances of meeting wild Pokémon of lower level when the Pokémon is in the team's lead position
Iron Fist	Increases power of punch attacks by 20% (Ice Punch, Mach Punch, Fire Punch, etc.)
Keen Eye	Protects Pokémon from Accuracy reduction/ Decreases chances of meeting wild Pokémon of lower level when the Pokémon is in the team's lead position
Klutz	Pokémon can't use held items except those that improve base stats or affect experience
Leaf Guard	Prevents status conditions during strong sunlight
Levitate	Prevents Pokémon from getting struck by Ground-type attacks
Lightningrod	Draws Electric-type attacks away from partner when it's in a two-on-two battle
Limber	Prevents Pokémon from getting a Paralyze condition
Liquid Ooze	Causes damage when opponent Pokémon absorbs its HP
Magic Guard	Prevents all damage except from direct-attack moves
Magma Armor	Prevents Pokémon from getting a Freeze condition/ Increases chances of hatching the Pokémon's Egg when the Pokémon is on the team
Magnet Pull	Prevents Steel-type opponents from escaping/ Increases chances of meeting wild Steel-type Pokémon when the Pokémon is in the team's lead position

Abilities (continued) Marvel Scale – Synchronize

Item	Description
Marvel Scale	Multiplies Defense by 1.5 when the Pokémon has a status condition
Minus	Multiplies Special Attack by 1.5 when positively charged Pokémon is also in battle
Mold Breaker	Prevents Pokémon from being affected by foe Pokémon's abilities during battle
Motor Drive	Prevents damage from Electric-type attacks and increases Speed by 1 level
Natural Cure	Cures a Pokémon's status condition when the Pokémon is withdrawn from battle
No Guard	Pokémon and foe both have 100% accuracy/Increases chances of meeting wild Pokémon when the Pokémon is in the team's lead position
Normalize	Changes all of Pokémon's attacks to Normal-type
Oblivious	Prevents Pokémon from becoming attracted
Overgrow	Multiplies power of Grass-type attacks by 1.5 when its HP falls below 1/3 its maximum
Own Tempo	Prevents Pokémon from getting a Confuse condition
Pickup	Picks up items from opponent Pokémon while in battle/Picked-up items will vary based on defeated Pokémon's level (see page 156)
Plus	Multiplies Special Attack power by 1.5 when negatively charged Pokémon is also in battle
Poison Heal	Restores HP every turn while Pokémon has Poison condition
Poison Point	Afflicts opponent Pokémon with a Poison condition 30% of the time when attacked directly
Pressure	Reduces opponent Pokémon's PP by 2 every time it damages Pokémon/ Increases chances of meeting wild Pokémon of a higher level when the Pokémon is in the team's lead position
Pure Power	Increases power of Pokémon's attacks, but the effect is reduced by half if the Ability is changed (e.g., Skill Swap)
Quick Feet	Doubles a Pokémon's Speed when Pokémon has any status condition except Paralysis, which reduces Speed by 1/4 of maximum/ Decreases chances of meeting wild Pokémon when the Pokémon is in the team's lead position
Rain Dish	Recovers HP in every turn when it's raining during battle
Reckless	Increases attack power of moves but causes damage to Pokémon when an attack hits
Rivalry	Increases Attack if foe's gender is same as your Pokémon's; decreases Attack if foe's gender is different from your Pokémon's
Rock Head	Prevents Pokémon from incurring damage when it uses Submission, Take Down, or Double-Edge
Rough Skin	Inflicts damage to opponent Pokémon when attacked directly
Run Away	Allows Pokémon to escape from wild Pokémon
Sand Stream	Summons a sandstorm when user is sent into battle
Sand Veil	Allows Pokémon to evade moves more easily during sandstorms/ Decreases chances of meeting wild Pokémon in a sandstorm when the Pokémon is in the team's lead position
Scrappy	Makes opponent Ghost-types vulnerable to Normal-type attacks
Serene Grace	Doubles the chance that any attack's secondary effects will work
Shadow Tag	Prevents foe from changing Pokémon or escaping
Shed Skin	Pokémon has a 1 in 3 chance of curing its status conditions every turn
Shell Armor	Helps Pokémon avoid critical hits
Shield Dust	Shields Pokémon from the additional effects from moves
Simple	Doubles the effectiveness of all stat modifications
Skill Link	Always hit 5 times with a move that attacks 2-5 times
Slow Start	Halves Pokémon's Attack and Speed for the first five turns the Pokémon is in battle
Sniper	Triples the power of critical hits
Snow Cloak	Pokémon evades moves more easily when it's hailing/ Decreases chances of meeting wild Pokémon in hail when the Pokémon is in the team's lead position
Snow Warning	Summons Hail when user is sent into battle
Solar Power	Multiplies a Pokémon's Special Attack by 1.5 and decreases HP every turn during strong sunlight
Solid Rock	Reduces damage from supereffective attacks
Soundproof	Frees Pokémon from Grasswhistle, Growl, Heal Bell, Hyper Voice, Metal Sound, Perish Song, Roar, Screech, Sing, Snore, Supersonic and Uproar
Speed Boost	Increases Pokémon's Speed every turn
Stall	Always acts after foe
Static	Afflicts opponent Pokémon with a Paralyze condition 30% of the time when it is attacked directly/ Increases chances of meeting wild Electric-type Pokémon when the Pokémon is in the team's lead position
Steadfast	Raises Speed by 1 level every time Pokémon flinches
Stench	Decreases chances of meeting wild Pokémon when the Pokémon is in the team's lead position
Sticky Hold	Prevents opponent Pokémon from stealing an item/ Increases chances of catching wild Pokémon while fishing when the Pokémon is in the team's lead position
Storm Drain	Draws Water-type attacks away from ally Pokémon in a two-on-two battle
Sturdy	Shields Pokémon from attacks that KO the Pokémon in one hit
Suction Cups	Prevents Pokémon from swapping out when the opponent Pokémon uses Whirlwind or Roar/ Increases chances of catching wild Pokémon while fishing when the Pokémon is in the team's lead position
Super Luck	Increases chances of a dealing a critical hit; allows use of Dire Hit and Focus Energy at same time
Swarm	Multiplies power of Bug-type attacks by 1.5 when HP falls below 1/3 its maximum/ Increases chances of hearing the Pokémon's cry when the Pokémon is in the team's lead position
Swift Swim	Doubles the Pokémon's Speed when it's raining in battle
Synchronize	Causes opponent Pokémon that inflicts a Poison, Paralyze, or Burn condition to receive the same condition/ Increases chances of meeting wild Pokémon of same Nature when the Pokémon is in the team's lead position

Item	Description
Tangled Feet	Pokémon's Evasion increases while afflicted with Confuse condition
Technician	Multiplies power of moves that have an attack power of 60 or less by 1.5
Thick Fat	Reduces damage by half when Pokémon is attacked by Fire- or Ice-type attacks
Tinted Lens	Doubles damage of ineffective attacks
Torrent	Multiplies power of Water-type attacks by 1.5 when its HP falls below 1/3 its maximum
Trace	Duplicates Ability that opponent Pokémon has
Truant	Causes Pokémon to make its move only every other turn
Unaware	Ignores foe's stat modifications
Unburden	Doubles Pokémon's Speed after it uses it consumes a held item
Vital Spirit	Prevents Pokémon from getting a Sleep condition/ Increases chances of meeting wild Pokémon of higher level when the Pokémon is in the lead team position
Volt Absorb	Restores Pokémon's HP when Pokémon is attacked by Electric-type attacks
Water Absorb	Restores Pokémon's HP when Pokémon is attacked by Water-type attacks
Water Veil	Prevents Pokémon from getting a Burn condition
White Smoke	Prevents opponent's moves from reducing Pokémon's stats/ Decreases chances of meeting wild Pokémon when the Pokémon is in the lead team position
Wonder Guard	Prevents all damage except from supereffective hits

The Pickup Ability

When your Pokémon has the Pickup Ability (see page 155), the likelihood and type of item it may get from its opponent depends on the Pokémon's level.

Pickup Item	L1-10	L11-20	L21-30	L31-40	L41-50	L51-60	L61-70	L71-80	L81-90	L91-100
Potion	30%									
Antidote	10%	30%								
Super Potion	10%	10%	30%							
Great Ball	10%	10%	10%	30%						
Repel	10%	10%	10%	10%	30%					
Escape Rope	10%	10%	10%	10%	10%	30%				
Full Heal	10%	10%	10%	10%	10%	10%	30%			
Hyper Potion	4%	10%	10%	10%	10%	10%	10%	30%		
Ultra Ball	4%	4%	10%	10%	10%	10%	10%	10%	30%	
Revive		4%	4%	10%	10%	10%	10%	10%	10%	30%
Rare Candy			4%	4%	10%	10%	10%	10%	10%	10%
Dusk Stone				4%	4%	10%	10%	10%	10%	10%
Shiny Stone					4%	10%	10%	10%	10%	10%
Dawn Stone						4%	4%	10%	10%	10%
Full Restore							4%	4%	10%	10%
Max Revive								4%	4%	10%
PP Up									4%	4%
Max Elixir										4%
Hyper Potion	1%									
Nugget	1%	1%								
King's Rock		1%	1%							
Full Restore			1%	1%						
Ether				1%	1%					
White Herb					1%	1%				
TM44 (Rest)						1%	1%			
Elixir							1%	1%		
TM01 (Focus Punch)								1%	1%	
Leftovers									1%	1%
TM26 (Earthquake)										1%

Nature and Characteristics

The charts below show how a Pokémon's Nature and characteristics (as listed on the Trainer Memo page of its Summary) affect the growth of its stats.

Nature	Attack	Defense	Special Attack	Special Defense	Speed
Adamant	Rises quickly		Rises slowly		
Bashful					
Bold	Rises slowly	Rises quickly			
Brave	Rises quickly				Rises slowly
Calm	Rises slowly			Rises quickly	
Careful			Rises slowly	Rises quickly	
Docile					
Gentle		Rises slowly		Rises quickly	
Hardy					
Hasty		Rises slowly			Rises quickly
Impish		Rises quickly	Rises slowly		
Jolly			Rises slowly		Rises quickly
Lax		Rises quickly		Rises slowly	
Lonely	Rises quickly	Rises slowly			
Mild		Rises slowly	Rises quickly		
Modest	Rises slowly		Rises quickly		
Naive				Rises slowly	Rises quickly
Naughty	Rises quickly			Rises slowly	
Quiet			Rises quickly		Rises slowly
Quirky					
Rash			Rises quickly	Rises slowly	
Relaxed		Rises quickly			Rises slowly
Sassy				Rises quickly	Rises slowly
Serious					
Timid	Rises slowly				Rises quickly

Rises Quickly	Pokémon Characteristics
HP	Loves to eat / Often dozes off / Often naps / Scatters things often / Likes to relax
Attack	Proud of its power / Likes to thrash about / A little quick tempered / Likes to fight / Hot Tempered
Defense	Sturdy body / Capable of taking hits / Highly persistent / Good endurance /Good perseverance
Special Attack	Highly curious / Mischievous / Thoroughly cunning / Often lost in thought / Very finicky
Special Defense	Strong willed / Somewhat vain / Strongly defiant / Hates to lose / Somewhat stubborn
Speed	Likes to run / Alert to sounds / Impetuous and silly / Somewhat of a clown / Quick to flee

Underground Goods

Item	How to Get	Sphere Value
Alert Tool 1	Barter Exchange	Pale 20-50
Alert Tool 2	Barter Exchange	Pale 20-50
Alert Tool 3	Barter Exchange	Pale 20-50
Alert Tool 4	Barter Exchange	Pale 20-50
Beauty Cup	Mr. Goods (after you win Beauty Contest)	—
Big Bookshelf	Barter Exchange	Green 20-25
Big Oil Drum	Barter Exchange	Pale 10-40
Big Table	Barter Exchange	Blue 12-15
Big TV	Barter Exchange/Veilstone Dept. Store	Prism 9-10
Bike Rack	Barter Exchange	Green 35-49
Binoculars	Barter Exchange	Pale 10-40
Blue Crystal	Mr. Goods (after you meet 100 people)	—
Blue Cushion	Barter Exchange	Red 8-10
Blue Tent	Barter Exchange	Pale 20-70
Bonsai	Barter Exchange	Green 8-10
Bonsly Doll	Veilstone Dept. Store	—
Bronze Trophy	20 wins in Battle Tower	—
Bubble Tool	Barter Exchange	Blue 28-32
Buizel Doll	Barter Exchange/Underground Man	
Bulbasaur Doll	Barter Exchange	Green 25-30
Buneary Doll	Barter Exchange/Underground Man	Pale 15-30
Cardboard Box	Barter Exchange	Red 20-25
Charmander Doll	Barter Exchange	Red 25-30
Chatot Doll	Barter Exchange/Veilstone Dept. Store	—
Chikorita Doll	Barter Exchange	Green 25-30
Chimchar Doll	Barter Exchange/Underground Man	Red 25-40
Clear Tent	Barter Exchange	Pale 40-99
Clefairy Doll	Barter Exchange	Pale 40-70
Container	Barter Exchange	Pale 10-40
Cool Cup	Mr. Goods (after you win Cool Contest)	—
Crate	Barter Exchange	Red 33-40
Crater Tool	Barter Exchange	Blue 25-30
Cute Cup	Mr. Goods (after you win Cute Contest)	—
Cute Flowers	Barter Exchange	Green 12-15
Cyndaquil Doll	Barter Exchange	Red 25-30
Display Rack	Barter Exchange	Green 12-15
Drifloon Doll	Barter Exchange	Blue 33-40
Ember Tool	Barter Exchange	Red 15-18
Fluffy Bed	Barter Exchange	Blue 33-40
Fire Tool	Barter Exchange	Red 33-40
Flower Tool	Barter Exchange	Green 65-80
Foam Tool	Barter Exchange	Blue 12-14
Fog Tool	Barter Exchange	Red 28-32
Game System	Barter Exchange	Prism 48-50
Glameow Doll	Barter Exchange	Blue 15-20
Glitter Gem	Underground Man (after you get 50 flags)	—
Globe	Mr. Goods (after connecting via Wi-Fi)	—
Gold Trophy	100 wins in Battle Tower	—
Green Bike	Barter Exchange	Green 33-40
Gym Statue	Mr. Goods (after getting 8 Badges)	—
Happiny Doll	Barter Exchange	Pale 40-70
Healing Machine	Barter Exchange	Prism 90-99
Iron Beam	Barter Exchange	Prism 9-10
Jigglypuff Doll	Barter Exchange	Pale 40-70
Lab Machine	Barter Exchange	Prism 28-30
Lavish Flowers	Barter Exchange	Green 8-10
Leaf Tool	Barter Exchange	Green 30-38
Long Table	Barter Exchange	Blue 12-15
Lovely Flowers	Barter Exchange	Green 8-10
Mantyke Doll	Barter Exchange/Veilstone Dept. Store	—
Maze Block 1	Barter Exchange	Prism 48-50

Item	How to Get	Sphere Value
Maze Block 2	Barter Exchange	Prism 48-50
Maze Block 3	Barter Exchange	Prism 48-50
Maze Block 4	Barter Exchange	Prism 48-50
Maze Block 5	Barter Exchange	Prism 48-50
Meowth Doll	Barter Exchange	Red 15-20
Mime Jr. Doll	Barter Exchange/Veilstone Dept. Store	—
Minun Doll	Barter Exchange	Blue 60-70
Mudkip Doll	Barter Exchange	Blue 25-30
Munchlax Doll	Barter Exchange/Veilstone Dept. Store	—
Mystic Gem	Underground Man (after you get 10 flags)	—
Oil Drum	Barter Exchange	Pale 10-40
Pachirisu Doll	Barter Exchange	Pale 70-99
Pikachu Doll	Barter Exchange	Pale 70-99
Pink Crystal	Mr. Goods (after you've received 100 goods)	—
Pink Dresser	Barter Exchange	Green 50-60
Piplup Doll	Barter Exchange/Underground Man	Blue 35-40
Pit Tool	Barter Exchange	Blue 10-12
Plain Table	Barter Exchange/Underground Man	Blue 8-10
Pluse Doll	Barter Exchange	Red 60-70
Poké Center Flower	Barter Exchange	Pale 10-40
Poké Center Table	Barter Exchange	Blue 20-25
Potted Plant	Barter Exchange	Red 20-25
Pretty Flowers	Barter Exchange	Green 8-10
Pretty Gem	Underground Man (after you get a flag)	—
Pretty Sink	Barter Exchange/Veilstone Dept. Store	Prism 9-10
Red Bike	Barter Exchange	Red 33-40
Red Crystal	Mr. Goods (after you mine 100 times)	—
Red Tent	Barter Exchange	Pale 20-70
Refrigerator	Barter Exchange/Veilstone Dept. Store	Green 12-15
Research Shelf	Barter Exchange	Green 12-15
Rock Tool	Barter Exchange	Red 10-12
Shiny Gem	Underground Man (after you get 3 flags)	—
Shop Shelf	Barter Exchange	Green 35-49
Sideboard	Barter Exchange/Veilstone Dept. Store	Green 20-25
Silver Trophy	50 wins in Battle Tower	—
Skitty Doll	Barter Exchange	Green 15—20
Small Bookshelf	Barter Exchange/Underground Man	Green 8-10
Small Table	Barter Exchange	Blue 8-10
Smart Cup	Mr. Goods (after you win Smart Contest)	—
Smoke Tool	Barter Exchange	Red 12-14
Snorlax Doll	Barter Exchange	Red 80-99
Squirtle Doll	Barter Exchange	Blue 25-30
Test Machine	Barter Exchange	Prism 28-30
Torchic Doll	Barter Exchange	Red 25-30
Totodile Doll	Barter Exchange	Blue 25-30
Tough Cup	Mr. Goods (after you win Tough Contest)	—
Trash Can	Barter Exchange	Red 8-10
Treecko Doll	Barter Exchange	Green 25-30
Tumble Tool	Barter Exchange	Red 25-30
Turtwig Doll	Barter Exchange/Underground Man	Green 35-40
Vending Machine	Barter Exchange	Green 8-10
Wailord Doll	Barter Exchange	Blue 80-99
Weavile Doll	Barter Exchange	Prism 28-30
Wide Sofa	Barter Exchange	Blue 20-25
Wide Table	Barter Exchange	Blue 12-15
Wobbuffet Doll	Barter Exchange	Green 80-99
Wood Dresser	Barter Exchange	Green 20-25
Wooden Chair	Barter Exchange/Underground Man	Red 8-10
Yellow Crystal	Mr. Goods (after you use traps 100 times)	—
Yellow Cushion	Barter Exchange/Veilstone Dept. Store	Red 8-10

Battle Moves Absorb – Bug Bite

CAT=Category
P=Physical Attack move: Physical moves are attacks that derive their power from the user's Attack stat and the target's Defense stat.
S=Special Attack move: Special moves are attacks that derive their power from the user's Special Attack stat and the target's Special Defense stat.
O=Other move: The Other category includes moves that heal wounded Pokémon, alter stats, inflict conditions, and cause other effects.

BA=Basic Attack Power:
Basic Attack Power determines the base amount of damage an attack move will inflict. This number is then modified by the Pokémon's Attack or Special Attack (depending on the move's category) and damage modifiers to determine how effective the move is.

2-on-2 Battle range:
1=Move is effective on one foe or partner.
2=Move is effective against both foes at once.
(NOTE: Moves with this range deal less damage in Double Battles.)
3=Move is effective on both foes and partner at once.
4=Move is effective on all Pokémon at once.
S=Move is effective on only the Pokémon that executes the move.
R=Move affects random Pokémon chosen from both foes and partner.

DA=Direct Attack: Moves marked as direct attacks trigger the effects of some abilities, such as Rough Skin, that react to certain kinds of physical contact.

Move	Type	Cat	BA	AC	PP	2-on-2	DA	Effect
Absorb	GRS	S	20	100	20	1		Restores HP equal to half the damage caused to foe

AC=Accuracy: Accuracy determines the base chance that a move will hit its target. Odds of success may be altered by Pokémon abilities, held items, or status conditions.

PP=Power Points: Power Points dictate how many times a Pokémon can use a move before the move is tapped out.

Move	Type	Cat	BA	AC	PP	2-on-2	DA	Effect
Absorb	GRS	S	20	100	20	1		Restores HP equal to half the damage caused to foe
Acid	PSN	S	40	100	30	2		Has 10% chance of lowering foe's Defense by 1 level
Acid Armor	PSN	O	–	–	40	S		Raises Defense by 2 levels
Acupressure	NRM	O	–	–	30	1	=	Raises a random stat by 2 levels
Aerial Ace (TM40)	FLY	P	60	–	20	1	=	Hits foe unavoidably
Aeroblast	FLY	S	100	95	25	1	=	Has a high chance for a critical hit
Agility	PSY	O	–	–	30	S		Raises Pokémon's Speed by 2 levels
Air Cutter	FLY	S	55	95	25	2		Has a high chance for a critical hit
Air Slash	FLY	S	75	95	20	1		Has 30% chance of causing Flinch
Amnesia	PSY	O	–	–	20	S		Raises Special Defense by 2 levels
Ancientpower	RCK	S	60	100	5	1	=	Has 10% chance of raising Attack, Defense, Sp. Attack, Sp. Defense and Speed 1 level
Aqua Jet	WTR	P	40	100	20	1	=	Causes you to move first in a turn; if opponent uses it too, the higher Speed prevails
Aqua Ring	WTR	O	–	–	20	S		Restores a small amount of HP each turn
Aqua Tail	WTR	P	90	90	10	1	=	No extra effect beyond damaging foe
Arm Thrust	FTG	P	15	100	20	1	=	Attacks 2-5 times per turn
Aromatherapy	GRS	O	–	–	5	S		Heals all critical conditions of all Pokémon in party
Assist	NRM	O	–	100	20	–		Uses a random move of a Pokémon not in battle
Assurance	DRK	P	50	100	10	1	=	Inflicts 2x damage if the opponent has already taken damage in the same turn
Astonish	GHO	P	30	100	15	1	=	Has 30% chance of causing Flinch
Attack Order	BUG	P	90	100	15	1		Has a high chance for a critical hit
Attract (TM45)	NRM	O	–	100	15	1		Causes foe of opposite gender to become attracted (50% chance can't move each turn)
Aura Sphere	FTG	S	90	–	20	1		Will always strike foe successfully
Aurora Beam	ICE	S	65	100	20	1		Has 10% chance of lowering foe's Attack 1 level
Avalanche (TM72)	ICE	P	60	100	10	1	=	Doubles damage if it hits a Pokémon that hit your Pokémon in the same turn
Barrage	NRM	P	15	85	20	1		Attacks 2-5 times per turn
Barrier	PSY	O	–	–	30	S		Raises Defense by 2 levels
Baton Pass	NRM	O	–	–	40	S		Can switch Pokémon with another, passing on many status/skill changes
Beat Up	DRK	P	10	100	10	1		Attacks opponent a number of times equal to your number of healthy Pokémon
Belly Drum	NRM	O	–	–	10	S		Decreases HP by 50% and increases Attack to maximum possible
Bide	NRM	P	–	100	10	S	=	Doubles damage received while waiting 2 turns and inflicts it on foe
Bind	NRM	P	15	75	20	1	=	Damages foe for 2-5 turns; foe can't escape until effect wears off
Bite	DRK	P	60	100	25	1	=	Has 30% chance of causing Flinch
Blast Burn	FIRE	S	150	90	5	1		Causes massive damage but forfeits attacker's next move
Blaze Kick	FIRE	P	85	90	10	1	=	Has a high chance for a critical hit; 10% chance of causing Burn
Blizzard (TM14)	ICE	S	120	70	5	2		Has 10% chance of causing Freeze
Block	NRM	O	–	100	5	1		Prevents foe from switching out during battle or escaping
Body Slam	NRM	P	85	100	15	1	=	Has 30% chance of causing Paralyze
Bone Club	GRD	P	65	85	20	1		Has 10% chance of causing Flinch
Bone Rush	GRD	P	25	80	10	1		Attacks 2-5 times per turn
Bonemerang	GRD	P	50	90	10	1		Attacks twice per turn
Bounce	FLY	P	85	85	5	1	=	User leaves battlefield then strikes next turn; 30% chance of causing Paralyze
Brave Bird	FLY	P	120	100	15	1	=	Inflicts 1/3 of damage to user
Brick Break (TM31)	FTG	P	75	100	15	1	=	Shatters foe's Reflect and Light Screen protection
Brine (TM55)	WTR	S	65	100	10	1		Inflicts twice the damage if foe's HP is 1/2 or less full
Bubble	WTR	S	20	100	30	2		Has 10% chance of reducing foe's Speed 1 level
Bubblebeam	WTR	S	65	100	20	1		Has 10% chance of reducing foe's Speed 1 level
Bug Bite	BUG	P	60	100	20	1	=	Eats foe's held berry and gains its effect

Contest Equivalents Absorb – Bug Bite

Each battle move has a contest equivalent—a version of the move that is used when a player enters a Super Contest in Hearthome City. Each move will not only have a new type, but also a new purpose. To learn more about Super Contests, see page 34.

Effect in Super Contests: Each move's functions are explained here. The +3 refers to a bonus to its Appeal score.

Move	Type	AP	Effect in Super Contests
Absorb	Smart	1	Earn +3 if two Pokémon in a row raise the Voltage

AP=Appeal Points: Appeal Points are the hearts you win from judges. The higher a move's AP, the better. A * here indicates that AP varies and is detailed in the "Effect in Super Contests" column.

Move	Type	AP	Effect in Super Contests
Absorb	Smart	1	Earn +3 if two Pokémon in a row raise the Voltage
Acid	Smart	3	A basic performance using a move known by the Pokémon
Acid Armor	Tough	–	Earn double the score in the next turn
Acupressure	Cool	–	Earn double the score in the next turn
Aerial Ace (TM40)	Cool	2	Earn +2 if the Pokémon performs first in the turn
Aeroblast	Cool	2	Earn +3 if the Pokémon that just went hit max Voltage
Agility	Cool	2	Enables the user to perform first in the next turn
Air Cutter	Cool	3	A basic performance using a move known by the Pokémon
Air Slash	Cool	2	Earn +2 if the Pokémon performs first in the turn
Amnesia	Cute	–	Earn double the score in the next turn
Ancientpower	Tough	2	Earn +2 if the Pokémon performs last in the turn
Aqua Jet	Beauty	2	Enables the user to perform first in the next turn
Aqua Ring	Beauty	*	AP value equal to Voltage of targeted judge
Aqua Tail	Cute	3	A basic performance using a move known by the Pokémon
Arm Thrust	Tough	2	Allows performance of the same move twice in a row
Aromatherapy	Smart	*	AP value equal to Voltage of targeted judge
Assist	Cute	2	Randomizes order that all Pokémon move next round
Assurance	Beauty	2	Earns double the score if the performance comes last in the final round
Astonish	Smart	3	A basic performance using a move known by the Pokémon
Attack Order	Smart	2	Earn +2 if the judge's Voltage goes up
Attract (TM45)	Cute	2	Prevents the Voltage from going down in the same turn
Aura Sphere	Beauty	2	Earn +2 if the Pokémon performs first in the turn
Aurora Beam	Beauty	2	Earn +2 if the Pokémon performs first in the turn
Avalanche (TM72)	Cool	2	Earns double the score if the performance comes last in the final round
Barrage	Tough	2	Allows performance of the same move twice in a row
Barrier	Cool	2	Prevents the Voltage from going up in the same turn
Baton Pass	Cute	*	AP value equal to 4 minus targeted judge's Voltage
Beat Up	Smart	2	Allows performance of the same move twice in a row
Belly Drum	Cute	–	Earn double the score in the next turn
Bide	Tough	2	Earns double the score if the performance comes last in the final round
Bind	Tough	*	AP is 1 if performed first in a turn, 2 if second, 3 if third, and 4 if fourth
Bite	Tough	3	A basic performance using a move known by the Pokémon
Blast Burn	Beauty	2	Earn +3 if the Pokémon that just went hit max Voltage
Blaze Kick	Beauty	2	Earn +2 if the Pokémon performs first in the turn
Blizzard (TM14)	Beauty	2	Earn +2 if the Pokémon performs first in the turn
Block	Cute	2	Prevents the Voltage from going up in the same turn
Body Slam	Tough	3	A basic performance using a move known by the Pokémon
Bone Club	Tough	3	A basic performance using a move known by the Pokémon
Bone Rush	Tough	2	Allows performance of the same move twice in a row
Bonemerang	Tough	2	Allows performance of the same move twice in a row
Bounce	Cute	1	Earn +3 if no other Pokémon has chosen the same judge
Brave Bird	Cute	2	Earn +2 if the Pokémon performs last in the turn
Brick Break (TM31)	Cool	3	A basic performance using a move known by the Pokémon
Brine (TM55)	Smart	2	Earn +2 if the judge's Voltage goes up
Bubble	Cute	2	Enables the user to perform last in the next turn
Bubblebeam	Beauty	2	Enables the user to perform last in the next turn
Bug Bite	Tough	–	If previous performer hits its Voltage to the max, then you will earn points equal to its Voltage

Move	Type	Cat	BA	AC	PP	2-on-2	DA	Effect
Bug Buzz	BUG	S	90	100	10	1		Has 10% chance of lowering foe's Sp. Defense 1 level
Bulk Up (TM08)	FTG	O	–	–	20	S		Raises Attack and Defense by 1 level
Bullet Punch	STL	P	40	100	30	1	=	Causes you to move first in a turn; if opponent uses it too, the higher Speed prevails
Bullet Seed (TM09)	GRS	P	10	100	30	1		Attacks 2-5 times per turn
Calm Mind (TM04)	PSY	O	–	–	20	S		Raises Sp. Attack and Sp. Defense 1 level
Camouflage	NRM	O	–	100	20	S		Changes Pokémon's type (grass, Grass; sand, Ground; water, Water; caves, Rock; other, Normal)
Captivate (TM78)	NRM	O	–	100	20	2		Lowers opposite-gendered Pokémon's Sp. Attack 2 levels
Charge	ELC	O	–	100	20	S		Doubles power of the Electric-type move that's next used; raises Sp. Defense 1 level
Charge Beam (TM57)	ELC	S	50	90	10	1		Has 70% chance of raising Sp. Attack 1 level
Charm	NRM	O	–	100	20	1		Lowers foe's Attack by 2 levels
Chatter	FLY	S	60	100	20	1		Has a higher chance of causing Confuse based on volume of recording (Chatot only)
Clamp	WTR	P	35	75	10	1	=	Damages foe for 2-5 turns; foe can't escape until completed
Close Combat	FTG	P	120	100	5	1	=	Inflicts massive damage but lowers your Defense and Sp. Defense 1 level
Comet Punch	NRM	P	18	85	15	1	=	Attacks 2-5 times per turn
Confuse Ray	GHO	O	–	100	10	1		Causes foe to have Confuse condition
Confusion	PSY	S	50	100	25	1		Has 10% chance of causing Confuse condition
Constrict	NRM	P	10	100	35	1	=	Has 10% chance of lowering foe's Speed
Conversion	NRM	O	–	–	30	S		Changes Pokémon's type into one of its attack types
Conversion 2	NRM	O	–	100	30	S		Changes Pokémon's type into one that matches an attack type that its foe is weak against
Copycat	NRM	O	–	–	20	–		Uses same move that foe just used
Cosmic Power	PSY	O	–	–	20	S		Raises Defense and Sp. Defense 1 level
Cotton Spore	GRS	O	–	85	40	1		Lowers foe's Speed 2 levels
Counter	FTG	P	–	100	20	–	=	Attacks second, doing 2x physical attack damage that foe did to Pokémon
Covet	NRM	P	40	100	40	1		Takes a foe's held item (if any)
Crabhammer	WTR	P	90	85	10	1	=	Has a high chance for a critical hit
Cross Chop	FTG	P	100	80	5	1	=	Has a high chance for a critical hit
Cross Poison	PSN	P	70	100	20	1	=	Has 10% chance of causing Poison; has a high chance for critical hit
Crunch	DRK	P	80	100	15	1	=	Has 20% chance of lowering foe's Defense 1 level
Crush Claw	NRM	P	75	95	10	1	=	Has 50% chance of lowering foe's Defense 1 level
Crush Grip	NRM	P	–	100	5	1	=	Inflicts more damage if the higher the foe's HP
Curse	?	O	–	–	10	1		Raises Att/Def 1 level but reduces Speed 1 level; halves GHO's HP and quarters foe's HP each turn
Cut (HM01)	NRM	P	50	95	30	1	=	Cuts down small trees outside of battle
Dark Pulse (TM79)	DRK	S	80	100	15	1		Has 20% chance of causing Flinch
Defend Order	BUG	O	–	–	10	S		Raises Defense and Sp. Defense 1 level
Defense Curl	NRM	O	–	–	40	S		Raises Defense 1 level
Defog (HM05)	FLY	O	–	–	15	1		Lower's foe's Evasiveness 1 level; clears Light Screen, Reflect, Safeguard, Mist, Spikes, and Toxic Spikes; clears fog on field
Destiny Bond	GHO	O	–	–	5	S		Causes foe to faint if Pokémon faints
Detect	FTG	O	–	–	5	S		Wards off foe moves for 1 turn; success falls if used consecutively
Dig (TM28)	GRD	P	80	100	10	1	=	User leaves battlefield then strikes next turn; returns to overworld outside battle
Disable	NRM	O	–	80	20	1		Disables foe's most recently used move for several turns
Discharge	ELC	S	80	100	15	3		Has 30% chance of causing Paralyze
Dive	WTR	P	80	100	10	1	=	User leaves battlefield then strikes next turn
Dizzy Punch	NRM	P	70	100	10	1	=	Has 20% chance of causing Confuse condition
Doom Desire	STL	S	120	85	5	1		Waits 2 turns then inflicts damage on foe on third turn
Double Hit	NRM	P	35	90	10	1	=	Attacks twice per turn
Double Kick	FTG	P	30	100	30	1	=	Attacks twice per turn
Double Team (TM32)	NRM	O	–	–	15	S		Raises Evasiveness by 1 level
Double-Edge	NRM	P	120	100	15	1		Inflicts Pokémon with 1/3 damage inflicted on foe
Doubleslap	NRM	P	15	85	10	1		Attacks 2-5 times per turn
Draco Meteor	DRG	S	140	90	5	1		Lowers your Special Attack by 2 levels
Dragon Claw (TM02)	DRG	P	80	100	15	1	=	No extra effect beyond damaging foe
Dragon Dance	DRG	O	–	–	20	S		Raises Attack and Speed 1 level
Dragon Pulse (TM59)	DRG	S	90	100	10	1		No extra effect beyond damaging foe
Dragon Rage	DRG	S	–	100	10	1		Causes 40 points of damage regardless of other battle factors
Dragon Rush	DRG	P	100	75	10	1		Has 20% chance of causing Flinch
Dragonbreath	DRG	S	60	100	20	1		Has 30% chance of causing Paralyze condition
Drain Punch (TM60)	FTG	P	60	100	5	1	=	Damages foe and restores own HP equal to 1/2 inflicted damage
Dream Eater (TM85)	PSY	S	100	100	15	1		Damages foe and restores own HP equal to 1/2 inflicted damage, if foe has Sleep condition
Drill Peck	FLY	P	80	100	20	1	=	No extra effect beyond damaging foe

Contest Equivalents (continued) Bug Buzz – Drill Peck

Move	Type	AP	Effect in Super Contests
Bug Buzz	Cute	2	Earn +2 if the judge's Voltage goes up
Bulk Up (TM08)	Beauty	–	Earn double the score in the next turn
Bullet Punch	Smart	2	Enables the user to perform first in the next turn
Bullet Seed (TM09)	Cool	2	Allows performance of the same move twice in a row
Calm Mind (TM04)	Smart	–	Earn double the score in the next turn
Camouflage	Smart	2	Prevents the Voltage from going up in the same turn
Captivate (TM78)	Beauty	2	Prevents the Voltage from going down in the same turn
Charge	Smart	–	Earn double the score in the next turn
Charge Beam (TM57)	Beauty	2	Earn +2 if the Pokémon performs first in the turn
Charm	Cute	2	Prevents the Voltage from going down in the same turn
Chatter	Smart	1	Earn +3 if the Pokémon gets the lowest score
Clamp	Tough	3	A basic performance using a move known by the Pokémon
Close Combat	Smart	2	Earn +3 if the Pokémon that just went hit max Voltage
Comet Punch	Tough	2	Allows performance of the same move twice in a row
Confuse Ray	Smart	2	Lowers the Voltage of all judges by one each
Confusion	Smart	3	A basic performance using a move known by the Pokémon
Constrict	Tough	*	AP is 1 if performed first in a turn, 2 if second, 3 if third, and 4 if fourth
Conversion	Beauty	1	Earn +3 if the Pokémon gets the lowest score
Conversion 2	Beauty	1	Earn +3 if the Pokémon gets the lowest score
Copycat	Cool	–	If previous performer hits its Voltage to the max, then you will earn points equal to its Voltage
Cosmic Power	Cool	–	Earn double the score in the next turn
Cotton Spore	Beauty	2	Enables the user to perform first in the next turn
Counter	Tough	2	Earns double the score if the performance comes last in the final round
Covet	Cute	–	If previous performer hits its Voltage to the max, then you will earn points equal to its Voltage
Crabhammer	Tough	2	Earn +2 if the Pokémon performs last in the turn
Cross Chop	Cool	2	Earn +2 if the Pokémon performs last in the turn
Cross Poison	Cool	3	A basic performance using a move known by the Pokémon
Crunch	Tough	2	Earn +2 if the Pokémon performs last in the turn
Crush Claw	Cool	3	A basic performance using a move known by the Pokémon
Crush Grip	Tough	2	Earns double the score if the performance comes last in the final round
Curse	Tough	*	AP is 1 if performed first in a turn, 2 if second, 3 if third, and 4 if fourth
Cut (HM01)	Cool	3	A basic performance using a move known by the Pokémon
Dark Pulse (TM79)	Cool	2	Earn +2 if the Pokémon performs first in the turn
Defend Order	Smart	–	Earn double the score in the next turn
Defense Curl	Cute	2	Prevents the Voltage from going up in the same turn
Defog (HM05)	Beauty	2	Prevents the Voltage from going up in the same turn
Destiny Bond	Smart	–	Earn +15 if all the Pokémon choose the same judge
Detect	Cool	*	AP value equal to 4 minus targeted judge's Voltage
Dig (TM28)	Smart	1	Earn +3 if no other Pokémon has chosen the same judge
Disable	Smart	2	Prevents the Voltage from going down in the same turn
Discharge	Cool	2	Earn +2 if the Pokémon performs first in the turn
Dive	Beauty	1	Earn +3 if no other Pokémon has chosen the same judge
Dizzy Punch	Cool	*	AP value equal to 4 minus targeted judge's Voltage
Doom Desire	Cool	2	Earn +2 if the Pokémon performs first in the turn
Double Hit	Smart	2	Allows performance of the same move twice in a row
Double Kick	Cool	2	Allows performance of the same move twice in a row
Double Team (TM32)	Cool	2	Enables the user to perform first in the next turn
Double-Edge	Tough	–	Earn +15 if all the Pokémon choose the same judge
Doubleslap	Tough	2	Allows performance of the same move twice in a row
Draco Meteor	Smart	2	Earn +3 if the Pokémon that just went hit max Voltage
Dragon Claw (TM02)	Cool	2	Earn +2 if the Pokémon performs first in the turn
Dragon Dance	Cool	–	Earn double the score in the next turn
Dragon Pulse (TM59)	Smart	2	Earn +2 if the judge's Voltage goes up
Dragon Rage	Cool	3	A basic performance using a move known by the Pokémon
Dragon Rush	Cool	2	Earn +2 if the Pokémon performs last in the turn
Dragonbreath	Cool	2	Earn +2 if the Pokémon performs first in the turn
Drain Punch (TM60)	Beauty	1	Earn +3 if two Pokémon in a row raise the Voltage
Dream Eater (TM85)	Smart	1	Earn +3 if two Pokémon in a row raise the Voltage
Drill Peck	Cool	3	A basic performance using a move known by the Pokémon

Move	Type	Cat	BA	AC	PP	2-on-2	DA	Effect
Dynamicpunch	FTG	P	100	50	5	1	=	Causes foe to have Confuse condition
Earth Power	GRD	S	90	100	10	1		Has 10% chance of lowering foe's Sp. Defense 1 level
Earthquake (TM26)	GRD	P	100	100	10	3		Inflicts twice the damage if foe is using Dig
Egg Bomb	NRM	P	100	75	10	1		No extra effect beyond damaging foe
Embargo (TM63)	DRK	O	–	100	15	1		Prevents foe and Trainer from using items for 5 turns
Ember	FIRE	S	40	100	25	1		Has 10% chance of causing Burn
Encore	NRM	O	–	100	5	1		Forces foe to repeat most recently used move for 3-6 turns
Endeavor	NRM	P	–	100	5	1	=	Inflicts damage equal to your foe's HP minus your HP
Endure (TM58)	NRM	O	–	–	10	S		Keep 1 HP even if foe's next move would cause you to faint; success drops if used repeatedly
Energy Ball (TM53)	GRS	S	80	100	10	1		Has 10% chance of lowering foe's Sp. Defense 1 level
Eruption	FIRE	S	150	100	5	2		Inflicts less damage if your HP is lower
Explosion (TM64)	NRM	P	250	100	5	3		Inflicts a massive amount of damage but causes you to faint
Extrasensory	PSY	S	80	100	30	1		Has 10% chance of causing Flinch
Extremespeed	NRM	P	80	100	5	1	=	Causes you to move first in a turn; if opponent uses it too, the higher Speed prevails
Facade (TM42)	NRM	P	70	100	20	1	=	Doubles Attack if you have a Poison, Paralyze or Burn condition
Faint Attack	DRK	P	60	–	20	1		Will always strike foe successfully
Fake Out	NRM	P	40	100	10	1		Causes Flinch, but move causes its damage and effect only on the first turn
Fake Tears	DRK	O	–	100	20	1		Lowers foe's Sp. Defense 2 levels
False Swipe (TM54)	NRM	P	40	100	40	1	=	Leaves foe with 1 HP even if move would normally cause foe to Faint
Featherdance	FLY	O	–	100	15	1		Lowers foe's Attack 2 levels
Feint	NRM	P	50	100	10	1		Clears Protect or Detect conditions when it hits foes who are using either move
Fire Blast (TM38)	FIRE	S	120	85	5	1		Has 10% chance of causing Burn
Fire Fang	FIRE	P	65	95	15	1	=	Has 10% chance of causing Flinch or Burn, will thaw target with Freeze condition
Fire Punch	FIRE	P	75	100	15	1		Has 10% chance of causing Burn
Fire Spin	FIRE	S	15	70	15	1		Damages foe for 2-5 turns; foe can't escape until completed
Fissure	GRD	P	–	30	5	1		Causes foe to Faint if it is lower level than user; AC improves based on difference between levels
Flail	NRM	P	–	100	15	1	=	Inflicts higher damage if your HP is lower
Flame Wheel	FIRE	P	60	100	25	1	=	Has 10% chance of causing Burn; will thaw target with Freeze condition
Flamethrower (TM35)	FIRE	S	95	100	15	1		Has 10% chance of causing Burn; will thaw target with Freeze condition
Flare Blitz	FIRE	P	120	100	15	1	=	Inflicts 1/3 of damage to user; 10% chance of causing Burn; will thaw target with Freeze condition
Flash (TM70)	NRM	O	–	100	20	1		Lowers foe's Accuracy 1 level; lights up dark caves outside of battle
Flash Cannon (TM91)	STL	S	80	100	10	1		Has 10% chance of lowering foe's Sp. Defense 1 level
Flatter	DRK	O	–	100	15	1		Causes foe to become Confused and raises foe's Sp. Attack 1 level
Fling (TM56)	DRK	P	–	100	10	1		Throws held item; power and effect varies based on held item
Fly (HM02)	FLY	P	90	95	15	1	=	User leaves battlefield then strikes next turn; can fly to towns previously visited
Focus Blast (TM52)	FTG	S	120	70	5	1		Has 10% chance of lowering foe's Sp. Defense 1 level
Focus Energy	NRM	O	–	–	30	S		Increases chance of critical hit
Focus Punch (TM01)	FTG	P	150	100	20	1	=	Causes you to move last in turn and Flinch if foe's move connects
Follow Me	NRM	O	–	100	20	S		Pokémon moves first and draws all attacks to itself during a 2-on-2 battle
Force Palm	FTG	P	60	100	10	1	=	Has 30% chance of causing Paralyze
Foresight	NRM	O	–	100	40	1		Your moves ignore foe's Evasiveness; exposes Ghost-types to Normal- and Fighting-type attacks
Frenzy Plant	GRS	S	150	90	5	1		Causes massive damage but forfeits attacker's next move
Frustration (TM21)	NRM	P	–	100	20	1	=	Inflicts higher damage if your Pokémon likes its Trainer less
Fury Attack	NRM	P	15	85	20	1	=	Attacks 2-5 times per turn
Fury Cutter	BUG	P	10	95	20	1	=	Doubles damage from Fury Cutter's use in previous turn (if it hit foe)
Fury Swipes	NRM	P	18	80	15	1	=	Attacks 2-5 times per turn
Future Sight	PSY	S	80	90	15	1		Waits 2 turns then inflicts damage on foe on third turn
Gastro Acid	PSN	O	–	100	10	1		Nullifies effect of foe's Ability
Giga Drain (TM19)	GRS	S	60	100	5	1		Damages foe and restores own HP equal to 1/2 inflicted damage
Giga Impact (TM68)	NRM	P	150	90	5	1	=	Attacker forfeits next turn
Glare	NRM	O	–	75	30	1		Causes Paralyze condition
Grass Knot (TM86)	GRS	S	–	100	20	1	=	The heavier the foe, the higher the attack's power
Grasswhistle	GRS	O	–	55	15	1		Causes Sleep condition for five turns
Gravity	GRD	O	–	–	5	4		Raises all Pokémon's accuracy for 5 turns; Flying-type and Levitated Pokémon can be hit by Ground-type moves; Fly, Splash, Bounce, and Magnet Rise are cancelled and cannot be used
Growl	NRM	O	–	100	40	2		Lowers foe's Attack by 1 level
Growth	NRM	O	–	–	40	S		Raises Sp. Attack 1 level
Grudge	GHO	O	–	100	5	S		Eliminates all PP from move that causes you to Faint in battle
Guard Swap	PSY	O	–	–	10	1		Switches any modification of Defense and Sp. Defense with foe
Guillotine	NRM	P	–	30	5	1	=	Causes foe to Faint if it is lower level than use; AC improves based on difference between levels

Contest Equivalents (continued) Dynamicpunch – Guillotine

Move	Type	AP	Effect in Super Contests
Dynamicpunch	Cool	2	Earn +2 if the Pokémon performs last in the turn
Earth Power	Smart	2	Earn +2 if the Pokémon performs last in the turn
Earthquake (TM26)	Tough	2	Earn +2 if the Pokémon performs last in the turn
Egg Bomb	Tough	3	A basic performance using a move known by the Pokémon
Embargo (TM63)	Cute	2	Prevents the Voltage from going up in the same turn
Ember	Beauty	3	A basic performance using a move known by the Pokémon
Encore	Cute	1	Earn +3 if two Pokémon in a row raise the Voltage
Endeavor	Tough	2	Earns double the score if the performance comes last in the final round
Endure (TM58)	Tough	2	Prevents the Voltage from going up in the same turn
Energy Ball (TM53)	Beauty	2	Earn +2 if the Pokémon performs first in the turn
Eruption	Beauty	2	Earn +2 if the Pokémon performs last in the turn
Explosion (TM64)	Beauty	—	Earn +15 if all the Pokémon choose the same judge
Extrasensory	Cool	2	Earn +2 if the Pokémon performs first in the turn
Extremespeed	Cool	2	Enables the user to perform first in the next turn
Facade (TM42)	Cute	2	Earns double the score if the performance comes last in the final round
Faint Attack	Smart	2	Earn +2 if the Pokémon performs last in the turn
Fake Out	Cute	2	Earn +2 if the Pokémon performs first in the turn
Fake Tears	Smart	2	Prevents the Voltage from going down in the same turn
False Swipe (TM54)	Cool	*	AP value equal to 4 minus targeted judge's Voltage
Featherdance	Beauty	2	Prevents the Voltage from going down in the same turn
Feint	Beauty	*	AP value equal to 4 minus targeted judge's Voltage
Fire Blast (TM38)	Beauty	2	Earn +2 if the Pokémon performs first in the turn
Fire Fang	Beauty	3	A basic performance using a move known by the Pokémon
Fire Punch	Beauty	2	Earn +2 if the Pokémon performs first in the turn
Fire Spin	Beauty	*	AP is 1 if performed first in a turn, 2 if second, 3 if third, and 4 if fourth
Fissure	Tough	—	Earn +15 if all the Pokémon choose the same judge
Flail	Cute	2	Earns double the score if the performance comes last in the final round
Flame Wheel	Beauty	2	Allows performance of the same move twice in a row
Flamethrower (TM35)	Beauty	2	Earn +2 if the Pokémon performs first in the turn
Flare Blitz	Smart	2	Earn +3 if the Pokémon that just went hit max Voltage
Flash (TM70)	Beauty	2	Lowers the Voltage of all judges by one each
Flash Cannon (TM91)	Smart	2	Earn +2 if the Pokémon performs first in the turn
Flatter	Smart	2	Prevents the Voltage from going down in the same turn
Fling (TM56)	Tough	1	Earn +3 if the Pokémon gets the lowest score
Fly (HM02)	Smart	1	Earn +3 if no other Pokémon has chosen the same judge
Focus Blast (TM52)	Cool	2	Earn +2 if the Pokémon performs first in the turn
Focus Energy	Cool	—	Earn double the score in the next turn
Focus Punch (TM01)	Tough	1	Earn +3 if no other Pokémon has chosen the same judge
Follow Me	Cute	2	Makes the order of contestants random in the next turn
Force Palm	Cool	2	Earn +2 if the Pokémon performs last in the turn
Foresight	Smart	1	Earn +3 if two Pokémon in a row raise the Voltage
Frenzy Plant	Cool	2	Earn +3 if the Pokémon that just went hit max Voltage
Frustration (TM21)	Cute	2	Earn +2 if the Pokémon performs last in the turn
Fury Attack	Cool	2	Allows performance of the same move twice in a row
Fury Cutter	Cool	2	Allows performance of the same move twice in a row
Fury Swipes	Tough	2	Allows performance of the same move twice in a row
Future Sight	Smart	2	Earn +2 if the Pokémon performs first in the turn
Gastro Acid	Beauty	2	Prevents the Voltage from going up in the same turn
Giga Drain (TM19)	Smart	1	Earn +3 if two Pokémon in a row raise the Voltage
Giga Impact (TM68)	Beauty	2	Earn +3 if the Pokémon that just went hit max Voltage
Glare	Tough	2	Prevents the Voltage from going down in the same turn
Grass Knot (TM86)	Smart	2	Earn +2 if the judge's Voltage goes up
Grasswhistle	Smart	2	Prevents the Voltage from going down in the same turn
Gravity	Beauty	2	Prevents the Voltage from going up in the same turn
Growl	Cute	2	Prevents the Voltage from going down in the same turn
Growth	Beauty	—	Earn double the score in the next turn
Grudge	Tough	2	Lowers the Voltage of all judges by one each
Guard Swap	Cute	*	AP value equal to 4 minus targeted judge's Voltage
Guillotine	Cool	—	Earn +15 if all the Pokémon choose the same judge

Move	Type	Cat	BA	AC	PP	2-on-2	DA	Effect
Gunk Shot	PSN	P	120	70	5	1		Has 30% chance of causing Poison
Gust	FLY	S	40	100	35	1		Inflicts double damage if foe is using Fly
Gyro Ball (TM74)	STL	P	–	100	5	1	=	The lower your Speed compared to your foe, the more damage this move inflicts (max 150)
Hail (TM07)	ICE	O	–	–	10	S		Changes weather to hail, which damages non-Ice-type foes for 5 turns
Hammer Arm	FTG	P	100	90	10	1	=	Lowers your Speed 1 level
Harden	NRM	O	–	–	30	S		Raises Defense 1 level
Haze	ICE	O	–	–	30	4		Returns your and foe's stats to normal
Head Smash	RCK	P	150	80	5	1	=	Inflicts 1/2 of damage to user
Headbutt	NRM	P	70	100	15	1	=	Has 30% chance of causing Flinch
Heal Bell	NRM	O	–	–	5	S		Heals all critical conditions of all Pokémon in party
Heal Block	PSY	O	–	100	15	2		Prevents foe from regaining HP for five turns
Heal Order	BUG	O	–	–	10	S		Restores half of Pokémon's maximum HP
Healing Wish	PSY	O	–	–	10	S		Heals next Pokémon completely but causes you to faint
Heart Swap	PSY	O	–	–	10	1		Switches modification of all stats with foe
Heat Wave	FIRE	S	100	90	10	2		Has 10% chance of causing Burn
Helping Hand	NRM	O	–	100	20	S		Raises power of partner's move in 2-on-2 battle
Hi Jump Kick	FTG	P	100	90	20	1	=	Inflicts 1/4 damage on you if attack doesn't strike foe
Hidden Power (TM10)	NRM	S	–	100	15	1		Has type and effect that vary with the Pokémon that uses it
Horn Attack	NRM	P	65	100	25	1	=	No extra effect beyond damaging foe
Horn Drill	NRM	P	–	30	5	1	=	Causes foe to Faint if it is lower level than user; AC improves based on difference between levels
Howl	NRM	O	–	–	40	S		Raises Attack 1 level
Hydro Cannon	WTR	S	150	90	5	1		Causes massive damage but forfeits attacker's next move
Hydro Pump	WTR	S	120	85	5	1		No extra effect beyond damaging foe
Hyper Beam (TM15)	NRM	S	150	90	5	1		Causes massive damage but forfeits next move
Hyper Fang	NRM	P	80	90	15	1	=	Has 10% chance of causing Flinch
Hyper Voice	NRM	S	90	100	10	2		No extra effect beyond damaging foe
Hypnosis	PSY	O	–	70	20	1		Causes Sleep condition
Ice Ball	ICE	P	30	90	20	1	=	Repeats 5 turns unless misses; damages more each turn; x2 damage after using Defense Curl
Ice Beam (TM13)	ICE	S	95	100	10	1		Has 10% chance of causing Freeze
Ice Fang	ICE	P	65	95	15	1	=	Has 10% chance of causing Flinch or Freeze
Ice Punch	ICE	P	75	100	15	1	=	Has 10% chance of causing Freeze
Ice Shard	ICE	P	40	100	30	1		Causes you to move first in a turn; if opponent uses it too, the higher Speed prevails
Icicle Spear	ICE	P	10	100	30	1		Attacks 2-5 times per turn
Icy Wind	ICE	S	55	95	15	2		Lowers foe's Speed 1 level
Imprison	PSY	O	–	100	10	S		Prevents foe from using the four moves Pokémon knows
Ingrain	GRS	O	–	100	20	S		Restores some HP each turn but Pokémon can't switch out
Iron Defense	STL	O	–	–	15	S		Raises Defense 2 levels
Iron Head	STL	P	80	100	15	1	=	Has 30% chance of causing Flinch
Iron Tail (TM23)	STL	P	100	75	15	1	=	Has 30% chance of lowering foe's Defense 1 level
Jump Kick	FTG	P	85	95	25	1	=	Self-inflicts 1/4 damage if attack doesn't strike foe
Karate Chop	FTG	P	50	100	25	1	=	Has a high chance for a critical hit
Kinesis	PSY	O	–	80	15	1		Lowers foe's Accuracy 1 level
Knock Off	DRK	P	20	100	20	1	=	Removes a foe's held item (if any) and returns it when battle ends
Last Resort	NRM	P	130	100	5	1	=	Attack can only be used after all other learned moves have been used
Lava Plume	FIRE	S	80	100	15	3		Has 30% chance of causing Burn; will thaw target with Freeze condition
Leaf Blade	GRS	P	90	100	15	1	=	Has a high chance for a critical hit
Leaf Storm	GRS	S	140	90	5	1		Lowers your Sp. Attack 2 levels
Leech Life	BUG	S	20	100	15	1	=	Damages foe and restores own HP equal to 1/2 inflicted damage
Leech Seed	GRS	O	–	90	10	1		Siphons foe's HP into your HP every turn; effect persists if you switch out
Leer	NRM	O	–	100	30	2		Lowers foe's Defense 1 level
Lick	GHO	P	20	100	30	1	=	Has 30% chance of causing Paralyze
Light Screen (TM16)	PSY	O	–	–	30	S		Halves damage from foes' special attacks for 5 turns; effect persists if you switch out
Lock-On	NRM	O	–	100	5	1		Causes next move always to hit successfully
Lovely Kiss	NRM	O	–	75	10	1		Causes Sleep condition
Low Kick	FTG	P	–	100	20	1	=	Inflicts higher damage if your foe's weight is heavier
Lucky Chant	NRM	O	–	–	30	2		Prevents foe from landing critical hits for five turns
Lunar Dance	PSY	O	–	–	10	S		Heals next Pokémon completely but causes you to faint
Luster Purge	PSY	S	70	100	5	1		Has 50% chance of lowering foe's Sp. Defense 1 level
Mach Punch	FTG	P	40	100	30	1	=	Causes you to move first in a turn; if opponent uses it too, the higher Speed prevails
Magic Coat	PSY	O	–	100	15	–		Reflects Leech Seed and moves that cause Poison, Paralyze, Sleep and Confuse back at attacker

Contest Equivalents (continued) Gunk Shot – Magic Coat

Move	Type	AP	Effect in Super Contests
Gunk Shot	Cool	3	A basic performance using a move known by the Pokémon
Gust	Smart	3	A basic performance using a move known by the Pokémon
Gyro Ball (TM74)	Beauty	2	Earns double the score if the performance comes last in the final round
Hail (TM07)	Beauty	2	Prevents the Voltage from going up in the same turn
Hammer Arm	Cool	2	Enables the user to perform last in the next turn
Harden	Tough	2	Prevents the Voltage from going up in the same turn
Haze	Beauty	2	Prevents the Voltage from going up in the same turn
Head Smash	Tough	2	Earn +3 if the Pokémon that just went hit max Voltage
Headbutt	Tough	3	A basic performance using a move known by the Pokémon
Heal Bell	Beauty	*	AP value equal to Voltage of targeted judge
Heal Block	Cute	2	Prevents the Voltage from going up in the same turn
Heal Order	Smart	*	AP value equal to Voltage of targeted judge
Healing Wish	Cute	*	AP value equal to Voltage of targeted judge
Heart Swap	Cool	*	AP value equal to 4 minus targeted judge's Voltage
Heat Wave	Beauty	2	Earn +2 if the Pokémon performs first in the turn
Helping Hand	Smart	1	Earn +3 if two Pokémon in a row raise the Voltage
Hi Jump Kick	Cool	3	A basic performance using a move known by the Pokémon
Hidden Power (TM10)	Smart	1	Earn +3 if the Pokémon gets the lowest score
Horn Attack	Cool	3	A basic performance using a move known by the Pokémon
Horn Drill	Cool	–	Earn +15 if all the Pokémon choose the same judge
Howl	Cool	–	Earn double the score in the next turn
Hydro Cannon	Beauty	2	Earn +3 if the Pokémon that just went hit max Voltage
Hydro Pump	Beauty	2	Earn +2 if the Pokémon performs first in the turn
Hyper Beam (TM15)	Cool	2	Earn +3 if the Pokémon that just went hit max Voltage
Hyper Fang	Cool	2	Earn +2 if the Pokémon performs last in the turn
Hyper Voice	Cool	3	A basic performance using a move known by the Pokémon
Hypnosis	Smart	2	Prevents the Voltage from going down in the same turn
Ice Ball	Beauty	2	Allows performance of the same move twice in a row
Ice Beam (TM13)	Beauty	2	Earn +2 if the Pokémon performs first in the turn
Ice Fang	Cool	3	A basic performance using a move known by the Pokémon
Ice Punch	Beauty	2	Earn +2 if the Pokémon performs first in the turn
Ice Shard	Beauty	2	Enables the user to perform first in the next turn
Icicle Spear	Beauty	2	Allows performance of the same move twice in a row
Icy Wind	Beauty	2	Enables the user to perform last in the next turn
Imprison	Smart	1	Earn +3 if two Pokémon in a row raise the Voltage
Ingrain	Smart	*	AP is 1 if performed first in a turn, 2 if second, 3 if third, and 4 if fourth
Iron Defense	Tough	2	Prevents the Voltage from going up in the same turn
Iron Head	Tough	2	Earn +2 if the Pokémon performs last in the turn
Iron Tail (TM23)	Cool	2	Earn +2 if the Pokémon performs last in the turn
Jump Kick	Cool	3	A basic performance using a move known by the Pokémon
Karate Chop	Tough	3	A basic performance using a move known by the Pokémon
Kinesis	Smart	–	Earn double the score in the next turn
Knock Off	Smart	3	A basic performance using a move known by the Pokémon
Last Resort	Cute	*	AP is 1 if performed first in a turn, 2 if second, 3 if third, and 4 if fourth
Lava Plume	Tough	2	Earn +2 if the Pokémon performs first in the turn
Leaf Blade	Cool	2	Earn +2 if the Pokémon performs first in the turn
Leaf Storm	Cute	2	Earn +3 if the Pokémon that just went hit max Voltage
Leech Life	Smart	1	Earn +3 if two Pokémon in a row raise the Voltage
Leech Seed	Smart	*	AP is 1 if performed first in a turn, 2 if second, 3 if third, and 4 if fourth
Leer	Cool	2	Prevents the Voltage from going down in the same turn
Lick	Tough	*	AP value equal to 4 minus targeted judge's Voltage
Light Screen (TM16)	Beauty	2	Prevents the Voltage from going up in the same turn
Lock-On	Smart	1	Earn +3 if two Pokémon in a row raise the Voltage
Lovely Kiss	Beauty	2	Prevents the Voltage from going down in the same turn
Low Kick	Tough	3	A basic performance using a move known by the Pokémon
Lucky Chant	Cute	2	Prevents the Voltage from going up in the same turn
Lunar Dance	Beauty	*	AP value equal to Voltage of targeted judge
Luster Purge	Smart	2	Earn +3 if the Pokémon that just went hit max Voltage
Mach Punch	Cool	2	Enables the user to perform first in the next turn
Magic Coat	Beauty	2	Earns double the score if the performance comes last in the final round

Move	Type	Cat	BA	AC	PP	2-on-2	DA	Effect
Magical Leaf	GRS	S	60	–	20	1		Will always strike foe successfully
Magma Storm	FIRE	S	120	70	5	1		Damages foe for 2-5 turns; foe can't escape until completed; will thaw target with Freeze condition
Magnet Bomb	STL	P	60	–	20	1		Will always strike foe successfully
Magnet Rise	ELC	O	–	–	10	S		Prevents Ground-type attacks for 5 turns
Magnitude	GRD	P	–	100	30	3		Bases damage based on random power (10, 30, 50, 70, 90, 110 or 150)
Me First	NRM	O	–	–	20	S		Uses powered-up version of foe's chosen attack, but move fails if user does not go first
Mean Look	NRM	O	–	100	5	1		Prevents foe from escaping or switching while you remain on field
Meditate	PSY	O	–	–	40	S		Raises Attack by 1 level
Mega Drain	GRS	S	40	100	10	1		Damages foe and restores own HP equal to 1/2 inflicted damage
Mega Kick	NRM	P	120	75	5	1	=	No extra effect beyond damaging foe
Mega Punch	NRM	P	80	85	20	1	=	No extra effect beyond damaging foe
Megahorn	BUG	P	120	85	10	1	=	No extra effect beyond damaging foe
Memento	DRK	O	–	100	10	1		Lowers foe's Attack and Sp. Attack 2 levels but you Faint in battle
Metal Burst	STL	P	–	100	10	S		Deals to foe 1.5x the damage dealt to you this turn
Metal Claw	STL	P	50	95	35	1	=	Has 10% chance of raising Attack 1 level
Metal Sound	STL	O	–	85	40	1		Lowers foe's Sp. Defense 2 levels
Meteor Mash	STL	P	100	85	10	1	=	Has 20% chance of raising Attack 1 level
Metronome	NRM	O	–	–	10	–		Uses a random move from entire repertoire of all Pokémon moves
Milk Drink	NRM	O	–	–	10	S		Restores half of Pokémon's maximum HP; out of battle, splits 1/5 of its HP among your other Pokémon
Mimic	NRM	O	–	100	10	1		Adds foe's last move to Pokémon move repertoire (effect remains while in battle)
Mind Reader	NRM	O	–	100	5	1		Causes next move always to hit successfully
Minimize	NRM	O	–	–	20	S		Raises Evasiveness 1 level
Miracle Eye	PSY	O	–	–	40	S		Your moves ignore foe's Evasiveness; exposes Dark-types to Psychic-type attacks
Mirror Coat	PSY	S	–	100	20	–		Attacks 2nd, doing x2 special attack damage that foe did to Pokémon
Mirror Move	FLY	O	–	–	20	–		Uses same move that foe used
Mirror Shot	STL	S	65	85	10	1		Has 30% chance of lowering foe's Accuracy 1 level
Mist	ICE	O	–	–	30	S		Prevents stat reduction
Mist Ball	PSY	S	70	100	5	1		Has 50% chance of lowering foe's Sp. Attack
Moonlight	NRM	O	–	–	5	S		Restores HP based on weather (sunny=2/3; normal=1/2; rain, sandstorm or hail=1/4)
Morning Sun	NRM	O	–	–	5	S		Restores HP based on weather (sunny=2/3; normal=1/2; rain, sandstorm or hail=1/4)
Mud Bomb	GRD	S	65	85	10	1		Has 30% chance of lowering foe's Accuracy 1 level
Mud Shot	GRD	S	55	95	15	1		Lowers foe's Speed 1 level
Mud Sport	GRD	O	–	100	15	S		Lowers power of all Electric-type attacks while Pokémon is on field
Muddy Water	WTR	S	95	85	10	2		Has 30% chance of lowering foe's Accuracy 1 level
Mud-Slap	GRD	S	20	100	10	1		Lowers foe's Accuracy 1 level
Nasty Plot	DRK	O	–	–	20	S		Raises Sp. Attack 2 levels
Natural Gift (TM83)	NRM	P	–	100	15	1		Type and power vary by user's held berry; berry is consumed in process; if no held berry, move fails
Nature Power	NRM	O	–	95	20	–		Changes to a different move based on terrain Pokémon is in
Needle Arm	GRS	P	60	100	15	1	=	Has 30% chance of causing Flinch
Night Shade	GHO	S	–	100	15	1		Causes damage equal to Pokémon's level regardless of other battle factors
Night Slash	DRK	P	70	100	15	1	=	Has a high chance for a critical hit
Nightmare	GHO	O	–	100	15	1		Reduces foe HP every turn, works only when opponent is asleep
Octazooka	WTR	S	65	85	10	1		Has 50% chance of lowering foe's Accuracy 1 level for all moves
Odor Sleuth	NRM	O	–	100	40	1		Your moves ignore foe's Evasiveness; exposes Ghost-types to Normal-type moves
Ominous Wind	GHO	S	60	100	5	1		Has 10% chance of raising Attack, Defense, Sp. Attack, Sp. Defense and Speed 1 level
Outrage	DRG	P	120	100	15	R	=	Repeats 2-3 turns; you'll get a Confuse condition when attacks are completed
Overheat (TM50)	FIRE	S	140	90	5	1	=	Causes massive damage but lowers your Sp. Attack 2 levels
Pain Split	NRM	O	–	100	20	1		Combines attacker's HP with opponent's HP and splits total between both
Pay Day	NRM	P	40	100	20	1		Results in post-battle payoff; final payoff= (attacker's level) x (number of attacks) x 2
Payback (TM66)	DRK	P	50	100	10	1	=	Doubles damage if it hits a Pokémon that hit your Pokémon in the same turn
Peck	FLY	P	35	100	35	1	=	No extra effect beyond damaging foe
Perish Song	NRM	O	–	–	5	S		Causes you and foe to Faint after 3 turns; switch out to prevent effect on Pokémon in your team
Petal Dance	GRS	S	90	100	20	R	=	Repeats 2-3 turns; you'll get a Confuse condition when attacks are completed
Pin Missile	BUG	P	14	85	20	1		Attacks 2-5 times per turn
Pluck (TM88)	FLY	P	60	100	20	1	=	If target is holding a berry with a combat effect, eat that berry and gain its effect
Poison Fang	PSN	P	50	100	15	1	=	Has 30% chance of causing Toxic; amount of Poison damage increases each turn
Poison Gas	PSN	O	–	55	40	1		Causes Poison condition
Poison Jab (TM84)	PSN	P	80	100	20	1	=	Has 30% chance of causing Poison
Poison Sting	PSN	P	15	100	35	1		Has 30% chance of causing Poison
Poison Tail	PSN	P	50	100	25	1	=	Has 10% chance of causing Poison; has a high chance for critical hit

Contest Equivalents (continued) Magical Leaf – Poison Tail

Move	Type	AP	Effect in Super Contests
Magical Leaf	Beauty	2	Earn +2 if the Pokémon performs first in the turn
Magma Storm	Tough	2	Allows performance of the same move twice in a row
Magnet Bomb	Cool	3	A basic performance using a move known by the Pokémon
Magnet Rise	Cute	2	Prevents the Voltage from going up in the same turn
Magnitude	Tough	2	Earn +2 if the Pokémon performs last in the turn
Me First	Cute	2	Enables the user to perform first in the next turn
Mean Look	Beauty	2	Lowers the Voltage of all judges by one each
Meditate	Beauty	–	Earn double the score in the next turn
Mega Drain	Smart	1	Earn +3 if two Pokémon in a row raise the Voltage
Mega Kick	Cool	2	Earn +2 if the Pokémon performs last in the turn
Mega Punch	Tough	2	Earn +2 if the Pokémon performs last in the turn
Megahorn	Cool	2	Earn +2 if the Pokémon performs last in the turn
Memento	Tough	–	Earn +15 if all the Pokémon choose the same judge
Metal Burst	Beauty	2	Earns double the score if the performance comes last in the final round
Metal Claw	Cool	2	Earn +2 if the Pokémon performs last in the turn
Metal Sound	Smart	2	Lowers the Voltage of all judges by one each
Meteor Mash	Cool	2	Earn +2 if the Pokémon performs last in the turn
Metronome	Cute	2	Makes the order of contestants random in the next turn
Milk Drink	Cute	*	AP value equal to Voltage of targeted judge
Mimic	Cute	–	If previous performer hits its Voltage to the max, then you will earn points equal to its Voltage
Mind Reader	Smart	1	Earn +3 if two Pokémon in a row raise the Voltage
Minimize	Cute	2	Prevents the Voltage from going up in the same turn
Miracle Eye	Cute	1	Earn +3 if two Pokémon in a row raise the Voltage
Mirror Coat	Beauty	2	Earns double the score if the performance comes last in the final round
Mirror Move	Smart	2	Earns double the score if the performance comes last in the final round
Mirror Shot	Cute	2	Earn +2 if the Pokémon performs first in the turn
Mist	Beauty	2	Prevents the Voltage from going up in the same turn
Mist Ball	Smart	2	Earn +3 if the Pokémon that just went hit max Voltage
Moonlight	Beauty	*	AP value equal to Voltage of targeted judge
Morning Sun	Beauty	*	AP value equal to Voltage of targeted judge
Mud Bomb	Smart	2	Earn +2 if the Pokémon performs last in the turn
Mud Shot	Tough	2	Enables the user to perform last in the next turn
Mud Sport	Cute	2	Prevents the Voltage from going up in the same turn
Muddy Water	Tough	2	Earn +2 if the Pokémon performs last in the turn
Mud-Slap	Cute	3	A basic performance using a move known by the Pokémon
Nasty Plot	Cute	–	Earn double the score in the next turn
Natural Gift (TM83)	Cool	2	Earn +2 if the Pokémon performs last in the turn
Nature Power	Beauty	2	Makes the order of contestants random in the next turn
Needle Arm	Smart	3	A basic performance using a move known by the Pokémon
Night Shade	Smart	3	A basic performance using a move known by the Pokémon
Night Slash	Beauty	3	A basic performance using a move known by the Pokémon
Nightmare	Smart	2	Prevents the Voltage from going down in the same turn
Octazooka	Tough	2	Earn +2 if the judge's Voltage goes up
Odor Sleuth	Smart	1	Earn +3 if two Pokémon in a row raise the Voltage
Ominous Wind	Smart	–	Earn double the score in the next turn
Outrage	Cool	2	Allows performance of the same move twice in a row
Overheat (TM50)	Beauty	2	Earn +3 if the Pokémon that just went hit max Voltage
Pain Split	Smart	2	Lowers the Voltage of all judges by one each
Pay Day	Smart	1	Earn +3 if the Pokémon gets the lowest score
Payback (TM66)	Cool	1	Earn +3 if no other Pokémon has chosen the same judge
Peck	Cool	3	A basic performance using a move known by the Pokémon
Perish Song	Beauty	2	Lowers the Voltage of all judges by one each
Petal Dance	Beauty	*	AP is 1 if performed first in a turn, 2 if second, 3 if third, and 4 if fourth
Pin Missile	Cool	2	Allows performance of the same move twice in a row
Pluck (TM88)	Cute	–	If previous performer hits its Voltage to the max, then you will earn points equal to its Voltage
Poison Fang	Smart	2	Earn +2 if the judge's Voltage goes up
Poison Gas	Smart	3	A basic performance using a move known by the Pokémon
Poison Jab (TM84)	Smart	2	Earn +2 if the judge's Voltage goes up
Poison Sting	Smart	2	Prevents the Voltage from going down in the same turn
Poison Tail	Smart	2	Earn +2 if the judge's Voltage goes up

Move	Type	Cat	BA	AC	PP	2-on-2	DA	Effect
Poisonpowder	PSN	O	–	75	35	1		Causes Poison condition
Pound	NRM	P	40	100	35	1	=	No extra effect beyond damaging foe
Powder Snow	ICE	S	40	100	25	2		Has 10% chance of causing Freeze
Power Gem	RCK	S	70	100	20	1		No extra effect beyond damaging foe
Power Swap	PSY	O	–	–	10	1		Switches modification of Attack and Sp. Attack with foe
Power Trick	PSY	O	–	–	10	S		Switches own Attack and Defense
Power Whip	GRS	P	120	85	10	1	=	No extra effect beyond damaging foe
Present	NRM	P	–	90	15	1		Causes damage randomly (40, 80, or 120 points) or restores defender's HP by 1/4
Protect (TM17)	NRM	O	–	–	10	S		Wards off foe moves for 1 turn; success falls if used consecutively
Psybeam	PSY	S	65	100	20	1		Has 10% chance of causing Confuse condition
Psych Up (TM77)	NRM	O	–	–	10	1		Duplicates foe's stat modifications
Psychic (TM29)	PSY	S	90	100	10	1		Has 10% chance of lowering foe's Sp. Defense 1 level
Psycho Boost	PSY	S	140	90	5	1		Causes massive damage but lowers attacker's Sp. Attack 2 levels
Psycho Cut	PSY	P	70	100	20	1		Has a high chance for a critical hit
Psycho Shift	PSY	O	–	90	10	1		Transfers Pokémon's condition (Poison, Sleep, Paralyze, Burn) to foe
Psywave	PSY	S	–	80	15	1		Bases damage on random multiplier (0.5 to 1.5) times your level
Punishment	DRK	P	–	100	5	1	=	Inflicts higher damage the more the foe has raised its stats
Pursuit	DRK	P	40	100	20	1	=	Inflicts double damage if foe is withdrawn during turn
Quick Attack	NRM	P	40	100	30	1	=	Causes you to move first in a turn; if opponent uses it too, the higher Speed prevails
Rage	NRM	P	20	100	20	1	=	Increases damage for next use if you're hit and you use it consecutively
Rain Dance (TM18)	WTR	O	–	–	5	S		Changes weather to rain for 5 turns, which raises power of Water-type moves
Rapid Spin	NRM	P	20	100	40	1	=	Frees you from foe's Bind, Wrap, Leech Seed and Spikes
Razor Leaf	GRS	P	55	95	25	2		Has a high chance for a critical hit
Razor Wind	NRM	S	80	100	10	2		Prepares attack on 1st turn then attempts strike on 2nd; has a high chance for a critical hit
Recover	NRM	O	–	–	20	S		Restores half of Pokémon's maximum HP
Recycle (TM67)	NRM	O	–	100	10	S		Reuses an item that has been used earlier in battle
Reflect (TM33)	PSY	O	–	–	20	S		Halves physical attack damage to your team for 5 turns
Refresh	NRM	O	–	100	20	S		Heals Poison, Paralyze and Burn conditions
Rest (TM44)	PSY	O	–	–	10	S		Restores all HP, then puts Pokémon to sleep for next 2 turns
Return (TM27)	NRM	P	–	100	20	1	=	Inflicts higher damage if your Pokémon likes you more
Revenge	FTG	P	60	100	10	1	=	Power of move is doubled if attacker was damaged on same turn
Reversal	FTG	P	–	100	15	1	=	Inflicts higher damage if your HP is lower
Roar (TM05)	NRM	O	–	100	20	1		Ends battle with wild Pokémon; forces random foe switch in Trainer battle
Roar of Time	DRG	S	150	90	5	1		Causes massive damage but forfeits attacker's next move
Rock Blast	RCK	P	25	80	10	1		Attacks 2-5 times per turn
Rock Climb (HM08)	NRM	P	90	85	20	1	=	Has 20% chance of causing Confuse; allows party to climb rocky slopes outside battle
Rock Polish (TM69)	RCK	O	–	–	20	S		Raises Speed 2 levels
Rock Slide (TM80)	RCK	P	75	90	10	2		Has 30% chance of causing Flinch
Rock Smash (HM06)	FTG	P	20	100	15	1	=	Has 50% chance of lowering foe's Defense by 1 level; smashes rocks in overworld
Rock Throw	RCK	P	50	90	15	1		No extra effect beyond damaging foe
Rock Tomb (TM39)	RCK	P	50	80	10	1		Lowers foe's Speed 1 level
Rock Wrecker	RCK	P	150	90	5	1		Causes massive damage but attacker forfeits next move
Role Play	PSY	O	–	100	10	1		Copies foe's Ability
Rolling Kick	FTG	P	60	85	15	1	=	Has 30% chance of causing Flinch
Rollout	RCK	P	30	90	20	1	=	Repeats 5 turns unless misses; damages more each turn; x2 damage after using Defense Curl
Roost (TM51)	FLY	O	–	–	10	S		Restores 1/2 of Pokémon's maximum HP, but grounds Flying-types for the turn
Sacred Fire	FIRE	S	100	95	5	1		Has 50% chance of causing Burn; will thaw target with Freeze condition
Safeguard (TM20)	NRM	O	–	–	25	S		Prevents all critical conditions to team for 5 turns
Sand Tomb	GRD	P	15	70	15	1		Damages foe for 2-5 turns; foe can't escape until completed
Sand-Attack	GRD	O	–	100	15	1		Lowers foe's Accuracy 1 level
Sandstorm (TM37)	RCK	O	–	–	10	S		Changes weather to sandstorm for 5 turns, which damages all but Rock-, Steel- & Ground-types
Scary Face	NRM	O	–	90	10	1		Lowers foe's Speed 2 levels
Scratch	NRM	P	40	100	35	1	=	No extra effect beyond damaging foe
Screech	NRM	O	–	85	40	1		Lowers foe's Defense 2 levels
Secret Power (TM43)	NRM	P	70	100	20	1		Has 30% chance of causing a 2nd effect; effect based on terrain
Seed Bomb	GRS	P	80	100	15	1		No extra effect beyond damaging foe
Seismic Toss	FTG	P	–	100	20	1	=	Causes damage equal to your level regardless of other battle factors
Selfdestruct	NRM	P	200	100	5	3		Inflicts a massive amount of damage but causes you to faint
Shadow Ball (TM30)	GHO	S	80	100	15	1		Has 20% chance of lowering foe's Sp. Defense 1 level
Shadow Claw (TM65)	GHO	P	70	100	15	1	=	Has a high chance for a critical hit

Contest Equivalents (continued) Poisonpowder – Shadow Claw (TM65)

Move	Type	AP	Effect in Super Contests
Poisonpowder	Smart	2	Prevents the Voltage from going down in the same turn
Pound	Tough	3	A basic performance using a move known by the Pokémon
Powder Snow	Beauty	3	A basic performance using a move known by the Pokémon
Power Gem	Beauty	3	A basic performance using a move known by the Pokémon
Power Swap	Beauty	*	AP value equal to 4 minus targeted judge's Voltage
Power Trick	Cool	*	AP value equal to 4 minus targeted judge's Voltage
Power Whip	Beauty	3	A basic performance using a move known by the Pokémon
Present	Cute	*	AP value equal to 4 minus targeted judge's Voltage
Protect (TM17)	Cute	*	AP value equal to 4 minus targeted judge's Voltage
Psybeam	Beauty	2	Earn +2 if the Pokémon performs first in the turn
Psych Up (TM77)	Smart	–	Earn double the score in the next turn
Psychic (TM29)	Smart	2	Earn +2 if the Pokémon performs first in the turn
Psycho Boost	Smart	2	Earn +3 if the Pokémon that just went hit max Voltage
Psycho Cut	Cool	2	Earn +2 if the Pokémon performs first in the turn
Psycho Shift	Cool	*	AP value equal to 4 minus targeted judge's Voltage
Psywave	Smart	3	A basic performance using a move known by the Pokémon
Punishment	Smart	1	Earn +3 if the Pokémon gets the lowest score
Pursuit	Smart	1	Earn +3 if two Pokémon in a row raise the Voltage
Quick Attack	Cool	2	Enables the user to perform first in the next turn
Rage	Cool	–	Earn double the score in the next turn
Rain Dance (TM18)	Tough	2	Prevents the Voltage from going up in the same turn
Rapid Spin	Cool	2	Earn +2 if the Pokémon performs first in the turn
Razor Leaf	Cool	3	A basic performance using a move known by the Pokémon
Razor Wind	Cool	1	Earn +3 if no other Pokémon has chosen the same judge
Recover	Smart	*	AP value equal to Voltage of targeted judge
Recycle (TM67)	Smart	–	If previous performer hits its Voltage to the max, then you will earn points equal to its Voltage
Reflect (TM33)	Smart	2	Prevents the Voltage from going up in the same turn
Refresh	Cute	*	AP value equal to Voltage of targeted judge
Rest (TM44)	Cute	*	AP value equal to Voltage of targeted judge
Return (TM27)	Cute	2	Earn +2 if the Pokémon performs first in the turn
Revenge	Tough	2	Earns double the score if the performance comes last in the final round
Reversal	Cool	2	Earns double the score if the performance comes last in the final round
Roar (TM05)	Cool	2	Prevents the Voltage from going down in the same turn
Roar of Time	Cool	2	Earn +3 if the Pokémon that just went hit max Voltage
Rock Blast	Tough	2	Allows performance of the same move twice in a row
Rock Climb (HM08)	Cool	2	Earn +2 if the Pokémon performs last in the turn
Rock Polish (TM69)	Tough	2	Enables the user to perform first in the next turn
Rock Slide (TM80)	Tough	3	A basic performance using a move known by the Pokémon
Rock Smash (HM06)	Tough	2	Earn +2 if the Pokémon performs last in the turn
Rock Throw	Tough	3	A basic performance using a move known by the Pokémon
Rock Tomb (TM39)	Smart	2	Enables the user to perform last in the next turn
Rock Wrecker	Tough	2	Earn +3 if the Pokémon that just went hit max Voltage
Role Play	Cute	1	Earn +3 if the Pokémon gets the lowest score
Rolling Kick	Cool	3	A basic performance using a move known by the Pokémon
Rollout	Tough	2	Allows performance of the same move twice in a row
Roost (TM51)	Cool	*	AP value equal to Voltage of targeted judge
Sacred Fire	Beauty	2	Earn +3 if the Pokémon that just went hit max Voltage
Safeguard (TM20)	Beauty	2	Prevents the Voltage from going up in the same turn
Sand Tomb	Smart	*	AP is 1 if performed first in a turn, 2 if second, 3 if third, and 4 if fourth
Sand-Attack	Cute	2	Prevents the Voltage from going down in the same turn
Sandstorm (TM37)	Tough	2	Prevents the Voltage from going up in the same turn
Scary Face	Tough	2	Enables the user to perform last in the next turn
Scratch	Tough	3	A basic performance using a move known by the Pokémon
Screech	Smart	2	Lowers the Voltage of all judges by one each
Secret Power (TM43)	Smart	2	Makes the order of contestants random in the next turn
Seed Bomb	Smart	3	A basic performance using a move known by the Pokémon
Seismic Toss	Tough	3	A basic performance using a move known by the Pokémon
Selfdestruct	Beauty	–	Earn +15 if all the Pokémon choose the same judge
Shadow Ball (TM30)	Smart	2	Earn +2 if the Pokémon performs first in the turn
Shadow Claw (TM65)	Cute	2	Earn +2 if the Pokémon performs first in the turn

Battle Moves (continued) Shadow Force – Swift

Move	Type	Cat	BA	AC	PP	2-on-2	DA	Effect
Shadow Force	GHO	P	120	100	5	1	=	User leaves battlefield then strikes next turn; ignore foe's Protect or Detect
Shadow Punch	GHO	P	60	–	20	1	=	Will always strike foe successfully
Shadow Sneak	GHO	P	40	100	30	1	=	Causes you to move first in a turn; if opponent uses it too, the higher Speed prevails
Sharpen	NRM	O	–	–	30	S		Raises Attack 1 level
Sheer Cold	ICE	S	–	30	5	1		Causes foe to Faint if it is lower level than user; AC improves based on difference between levels
Shock Wave (TM34)	ELC	S	60	–	20	1		Will always strike foe successfully
Signal Beam	BUG	S	75	100	15	1		Has 10% chance of causing Confuse condition
Silver Wind (TM62)	BUG	S	60	100	5	1		Has 10% chance of raising Attack, Defense, Sp. Attack, Sp. Defense and Speed 1 level
Sing	NRM	O	–	55	15	1		Causes Sleep condition
Sketch	NRM	O	–	–	1	1		Adds foe's last move to Pokémon move repertoire (effect remains after battle)
Skill Swap (TM48)	PSY	O	–	100	10	1		Switches abilities with foe
Skull Bash	NRM	P	100	100	15	1	=	Raises Defense 1 level; prepares attack on 1st turn then attempts strike on 2nd
Sky Attack	FLY	P	140	90	5	1		Prepares attack on 1st turn then attempts strike on 2nd; has a 30% chance of causing Flinch
Sky Uppercut	FTG	P	85	90	15	1	=	Inflicts damage even if foe is using Fly
Slack Off	NRM	O	–	100	10	S		Restores half of your maximum HP
Slam	NRM	P	80	75	20	1	=	No extra effect beyond damaging foe
Slash	NRM	P	70	100	20	1	=	Has a high chance for a critical hit
Sleep Powder	GRS	O	–	75	15	1		Causes Sleep condition
Sleep Talk (TM82)	NRM	O	–	–	10	–		Protects oneself by using moves randomly, if you have Sleep condition
Sludge	PSN	S	65	100	20	1		Has 30% chance of causing Poison
Sludge Bomb (TM36)	PSN	S	90	100	10	1		Has 30% chance of causing Poison
Smellingsalt	NRM	P	60	100	10	1	=	Inflicts double damage on foes with Paralyze; then cures foe of Paralyze
Smog	PSN	S	20	70	20	1		Has 40% chance of causing Poison
Smokescreen	NRM	O	–	100	20	1		Lowers foe's Accuracy 1 level
Snatch (TM49)	DRK	O	–	100	10	–		Steals and uses special effect (if any) from foe's move
Snore	NRM	S	40	100	15	1		Has 30% chance of causing Flinch; can be used only if you have the Sleep condition
Softboiled	NRM	O	–	100	10	S		Restores half of Pokémon's maximum HP; out of battle, splits 1/5 of its HP among your other Pokémon
Solarbeam (TM22)	GRS	S	120	100	10	1		Preps attack on 1st then attempts strike on 2nd; no wait if sunny weather; less powerful in rain
Sonicboom	NRM	S	–	90	20	1		Causes 20 pts. of damage regardless of other battle factors
Spacial Rend	DRG	S	100	95	5	1		Has a high chance for a critical hit
Spark	ELC	P	65	100	20	1	=	Has 30% chance of causing Paralyze
Spider Web	BUG	O	–	100	10	1		Prevents foe from switching out during battle
Spike Cannon	NRM	P	20	100	15	1		Attacks 2-5 times per turn
Spikes	GRD	O	–	–	20	2		Damages foe that switches in; effect persists until battle is over; use again to increase damage
Spit Up	NRM	S	–	100	10	1		Inflicts damage by amount fueled by Stockpile power
Spite	GHO	O	–	100	10	1		Lowers PP of foe's last move 2 to 5 pts.
Splash	NRM	O	–	–	40	S		Inflicts no damage and has no effect
Spore	GRS	O	–	100	15	1		Causes Sleep condition
Stealth Rock (TM76)	RCK	O	–	–	20	2		Damages foe that switches in; effect persists until battle is over; damage affected by type
Steel Wing (TM47)	STL	P	70	90	25	1	=	Has 10% chance of raising Defense 1 level
Stockpile	NRM	O	–	–	10	S		Raises Defense and Sp. Defense 1 level; can be used up to three times to fuel Spit Up and Swallow
Stomp	NRM	P	65	100	20	1	=	Has 30% chance of causing Flinch
Stone Edge (TM71)	RCK	P	100	80	5	1		Has a high chance for a critical hit
Strength (HM04)	NRM	P	80	100	15	1	=	No extra effect beyond damaging foe; shoves boulders in overworld
String Shot	BUG	O	–	95	40	2		Lowers foe's Speed 1 level
Struggle	NRM	P	50	100	1	1	=	Inflicts 1/4 of damage on user; move opens to all that lose all PP for all moves
Stun Spore	GRS	O	–	75	30	1		Causes Paralyze condition
Submission	FTG	P	80	80	25	1	=	Damages foe but inflicts you with 1/4 damage
Substitute (TM90)	NRM	O	–	–	10	S		Creates a battle decoy from 1/4 of your maximum HP
Sucker Punch	DRK	P	80	100	5	1	=	Causes you to move first in turn when foe selects attack move
Sunny Day (TM11)	FIRE	O	–	–	5	S		Changes weather to sunny for 5 turns, which raises power of Fire-type moves
Super Fang	NRM	P	–	90	10	1	=	Slashes opponent's HP to half of its current total
Superpower	FTG	P	120	100	5	1	=	Inflicts a massive amount of damage but lowers your Attack and Defense 1 level
Supersonic	NRM	O	–	55	20	1		Causes foe to have Confuse condition
Surf (HM03)	WTR	S	95	100	15	3		No extra effect beyond damaging foe; allows travel across water
Swagger (TM87)	NRM	O	–	90	15	1		Causes foe to have Confuse condition and causes it to hurt itself worse by raising its Attack 2 levels
Swallow	NRM	O	–	–	10	S		Restores HP by amount fueled by Stockpile power
Sweet Kiss	NRM	O	–	75	10	1		Causes foe to have Confuse condition
Sweet Scent	NRM	O	–	100	20	2		Lowers foe's Evasiveness 1 level; draws wild Pokémon into the open in overworld
Swift	NRM	S	60	–	20	2		Will always strike foe successfully

Contest Equivalents (continued) Shadow Force – Swift

Move	Type	AP	Effect in Super Contests
Shadow Force	Smart	2	Earn +3 if the Pokémon that just went hit max Voltage
Shadow Punch	Smart	2	Earn +2 if the Pokémon performs first in the turn
Shadow Sneak	Smart	2	Enables the user to perform first in the next turn
Sharpen	Cute	–	Earn double the score in the next turn
Sheer Cold	Beauty	–	Earn +15 if all the Pokémon choose the same judge
Shock Wave (TM34)	Cool	2	Earn +2 if the Pokémon performs first in the turn
Signal Beam	Beauty	2	Earn +2 if the judge's Voltage goes up
Silver Wind (TM62)	Beauty	2	Earn +2 if the judge's Voltage goes up
Sing	Cute	2	Prevents the Voltage from going down in the same turn
Sketch	Smart	1	Earn +3 if the Pokémon gets the lowest score
Skill Swap (TM48)	Smart	–	If previous performer hits its Voltage to the max, then you will earn points equal to its Voltage
Skull Bash	Tough	1	Earn +3 if no other Pokémon has chosen the same judge
Sky Attack	Cool	1	Earn +3 if no other Pokémon has chosen the same judge
Sky Uppercut	Cool	2	Earn +2 if the Pokémon performs first in the turn
Slack Off	Cute	*	AP value equal to Voltage of targeted judge
Slam	Tough	3	A basic performance using a move known by the Pokémon
Slash	Cool	3	A basic performance using a move known by the Pokémon
Sleep Powder	Smart	2	Prevents the Voltage from going down in the same turn
Sleep Talk (TM82)	Cute	3	A basic performance using a move known by the Pokémon
Sludge	Tough	2	Earn +2 if the Pokémon performs last in the turn
Sludge Bomb (TM36)	Tough	2	Earn +2 if the Pokémon performs last in the turn
Smellingsalt	Smart	*	AP value equal to 4 minus targeted judge's Voltage
Smog	Tough	3	A basic performance using a move known by the Pokémon
Smokescreen	Smart	2	Lowers the Voltage of all judges by one each
Snatch (TM49)	Smart	–	If previous performer hits its Voltage to the max, then you will earn points equal to its Voltage
Snore	Cute	3	A basic performance using a move known by the Pokémon
Softboiled	Beauty	*	AP value equal to Voltage of targeted judge
Solarbeam (TM22)	Cool	1	Earn +3 if no other Pokémon has chosen the same judge
Sonicboom	Cool	3	A basic performance using a move known by the Pokémon
Spacial Rend	Tough	2	Earn +2 if the judge's Voltage goes up
Spark	Cool	3	A basic performance using a move known by the Pokémon
Spider Web	Smart	2	Prevents the Voltage from going up in the same turn
Spike Cannon	Cool	2	Allows performance of the same move twice in a row
Spikes	Smart	2	Prevents the Voltage from going up in the same turn
Spit Up	Tough	2	Earn +2 if the Pokémon performs last in the turn
Spite	Tough	2	Prevents the Voltage from going down in the same turn
Splash	Cute	*	AP value equal to 4 minus targeted judge's Voltage
Spore	Beauty	2	Lowers the Voltage of all judges by one each
Stealth Rock (TM76)	Cool	2	Prevents the Voltage from going up in the same turn
Steel Wing (TM47)	Cool	3	A basic performance using a move known by the Pokémon
Stockpile	Tough	–	Earn double the score in the next turn
Stomp	Tough	3	A basic performance using a move known by the Pokémon
Stone Edge (TM71)	Tough	2	Earn +2 if the judge's Voltage goes up
Strength (HM04)	Tough	3	A basic performance using a move known by the Pokémon
String Shot	Smart	2	Prevents the Voltage from going down in the same turn
Struggle	–	–	(Struggle is not available in contest)
Stun Spore	Smart	2	Prevents the Voltage from going down in the same turn
Submission	Cool	3	A basic performance using a move known by the Pokémon
Substitute (TM90)	Smart	1	Earn +3 if the Pokémon gets the lowest score
Sucker Punch	Smart	2	Enables the user to perform first in the next turn
Sunny Day (TM11)	Beauty	2	Prevents the Voltage from going up in the same turn
Super Fang	Tough	3	A basic performance using a move known by the Pokémon
Superpower	Tough	2	Earn +2 if the Pokémon performs last in the turn
Supersonic	Smart	2	Prevents the Voltage from going down in the same turn
Surf (HM03)	Beauty	2	Earn +2 if the Pokémon performs first in the turn
Swagger (TM87)	Cute	2	Prevents the Voltage from going down in the same turn
Swallow	Tough	*	AP value equal to Voltage of targeted judge
Sweet Kiss	Cute	2	Prevents the Voltage from going down in the same turn
Sweet Scent	Cute	2	Prevents the Voltage from going down in the same turn
Swift	Cool	2	Earn +2 if the Pokémon performs first in the turn

Battle Moves (continued) Switcheroo – Zen Headbutt

Move	Type	Cat	BA	AC	PP	2-on-2	DA	Effect
Switcheroo	DRK	O	–	100	10	1		Switches foe's held items with yours
Swords Dance (TM75)	NRM	O	–	–	30	S		Raises Attack 2 levels
Synthesis	GRS	O	–	–	5	S		Restores HP based on weather (sunny=2/3; normal=1/2; rain, sandstorm or hail=1/4)
Tackle	NRM	P	35	95	35	1	=	No extra effect beyond damaging foe
Tail Glow	BUG	O	–	100	20	S		Raises Sp. Attack 2 level
Tail Whip	NRM	O	–	100	30	2		Lowers foe's Defense 1 level
Tailwind	FLY	O	–	–	30	2		Doubles Speed for 3 turns; affects both of your Pokémon in Double Battle
Take Down	NRM	P	90	85	20	1	=	Inflicts 1/4 of damage to user
Taunt (TM12)	DRK	O	–	100	20	1		Forces foe to use attack (not defensive) moves for current and next turn
Teeter Dance	NRM	O	–	100	20	3		Causes all Pokémon on field except you to have Confuse condition
Teleport	PSY	O	–	–	20	S		Ends battle with wild Pokémon; teleports you to last visited Pokémon Center in overworld
Thief (TM46)	DRK	P	40	100	10	1	=	Takes a foe's held item (if any)
Thrash	NRM	P	90	100	20	R	=	Repeats 2-3 turns; you'll get Confuse condition when attacks are completed
Thunder (TM25)	ELC	S	120	70	10	1		Has 100% AC in rainy weather and 50% AC in sunny; has 30% chance of causing Paralyze
Thunder Fang	ELC	P	65	95	15	1	=	Has 10% chance of causing Flinch or Paralyze
Thunder Wave (TM73)	ELC	O	–	100	20	1		Causes Paralyze condition
Thunderbolt (TM24)	ELC	S	95	100	15	1		Has 10% chance of causing Paralyze
Thunderpunch	ELC	P	75	100	15	1	=	Has 10% chance of causing Paralyze
Thundershock	ELC	S	40	100	30	1		Has 10% chance of causing Paralyze
Tickle	NRM	O	–	100	20	1	=	Lowers foe's Attack and Defense 1 level
Torment (TM41)	DRK	O	–	100	15	1		Prevents foe from using the same move twice in a row
Toxic (TM06)	PSN	O	–	85	10	1		Causes Toxic condition; amount of poison damage increases each turn
Toxic Spikes	PSN	O	–	–	20	2		Causes Poison to foes that switch in; causes Toxic if you use it twice; effect ends when a Poison-type switches in
Transform	NRM	O	–	–	10	1		Changes to same Pokémon as opponent with same attacks, all PP at 5
Tri Attack	NRM	S	80	100	10	1		Has 20% cause of causing one random condition: Freeze, Burn or Paralyze
Trick	PSY	O	–	100	10	1		Switches foe's held items with yours
Trick Room (TM92)	PSY	O	–	–	5	4		Slower Pokémon act first for 5 turns; effect ends if used a second time
Triple Kick	FTG	P	10	90	10	1	=	Attacks 3 times per turn, damage increases each time
Trump Card	NRM	S	–	–	5	1	=	Will always strike foe successfully; causes higher damage when move's PP is low
Twineedle	BUG	P	25	100	20	1		Attacks 2 times per turn, has 20% chance of causing Poison
Twister	DRG	S	40	100	20	2		Has 20% chance of causing Flinch; inflicts double damage if foe is using Fly
Uproar	NRM	S	50	100	10	R		Repeats 2 to 5 turns; no Pokémon can inflict a Sleep condition during the uproar
U-turn (TM89)	BUG	P	70	100	20	1	=	Attacks foe, then switches out attacker for another Pokémon
Vacuum Wave	FTG	S	40	100	30	1		Causes you to move first in a turn; if opponent uses it too, the higher Speed prevails
Vicegrip	NRM	P	55	100	30	1	=	No extra effect beyond damaging foe
Vine Whip	GRS	P	35	100	10	1	=	No extra effect beyond damaging foe
Vital Throw	FTG	P	70	100	10	1	=	Causes you to strike 2nd but move will always strike foe successfully
Volt Tackle	ELC	P	120	100	15	1	=	Self-inflicts 1/3 of the damage
Wake-Up Slap	FTG	P	60	100	10	1	=	Inflicts double damage on foes with Sleep, then cures foe of Sleep
Water Gun	WTR	S	40	100	25	1		No extra effect beyond damaging foe
Water Pulse (TM03)	WTR	S	60	100	20	1		Has 20% chance of causing Confuse
Water Sport	WTR	O	–	100	15	S		Lowers power of all Fire-type attacks while Pokémon is on field
Water Spout	WTR	S	150	100	5	2		Inflicts less damage if your HP is weaker
Waterfall (HM07)	WTR	P	80	100	15	1	=	Has 20% chance of causing Flinch; allows you to climb waterfalls outside of battle
Weather Ball	NRM	S	50	100	10	1		Doubles damage for move types in specific weather (sunny=Fire; rain=Water; sandstorm=Rock; hail=Ice)
Whirlpool	WTR	S	15	70	15	1		Damages foe for 2-5 turns; foe can't escape until completed
Whirlwind	NRM	O	–	100	20	1		Ends battle with wild Pokémon; forces random foe switch in Trainer battle
Will-O-Wisp (TM61)	FIRE	O	–	75	15	1		Causes Burn condition
Wing Attack	FLY	P	60	100	35	1	=	No extra effect beyond damaging foe
Wish	NRM	O	–	100	10	S		Restores half of max HP on next turn; effect transfers if you switch Pokémon for next turn
Withdraw	WTR	O	–	–	40	S		Raises Defense 1 level
Wood Hammer	GRS	P	120	100	15	1	=	Self-inflicts 1/3 of the damage
Worry Seed	GRS	O	–	100	10	1		Changes Ability into Insomnia; doesn't work if original Ability is Truant
Wrap	NRM	P	15	85	20	1	=	Damages foe for 2-5 turns; foe can't escape until completed
Wring Out	NRM	S	–	100	5	1	=	Inflicts higher damage the higher the foe's HP (max 120)
X-Scissor (TM81)	BUG	P	80	100	15	1	=	No extra effect beyond damaging foe
Yawn	NRM	O	–	100	10	1		Causes foe to get Sleep condition on next turn
Zap Cannon	ELC	S	100	50	5	1		Causes foe to have Paralyze condition
Zen Headbutt	PSY	P	80	90	15	1	=	Has 20% chance of causing Flinch

Contest Equivalents (continued) Switcheroo – Zen Headbutt

Move	Type	AP	Effect in Super Contests
Switcheroo	Cool	–	If previous performer hits its Voltage to the max, then you will earn points equal to its Voltage
Swords Dance (TM75)	Beauty	–	Earn double the score in the next turn
Synthesis	Smart	*	AP value equal to Voltage of targeted judge
Tackle	Tough	3	A basic performance using a move known by the Pokémon
Tail Glow	Beauty	–	Earn double the score in the next turn
Tail Whip	Cute	2	Prevents the Voltage from going down in the same turn
Tailwind	Smart	2	Enables the user to perform first in the next turn
Take Down	Tough	3	A basic performance using a move known by the Pokémon
Taunt (TM12)	Smart	*	AP value equal to 4 minus targeted judge's Voltage
Teeter Dance	Cute	2	Makes the order of contestants random in the next turn
Teleport	Cool	2	Enables the user to perform first in the next turn
Thief (TM46)	Tough	–	If previous performer hits its Voltage to the max, then you will earn points equal to its Voltage
Thrash	Tough	2	Allows performance of the same move twice in a row
Thunder (TM25)	Cool	2	Earn +2 if the Pokémon performs first in the turn
Thunder Fang	Smart	3	A basic performance using a move known by the Pokémon
Thunder Wave (TM73)	Cool	2	Prevents the Voltage from going down in the same turn
Thunderbolt (TM24)	Cool	2	Earn +2 if the Pokémon performs first in the turn
Thunderpunch	Cool	2	Earn +2 if the Pokémon performs first in the turn
Thundershock	Cool	3	A basic performance using a move known by the Pokémon
Tickle	Cute	2	Prevents the Voltage from going down in the same turn
Torment (TM41)	Tough	*	AP value equal to 4 minus targeted judge's Voltage
Toxic (TM06)	Smart	2	Prevents the Voltage from going down in the same turn
Toxic Spikes	Smart	2	Prevents the Voltage from going up in the same turn
Transform	Smart	1	Earn +3 if the Pokémon gets the lowest score
Tri Attack	Beauty	3	A basic performance using a move known by the Pokémon
Trick	Smart	–	If previous performer hits its Voltage to the max, then you will earn points equal to its Voltage
Trick Room (TM92)	Cute	2	Makes the order of contestants random in the next turn
Triple Kick	Cool	2	Allows performance of the same move twice in a row
Trump Card	Cool	–	AP is 1 if performed first in a turn, 2 if second, 3 if third, and 4 if fourth
Twineedle	Cool	2	Allows performance of the same move twice in a row
Twister	Cool	3	A basic performance using a move known by the Pokémon
Uproar	Cute	2	Lowers the Voltage of all judges by one each
U-turn (TM89)	Cute	*	AP value equal to 4 minus targeted judge's Voltage
Vacuum Wave	Smart	2	Enables the user to perform first in the next turn
Vicegrip	Tough	3	A basic performance using a move known by the Pokémon
Vine Whip	Cool	3	A basic performance using a move known by the Pokémon
Vital Throw	Cool	2	Enables the user to perform last in the next turn
Volt Tackle	Cool	2	Earn +3 if the Pokémon that just went hit max Voltage
Wake-Up Slap	Smart	*	AP value equal to 4 minus targeted judge's Voltage
Water Gun	Cute	3	A basic performance using a move known by the Pokémon
Water Pulse (TM03)	Beauty	2	Earn +2 if the Pokémon performs first in the turn
Water Sport	Cute	2	Prevents the Voltage from going up in the same turn
Water Spout	Beauty	2	Earn +3 if the Pokémon that just went hit max Voltage
Waterfall (HM07)	Tough	3	A basic performance using a move known by the Pokémon
Weather Ball	Smart	2	Earn +2 if the judge's Voltage goes up
Whirlpool	Beauty	*	AP is 1 if performed first in a turn, 2 if second, 3 if third, and 4 if fourth
Whirlwind	Smart	–	Earn +15 if all the Pokémon choose the same judge
Will-O-Wisp (TM61)	Beauty	2	Earn +2 if the Pokémon performs first in the turn
Wing Attack	Cool	3	A basic performance using a move known by the Pokémon
Wish	Cute	*	AP value equal to Voltage of targeted judge
Withdraw	Cute	2	Prevents the Voltage from going up in the same turn
Wood Hammer	Tough	2	Earn +2 if the Pokémon performs last in the turn
Worry Seed	Beauty	2	Prevents the Voltage from going down in the same turn
Wrap	Tough	*	AP is 1 if performed first in a turn, 2 if second, 3 if third, and 4 if fourth
Wring Out	Smart	2	Earn +3 if the Pokémon that just went hit max Voltage
X-Scissor (TM81)	Beauty	2	Earn +2 if the Pokémon performs first in the turn
Yawn	Cute	2	Prevents the Voltage from going down in the same turn
Zap Cannon	Cool	2	Earn +2 if the judge's Voltage goes up
Zen Headbutt	Beauty	2	Earn +2 if the Pokémon performs last in the turn

Pokémon Egg Groups

Once you know the basics of breeding, use this chart to help you to find compatible Pokémon to match and breed at the Pokémon Day Care in Solaceon Town. See page 32 for more on breeding Pokémon.

Amorphous

#	Name	Other Type
354	Banette	–
351	Castform	Fairy
358	Chimecho	–
426	Drifblim	–
425	Drifloon	–
356	Dusclops	–
477	Dusknoir	–
355	Duskull	–
475	Gallade	–
282	Gardevoir	–
092	Gastly	–
423	Gastrodon	Water 1
094	Gengar	–
088	Grimer	–
316	Gulpin	–
093	Haunter	–
281	Kirlia	–
109	Koffing	–
219	Magcargo	–
200	Misdreavus	–
429	Mismagius	–
089	Muk	–
280	Ralts	–
479	Rotom	–
422	Shellos	Water 1
353	Shuppet	–
218	Slugma	–
442	Spiritomb	–
317	Swalot	–
110	Weezing	–
202	Wobbuffet	–

Bug

#	Name	Other Type
168	Ariados	–
267	Beautifly	–
015	Beedrill	–
412	Burmy	–
012	Butterfree	–
268	Cascoon	–
010	Caterpie	–
415	Combee	–
452	Drapion	Water 3
269	Dustox	–
330	Flygon	–
205	Forretress	–
207	Gligar	–
472	Gliscor	–
214	Heracross	–
314	Illumise	Human-Like
014	Kakuna	–
401	Kricketot	–
402	Kricketune	–
166	Ledian	–
165	Ledyba	–
284	Masquerain	Water 1
011	Metapod	–
414	Mothim	–
290	Nincada	–
291	Ninjask	–
046	Paras	Grass
047	Parasect	Grass
204	Pineco	–
127	Pinsir	–
212	Scizor	–
123	Scyther	–
213	Shuckle	–
266	Silcoon	–
451	Skorupi	Water 3
167	Spinarak	–
283	Surskit	Water 1
328	Trapinch	–
049	Venomoth	–
048	Venonat	–
416	Vespiquen	–
329	Vibrava	–
313	Volbeat	Human-Like
013	Weedle	–
413	Wormadam	–
265	Wurmple	–
193	Yanma	–
469	Yanmega	–

Ditto

#	Name	Other Type
132	Ditto	–

Dragon

#	Name	Other Type
334	Altaria	Flying
024	Arbok	Field
371	Bagon	–
006	Charizard	Monster
004	Charmander	Monster
005	Charmeleon	Monster
148	Dragonair	Water 1
149	Dragonite	Water 1
147	Dratini	Water 1
023	Ekans	Field
349	Feebas	Water 1
444	Gabite	Monster
445	Garchomp	Monster
443	Gible	Monster
253	Grovyle	Monster
130	Gyarados	Water 2
116	Horsea	Water 1
230	Kingdra	Water 1
129	Magikarp	Water 2
350	Milotic	Water 1
373	Salamence	–
254	Sceptile	Monster
117	Seadra	Water 1
336	Seviper	Field
372	Shelgon	–
333	Swablu	Flying
252	Treecko	Monster

Fairy

#	Name	Other Type
184	Azumarill	Water 1
242	Blissey	–
286	Breloom	Grass
351	Castform	Amorphous
113	Chansey	–
421	Cherrim	Grass
420	Cherubi	Grass
036	Clefable	–
035	Clefairy	–
301	Delcatty	Field
478	Froslass	Mineral
362	Glalie	Mineral
210	Granbull	Field
187	Hoppip	Grass
039	Jigglypuff	–
189	Jumpluff	Grass
490	Manaphy	Water 1
183	Marill	Water 1
303	Mawile	Field
312	Minun	–
417	Pachirisu	Field
489	Phione	Water 1
025	Pikachu	Field
311	Plusle	–
026	Raichu	Field
315	Roselia	Grass
407	Roserade	Grass
285	Shroomish	Grass
188	Skiploom	Grass
300	Skitty	Field
361	Snorunt	Mineral
209	Snubbull	Field
468	Togekiss	Flying
176	Togetic	Flying
040	Wigglytuff	–

Field

#	Name	Other Type
359	Absol	–
190	Aipom	–
424	Ambipom	–
181	Ampharos	Monster
024	Arbok	Dragon
059	Arcanine	–
400	Bibarel	Water 1
399	Bidoof	Water 1
257	Blaziken	–
418	Buizel	Water 1
427	Buneary	Human-Like
323	Camerupt	–
390	Chimchar	Human-Like
256	Combusken	–
155	Cyndaquil	–
301	Delcatty	Fairy
225	Delibird	Water 1
087	Dewgong	Water 1
050	Diglett	–
232	Donphan	–
051	Dugtrio	–
206	Dunsparce	–
133	Eevee	–
023	Ekans	Dragon
309	Electrike	–
395	Empoleon	Water 1
196	Espeon	–
295	Exploud	Monster
083	Farfetch'd	Flying
180	Flaaffy	Monster
136	Flareon	–
419	Floatzel	Water 1
162	Furret	–
203	Girafarig	–
471	Glaceon	–
431	Glameow	–
055	Golduck	Water 1
210	Granbull	Fairy
058	Growlithe	–
326	Grumpig	–
449	Hippopotas	–
450	Hippowdon	–
229	Houndoom	–
228	Houndour	–
392	Infernape	Human-Like
135	Jolteon	–
352	Kecleon	–
470	Leafeon	–
264	Linoone	–
428	Lopunny	Human-Like
294	Loudred	Monster
448	Lucario	Human-Like
404	Luxio	–
405	Luxray	–
473	Mamoswine	–
310	Manectric	–
056	Mankey	–
179	Mareep	Monster
303	Mawile	Fairy
052	Meowth	–
262	Mightyena	–
241	Miltank	–
391	Monferno	Human-Like
034	Nidoking	Monster
029	Nidoran ♀	Monster
032	Nidoran ♂	Monster
033	Nidorino	Monster
038	Ninetales	–
322	Numel	–
274	Nuzleaf	Grass
417	Pachirisu	Fairy
053	Persian	–
231	Phanpy	–
025	Pikachu	Fairy
221	Piloswine	–
393	Piplup	Water 1
077	Ponyta	–
261	Poochyena	–
057	Primeape	–
394	Prinplup	Water 1
054	Psyduck	Water 1
432	Purugly	–
195	Quagsire	Water 1
156	Quilava	–
026	Raichu	Fairy
078	Rapidash	–
020	Raticate	–
019	Rattata	–
112	Rhydon	Monster
111	Rhyhorn	Monster
464	Rhyperior	Monster
027	Sandshrew	–
028	Sandslash	–
364	Sealeo	Water 1
273	Seedot	Grass
086	Seel	Water 1
161	Sentret	–
336	Seviper	Dragon
275	Shiftry	Grass
403	Shinx	–
300	Skitty	Fairy
435	Skuntank	–
289	Slaking	–
287	Slakoth	–
235	Smeargle	–
215	Sneasel	–
209	Snubbull	Fairy
363	Spheal	Water 1
327	Spinda	Human-Like
325	Spoink	–
234	Stantler	–
434	Stunky	–
220	Swinub	–
128	Tauros	–
216	Teddiursa	–
255	Torchic	–
324	Torkoal	–
157	Typhlosion	–
197	Umbreon	–
217	Ursaring	–
134	Vaporeon	–
288	Vigoroth	–
037	Vulpix	–
320	Wailmer	Water 2
321	Wailord	Water 2
365	Walrein	Water 1
461	Weavile	–
293	Whismur	Monster
194	Wooper	Water 1
335	Zangoose	–
263	Zigzagoon	–

Flying

#	Name	Other Type
142	Aerodactyl	–
334	Altaria	Dragon
441	Chatot	–
169	Crobat	–
085	Dodrio	–
084	Doduo	–
083	Farfetch'd	Field
022	Fearow	–
042	Golbat	–
430	Honchkrow	–
163	Hoothoot	–
198	Murkrow	–
177	Natu	–
164	Noctowl	–
279	Pelipper	Water 1
018	Pidgeot	–
017	Pidgeotto	–
016	Pidgey	–
227	Skarmory	–
021	Spearow	–
398	Staraptor	–
397	Staravia	–
396	Starly	–
333	Swablu	Dragon
277	Swellow	–
276	Taillow	–
468	Togekiss	Fairy
176	Togetic	Fairy
278	Wingull	Water 1
178	Xatu	–
041	Zubat	–

Grass

#	Name	Other Type
460	Abomasnow	Monster
153	Bayleef	Monster
182	Bellossom	–
069	Bellsprout	–
286	Breloom	Fairy
001	Bulbasaur	Monster
331	Cacnea	Human-Like
332	Cacturne	Human-Like
455	Carnivine	–
421	Cherrim	Fairy
420	Cherubi	Fairy
152	Chikorita	Monster
102	Exeggcute	–
103	Exeggutor	–
044	Gloom	–
388	Grotle	Monster
187	Hoppip	Fairy
002	Ivysaur	Monster
189	Jumpluff	Fairy
271	Lombre	Water 1
270	Lotad	Water 1
272	Ludicolo	Water 1
154	Meganium	Monster
274	Nuzleaf	Field
043	Oddish	–
046	Paras	Bug
047	Parasect	Bug
315	Roselia	Fairy
407	Roserade	Fairy
273	Seedot	Field
275	Shiftry	Field
285	Shroomish	Fairy
188	Skiploom	Fairy
459	Snover	Monster
192	Sunflora	–
191	Sunkern	–
114	Tangela	–
465	Tangrowth	–
389	Torterra	Monster
357	Tropius	Monster
387	Turtwig	Monster
003	Venusaur	Monster
071	Victreebel	–
045	Vileplume	–
070	Weepinbell	–

Human-Like

#	Name	Other Type
063	Abra	–
065	Alakazam	–
427	Buneary	Field
331	Cacnea	Grass
332	Cacturne	Grass
390	Chimchar	Field
453	Croagunk	–
096	Drowzee	–
125	Electabuzz	–
466	Electivire	–
297	Hariyama	–
107	Hitmonchan	–
106	Hitmonlee	–
237	Hitmontop	–
097	Hypno	–
314	Illumise	Bug
392	Infernape	Field
124	Jynx	–
064	Kadabra	–
428	Lopunny	Field
448	Lucario	Field
068	Machamp	–
067	Machoke	–
066	Machop	–
126	Magmar	–
467	Magmortar	–
296	Makuhita	–
308	Medicham	–
307	Meditite	–
391	Monferno	Field
122	Mr. Mime	–
302	Sableye	–
327	Spinda	Field
454	Toxicroak	Bug
313	Volbeat	Bug

Mineral

#	Name	Other Type
343	Baltoy	–
374	Beldum	–
437	Bronzong	–
436	Bronzor	–
344	Claydol	–
101	Electrode	–
478	Froslass	Fairy
074	Geodude	–
362	Glalie	Fairy
076	Golem	–
075	Graveler	–
337	Lunatone	–
081	Magnemite	–
082	Magneton	–
462	Magnezone	–
376	Metagross	–
375	Metang	–
299	Nosepass	–
095	Onix	–
137	Porygon	–
233	Porygon2	–
474	Porygon-Z	–
476	Probopass	–
292	Shedinja	–
361	Snorunt	Fairy
338	Solrock	–
208	Steelix	–
185	Sudowoodo	–
100	Voltorb	–

Monster

#	Name	Other Type
460	Abomasnow	Grass
306	Aggron	–
181	Ampharos	Field
304	Aron	–
411	Bastiodon	–
153	Bayleef	Grass
009	Blastoise	Water 1
001	Bulbasaur	Grass
006	Charizard	Dragon
004	Charmander	Dragon
005	Charmeleon	Dragon
152	Chikorita	Grass
408	Cranidos	–
159	Croconaw	Water 1
104	Cubone	–
295	Exploud	Field
160	Feraligatr	Water 1
180	Flaaffy	Field
444	Gabite	Dragon
445	Garchomp	Dragon
443	Gible	Dragon
388	Grotle	Grass
253	Grovyle	Grass
002	Ivysaur	Grass
115	Kangaskhan	–
305	Lairon	–
131	Lapras	Water 1
246	Larvitar	–
463	Licklicky	–
108	Lickitung	–
294	Loudred	Field
179	Mareep	Field
105	Marowak	–
259	Marshtomp	Water 1
154	Meganium	Grass
258	Mudkip	Water 1
034	Nidoking	Field
029	NidoranF	Field
032	NidoranM	Field
033	Nidorino	Field

#	Name	
247	Pupitar	–
409	Rampardos	–
112	Rhydon	Field
111	Rhyhorn	Field
464	Rhyperior	Field
254	Sceptile	Grass
410	Shieldon	–
080	Slowbro	Water 1
199	Slowking	Water 1
079	Slowpoke	Water 1
143	Snorlax	–
459	Snover	Grass
007	Squirtle	Water 1
260	Swampert	Water 1
389	Torterra	Grass
158	Totodile	Water 1
252	Treecko	Grass
357	Tropius	Grass
387	Turtwig	Grass
248	Tyranitar	–
003	Venusaur	Grass
008	Wartortle	Water 1
293	Whismur	Field

None

#	Name	Other Type
144	Articuno	–
482	Azelf	–
298	Azurill	–
438	Bonsly	–
406	Budew	–
251	Celebi	–
433	Chingling	–
173	Cleffa	–
488	Cresselia	–
386	Deoxys	–
483	Dialga	–
239	Elekid	–
244	Entei	–
487	Giratina	–
383	Groudon	–
485	Heatran	–
250	Ho-Oh	–
174	Igglybuff	–
385	Jirachi	–
382	Kyogre	–
380	Latias	–
381	Latios	–
440	Happiny	–
249	Lugia	–
240	Magby	–
458	Mantyke	–
481	Mesprit	–
151	Mew	–
150	Mewtwo	–
439	Mime Jr.	–
146	Moltres	–
446	Munchlax	–
031	Nidoqueen	–
030	Nidorina	–
484	Palkia	–
172	Pichu	–
243	Raikou	–
384	Rayquaza	–
378	Regice	–
486	Regigigas	–
377	Regirock	–
379	Registeel	–
447	Riolu	–
238	Smoochum	–
245	Suicune	–
175	Togepi	–
236	Tyrogue	–
201	Unown	–
480	Uxie	–
360	Wynaut	–
145	Zapdos	–

Water 1

#	Name	Other Type
184	Azumarill	Fairy
400	Bibarel	Field
399	Bidoof	Field
009	Blastoise	Monster
418	Buizel	Field
366	Clamperl	–
341	Corphish	Water 3
222	Corsola	Water 3
342	Crawdaunt	Water 3
159	Croconaw	Monster
225	Delibird	Field
087	Dewgong	Field
148	Dragonair	Dragon
149	Dragonite	Dragon
147	Dratini	Dragon
395	Empoleon	Field
349	Feebas	Dragon
160	Feraligatr	Monster
419	Floatzel	Field
423	Gastrodon	Amorphous
055	Golduck	Field

#	Name	
368	Gorebyss	–
116	Horsea	Dragon
367	Huntail	–
140	Kabuto	Water 3
141	Kabutops	Water 3
230	Kingdra	Dragon
131	Lapras	Monster
271	Lombre	Grass
270	Lotad	Grass
272	Ludicolo	Grass
490	Manaphy	Fairy
226	Mantine	–
183	Marill	Fairy
259	Marshtomp	Monster
284	Masquerain	Bug
350	Milotic	Dragon
258	Mudkip	Monster
224	Octillery	Water 1
138	Omanyte	Water 3
139	Omastar	Water 3
279	Pelipper	Flying
489	Phione	Fairy
393	Piplup	Field
186	Politoed	–
060	Poliwag	–
061	Poliwhirl	–
062	Poliwrath	–
394	Prinplup	Field
054	Psyduck	Field
195	Quagsire	Field
369	Relicanth	Water 2
223	Remoraid	Water 2
117	Seadra	Dragon
364	Sealeo	Field
086	Seel	Field
422	Shellos	Amorphous
080	Slowbro	Monster
199	Slowking	Monster
079	Slowpoke	Monster
363	Spheal	Field
007	Squirtle	Monster
283	Surskit	Bug
260	Swampert	Monster
158	Totodile	Monster
365	Walrein	Field
008	Wartortle	Monster
278	Wingull	Flying
194	Wooper	Field

Water 2

#	Name	Other Type
339	Barboach	–
318	Carvanha	–
170	Chinchou	–
456	Finneon	–
118	Goldeen	–
130	Gyarados	Dragon
171	Lanturn	–
457	Lumineon	–
370	Luvdisc	–
129	Magikarp	Dragon
224	Octillery	Water 1
211	Qwilfish	–
369	Relicanth	Water 1
223	Remoraid	Water 1
119	Seaking	–
319	Sharpedo	–
320	Wailmer	Field
321	Wailord	Field
340	Whiscash	–

Water 3

#	Name	Other Type
347	Anorith	–
348	Armaldo	–
091	Cloyster	–
341	Corphish	Water 1
222	Corsola	Water 1
346	Cradily	–
342	Crawdaunt	Water 1
452	Drapion	Bug
140	Kabuto	Water 1
141	Kabutops	Water 1
099	Kingler	–
098	Krabby	–
345	Lileep	–
138	Omanyte	Water 1
139	Omastar	Water 1
090	Shellder	–
451	Skorupi	Bug
121	Starmie	–
120	Staryu	–
072	Tentacool	–
073	Tentacruel	–

Alphabetical Sinnoh Pokémon List

#	Name	Sinnoh Pokédex Page
143	Abomasnow	142
020	Abra	128
063	Aipom	133
022	Alakazam	129
064	Ambipom	133
148	Azelf	143
126	Azumarill	140
124	Azurill	140
080	Barboach	135
039	Bastiodon	130
050	Beautifly	132
014	Bibarel	128
013	Bidoof	128
098	Blissey	137
092	Bonsly	137
089	Bronzong	136
088	Bronzor	136
025	Budew	129
056	Buizel	133
067	Buneary	134
045	Burmy	131
131	Carnivine	141
051	Cascoon	132
097	Chansey	137
102	Chatot	138
059	Cherrim	133
058	Cherubi	133
004	Chimchar	127
083	Chimecho	136
082	Chingling	135
101	Clefable	138
100	Clefairy	137
099	Cleffa	137
053	Combee	132
036	Cranidos	130
129	Croagunk	141
030	Crobat	129
149	Dialga	143
128	Drapion	141
066	Drifblim	134
065	Drifloon	134
052	Dustox	132
009	Empoleon	127
138	Feebas	142
134	Finneon	141
057	Floatzel	133
110	Gabite	139
111	Garchomp	139
069	Gastly	134
061	Gastrodon	133
071	Gengar	134
031	Geodude	130
109	Gible	138
121	Girafarig	140
076	Glameow	135
029	Golbat	129
078	Goldeen	135
044	Golduck	131
033	Golem	130
032	Graveler	130
002	Grotle	126
024	Gyarados	129
096	Happiny	137
070	Haunter	134
062	Heracross	133
122	Hippopotas	140
123	Hippowdon	140
075	Honchkrow	135
106	Hoothoot	138
006	Infernape	127
021	Kadabra	128
015	Kricketot	128
016	Kricketune	128
068	Lopunny	134
116	Lucario	139
135	Lumineon	141

#	Name	Sinnoh Pokédex Page
018	Luxio	128
019	Luxray	128
042	Machamp	131
041	Machoke	131
040	Machop	131
023	Magikarp	129
151	Manaphy	143
141	Mantine	142
140	Mantyke	142
125	Marill	140
087	Medicham	136
086	Meditite	136
147	Mesprit	143
139	Milotic	142
094	Mime Jr.	137
072	Misdreavus	134
073	Mismagius	134
005	Monferno	127
047	Mothim	132
095	Mr. Mime	137
112	Munchlax	139
074	Murkrow	135
107	Noctowl	138
133	Octillery	141
034	Onix	130
055	Pachirisu	132
150	Palkia	143
120	Pelipper	140
103	Pichu	138
104	Pikachu	138
007	Piplup	127
090	Ponyta	136
008	Prinplup	127
043	Psyduck	131
077	Purugly	135
118	Quagsire	139
105	Raichu	138
037	Rampardos	130
091	Rapidash	136
132	Remoraid	141
115	Riolu	139
026	Roselia	129
027	Roserade	129
079	Seaking	135
060	Shellos	133
038	Shieldon	130
017	Shinx	128
049	Silcoon	132
127	Skorupi	140
085	Skuntank	136
144	Sneasel	142
113	Snorlax	139
142	Snover	142
108	Spiritomb	138
012	Staraptor	127
011	Staravia	127
010	Starly	127
035	Steelix	130
084	Stunky	136
093	Sudowoodo	137
136	Tentacool	141
137	Tentacruel	142
003	Torterra	126
130	Toxicroak	141
001	Turtwig	126
114	Unown	139
146	Uxie	143
054	Vespiquen	132
145	Weavile	142
081	Whiscash	135
119	Wingull	140
117	Wooper	139
046	Wormadam	131
048	Wurmple	132
028	Zubat	129